A Brilliant Little
Operation

A Brilliant Little Operation

The Cockleshell Heroes and
the Most Courageous Raid of WW2

PADDY ASHDOWN

First published in Great Britain
2012 by Aurum Press Ltd
7 Greenland Street
London NW1 0ND
www.aurumpress.co.uk

A catalogue record for this book is available from the British Library.

ISBN 978 1 84513 701 4

3 5 7 9 10 8 6 4 2
2012 2014 2016 2015 2013

Typeset in Dante MT Std by Saxon Graphics Ltd, Derby
Printed by Clays Ltd, St Ives plc

Barbed wire enclosed an arbitrary spot
Where bored officials lounged (one cracked a joke)
And sentries sweated for the day was hot:
A crowd of ordinary decent folk
Watched from without and neither moved nor spoke
As three pale figures were led forth and bound
To three posts driven upright in the ground.

The mass and majesty of this world, all
That carries weight and always weighs the same
Lay in the hands of others; they were small
And could not hope for help and no help came:

W.H. Auden, *The Shield of Achilles*

It is the plain truth which will be denied by no honest person inside our various propaganda organisations, that most of the energy which should have been directed against the enemy has been dissipated in inter-departmental strife and jealousies.

Minute of 22 August 1941 from Bruce Lockhart to Anthony Eden, Minister for War and Foreign Secretary

Contents

List of Maps

Acknowledgements

This book has been part labour of love, part homage to the young men who paddled into the Gironde in December 1942 and the French men and women who helped them and part a means to return thanks to my old unit, the Royal Marines Special Boat Service. It has also been a journey of revelation in the joy of discovery as I have attempted to unearth the full story of the extraordinary Frankton raid and the people who played a part in the events which took place on and around the Bordeaux quays during the nine months from August 1942 to April 1943.

Much of this story has been hidden in files now open for public scrutiny in that national treasure, the National Archives in Kew. I have spent many long and absorbed hours there and am immensely grateful to the staff who were so unfailing in the helpfulness and patience with which they responded to my pestering and inexperience, especially Neil Cobbett, expert on SOE, and William Spencer, principal military specialist. I am also grateful to Jim Daly and Christine Ferguson of the FCO Information Management Department, who helped me access files which would otherwise not yet be open to public scrutiny; to Dr Roderick Bailey, Stephen Walton, Matthew Lee and their colleagues at the Imperial War Museum for access to their sound and film archives; to Richard Wooldridge, who with his staff facilitated my several visits to his remarkable Combined Services Military Museum at Maldon in Essex. It was here that we made the first tentative identification of the Mark II Cockle in the museum as *Cachalot*, the canoe which was damaged and left behind on HM Submarine *Tuna* on the night Operation Frankton was launched; to Boris Pretzel of the V&A Museum for his assistance in obtaining the services of Paul Garside of the British Library, who helped carry out initial tests on *Cachalot*; to Emma Schmuecker of the Imperial War Museum for facilitating the involvement of Dr Sonia O'Connor,

Archaeological Sciences Division of the University of Bradford, who with her university colleague Lucy Martin (together with husband Alan and baby Freddy) and Nathan Bradley of 3DX-Ray Ltd of Loughborough spent a long afternoon making the X-ray and photographic images of *Cachalot*'s paintwork.

Museums and archives have been, rather unexpectedly, a most enjoyable part of my life in the nearly two years it has taken me to write this book. Not all of these have been in London, or even in Britain. Matt Little, archivist of the Royal Marines Museum at Eastney, Portsmouth has gone out of his way to provide me with advice and invaluable reference material, as has George Malcolmson, archivist of the Royal Navy Submarine Museum in Portsmouth. The assistance of Andy Godfrey, head of the Navy Disclosure Cell at Whale Island, was crucial in obtaining the service records of Hasler's men, as was that of Lieutenant-Colonel Norman Bonney, who provided me with information on the history, development and operation of the limpet mines used on Operation Frankton.

I am indebted, too, to General Gilles Robert, Lieutenant-Colonel Christophe Poujol, André Rakoto, Pascal Gallien, Odile Jurbert and François-Xavier Guenot of the *Service Historique de la Défense* at Château de Vincennes in Paris for their kindness and courtesy during my visits there, and to Jean-Marie Linsolas, the *Chef du département interarmées du Bureau de la Résistance* of the *Service Historique de la Défense*, and Bernard Mouraz of the French Gendarmerie archives for their work in uncovering the file of Gendarme Pierre Hennequin. Colonel Michael J. Haller, the Military Attaché of the German Embassy in London, his colleagues Dr Sabine Dumschat and Mrs Jana Blumberg of the Bundesarchiv in Berlin and Arne Schrader, Daniel Hauser and Ms Kalbhenn of the *Volksbund Deutsche Kriegsgräberfürsorge* (German War Graves Commission) have, together with Simon McDonald, the British Ambassador in Berlin, all been of great assistance in facilitating my attempts to find the graves of those executed by the Germans after the Frankton raid. As have Édouard Vergriète, *Conservateur* of the Bagneux cemetery archives and Pascal-Hervé Daniel, *Chef du Service Cimetières* in Paris. Peter Monte and Horst Bredow kindly provided access to the Walter Schnöppe Collection of documents and photographs held at the German U-Boat Museum in

Cuxhaven, many of which appear in this book, and Peter Lieb has kindly provided advice and checked the German texts.

One of my hopes was to be able to reconstruct with accuracy the precise tidal, hydrographical, astronomical and meteorological conditions which prevailed in the Gironde area over the period of Operation Frankton and the following days. In this I have been especially assisted by Dr Steve Bell, Guy Hannaford, Christopher Jones, Tim Smith and their colleagues at the UK Hydrographic Office in Taunton, Joan Self and Mark Beswick of the National Meteorological Archive in Exeter and Captain M.K. Barritt RN, retd, an ex-Chief Hydrographer of the Royal Navy. My old Royal Marine colleague Ewen Southby-Tailyour, the author of *Blondie*, Hasler's biography (among other excellent books on military history), has been most generous in providing me with his thoughts, based on personal experience, on the hydrographic conditions in the Gironde estuary, and in providing corrections and useful pointers on a wide variety of matters, not least the complex character of Blondie Hasler himself.

I am also much indebted to four old colleagues who joined the Royal Marines in the same year as I did: Peter Cameron, Jake Hensman, Mike Hodder and Brian Mollan. In 1960, they followed the Frankton route (the first after Blondie to do so) all the way from Le Verdon to Ruffec. At that time nearly all the main players in the story were still alive. The report they wrote, which is held in the Royal Marines Museum, Eastney, has proved an invaluable source of information, witness testimony and photographs.

While my background gave me reasonable personal knowledge of the Royal Marines and canoe-based operations, I started from a position of near-perfect ignorance on the second major strand of this story: SOE – and especially its circuit in Bordeaux, the *Scientist* network. Here I have been helped immensely by, among others, the doyen of SOE historians, the late and much-missed Professor M.R.D. Foot, himself a Combined Operations officer during the war, who was kind enough, even when writing his own book, to spare time to read and correct key passages of mine. Noreen Riols, who was an SOE operative at its 'finishing' school in Beaulieu and an author in her own right, also helped in this way – as well as introducing me both to Clothilde Blanc, who provided fascinating insights into the character and history of the de Baissac family (especially

Lise), and to Marcel Jaurment-Singer, *Président Libre Résistance* in Paris. He hosted a memorable lunch for my daughter and me, whose conviviality was matched only by the wealth of moving and often amusing stories about SOE's F Section which accompanied it.

Others who provided generous assistance in this field were SOE expert Duncan Stuart and Jenny Kauntze, Records Archivist for the FANY, the Second World War parent organisation for many of SOE's women agents; David Harrison, who allowed me to pillage his astonishing library of SOE files; and ex-SOE agent Yvonne Burney (Baseden when she was in SOE), who was kind enough to allow me to interview her. She provided some valuable insights, especially on Mary Lindell, whom she met in Dijon prison and Ravensbrück concentration camp in 1945.

Next I need to acknowledge the enormous help I have had from the relatives and descendants of Blondie Hasler and his men. Chief among them is Blondie's widow Bridget, who was kind enough to allow me to spend the best part of a day with her at the Hasler family home in Argyll and generously gave me access not only to her own memories but also to the Hasler archive. I am also indebted to Blondie and Bridget's daughter Dinah and son Tom, who enabled me to maintain email contact with their mother so that I could submit texts and questions to her as they arose in the writing of the book. The other person to whom I owe an immense debt of gratitude is the late Peter Siddall, nephew of George Sheard, long-time researcher into Frankton (especially the circumstances of his uncle's death) and an accomplished linguist in both French and German. He is responsible not only for helping to shape this book, but also for correcting its many early mistakes (including textual ones) and for many of the translations it contains. I miss him.

Other relatives who have helped with advice, corrections, information and photographs include Eileen Kiltie, Judy and Ken Simms, David Moffatt, the late Eddie Ward, Terry Sparks, Frank Sparks, George Ewart, Peter Ellery and Olive Pyne, Ken Brotherhood and the Conway family descendants in Stockport.

I have had many, many French advisors and helpers in writing this book. Chief among them is François Boisnier, ex-President of Frankton Souvenir, a Bordeaux-based French organisation dedicated to keeping alive the memories of Hasler and his men. François' commitment to this task and to researching what happened to each of those young men has – not before time – earned him recognition from Her Majesty the Queen in the award of the MBE in 2011. Without his work and the formidable archive he has accumulated in his home in Barbézieux-St-Hilaire in the Charente, it would never have been possible for me to record these stories and they would have been lost for ever. I owe him and the new President of Frankton Souvenir, Erick Poineau (whose professional local knowledge of the Gironde tides around the Pointe de Grave has also been invaluable), an immense debt, not only for their information but also for their many kindnesses to me on my visits to the area.

Others who should also be mentioned in this context include Alia El Khafafi, who has translated for me on several occasions; Yves Leglise, who was so generous with his help and hospitality during the visit my daughter Kate and I made to Nice to see his mother Suzanne (née Duboué); Jean Fernandez; Jeanette Baudray; Monique Marcellin; Jean Trocard; Amélie Dubreuille; Dénise, Nicole and Pierre Hèches, who looked after my wife and me on our visit to Tarbes in the spring of 2011; Michel St Marc of Cauderon, for his immense help in uncovering the story of MacKinnon and Conway; the late and much-missed Anne-Marie Farré (née Bernadet) and her son Hervé and his family of St Médard d'Eyrans, who gave us a delicious dinner when we visited them; Val and Vito Traille at Le Moulin de Saquet; David Devigne; Anne-Marie Gillet of Château La Bertrande, Omet; Marie-Thérèse Sénac, *Attachée de conservation du patrimoine* of *Les Archives Communales*, Martignas-sur-Jalle, and her staff; Jean-Louis Lamouliatte for taking me round Souges; and Jacques Loiseau and Philippe Saujeon of the Bibliothèque Municipale at La Réole, for sending such useful information on their town during the war.

Fairness demands that I should also include here my grandson Matthias Theurel and his sister Loïs, who, together with their mother Kate and father Sébastien have provided unofficial and – mostly – uncomplaining French translation services when I needed them. They all put up with my obsession with this project during our precious holidays together with saintly patience and only an occasional resignatory Gallic shrug.

I have been blessed by having a small team of 'readers' to whom I have sent some or all chapters as they were written. If it had not been for their patience with me, the mistakes in this manuscript would have tripled in number and increased in seriousness by a factor of ten.

Those not so far mentioned include Mark Bentinck (Royal Marines Corps historian), Stephanie Bailey, Rosemary Billinge, Harriett McDougal (who also drew the maps in this book), Janet Smith, Ellen Dahrendorf, Malcolm Cavan, Norman Colley (the only survivor of Hasler's team) and his friend Jean, Steve Radley, two old Royal Marines colleagues Rupert van der Horst and Chris Nunn (who walked the Frankton escape route with my text in their hands, correcting it as they went) and Linda Siegle, who apart from acting as a scrupulous and demanding reader has also helped me hugely with the research at the National Archives, especially when it came to disentangling the details of the parachute jumps and supply drops which reinforced and sustained the *Scientist* network in Bordeaux.

I am also indebted to my publisher Graham Coster, of Aurum, who suggested that I should write this book and has given me unfailing support and advice on its construction and flow; to Steve Gove who copy-edited my text, correcting its many errors and insisting with courteous determination that I stuck to the main strand of the story and did not wander off into the many thickets of my own enthusiasm; to my agent Michael Sissons and all at Peter Fraser Dunlop (PFD), who have once again looked after my interests with care, encouragement and diligence; and to my wife Jane who has, with her usual patience and equanimity, put up with a husband who has spent the past two years or so on, as she has christened it, 'Planet Blondie'.

Finally, more thanks than I can express go to the man without whose help this book in its present form simply could not have been written: Dr Tom Keene. It was Tom who first unearthed the SOE files revealing that a key element of this story had remained hidden since 1942 – the fact that, at the same time as Blondie Hasler was conducting his daring raid, SOE had a parallel and generously resourced operation in place on the Bordeaux quays, which no one knew about. It was Tom who pulled out the first thread of this fascinating story, which I have (with his help) been able to tug on to unravel the existence and scale of the whole *Scientist* network so that it could be set alongside the epic of Blondie Hasler's men. Tom, an author in his own right, has in addition been most generous in offering suggestions and corrections to my text and permitted me freely to pillage his outstanding PhD thesis on the wartime rivalry between SOE and Combined Operations. As though that were not enough, he has in addition helped me with my research, not least by introducing me to the wonders of the National Archives and discovering the whereabouts of some of the hitherto unknown Frankton relatives. This has been, for me at least, a fruitful and enjoyable collaboration which is now underpinned by friendship. I hope we will be able to pursue other projects in the near future.

To all of these people, and probably many more I have omitted, I owe a great debt in producing this book – a process which has given me huge pleasure, not least because of the new friends I have made in the process. Where the book succeeds – if it does – it is in large measure due to them. But its mistakes and infelicities are all my own.

Notes and Conventions

Times. Since this is the story of a primarily military operation, I have thought it appropriate to use the 24-hour clock throughout. During the Second World War all British forces in the European theatre used Greenwich Mean Time (GMT), while all German forces used Central European Time (CET), which in that era was GMT +2 hours. All times in the text are given in GMT (i.e. two hours have been taken off the times shown in German records to make them consistent with GMT).

Tides. Tide times, flows and levels, together with pilotage and chart details, are based on those provided by the archive department of the UK Hydrographic Office for the period concerned. This information has been supplemented by tidal information from the French Hydrographic Office (SHOM). On the rare occasions where these do not closely coincide, I have chosen to follow the UK hydrographers in respect of the open sea and the French in respect of the closed waters of the Gironde. In the latter case this information has been checked against local knowledge and especially the advice of M. Erick Poineau, *Responsable Magasin et Contrôleur Marégraphique* of buoys and lights at Le Verdon.

Weather and Astronomy. Weather and astronomical details are based on information provided by the archive department of the Met Office, supplemented where available by German weather information and charts of the period, which are also held in Met Office archives.

Measurements. Given that this was a British operation which took place before the European Union existed, I have thought it right to use imperial measurements in preference to metric ones throughout.

Code words. Combined Operations code words were straightforward. Each operation was assigned a code word, chosen by a purely random process, and this threw up the name, Frankton, by which this operation was known.

SOE code words were more complicated. Each SOE agent had two code names. The first was that by which they were referred to in SOE internal communications. In the south of France these were taken from an occupation; hence the chief agent operating in Bordeaux in the autumn of 1942, Claude de Baissac, was known as *Scientist*, while his courier, Mary Herbert, was *Jeweller*, etc.

Each also had a *nom de guerre* by which they were known locally. De Baissac was known to his local collaborators in France as '*David*' and Mary Herbert as '*Claudine*'.

In addition, each agent was also equipped with a false identity, backed by the appropriate papers and identity cards and supported by a cover story, or 'legend'. De Baissac posed as a travelling publicity agent called Claude Marc Boucher and Mary Herbert was Marie-Louise Vernier, a young widow from Alexandria.

SOE agent networks – they were interchangeably known as 'circuits', or *réseaux* in French – also had their own code name, taken from that of the circuit head. Thus the network operating in Bordeaux in late 1942 was known after its chief, as the *Scientist* network.

Dialogue. I have only used dialogue in quotation marks where this has been taken from a record made by, or approved by, one of the participants in Frankton. Since Hasler worked with Lucas Phillips in the production of *Cockleshell Heroes*, I have presumed that the dialogue in that book was approved by him as an accurate representation of what was said at the time.

Sketches. The sketches included at certain points in the text are by Hasler himself.

Prologue

Over the Easter weekend of 1965, just after I had qualified as a Swimmer Canoeist in the Royal Marines Special Boat Section (SBS), I took part in the Devizes to Westminster canoe race. My partner and I competed in the collapsible canoe class, which involved paddling 125 miles non-stop and carrying our fully laden canoe around seventy-seven locks. We were lucky enough to win in our class. But it was one of the most gruelling twenty-four hours I have ever experienced.

After the race I boarded the train at Waterloo station, heading back to the SBS base in Poole. I dumped my rucksack on the luggage rack and slumped into the window seat of my compartment, pulled my service-issue camouflaged canoe smock around me and fell immediately into an exhausted sleep. The train was not crowded and there was, I vaguely recall before sleep dragged me down, only one other person in the carriage. At a station not far out of London – Woking perhaps – the train was severely jolted as it stopped at a station and I woke with a start to find my travelling companion studying me carefully.

He was an imposing man with broad shoulders, a bald head, piercing, craggy eyes, an athletic-looking figure for his age – which I judged to be around fifty – and a tidily trimmed greying moustache. I cannot now remember how our conversation started, or who started it – I think he did. But I can remember that it was not long before I felt I was being rather firmly interrogated.

'Judging from your camouflage smock, you're a Royal Marine, I suppose?'
'I am.'
'What rank are you?'
'I'm a lieutenant.'
'So you are coming down from London?'
'Yeah. I've just done the Devizes to Westminster canoe race.'

'Hmm. That's quite tough, isn't it?'

'It's a hundred and twenty-five miles – and it's completely exhausting, I can tell you.'

'I imagine it is. So you are off to Poole, I suppose?'

'Yes.'

'SBS?'

'Look, I'm not at liberty to tell you the details of my job. It's confidential and not to be discussed with those not entitled to know,' I replied in a pompous and irritable tone which I did not mean and immediately regretted.

Not surprisingly, our conversation ended there and we relapsed into what was, for me at least, an uncomfortable silence until he left the train – I think at Winchester – while I continued on to Poole. On disembarking, I hitched my rucksack on my back and headed for the taxi rank. Here a fellow SBS colleague who had been on the same train bounded up to me.

'What was he like?' he said.

'Who?' I asked.

'Blondie Hasler,' he replied. 'You were sharing a compartment with him!'

Even today it gives me embarrassment and pain to remember that the travelling companion to whom I had been so gratuitously rude had been one of the most extraordinary figures of the Second World War. He was the leader and one of only two survivors of the 'Cockleshell Heroes' raid – a man who had not only become a legend in his own lifetime, but whose exploits had laid the foundations for the modern SBS, creating both its ethos and its culture.

That chance meeting was not my only contact with the ten men who took part in that iconic raid on Axis shipping in Bordeaux. During my recently completed SBS course I had paddled at night, as had they, from submarines up Loch Long and Loch Fyne in Scotland. I had taken part in night marches through the woods and heaths of the Argyll peninsula, where they had carried out their pre-raid training. Their ghosts were everywhere.

What was more, the first Royal Marines to complete the Devizes to Westminster canoe race non-stop,* as I had just done, had paddled it

---

* Captain H.G. Bruce and Corporal J.F. Litherland, in a time of 35 hours, 12 minutes. The following year they again came second in their class with a time of 24 hours, 21 minutes.

fifteen years previously in one of the very same Cockle Mark II canoes launched by Hasler and his raiders from Her Majesty's Submarine *Tuna* off the mouth of the Gironde estuary on that cold December night in 1942. And later on, when I commanded my own SBS unit on operational duties in the Far East, the headquarters ship of the Seventh Submarine Squadron with whom we worked had been HMS *Forth* – the same ship Blondie Hasler's team had used as their training base in the Clyde and from which their raid was launched.*

Operation Frankton, 'a brilliant little operation' in the words of Lord Mountbatten,† has I think an unrivalled claim to be the greatest small raid of the Second World War. Up to 1942, almost all British commando raids had been brief, limited in scope and designed more to boost morale at home, rather than do serious damage to the enemy – they were christened 'butcher and bolt' affairs. But Frankton had genuine strategic purpose: damaging blockade runners which were providing vital material to the Axis war effort. As far as we know, Blondie's men killed no one. But their success did serious damage to the sense of invincibility of Britain's enemies at a moment when they seemed to be triumphant everywhere. It also gave renewed hope and offensive spirit to our allies among the French people.

Few other raids in the Second World War could match the audacity of an assault on the massive German naval port of Bordeaux with just ten men in five fragile canoes. And none required such a deep and prolonged penetration of enemy territory. Finally, the epic post-raid escape and evasion of Hasler and his canoe companion Bill Sparks across enemy-occupied France, over the Pyrenees, through Spain and back to Britain, remains a classic that has never been surpassed.

Immediately after the war, one German officer present in Bordeaux when the raid took place described Operation Frankton as the

---

* My son Simon was christened on HMS *Forth*, whose commander at the time, the much-loved Captain John Moore RN, died on 8 July 2010. The christening party, held on *Forth*'s wooden-planked quarterdeck, was such a good one that it was only as we passed through the gates of Singapore's Royal Naval Dockyard that my wife remembered we had left something behind on the great ship – our newly christened son!

† In the foreword to Hasler's post-operation report, Mountbatten used these terms to describe Frankton.

'outstanding Commando raid of the war'. Later, in the early 1950s, a rather good, if monochromatic book was written about the exploits of Blondie Hasler and his men. Later still, in 1955, a badly flawed and inaccurate film was also made on the subject. They both bore the same name: *Cockleshell Heroes* – a title which Hasler intensely disliked.

The tale told by both the *Cockleshell Heroes* book and film was, necessarily, a partial one, based on Hasler's own account and the skimpy information available at the time. But seventy years on, we have access to sources which were not available to Hasler and his chroniclers. We can now consult the German records of the time which tell the story from their point of view and record in detail the fate of each of Hasler's Marines; French records which reveal how his men were helped – and betrayed. And newly opened files in Britain's National Archives which expose a shocking level of deceit, duplication and inter-departmental rivalry on the part of those in London who sent Hasler's Royal Marines off on a mission that may never have been necessary or, at the very least, did not need to cost so many of their young lives.

In researching and writing this book I have been privileged to meet people who themselves played a part in this story and remember every remarkable and sometimes tragic detail of what happened; to record the accounts of relatives, handed down from their families, which have never been heard before; and to work with an extraordinary group of French men and women in the Bordeaux area who have made it their business to gather the last living testimonies of what happened to Blondie and his men, so that these memories are not sucked forever down the black hole of the past.

As a result we now know that this story is not just about the courage and indomitable spirit of the Cockleshell Heroes. It is also about their very human flaws. And we know, too, that their leader, Blondie Hasler, was not the chromium-plated hero beloved of action comics and war films. He was, rather, a deeply complex and compassionate man who, despite doubting his own leadership qualities, was able to inspire very ordinary men to undertake this truly extraordinary – almost super-human – mission.

The full story of Operation Frankton – the Cockleshell Heroes raid – is, we now know, not a simple picture of 'Boy's Own' derring-do. There are blacks here as well as whites; not all is unvarnished glory, unflinching resistance or impeccable judgement.

But through it all – through the vicissitudes, the misjudgements and the pain, the setbacks, the tragedies and the bad luck – one light cannot be extinguished. That is the raw courage and unbreakable determination of the nine men who hazarded their lives with my inquisitive train companion of that spring day in 1965. It is to them, to the brave people of France who helped them and to all those who have sought to follow their example in today's Special Boat Service, that this book is dedicated.

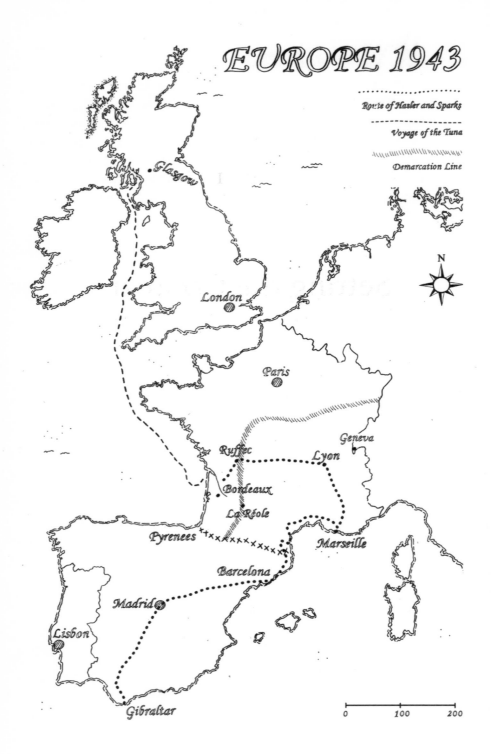

EUROPE 1943

Route of Hasler and Sparks
Voyage of the Tuna
Demarcation Line

N

Glasgow

London

Paris

Geneva

Ruffec   Lyon

Bordeaux

La Réole

Pyrenees   Marseille

Barcelona

Madrid

Lisbon

Gibraltar

0   100   200

PART I

Setting the Context

I

London 1942

The early months of 1942 were, arguably, Britain's darkest period of the Second World War. The heady days of solitary defiance, of Dunkirk and the Battle of Britain, were over. Now the country was into the long, grinding slog of protracted conflict. And all the signs were that it was losing.

After the loss of France, one defeat after another confirmed the triumph first of Germany and then of Japan against a Britain unfit for battle and staggering on her feet. In the Far East, the pride of the Royal Navy, HMS *Prince of Wales* and HMS *Repulse*, had been sunk by Japanese bombers on 10 December 1941, three days after the attack on Pearl Harbor. The Japanese then stormed through Malaya to the gates of Singapore, which fell on 15 February 1942; Churchill declared it 'the worst disaster and the largest capitulation in British history'. The Japanese swept on to capture Burma, the British and Dutch East Indies, and to deliver reverse after reverse to the United States in a series of crushing defeats redeemed only by a single American victory in the Coral Sea. Britain's other ally, Russia, was also in headlong retreat before Hitler's armoured columns, aimed straight for the gates of Moscow and sweeping all before them.

Until the massive weight of the United States could be mobilised, Britain had only two assets with which to turn this almost overwhelming tide of defeats: the unquenchable, bloody-minded pugnacity of her Prime Minister, Winston Churchill, and that age-old bastion of British power, the Royal Navy, which despite its reverses remained the one British arm capable of matching its German counterparts. But in early

1942 naval pride took a second blow when the German warships *Scharnhorst*, *Gneisenau* and *Prinz Eugen* ran the British gauntlet up the English Channel, swatting aside Britain's puny attempts to stop them and reaching their home port largely unscathed.

Worse was to follow as U-boat packs, many operating from newly constructed submarine pens in Bordeaux, tore into convoys of British ships, men and vital war materiel in the Battle of the Atlantic. That early battle too was a one-sided affair. Between January and March 1942 alone, 225 merchantmen were sunk for the loss of just 11 U-boats.[1]

In the Mediterranean, the little British fortress of Malta, under desperate siege, was fighting for survival and became briefly the most bombed place on earth. In North Africa, Rommel drove the British Eighth Army back to El Alamein, capturing Tobruk and causing the panicky packing of suitcases and burning of files in Cairo offices.

With an army still rebuilding after Dunkirk, an RAF whose resources were still insufficient even to defend our skies and a Royal Navy whose hands were full saving the country from starvation in the icy wastes of the north Atlantic, counter-attack was not yet an option. But even the next best strategy – a blockade aimed at denying Germany access to essential raw materials for its war machine – had failed. Until mid-1941 Hitler didn't need to use the high seas to ship in what he needed. He simply seized it from the lands his triumphant armies had so swiftly overrun: iron ore from Scandinavia; heavy water for a future atomic programme from the hydroelectric stations of Norway; food from France and the Low Countries; oil from Romania. The German counter-strategy of seizure by conquest enabled her to bypass Britain's attempts at naval blockade in obtaining 90 per cent of what she needed to prosecute her war. Even those specialised materials which could not be obtained from her European satraps – rubber, opium for medicines, tin, tungsten, antimony, molybdenum and animal and vegetable oils – could, in the early years of the war, be transported overland direct from the Far East, over the Trans-Siberian Railway.

But Operation Barbarossa, the German invasion of Russia in June 1941, changed all that – to Hitler's disadvantage. A system of exchange between the Axis powers had already been agreed in principle under the Tripartite Pact signed in September 1940. The Japanese referred to this as the *Yanagi* trade and it was now brought into full operation, with the Japanese exchanging specialised raw materials from their captured territories in Malaya, Indonesia, the Philippines and Indo-China for their own war necessities: German ball-bearings, chemicals, blueprints and advanced war technology like proximity fuses and radar. A paper based on intelligence of German-Japanese trading intentions, written by the Ministry of Economic Warfare for the Admiralty in mid-1942, estimated that 'during the next 12 months Germany wishes to obtain 250,000 tons of cargo from Japan. This is a substantial increase on the original figure of 100,000 tons',[2] while Japanese requirements from Germany were due to increase, they predicted, from 40,000 tons to 100,000 in the same period.

Suddenly, after the German invasion of Russia, blockade was back on Britain's war agenda again. But a purely naval blockade was not as easy as it sounded.

Britain's previous attempts at blockade in the Napoleonic and First World Wars had been largely north Atlantic and Mediterranean affairs. But now an effective blockade had to have global reach. And mounting a blockade on this scale, while simultaneously fighting the Battle of the Atlantic, was beyond the naval resources available to the Allies at the time. German-crewed[3] blockade runners (an estimate of October 1942 calculated that there were twenty-six[4]) were mostly requisitioned or captured ships. They were replenished during their voyages of around three months' duration, by mid-ocean German supply ships and tankers, were substantially armed[5] and, with speeds of up to seventeen knots, were often capable of outrunning British warships. So the prosecution of a successful blockade strategy had to rely, not just on catching the blockade runners on the high seas, but also on hitting them when they were in port.

And especially the great port of Bordeaux in southwest France. With the Allies still in possession of the Suez Canal, all German shipping from the Far East had to come round the Cape of Good Hope. One near port of disembarkation might have been Marseille, but this would have involved running the gauntlet of British guns on Gibraltar. So Bordeaux,[6] positioned on the Garonne river a few miles upstream from where it joins the Dordogne to form Europe's largest estuary, the Gironde, was now important not merely as a port for coastal traffic carrying, for instance iron ore, from Spain; it was also the nearest German-controlled port for unloading her precious Far Eastern cargoes. Bordeaux was, in short, strategically central both to Germany's struggle to get the specialised materials she needed for her prosecution of the war and to Britain's attempts to deny her these.

The importance to both sides of this traffic can be illustrated by the resources each was prepared to devote to it. A single blockade runner, the merchant cargo vessel *Osorno*, was protected on her approach to Bordeaux by no less than thirteen U-boats and eleven German surface ships, while the Allies were trying to find and sink her with forces which included a US carrier, three destroyers, eight Halifax bombers and fifty-three sorties by Mosquitoes and Beaufighters[7] – yet still she got through.

Berlin attached considerable propaganda importance to successful 'blockade runs'. When the Japanese submarine I-52 *Momi*[8] arrived in Lorient with a cargo of gold (to pay for the goods Japan had purchased from Germany) in late 1943, her crew was invited to Berlin to meet Hitler and, amid great publicity, spent a few days sightseeing in Paris on their way back. On her successful return journey (also much publicised in Germany) she carried a cargo of radar, sonar, optical equipment, 800 lb of uranium oxide (said to be for use in a 'dirty bomb' targeted on the US) and blueprints, along with samples of some of Germany's most advanced weaponry.

But blockade, though necessary, was a passive strategy. Churchill's pugnacious spirit demanded a way to move onto the offensive as well. Here his options were savagely limited by lack of resources. Since conventional offensive operations against an enemy now firmly dug in behind the walls of *Festung Europa* (Fortress Europe) were clearly beyond Britain's military means at this stage, he had to turn instead to unconventional means and irregular forces. The next phase of the European ground war would, he concluded, have to be secret, irregular and clandestine.

In mid-1940 Churchill created two new organisations at very nearly the same time to pursue this secret war. He even used strikingly similar language when setting out their tasks. Combined Operations, launched on 14 June 1940, was told to 'develop a reign of terror'[9] all along the coasts of Occupied Europe, while the Special Operations Executive (SOE), brought into existence a little over a month later on 22 July, was instructed to 'set Europe ablaze'.

Despite this cat's cradle of overlapping responsibilities, SOE, under its chief, the abrasive, egotistical, driven, left-wing, power-hungry Dr Hugh Dalton, felt neither need nor obligation to tell anyone what it did; as he put it, 'the organisation should ... be entirely independent of the War Office machine'.[10] SOE, with headquarters at 64 Baker Street, off the Marylebone Road and well away from the centre of government in Whitehall, viewed sharing information with others not only as a danger to its agents in the field, but also as a potential threat to its own political survival. This view was not without justification: there really *were* powerful forces out to get SOE by strangling its resources, snuffing out its operations and spreading damaging rumours around the Whitehall establishment, even as far as No. 10 Downing Street itself.

The truth was that, by mid-1941, despite having been established for almost a year and having consumed considerable resources (not least precious aircraft), SOE had achieved very little beyond minor pinpricks against the enemy which contributed almost nothing to the main war effort.

Combined Operations, whose headquarters were in Richmond Terrace, Whitehall, had already by May 1942 carried out more than twenty raids against Europe's enemy-occupied coastline in places that stretched from north of the Arctic Circle to south of the Bay of Biscay. Churchill's 'hand of steel', which he commanded to 'come out of the sea from time to time [and] turf the German sentries from their posts with growing efficiency', was now doing just that somewhere along the Atlantic coastline, on average, once every two weeks. But these raids were, almost without exception, mere 'butcher and bolt' affairs which, though dashing and no doubt demoralising to the enemy, had little or no impact on the strategic direction of the war. Many in Whitehall were openly questioning whether, at a time of extreme shortage of resources, these small raids were worth the return they gave in strategic terms. Combined Operations, like SOE, were under pressure to show that they could make a worthwhile contribution to the war effort.

The new Chief of Combined Operations (CCO), appointed in March 1942 with a coveted place on the all-powerful Chiefs of Staff Committee,[11] was the thrusting, young, good-looking, royally connected ex-destroyer commander Louis Mountbatten. In the early months of Mountbatten's tenure he met SOE chief Hugh Dalton to discuss cooperation between their two organisations. But this achieved little beyond establishing a relationship of guarded congeniality between the two men. When, in February 1942, Churchill removed Dalton from his position as Minister of Economic Warfare[12] and Chairman of SOE and replaced him with the more emollient Lord Selborne, the high-level relationship between the two organisations improved somewhat: Selborne was acutely aware that, after Dalton's abrasive approach, he had much ground to recover when it came to improving Whitehall relations with the other services, both in and out of uniform.

Day-to-day relationships between the staffs of SOE and Combined Operations were much more functional. SOE placed one of its secret establishments, Technical Section IX, based at a country house hotel called The Frythe at Welwyn Garden City in Hertfordshire, at Combined Operations' disposal. It was this organisation which was responsible for the development, manufacture and supply of new weapons for use in the clandestine war, such as the anti-ship 'limpet' mine and its smaller, less powerful cousin used for attacking railway lines, the 'clam' charge.

One other 'common user' organisation crucial to both SOE and Combined Operations at this time was the Inter-Services Topographical Department or ISTD, which was effectively run by Britain's Secret Intelligence Service (SIS).* Based in the School of Geography in Oxford and staffed in the main by the university's geography dons, this unit was tasked with bringing together all available information, from pre-war holiday snaps to the latest aerial photography and agent information, in order to produce detailed topographical reports on areas where prospective operations were under consideration. Despite such low-level cooperation on operational matters, however, the high-level relationships between Richmond Terrace and Baker Street remained guarded and suspicious.

This climate of rivalry, duplication and competition was not confined to Combined Operations and SOE. It also existed between SOE and SIS. The latter saw the newcomer as an upstart, intent not only upon taking

---

*   Also known as MI6 (originally Military Intelligence 6), to distinguish it from MI5 (Military Intelligence 5) and – as we shall see later – MI9 (Military Intelligence 9). But I shall refer to it by its more commonly used name today, SIS.

over its own role, but also doing this in a nasty, noisy way which involved letting off bangs and killing Germans, thus disturbing the quiet, felt-shoed business of 'real' espionage. Commenting on this enmity after the war, Malcolm Muggeridge, himself an SIS officer, said: 'Though SOE and SIS were nominally on the same side in the war, they were, generally speaking, more abhorrent to one another than the Abwehr was to either of them.'[13]

The dysfunctional institutional relationship between the two organisations was exacerbated by personal dislike on a grand scale. Claude Dansey, who despite being SIS's deputy was effectively the organisation's head, referred to SOE as 'amateur bandits' and took much pleasure in every Baker Street reverse.[14]

SOE was, like SIS, a 'non-avowed' organisation; that is, its founding was not the subject of parliamentary approval, its budget was secret and its existence was nowhere publicly acknowledged. Born in secrecy, preserved in secrecy, secrecy very quickly became SOE's obsession, its code, its culture and its means of survival in the jungle of 1940s Whitehall. Its officers even used aliases when they attended meetings or did business with their opposite numbers in Whitehall. Nor was SOE's culture of exclusion and secrecy confined to its external relations. The organisation's internal structure was largely based on 'Country sections', each responsible for the training, insertion and running of agents in different occupied countries in Europe. There was one agent-running section for each occupied country, except for France, which had two: SOE F (for France) Section and SOE RF (for *République Française*) Section.[15] The former, run by Colonel Maurice Buckmaster, was staffed predominantly by British officers and agents and, at the insistence of General de Gaulle, was heavily discouraged from recruiting French citizens.[16] These were supposed to be the preserve of RF Section.[17] Although on the ground F and RF Sections would often cooperate, their London headquarters distrusted each other completely, disliked each other heartily and shared their intelligence almost never.

There was, in addition, a third SOE section operating into France at this time: DF Section. This was a Europe-wide organisation which reported directly to Brigadier Colin Gubbins, SOE's Director of Operations and Training, and was dedicated to providing escape lines, principally for SOE's own agents. It was also, from time to time, used to help others such as escaping prisoners and downed pilots trying to get back home.

But the duplication and rivalry between competing clandestine organisations did not end there. There were no less than three other secret organisations also operating in France at the time.

The first was de Gaulle's independent Free French *Bureau Central de Renseignement et d'Action* (BCRA), established in 1940[18] and run from de Gaulle's London headquarters in 4 Carlton Terrace by Colonel Dewavrin (code name *Passy*). BCRA's networks, or *réseaux* were split into *réseaux des actions* and *réseaux des renseignements*. The former concentrated on sabotage and offensive action, while the latter gathered intelligence, the greater part of which was passed back to SOE's deadly rivals, SIS.

Then there were SIS's own intelligence organisations, the most famous of which at this time was 'Noah's Ark' (so christened by the Germans because all its agents were named after animals), run by Marie-Madeleine Fourcade-Bridou.

And finally – and not to be confused with SOE's DF Section – there was MI9, headed by Major Norman Crockatt, which ran its own independent secret organisation dedicated to helping escaped prisoners of war and downed airmen back to Britain.

Rivalry, duplication, suspicion and a desperation to prove their worth; these were the prevailing characteristics of the secret organisations which proliferated and competed in the London of 1941. Then, suddenly, in the late summer of that year – just when SOE needed it most – Baker Street started receiving secret messages from Bordeaux which were of vital relevance to the British strategy of blockade, to Churchill's secret war, and to SOE's battle to survive in Whitehall as well ...

2

Bordeaux 1940–1942

The Bordeaux element of our story starts, as great stories often do, with a single man.

Jean Duboué was forty-three when the Second World War began. A self-made man, he had started his working life as a boy down the coal mines in the Basque country of Spain, from where he was rescued and educated by the Jesuits. Daboué arrived in Bordeaux between the wars and began a new career as a restaurateur, managing the Café du Commerce, the city's most famous restaurant. From here he branched out with his own businesses. One of these was the Café des Marchands, a small restaurant and boarding house frequented by dockers, truckers and travelling salesmen, which he ran with his wife on the city's waterfront – known locally as *Le Port de la Lune* because of its sweeping crescent shape.

At about the time Jean Duboué first arrived in Bordeaux, the city's mayor was engaged in a major programme of renovation. The old tumbledown quays which had shipped iron and tin in Roman times, wine from the eighth century (chiefly to Bristol), slaves to the New World and coffee, sugar, cocoa, cotton and indigo to most of Europe in the centuries that followed, were being torn down. In a huge programme of public works, the wharves on both sides of the river were replaced by new stone quays almost four and a half miles in length. These were served by over a hundred and fifty of the most up-to-date electric rolling cranes, supported by six floating cranes and other equipment for the loading and discharge of coal, sand, grain, iron ore and other commodities. Behind these, a line of large concrete hangars were constructed which acted as warehouses and passenger terminals. Further behind still, the old dockside cobbled road was torn up and replaced by a broad tarmacadamed highway which ran the full length of Bordeaux's magnificent eighteenth-century waterfront.[1] Here were ships' chandlers and the offices of the great shipping lines, cafés and luxury hotels and merchants (especially wine merchants), and, at the upstream Pont de Pierre end, elegant balconied apartments set around with parks, middle-class amusements and genteel walks. At the other end of the waterfront, known as the Quai des Chartrons, lay the Bacalan district with its jumble of working-class homes housing the two thousand dockers who earned their living from the port. In Bacalan life was tough, livelihoods murky, the streets dimly lit, the cafés small, smokey and cheap and the red wine as rough as the clientele who drank it.

Jean Duboué's Café des Marchands was located halfway along this crescent of social gradation, reflecting his own position as an upwardly mobile middle-class Bordeaux entrepreneur. By the time war broke out, the Duboué businesses were doing well enough for him to have purchased a little *villégiature*, or *maison de campagne*, called Ancienne Villa Roucoule, at Lestiac-sur-Garonne, twelve and a half miles southwest of Bordeaux.

The war, when it finally started in France, came swiftly to Bordeaux. The city was briefly declared France's temporary wartime capital after the fall of Paris.[2] But it couldn't last. On 17 June 1940 Charles de Gaulle took a plane, 100,000 gold francs, a spare pair of trousers, four clean shirts, and, many argue, the honour of France, and fled to Britain from Bordeaux's Mérignac airport.

The armistice which Marshal Pétain signed five days later divided France in two. The northern and western part (known as the *Zone Occupée*, or ZO) included its entire Atlantic seaboard and was placed under direct German rule. The southern two-fifths (the *Zone Non-Occupée*, or ZNO) was governed by Pétain's puppet government from its '*capitale*' in Vichy. The two were separated by a line of demarcation which ran from the Swiss border opposite Geneva to a point on the Spanish frontier close to St Jean-Pied-de-Port.

This line – effectively an interior frontier – was manned at each crossing point by a permanent German guard post complete with a swastika-emblazoned flag and large notice carrying the stern declaration:

'*Demarkationsline. Überschritten verboten* – *Ligne de démarcation, défense de traverser*'. The equivalent Vichy post on the ZNO side, positioned usually within five hundred yards of the German one, was a more informal affair which was often left unmanned for several hours at a time. In the Bordeaux area, this line of control ran more or less north–south some nineteen miles east of the city, crossing the Dordogne at Castillon la Bataille and the Garonne at Langon.

The formal implementation of the division of France began at midnight on 26 June 1940, but it was not until 1 July that German troops arrived in Bordeaux in substantial numbers, swiftly imposing a heavy hand over the town's people, economy and lines of communication. A curfew was established between 11 p.m. and 5 a.m. German time (2100–0300 GMT) with curfew-breakers suffering terms of imprisonment or forced labour. All firearms, including hunting weapons, had to be deposited in the local *mairie*. All official notices were required to be published in German as well as French. The swastika was hoisted over all principal buildings. Strict controls were established at the port of Bordeaux, the Gironde estuary, all major transport intersections and on the railways. In due course every aspect of ordinary life would fall under German control, including posts and telecommunications, newspapers, cinemas, cultural events, agriculture (including wine), commercial transactions, the refining and distribution of petroleum products and the passage of goods to and from Vichy France. There were countless fixed road blocks (*contrôles*) supplemented by spot checks (known as *rafales*) at which an identity card, accompanied by a *laissez-passer* or *Ausweis*, had to be presented.

Food (now rationed) became increasingly scarce, especially for those living in the towns and cities of German-occupied France, for whom the struggle to obtain enough sustenance for themselves and their families became a major preoccupation. It was not long before this resulted in the growth of a flourishing black market.

South of the Demarcation Line, in the ZNO – also known as the *Zone Libre* – things were more relaxed. Travel here was, despite occasional *contrôles* and *rafales*, much freer and the hand of the Vichy administration much lighter.

Despite its recent history as the effective capital of France – and contrary to the wishful thinking of the then head of SOE, Hugh Dalton, who claimed that 'occupied Europe was smouldering with resistance to the Nazis and ready to erupt at the slightest support or encouragement'[3] – Bordeaux was not an early hotbed of resistance to the Germans. In fact, in the early years of the war most of France seemed at ease with their occupiers and most German soldiers posted there regarded it as a 'cushy number'. Secret feelers put out by SIS and de Gaulle's Free French into the area all complain that the spirit of resistance among the Bordelais at this time was depressingly frail. At first, local opposition to the German occupation was largely confined to individual acts of defiance.

Things began to change when the Germans started to react to minor provocations with increasing severity. On 27 August 1940, Leizer Karp, a Jew, was summarily condemned to death for raising his fist at a German parade. In December, a brilliant local mathematics student, Pierre Germin, was convicted of organising resistance and shot at Souges, just outside the city, soon to become infamous as a place of execution for those prepared to risk death in the struggle against France's occupiers. On 20 October 1941, a German military advisor, Hans Reimer, was assassinated in Bordeaux.[4] The Germans responded with terrible severity: fifty French civilian hostages were taken to Souges and shot in reprisal.[*] Slowly, organised resistance against the occupiers in the Bordeaux area began to grow.

After Operation Barbarossa in June 1941, a Communist-led organisation called *Franc-tireurs et Partisans* (FTP)[5] was formed with many activists among the dockers, railwaymen and Post Office workers from the Bordeaux area. Shortly afterwards, a second left-wing organisation, this time linked to de Gaulle under the title *Confédération Général du Travail* (CGT), emerged. The right wing responded by forming its own network, the *Organisation Civile et Militaire* (OCM), with a branch in the Charente area which called itself *Le Groupe Ouest*.

In due course, all this confusion of organisations would resolve into a broadly based armed Resistance – albeit a highly fractured one – peopled by thousands of individual agents, many of whom were often unaware even of the name of the organisation to which they belonged. Some of

---

[*]   According to the 1907 Hague Convention, it was, in principle, legal to take hostages from the civilian population and execute them in cases where violent action was committed by an occupied population against an occupying power.

these were little more than clubs of friends who combined to express their comradeship, patriotism, anger, or even political (mostly Communist) affiliations through resistance to their oppressors. It has been estimated[6] that, by the end of the war, there were 266 Resistance *réseaux* of one kind or another – armed, equipped and directed by the various rival secret organisations back in Britain – with perhaps over 100,000 agents, in almost every locality across the whole of France.[7]

Jean Duboué was one of the very first in Bordeaux to start organising resistance to his country's occupiers. This was not his first war. In 1914–18 he had been wounded at one of France's bloodiest calvaries, the battle of Chemin des Dames, and was awarded the Légion d'Honneur for bravery. In August 1940, less than six weeks after de Gaulle left for England, he joined forces with his friend Léo Paillère who lived next door to his restaurant on the Quai des Chartrons waterfront, to form one of the earliest secret Resistance networks. In 1941 this was subsumed into what later became known as the *A.S.* (short for *Armée Secrète*) network. In mid-1941, however, there was neither the equipment nor the strength in numbers for armed resistance. So Duboué's *A.S. Réseau*, which had grown to thirty-six operatives before the end of 1940,[8] started off as a *réseau de renseignements* (intelligence network). In 1940 and during the summer of 1941, Duboué and Paillère worked to strengthen and expand their *réseau* to a hundred members, establishing three sites for receiving parachute drops and a 'post box' for clandestine messages. Duboué established a network of contacts among the dock labourers frequenting his café which kept him informed about the movement of ships and their cargoes.

But Duboué and Paillère's organisation was not the only *réseau de renseignements* operating in Bordeaux at the time. De Gaulle's Free French BCRA also had its own agents in the city, including two Gironde pilots, Jean Fleuret and Ange-Marie Gaudin,[9] who provided detailed information on shipping in and out of the port, hydrographical and topographical information about the Gironde and details of the disposition of German forces in the area.[10] This 'product' was passed back to de Gaulle's BCRA in London, who passed it on to SOE's deadly rivals in SIS.

SIS, however, had its own independent circuits in the city. These included the Polish F2 network run by Tadeusz Jekiel, who reported back on shipping movements through Marseille, and an intelligence *réseau* called Jade-Amicol.

At about the same time as Duboué started his resistance work in 1941, an elegant 49-year-old named Raymond Brard set up a separate intelligence *réseau* concentrating chiefly on the docks area.[11] Brard, a well-known and respected figure in Bordeaux, was head of the port's Fire Defence Service and as such, had free access to all the ships berthed at the quays. Initially he passed his information to the SIS-run Jade circuit, but subsequently set up his own SIS-controlled *réseau*, called *Phidias-Phalanx*,[12] which later also undertook minor sabotage in the port.[13] Although Brard doubtless knew of Duboué and his connection with SOE there was no contact between the two organisations. As one of Brard's key agents, Albert Juenbekdjian, was to write after the war, Duboué and his colleagues 'reported directly to Section "F" of S.O.E. (Buckmaster) who not only had no link with us, but actually hid from us all activities they carried out'.[14]

Disparate, secretive and exclusive, all these multiple networks had one thing in common. They were as jealous of their reputations and conspiratorial with each other as were their masters in London.

Sometime in 1941, Duboué further expanded his network by linking up with another early resister, Gaston Hèches in Tarbes, some hundred miles to the south of Bordeaux and close to the Pyrenees and the Spanish border. Hèches, a small man so severely incapacitated with rheumatism that he found it impossible to turn his head and could only walk with the aid of two sticks,[15] was *chef* and *patron* of a modest restaurant and occasional boarding house which he ran with his wife and two daughters in the centre of the town.

In 1939, when Tarbes was flooded with refugees from the Spanish Civil War, Gaston and his wife Mimi set up a day-and-night soup kitchen to feed and care for them. In mid-May 1940 the town was again flooded with refugees – but this time from the opposite direction. Thousands of the destitute and the terrified, fleeing the advancing German armies in the hope of crossing into Spain, flooded into the town. Gaston and Mimi re-established their soup kitchen to feed them.

In early June 1940, just weeks before France fell, two men dressed in British uniforms walked into Hèches' restaurant, ordered some soup and asked for a bed for the night. When all the other clients had left, the strangers sought Hèches out and introduced themselves as 'Colonel R' from the 'War Office' and Mr 'Gabriel', from SIS in Paris.[16] They explained that they were setting up an escape line from Nancy in Lorraine, through Argenteuil in Paris, to Tarbes and over the Pyrenees to Spain. They had heard that Hèches was a patriot and anti-Nazi. Would he be their organiser in the area and set up a network which would courier intelligence to London and assist in getting people and documents over the Pyrenees into Spain? Hèches agreed without hesitation. Before leaving they asked him to swear an oath of allegiance to 'The Franco-British Forces for the Liberation of Europe'[17] and told him that he would have two code names: *Thomas* and *Tristan*. His organisation would be known as the *Édouard* line.[18]

By mid-1941, Hèches' *Édouard* network (motto: *Chercher: Passer: Recevoir* – 'To seek, to receive, to pass on to England') had set up a widespread organisation extending into the *Zone Occupée*. This facility was supplemented by six crossing points on the Demarcation Line and sixteen safe houses close to La Réole, some twenty-five miles southeast of Bordeaux. One of the *Édouard* line's key agents in La Réole was a gendarme in the town called Albert Rigoulet.[19]

By early 1941, SOE had taken over the *Édouard* line and subsumed it into their DF Section, as part of the escape network for agents in need of an emergency back door out of France. As well as fugitives, the *Édouard* line also acted as a conduit for passing documents and messages back to London. From 4 April 1941 to June 1943, a sixty-year-old Briton of Maltese extraction called Egbert V.H. Rizzo (code name *Édouard II*), acted as SOE's full-time liaison officer with Hèches and his team. By late 1941 the *Édouard* line was running regular weekly courier services carrying messages and documents across the Pyrenees into Spain. Eventually its escape tentacles reached as far north as Paris and as far east as Albertville and Annecy in the Savoie.[20] It is estimated that during the course of the war, the *Édouard* line helped more than five hundred escapers, ranging from agents to prisoners of war and downed airmen, over the Pyrenees and into Spain.[21]

Among Hèches' earliest and most frequent customers were Duboué's *A.S. Réseau* in Bordeaux, who used this route to pass people and messages to Barcelona; there the British Consul, Sir Henry Farquhar, operated as post box and transit point for onward passage to Gibraltar and thence to

SOE headquarters in London. The first messages from Duboué's organisation – the ones which were to cause such a stir in Baker Street – were reports on the docks and blockade runners at Bordeaux, carried to Tarbes for onward transmission to London in the summer of 1941 by Duboué's daughter, Suzanne (whose code name was *Mouton*), then aged seventeen. By the end of 1941 a second line was established for passing Duboué's information back to Baker Street. This used Suzanne Duboué to courier her father's reports to the city of Tours, where *Robert*,[22] one of the first British wireless operators to be parachuted into the region, had set up a clandestine radio station. In January 1942, a courier (we do not know his or her identity) made the journey from Bordeaux, through Tarbes all the way back to London, duly sending back through the BBC[23] the prearranged code phrase, '*Bonjour à Mouton*',[24] indicating his safe arrival.

In September 1941, SOE responded to all this activity and intelligence by sending in an agent to find out more about what was happening on the quays of Bordeaux.[25]

Robert Yves Marie Leroy, born in Brest on 27 February 1911, was clearly something of an adventurer. He joined the French Navy at seventeen, specialising as an Engine Room Artificer. He left after five years to become a merchant seaman and then an arms smuggler during the Spanish Civil War. The outbreak of the wider conflict found him on a banana boat in the Cameroons, from where he returned home to Brest just in time to have to flee again when the Germans arrived in June 1940. When he reached Britain he joined the Free French Navy under General de Gaulle.

This must not have suited him, however, as he appears to have deserted shortly afterwards. He was recruited by SOE on 11 April 1941 and sent almost immediately to their training schools, finishing at Ringway for his parachute course. He refused his second jump and was removed from the course. It is clear, however that, despite this, SOE valued what Leroy – something of a rough diamond – could offer, describing him in its reports as 'very tough and intelligent of the sailor type, a man of great resource and native wit'. A later, less flattering report describes him as 'shrewd ... [but] suffering from the weaknesses of his class – a proneness to alcoholic indulgence and women'.

On the night of 19 September 1941, Robert Leroy, equipped with a quantity of explosives, was landed from the undercover ship 'Q' HMS

Fidelity[26] at Barcarès near Perpignan, one of the earliest SOE agents to be landed on French soil.[27] Leroy, for all his faults, was later described by Maurice Buckmaster as one of the four most important agents operating in France at that time. His orders were to make his way to Bordeaux where he was to find information on the blockade runners and investigate the possibility of attacking the *bassin*, or dock, at the mouth of the port, in which the Germans were at that time constructing concrete submarine pens. Unfortunately the explosives Leroy was supposed to take with him somehow got misplaced during the landing, leaving him to set off for Tarbes without them the following day.

In November Egbert Rizzo, the head of the *Édouard* line, reported to London that Leroy – 'a queer looking fellow with a tooth-swollen jaw [and] neither food, card nor tickets'[28] – had turned up in Tarbes and had, with the help of false papers arranged by Gaston Hèches, moved on to Bordeaux where he made contact with Jean Duboué. It appears[29] that it was about this time also that, at the instigation of Leroy, Jean Duboué's *réseau* formally joined SOE's British-run F Section. A month later, thanks to widespread arrests among SOE's meagre stock of agents, Leroy was, for a short period, their only operating agent left in southwest France.

Leroy got a job as a tractor driver on the Bordeaux docks, almost certainly with the help of Duboué and his contacts. He built up an extensive network of informal contacts, describing the dockers as Anglophile, anti-German and, in large measure, Communist. Quickly deciding that it would not be possible to attack the submarine base and the *bassin*, due both to the difficulty of access and the lack of viable targets, he investigated instead the possibility of an attack on 'the big ships which left from time to time for Japan and the Middle East and began passing detailed intelligence on these blockade runners … back to London'.[30]

Sometime in early May 1942, London decided that Leroy's information was so important that he should be recalled for a full debrief. Leroy returned over the Pyrenees with the help of Hèches and the *Édouard* line, arriving in London on 29 May bearing, among other things, a full report on the blockade runners and a map showing the detailed layout of the Bordeaux docks. It is with this tiny thread of information that our story really begins.

3

Blondie Hasler and the Blockade Runners

To the Prime Minister   **9 May 1942**

BLOCKADE RUNNERS

I attach a note, based on the evidence available, showing that:

1 Blockade running, both ways, between German Europe and the Far East is beginning and is likely to increase;
2 Even a few cargoes will appreciably strengthen both Germany and Japan;
3 The first cargoes to sail are likely to be much more important.

I submit, therefore, that everything practicable should be done quickly to ensure that blockade-runners in either direction shall be located and intercepted.

I know that the Admiralty is fully alive to the danger and that measures for facilitating transmission of reports from Spain, the location of blockade-runners at sea and attacks in neutral waters are now being considered.

I submit that in addition to these proposals, the implementing of which is an urgent need, the Defence Committee should consider how to … ensure interception of the next ships to sail, thus catching the most vital cargoes and perhaps stopping the trade altogether.[1]

Attached to this letter from Lord Selborne (who was at the time both Minister for Economic Warfare and head of SOE) was an explanatory note identifying the number and details of blockade runners currently on the high seas and alongside at Bordeaux – an analysis assembled, he said, from 'numerous communications' (almost certainly German signals decrypted by Britain's codebreakers at Bletchley Park) indicating that the Axis powers planned to increase this trade over the coming months. This was followed by an estimation of the importance of the trade to both sides, which, the note concluded, was 'out of all proportion to the size of the cargoes carried'. Selborne ended with a final call for immediate action; 'Of cargoes to Germany, only those which arrive within the next few months can affect this year's campaign; whilst ... cargoes to Japan ... contain machinery ... which, if intercepted, cannot be replaced for many months.'

The significance of Selborne's letter went far beyond its plea for urgency, its wealth of detail, or the evident fact that much of it was based on reports from Britain's various secret sources in Bordeaux.[2] What it confirmed was that the destruction of the German blockade runners was now a key aim of Britain's war strategy. Moreover, since the Royal Navy could not guarantee that seaborne action alone could be relied on to achieve this objective, a double-pronged strategy would be required. Those blockade runners which could be caught at sea would be sunk there; those which got through should be attacked in harbour in Bordeaux.

Whitehall departments now began to give active consideration to Selborne's demands 'that everything practicable should be done quickly' to tackle what was becoming known as 'the Bordeaux problem', now considered important enough to be assigned a code name of its own – Operation Frankton.

During June 1942, Frankton was considered by both the Admiralty and the RAF. The first turned it down because Bordeaux was considered to be too far up a heavily defended estuary for a raid to have any chance of success. The second swiftly followed suit: given the inaccuracy of bombing at this stage of the war, it was concluded there would be no certainty of hitting the target and every possibility of causing significant civilian casualties in the process. This latter view was supported by the Foreign Office, who were concerned at the effect excessive French civilian casualties would have on anti-British feeling in a France still smarting from the Royal Navy's destruction of the French fleet at Mers el Kebir in July 1940. In this operation, taken to prevent French warships falling into German hands, three French battleships were destroyed and 1297 French sailors killed in ten minutes of British shelling.[3]

There had, moreover, already been attempts to bomb the Bordeaux docks and other installations from as early as December 1940, but these had been ineffectual and involved significant civilian casualties. By the middle of 1942, the Director of Naval Plans effectively closed the bombing option by pointing out to the First Sea Lord that the '"blitzing" of [blockade runners'] terminal ports has been ruled out by Cabinet decision'.[4] On 26 June Sir Charles Portal, then Chief of the Air Staff, suggested at a meeting of the Chiefs of Staff Committee that 'this was a matter in which the SOE might be able to give valuable assistance by devising special means of dealing with these ships',[5] little realising that that was exactly what SOE was already doing.

In early July 1942, Combined Operations' Examinations Committee (who considered all operations before they were passed to the Chiefs of Staff for approval) looked at the 'Bordeaux problem' and concluded that a Combined Operations raid on the port could only succeed if three divisions or some 50,000 men were committed to it.[6] At this point in the war, with resources so constrained, this was no more than a polite way of declaring that such an operation could not be done by this means. On 27 July 1942, Combined Operations' Search Committee (which identified possible targets and passed them to the Examination Committee for a judgement on viability) revisited the problem and added their own lukewarm opinion:

1 Bombing. But … a large number of bombers would be required to have any marked effect.
2 Mining the mouth of the Gironde.
3 Submarine patrol … but (this) … would require a large number of submarines.
4 SOE or Commando Saboteurs.[7]

What no one in Whitehall could have known was that the answer to the 'Bordeaux problem' would lie not in any of these means, but in a paper on the use of canoes to attack ships in harbour, written by a young, unknown and largely unregarded Royal Marines officer, which the Admiralty had rejected as unworkable more than a year previously.

The author of that rejected Admiralty paper had built his first canoe and paddled it around Portsmouth and Langstone harbours at the age of twelve.

Christened Herbert George Hasler,[8] he was born in Dublin on 27 February 1914, the second son of Annie and Arthur Hasler. Despite being in a non-combat arm – the Royal Army Medical Corps – Lieutenant (Quartermaster) Arthur Hasler, who had gained his commission from the ranks, had, by the third year of the First World War, been awarded the Military Cross and the French Military Medal in addition to being twice mentioned in dispatches. All these awards were given for saving lives rather than for offensive action. In 1917, Lieutenant Hasler was drowned when his troopship, the *Transylvania*, was torpedoed in the Mediterranean. Herbert, then only three, and his brother John were left to be brought up by their mother on a meagre widow's pension in a modest part of the Portsmouth suburb of Southsea, within sight and sound of the sea.

It was the sea which became, from a very early age, Hasler's passion. His home-made canoe was followed in his early teens by an inelegant flat-bottomed, tub-shaped sailing boat, built from a plan he found in *Boy's Own Paper*. In this he could go further afield, exploring Portsmouth Harbour and making trips across the Solent to the Isle of Wight. Often he would be away for two or three days at a time, leading his mother to comment during a later and much more prolonged absence that she 'always knew he would turn up, sooner or later'.

Hasler's second obsession – also evident from an early age – was to discover how things worked and, in particular, how they could be made to work better. Writing in the mid-1950s, C.E. Lucas Phillips, the author of *Cockleshell Heroes* and first chronicler of Hasler's exploits, captures the essence of these two primary elements of his subject's personality in a passage whose insight is not diminished by the flowery idiom of the time:

> The impulse of the moving waters was in his veins. Together with this passion went an ardour for contriving and devising things. He

was not content to accept things ready made, but worked them out for himself, and they had to pass every test. He loved making things with his own hands from the beginning up, and to whatever problem he turned – whether it was a point of ceremonial drill, the rig of a dinghy, the fastening of a ski, the modification of a car, the diet needed for a long cruise – he devoted an intensity and singleness of purpose that was not satisfied with any ready-offered solution, but impelled him to probe the smallest details of invention, whether it were a screw, a cord, a strap or a grain of wheat.[9]

The young Herbert was by all accounts a serious and assiduous child, who did well at his early schools. So well, in fact, that it was recommended he should try for one of the scholarships reserved for officers' sons at Wellington, the well-known public school which specialised in preparing boys to be officers in Britain's armed services. He passed his scholarship exams comfortably but was rejected on the grounds that he was not the son of a 'real' officer (meaning that his father had come up through the ranks, rather than being given a King's Commission on joining). His mother, whose outwardly gentle demeanour hid an iron determination when it came to the well-being of her family, insisted that the terms of the scholarship made no such distinction. Whether the authorities at Wellington were persuaded by the argument, the mother's determination or the child's accomplishments is not known, but Mrs Annie Hasler's younger son duly began at the school in 1928.

In his first term young Herbert was known as 'Bert' and had a broad Portsmouth accent, for which he was teased (and no doubt worse) by his more 'well spoken' fellow pupils. By the second term, the accent had gone and so had 'Bert'. He now insisted on being known by his second name, George, which was how his friends referred to him for the rest of his school days. One junior Wellington contemporary who was in the same boarding house as Hasler described him in these years as 'kind, fearless and tough'.[10]

Having finished Wellington with good results, Hasler was commissioned as a probationary second lieutenant into His Majesty's Corps of Royal Marines (known as 'The Corps' for short) and began his training on 1 September 1932.[11]

The adult Hasler who joined the Royal Marines at eighteen was a little over six feet tall and of athletic build, with receding fair hair; sometime after joining he grew a magnificent blond moustache, which swiftly became his most distinguishing feature. Thanks to the Royal Marines' love of nicknames, Hasler's two first names, Herbert George, seem to have been rather quickly mislaid and replaced with 'Blondie' after the colour of his hair.[12] From this moment onwards 'Blondie' was the name by which he was known to all, except his mother, his brother and his blood family. The serious and assiduous schoolboy now became, at a princely six shillings and eightpence a day, a serious and assiduous young Royal Marines officer, eventually 'passing out' top of his year.

But Hasler soon showed he was no conventional young officer. Right from the start he stood out among his fellows as different – even eccentric. Indeed, his tendency to behave in ways which more conventional people regarded as verging on the bizarre is one of the characteristics most commonly ascribed to him by his contemporaries. After the war, one close associate would comment that he came from a 'long breed of intrepid (British) eccentrics who always come to the fore in times of crisis'.[13] Another, perhaps more perceptively, would take this further: 'I think he may have had an ultimate belief in his own sense of right and wrong that would have made him capable of even reacting against the highest authority – the State – if he had thought it necessary.'[14]

It is often the case that complex characters are formed at the collision point between opposing forces. And so it was with Blondie Hasler. Throughout his service career – and arguably in later life, too – the pressure for order, discipline and convention which was required by his profession, and the contrary pull of the loner dedicated to life on his own terms, were the two opposing forces that constantly played against each other in the crucible in which his singular, complex and most unusual character was formed.

One disconcerting habit he had at this time was testing his limits by staying awake for long periods and forcing himself to the boundaries of physical endurance. Later on, he would try taking salt with his water at meals to see if he could create sufficient tolerance in his body to enable him to survive on seawater.[15] On one occasion, when his officer training shifted from Plymouth to Portsmouth, Hasler decided not to travel to his new posting by conventional means, but instead to sail there single-handed in his latest sailing boat, an open dinghy called *Trivia*. In the process he had to hazard a risky passage through the tidal overfalls around the end of Portland Bill and spend a night with his boat anchored, all sails still standing, right under its forbidding cliffs.[16] It was an experience he would have cause to remember later in his life.

Hasler's reserves were formidable. But they were sustained not so much by physical strength as by an iron will and unbreakable determination. Once Blondie Hasler had settled on an objective, nothing physical could divert him from it.

There was, above all, nothing of the dilettante about Hasler. He regarded soldiering as a deeply professional business, in which those who hazarded their lives in combat were entitled to expect from those who led them the proper exercise of good judgement, learnt skills, attention to detail, careful preparation and above all, meticulous planning. He had little in common with those (rather prevalent in the early days of the war) who came largely from the upper reaches of society and believed that the qualities of a gifted amateur were sufficient, provided they were supported by dash, daring and a devil-may-care attitude to danger. It is significant that when, in the coming months, Hasler chose the men who were to join him in leading the enterprise ahead, he would select mostly officers who had shown their soldierly professionalism by coming up through the ranks, as his own father had done.

But it would be wrong to conclude from this that he was some gimlet-eyed, gung-ho military obsessive. Soldiering was his chosen profession – yet he abhorred violence and took great pains to avoid it where he could. His much-decorated father had shown his courage in saving lives in the RAMC, rather than destroying them on the front line. Hasler may have been driven by the same instinct when he chose to conduct his war through the stealth and guile of Special Forces, rather than through the exercise of total violence which is necessary for success in conventional warfare. If so, he would not have been the last Special Forces soldier to feel this way.

He was awarded the OBE in his first active service engagement in the Norwegian campaign of 1940. And the Légion d'Honneur for his work with a French Foreign Legion unit who were also part of the Allied forces in the Norway operation. Yet he confided to a friend afterwards that he doubted his leadership abilities and feared letting his men down if these were tested too severely at some time in the future.[17] It may have been because of this that he never asked his men to do anything he had not first done himself – as though he was testing the limits of his courage and leadership, just as he had those of his physical endurance.

Though he worked hard at learning the skills of his profession, he was a man of many other accomplishments. He was passionate about cars and loved tinkering with them. A gifted cartoonist, he painted with skill and insight, played the clarinet, taught himself the piano (jazz in both cases; his favourite tune was 'Sweet Georgia Brown') and was later to write frequently for national newspapers who valued his clear, unfussy and surprisingly elegant prose.[18]

I doubt that Hasler was a comfortable colleague to most of his fellow officers. A deeply private man who was painfully shy in the presence of women (whom he held in romantic awe), he was known intimately only by those closest to him. I suspect his fellows found him a little unbending at times and too constantly challenging for easy friendship; in consequence he was probably more respected than loved by those he commanded. Not especially 'clubbable', his close friends were very close – and comparatively few.

Some commentators have overlooked Hasler's sense of humour, perhaps because it was not obvious to the casual acquaintance. However, those who knew him well speak of his wickedly dry wit when among intimate friends and family. There are, among his papers, some rather good and impishly saucy limericks, with which he used to amuse his close circle:

> Miss Mainwairing stopped wearing mauve
> When the Brighton police said it drove
> Young men mad to seduce
> Her. So she wore puce
> And was laid, like a carpet in Hove.

And

> A popular girl from South Mimms
> Had several remarkable whims.
> The most entertaining

One called for strict training
And frightfully flexible limbs.

Later in life Hasler would find himself uncomfortable with fame, which he did his best to avoid or play down altogether, causing him to be judged a modest man. This he almost certainly was. But modesty may also have been a convenient mechanism for preventing fame from violating his private space.

Above all, Blondie Hasler was an individualist. At a time when it would have been regarded as almost an act of treachery for one of Her Majesty's Officers not to vote Conservative, Hasler, according to his wife Bridget, was a lifelong Liberal. In due course he would also be far ahead of his time in believing in – and practising – a more sustainable life-style. Later on, in a revealing comment he would write to a friend: 'if the whole world is going in one direction – it's time to set off on the reciprocal'.[19]

Blondie Hasler was a loner; neither afraid of solitude, nor frightened of taking lonely positions. He set his own course, charted his own voyages and – both metaphorically and literally – paddled his own canoe.

4

Buttercup and Her Daughters

In fact, although Blondie Hasler's name more than any other was to become indelibly linked with the use of canoes for offensive purposes in the Second World War, the true lineage of the idea goes back to the pre-war years and a 1938 Klepper,[1] a German-manufactured *Faltboot* or collapsible canoe, called *Buttercup*.

In June of that year, Roger Courtney (known to his friends as 'Jumbo') and his new wife Dorrise decided to spend their honeymoon canoeing down the Danube to the Black Sea. *Buttercup* was their chosen vehicle of newly married bliss. The escapade made Roger Courtney an enthusiastic devotee of canoes and their uses. Whether this enthusiasm extended to his long-suffering bride, history does not relate.

When the Second World War broke out a little over a year later, Jumbo Courtney, his larger-than-life personality and appetite for adventure undiminished though he was already forty years old, was big-game hunting in Africa. He left for England immediately and offered himself to the Army as, in his words, a 'commando kayaker'. Rejected, he joined the King's Royal Rifle Corps as an ordinary rifleman. He was quickly promoted to corporal and commissioned as an officer only two months after war started. He joined the Army Commandos in mid-1940 and was sent to the Combined Training Centre in Scotland, determined to get *someone* to listen to his ideas about using canoes for offensive special operations.

At about the same time, Lieutenant G.M.D. Wright, Royal Navy, was thinking along similar lines. In response to a 1939 Admiralty Fleet Order calling for suggestions 'for the further prosecution of the war',[2] Wright volunteered himself for any undertaking which used canoes to attack ships in enemy harbours. On the face of it, he was the ideal person for such a mission, since he had considerable knowledge of Stavanger and other German-occupied Norwegian ports, had used canoes (or 'folbots' as they were known at the time) extensively before the war and was an expert in the use of the new powerful lightweight plastic explosive, having already proposed that this should be used to create limpet mines to attach to enemy ships.

In Wright's correspondence with the Admiralty of July 1940, he pointed out that canoes had a number of advantages when used for clandestine purposes: they were silent, had a very low silhouette, were easily manoeuvred, could travel at around three to four knots, were seaworthy in light seas, could be loaded with up to 320 lb of demolition charges as well as their two paddlers and, being collapsible, could be easily stowed and launched from a submarine. It was this last feature, rather than the canoe's offensive potential, which caught the eye of the Lords of the Admiralty, who were at the time under increasing pressure to use their submarines for landing agents on enemy coastlines. The Naval Director of Tactical Staff Duties duly issued instructions for a canoe to be purchased from Folbots Folding Boats Limited of Golden Lane, London and ordered it to be sent to the submarine depot ship HMS *Forth*. After trials, these 'folbots' were issued to certain submarines in the 1st, 2nd, 3rd and 9th Submarine Flotillas.

But it was the canoe's utility as an instrument for commando raiding, rather than for landing agents, that interested Second Lieutenant Roger Courtney, as he now was. He tried to persuade the then head of Combined Operations, Admiral Sir Roger Keyes, of his ideas – but failed conspicuously. So he decided to take matters into his own hands. He paddled out undetected one night to the landing ship HMS *Glenfoyle*, then lying in the Clyde, clambered on board unseen, allegedly wrote his initials on the captain's door and stole a canvas gun cover (along with a pair of officer's trousers, according to some reports), later presenting these trophies to a gathering of high-ranking naval officers dining in a nearby Inveraray hotel.

History does not reveal how he was received by his superiors when he barged, dripping wet, into the middle of their dinner. But it cannot have been too badly, for Courtney was immediately promoted to captain and told to form a twelve-man unit at Arran in the Clyde in order to exploit the use of canoes for clandestine operations. And so the first Special Boat Section (SBS)[3] was born.

Courtney's first action was to visit Folbots Ltd and propose alterations to their standard craft, based on his honeymoon experience with *Buttercup*. The resulting canoes were duly provided at £15 each and subsequently became known as the Cockle Mark I.[4] The problem with the Mark I Cockle (the name was not formally adopted until March 1942) was that it was too wide in the beam to pass fully assembled through the forward torpedo-loading hatch of a submarine. This meant it had to be made up and broken down on the submarine's casing, keeping the parent 'boat'[5] on the surface in hostile waters for longer than any submarine captain interested in survival would wish.

Nevertheless, the Mark I more than proved its worth as a weapon of war. In February 1941, Courtney and his small section of commando canoeists – now called No. 1 SBS – sailed from the Clyde for active service in the Mediterranean. After a period of training in the African Great Lakes, No. 1 SBS was attached to the 1st Submarine Flotilla in Alexandria harbour. They were used extensively for reconnaissance and sabotage purposes throughout 1941 and 1942. Courtney and his team were involved in many offensive actions – blowing up railway tunnels, attacking coast roads, creating mayhem on enemy airfields and on one occasion, even attempting to capture Field Marshal Erwin Rommel.[6]

While Courtney and his team were using canoes to create mayhem on the Mediterranean coast, two young officers in the UK were applying their minds to the use of canoes for attacking ships in enemy harbours. The first of these was Captain Gerald Charles Stokes Montanaro, Royal Engineers. A colleague and friend of Courtney's, Montanaro commanded No. 101 (Folboat) Troop of No. 6 Army Commando – at the time also based at Arran in the Clyde. He began working out techniques for attacking large ships using limpet mines supplied by SOE. In fact, the first submarine and canoe-based limpet mine attack on an enemy ship was undertaken by two Royal Marines as early as July 1941 in Benghazi harbour, and was followed up by another, four months later, in Navarino.

Montanaro began developing these techniques in home waters, using as delivery vehicles the fast patrol and motor torpedo boats which were in regular action in the narrow waters of the English Channel. The first use of the canoe on active service in home waters appears to have taken place on the night of 12–13 November 1941, when Lieutenant Keith Smith of Montanaro's No. 6 Commando was captured attempting a beach reconnaissance near Deauville.[7]

At this time, Acting Major Herbert George 'Blondie' Hasler, Royal Marines, newly returned from active service in Norway, was serving in No. 2 Mobile Naval Base Defence Organisation (MNBDO), a subsidiary unit of Combined Operations based on Hayling Island near Portsmouth. In the spring of 1941, at about the same time as Roger Courtney was preparing No. 1 SBS for operations in the Mediterranean, Hasler submitted his paper to the Admiralty proposing the use of submarine-launched canoes and underwater swimmers to attack enemy ships in harbours. The paper, which has subsequently been lost, was, as we have seen, summarily rejected.

But Hasler didn't give up. On 13 January 1942 he met Montanaro to discuss his ideas. Montanaro, who like Courtney believed that Hasler was too 'gadget minded',[8] was not impressed, noting in his diary for that day: 'Visit by Major Hasler RM. No authy [authority] behind him. Dam' nonsense of a scheme. Crackers! Led him on quite happily.' However, things cannot have been too bad between the two men, for only three weeks later, Montanaro agreed to second two of his people to HMS *Vernon* in Portsmouth to help Hasler develop his canoe ideas.

By now it was clear that a new canoe to replace the Mark I would have to be developed. The Folbot Folding Boat Company had gone into liquidation at the end of May 1941 and the search had begun for a replacement manufacturer. Two names were put forward. One was based in Richmond in Surrey and the second, a firm called Saro, an offshoot of the flying boat manufacturers Saunders Roe, on the Isle of Wight. Saro had on their books a retired designer called Fred Goatley, an expert in the construction of folding boats.[9] Goatley was brought back into service as a consultant and immediately started to propose new canoe designs.

In order to clarify what they needed, Hasler, Montanaro and Courtney met at Combined Operations headquarters in London on 9 March 1942.[10] They agreed 'that there was no reason why a single type of boat should not fulfil all existing requirements for canoe operations'[11] and went on to define in precise detail the common criteria on which this should be based. The craft should be 'capable of being transported to the scene of operations and then of landing a small party of men unopposed on an enemy coast' and able to 'stand up to a sea produced by a wind of Force 4 blowing in the open sea' while being capable of carrying two thirteen-stone men plus a hundredweight of cargo (i.e. a total weight of 480 lb); it had to be able to pass through the forward loading hatch of a submarine, be capable of assembly in less than thirty seconds and remain afloat even when flooded and fully laden.

The three men may have concluded what, in outline, they all wanted. But it was left to Hasler to develop it, and his work with Goatley, with some later development and refinement, laid down the general shape, design and details of all subsequent submarine-launched two-man and three-man canoes of the war.

On 30 March 1942, Hasler went to Dover at Montanaro's invitation to watch (and participate in) an exercise in which Montanaro's team carried out a mock ship attack with canoes. What Hasler may not have realised, as he watched Montanaro's demonstration, was that this was more than just a practice attack. It was almost certainly also a rehearsal for the real thing – Operation JV. Ten days later, on the night of 11–12 April, Montanaro and Sergeant Preece launched their canoe from a fast patrol boat in the Channel. They paddled into Boulogne harbour where they attacked and severely damaged a 5500-ton bulk ore carrier.

For this escapade, Montanaro was awarded the DSO and Preece the DSM. The Germans had no idea how the attack had been mounted and, presuming it to have been carried out by the French Resistance, are alleged to have shot a hundred Frenchmen in reprisal. This rumour, however, remains unconfirmed and no such reprisals are recorded by the *mairie* in Boulogne.

The race was now on to produce the new canoe. Hasler personally took charge of the process, forming a close relationship with Goatley and his team of canoe builders on the Isle of Wight. It turned out to be an inspired partnership, with Hasler using his knowledge of small boats to ensure that every detail of the new craft was exactly right and Goatley providing the design skill and craftsmanship to turn Hasler's ideas into a canoe which could withstand the rigours of the open sea and action against the enemy.

Hasler's attention to detail at this point is extraordinary, stipulating, altering and checking every detail until he was satisfied, down to the positioning of the cleats on the outside of the craft, the fact that the craft had to have a stern 'fairing' to prevent flooding from behind when beaching and the precise length of the painter. He paid special attention to the cockpit openings, as he knew that, in rough seas and heavy rain, it is through the gap between the canoeist and the edge of the cockpit that most of the water gets into a canoe. He insisted that the openings should be flared and stiffened so that the elasticised 'skirt' of a new canoeing jacket he was also designing could be hitched over and secured to the cockpit edges, making a near waterproof joint. Hasler also experimented with compasses to be fitted to the canoe, finally deciding on a P8 Spitfire compass, mounted on the front coaming.* The Cockle Mark II was substantially improved and developed during trials, before the first six production models were finally delivered to Hasler at a cost of £160 each (the equivalent cost for a bomber at the time was £70,000).[12]

The canoe Goatley and his craftsmen provided for Hasler conformed very closely to the criteria set out at the meeting between Hasler, Montanaro and Courtney. The double-ended, two-man craft (with the heavier man sitting in the front) was 16ft long, had a 28½in beam and a depth of 11¼in, making it big enough for two men to sleep in. But it could be vertically collapsed, like a top hat, to only six inches deep for stowage. Its sides were made of waterproofed canvas with a flat deck and bottom made of ⅛in plywood. The flat bottom, reinforced with timber runners, made it much stronger than the Mark I, enabling the canoe to be dragged, fully laden, across shingle, sand or mud without damage. This rigid top and bottom, strengthened by internal struts of seasoned mahogany or oak, also made the hull strong enough to enable the boat to be lifted for disembarkation from its parent craft by two strops positioned about a third of the way down the craft, even when fully loaded and with its two crew aboard.

Its paddles were 9ft long and capable of being broken in two for stealthier single-paddle approaches. It was, however, still capable of being paddled on double paddles, with a full cargo, at around five knots[13]

---

* The same model of both canoe jacket and compass was used right up to the time I left the SBS in 1967.

(though a wiser planning speed would have been around four knots) and had sufficient internal buoyancy to remain afloat even when fully loaded and totally flooded. The Mark II was, in short, a brilliant compromise between compactness for stowage on submarines, robustness for operational purposes and speed and manoeuvrability for long passage and silent approaches.

One of the compromises which, however, had to be made to give Hasler the robust flat bottom he needed to drag the canoe across mud and shingle, was that the canoe did not have a shaped or 'keeled' bottom. As a result the Mark II, as Hasler himself conceded, was less stable than the Mark I.[14] It was also more difficult for its operators to keep the craft's head to sea to prevent it 'broaching' – turning parallel to the waves, rather than staying head-on – in turbulent water and surf.[15]

It may have been this which caused some concern about the Mark II's seaworthiness in heavy seas. In November 1942, the Cockle Mark II was offered to Roger Courtney for use by his SBS teams. He firmly declined, commenting that the Mark II was 'an unsatisfactory boat; not seaworthy'.[16] On 16 December Lieutenant-Colonel David Stirling (the founder of the SAS) was again offered Mark II Cockles to fill in during a temporary shortage of Mark Is. He too declined, commenting that 'he did not consider the craft suitable for his operations as it was insufficiently seaworthy'.[17] After the war, the Admiralty declared that the Cockle Mark II was limited by weather conditions and most suitable for use in enclosed waters.[18]

This, however, was not the view of those who were later to paddle the Mark II with Hasler into the very mouth of danger. They regarded the Mark II as lower in silhouette, faster in the water and 'definitely better than the Mark 1 [being] very good in rough seas'.[19] They believed, in short, that their commander had given them the best craft available for the mission ahead: a mission that would tax their courage – and their canoes – to the limit.

5

An Idea Born in the Bath

Early in January 1942 – and out of the blue – Hasler received the orders which were to change his life and with it, the future of the humble canoe as a weapon of war.

On 26 January that year he joined a new unit, the Combined Operations Development Unit (CODU),[1] based at the Royal Marines Barracks at Eastney; its headquarters, in an art deco block of flats called Dolphin Court, overlooked Southsea Park and its Canoe Lake, on which Hasler had first learned to paddle a canoe. CODU's task at the time was to develop new weapons, craft and materiel for amphibious warfare; Hasler's role was to investigate the use of small craft to attack enemy ships in harbour.

Almost a year earlier, on 26 March 1941, Italian explosive motor boats (EMBs) sank the British cruiser HMS *York* and damaged the Norwegian freighter *Pericles* in the British naval base at Suda Bay in Crete. During a second, failed attack on Valletta harbour in Malta on 26 June, a number of these boats were captured intact. The British were impressed by the technical quality of the new Italian weapon but objected to its 'kamikaze' form of operation, believing that it was contrary to British traditions to ask men to undertake operations from which the best outcome would be capture.

Before further consideration could be given to ways of dealing with this new threat, the Italians struck again on 19 December 1941, carrying out successful underwater attacks which seriously damaged two British warships, the *Queen Elizabeth* and the *Valiant*, using another completely new weapon – the so-called 'human torpedo'.[2] A month later, on 18

January 1942, Churchill wrote a characteristically abrasive minute to General Ismay and the Chiefs of Staff Committee:

Please report what is being done to emulate the exploits of the Italians in Alexandria Harbour and similar methods of this kind ... Is there some reason why we should be incapable of the same kind of scientific aggressive action that the Italians have shown? One would have thought we should be in the lead.[3]

It must have been about this time that someone in Combined Operations, probably in response to Churchill's demands, remembered Hasler's rejected paper on canoes and sent for him.[4] As Blondie put it in a letter to a fellow Royal Marines officer after the war:

From my point of view it was a sheer stroke of luck that (a) the Italians demonstrated that ship attack by clandestine small craft could be successful and (b) that somebody in COHQ remembered having turned down similar proposals made by an unknown Captain, RM, serving in a non-combatant unit.[5]

On his second day in his new job Hasler, accompanied by his boss, Captain T.A. Hussey RN, met in London with Louis Mountbatten, the Chief of Combined Operations. According to C.E. Lucas Phillips, the conversation went as follows:

'We've got you in because you know a lot about small boats and seem to have some ideas about using them. Are you keen to have a shot at the job?'

'Very keen, Sir.'

'Good. I am sure you will fit in well at the CODU under Captain Hussey, and I am sure we shall see some results from you soon.'[6]

Hasler's new job description stipulated that he should concentrate primarily not on canoes, but on developing a British version of the EMB and on countering the threat from the Italian EMBs and human torpedoes. This did not stop him developing his ideas on canoes, or prevent him writing numerous and no doubt irksome letters to his superiors in which he returned again and again to his original proposal for the clandestine use of canoes to attack ships in harbour. Reading his diary for this period, it is difficult not to conclude that, though Hasler's head had to busy itself with Explore Motor Boats, his heart lay firmly with his beloved canoes.

On 2 March 1942 Hasler set up the headquarters of his new unit in Lumps Fort, an old Napoleonic defensive strongpoint adjacent to Southsea Canoe Lake.[7] Nine days later he tried yet again – this time verbally – to persuade his immediate boss, Captain Hussey, of the potential use of canoes with explosives to sink ships, noting in his diary that this was 'not well received' (Hasler's emphasis). It would not be unreasonable to imagine the more senior man telling his junior that their commander, Mountbatten, had told him to concentrate on explosive motor boats and that was precisely what he should do.

Undeterred, Hasler's diary shows that he spent the next five weeks taking delivery of his first canoes, paddling them in all weathers, learning how to strip them down for transport, traipsing round Portsmouth looking for canoe manufacturers, poring over new canoe drawings, inspecting the forward torpedo-loading hatch of an H class submarine for canoe loading problems and finding accommodation for the two commando canoe experts lent to him by Montanaro.

On 19 April, he took his oft-rejected and much-rewritten report on EMBs (now known under the cover name of 'Boom Patrol Boats' or BPBs) to Hussey for approval and, as his diary puts it, 'got it torn up'. The following day, 20 April, he caught the train to London with a revised version of the report. This time, at last, it seems to have been accepted.

Judging from his diaries this period seems to have been, for Hasler, rather sterile and unproductive. In one sense, he was doing what he loved: indulging his lifelong passion for small boats, tinkering with machinery, solving problems, inventing solutions, testing out techniques. But, despite having already seen more action than most of his contemporaries would until D-Day, he seems to have felt 'out of it' – without a command and unhappily separated from the action. There are scattered diary entries describing occasional parties with Wrens and sailing expeditions with girlfriends in this period – leading to the story related by some chroniclers that he became quite famous with the Portsmouth Harbour patrol who, on seeing his boat on the water, would dismiss it as a potential threat with the comment 'It's only the Major out with one of his floozies again.'[8]

Although Hasler's mind throughout these early months in his new job was fully engaged, his spirit was restlessly looking for something bigger to do. Irked at the prospect of spending the war as a 'back-room boy' developing equipment for others, he wanted to use them against the enemy himself.

On 20 April 1942, while taking his evening bath, he found the solution. His diary entry for what was to prove a genuine *Eureka* moment is brief and laconic: 'Birth of embryo idea for more active-service role for your's T[ruly] (in bath).'[9] Lucas Phillips gives weight to the moment by adding, presumably with his subject's permission, that Hasler's bath-time musings concluded with the following thought: 'Here [the canoe] is a new weapon, a very specialised weapon. But who is going to man it? There isn't an existing unit suited to it – why not yours truly?'[10]

Nevertheless he must have understood that, given his superiors' scepticism towards his ideas for canoe attack, another direct approach making the same proposal would once more be bound to fail. So the following day Hasler put to Hussey the idea of a canoe unit which would be used to support the explosive BPBs, explaining, according to Lucas Phillips, that these could be used to 'clear surface obstructions [for the BPBs] and take the chaps off after they have fired their charges'.

Whether Hussey was taken in about Hasler's real intentions we do not know, but by the end of the meeting he agreed that Hasler could submit a plan for forming a Royal Marines canoe unit which he would command and which would act under the cover name of 'The Royal Marine Harbour Patrol'.[11] He instructed Hasler to work up his plan and take it to Combined Operations for approval.

The following day Hasler was back at Combined Operations headquarters in London, where he managed to persuade the Chief of Staff, Brigadier G.E. Wildman-Lushington (a fellow Royal Marine), of his 'basic idea'.[12] The day after that (a Sunday) he returned to Eastney and spent two hours paddling a canoe around Portsmouth Harbour, getting arrested for his pains by an alert harbour patrol.

Despite the initial positive response to Hasler's ideas, gaining final approval was by no means a foregone conclusion. Hasler had to work hard to get his idea accepted, canvassing the support of the Commander-in-Chief, Plymouth; shrewdly playing on the Admiral's natural concern to protect his base from attack, he stressed that the unit would have 'a genuine defensive role'.[13]

Although the supposed purpose of Hasler's new unit was to complement the BPBs, there are almost no mentions in his diary of these craft in the four weeks from his '*Eureka* moment' on 20 April to the final submission of his 'canoe' proposal to Richmond Terrace in mid-May. This entire period was dedicated almost exclusively to developing, designing, paddling, load-testing, speed-measuring, camouflaging and equipping canoes, from an Eskimo kayak to a Canadian Indian war canoe. He met Courtney again on 8 May to discuss oared skiffs and (of course) canoes. Meanwhile, the Mark II canoe was now under full-scale development in the Saro factory in the Isle of Wight with the first model being launched in the Medina river on 13 May 1942.

Exactly a week after this auspicious event, Hasler, then in Manchester, learnt of another. His diary for 20 May records, 'Heard the glad news that ALL our ... proposals had been approved' by Mountbatten. His new unit was to be known, at Mountbatten's personal suggestion, by the more obtuse cover name of 'The Royal Marine Boom Patrol Detachment', or RMBPD, and was to be formed and begin training on 6 July, with the aim of being ready for 'simple canoe operations' by the end of August, more complex 'Boom Patrol Boat' operations by 'say the beginning of October' and 'other specialised operations against ships' later, 'according to progress'.[14]

It is easy to overlook the extraordinary success of Hasler's campaign to change the nature of his job from one of 'back room' research to one dedicated to active operations of the most dangerous sort against the enemy. Mountbatten's decision to allow him to go ahead was remarkable, too, since it ran contrary to the thrust of Whitehall policy at the time, which was aimed at closing down the proliferation of 'private armies' which had occurred in the early years of the war. Given the words in RMBPD's founding document – and especially the mention of 'specialised operations against ships' – there could be no doubt that this time Mountbatten knew very well what he was asking Hasler to create – a special force which used canoes for ship attack. In letting Hasler go ahead, Mountbatten was almost certainly backing a hunch. For him this was, one suspects, less about exploiting the strategic capabilities of the humble canoe and more about letting a remarkable young man have his head.

Once again, Hasler wasted no time. On 20 May 1942, the same day that he heard his scheme was approved, the Royal Marines Office at the Admiralty promulgated an order calling for 'volunteers for hazardous service' in Hasler's new unit. The order stipulated that applicants should be:

Eager to engage the enemy.
Indifferent to their personal safety.
Intelligent.
Nimble.
Free of strong family ties.
Able to swim.
Of good physique.

... the name of this unit, when published, should not be taken to indicate its true function.[15]

6

RMBPD

For Blondie Hasler, June 1942 must have provided a welcome respite from his efforts to persuade his superiors to allow him to form his own active special service unit.

Any mention of EMBs now vanishes almost completely from his diary. Every spare day of the first three weeks of June was filled with developing, testing, towing, altering, sailing, sinking, capsizing, maltreating, inserting into submarines, infiltrating into harbours (chiefly Portsmouth at night), camouflaging, dropping 5 lb depth charges and even firing machine guns and rocket launchers from the Cockle Mark II canoe. On the night of 4 June Hasler made his first successful clandestine entry into Portsmouth Harbour in a Cockle Mark I, repeating the exercise in a Mark II ten days later.

On 19 June, Hasler took his first key step in recruiting the people he needed for his new unit. Over dinner that night he persuaded a fellow Royal Marines officer, Temporary Lieutenant J.D. (Jock) Stewart, to join him as his second-in-command, following this up the next day with a visit to persuade Stewart's boss to release him from his current duties. Stewart, a London-born Scot of strong physique, had come up from the ranks and had served with Hasler in Norway. He proved an inspired choice. As Hasler's deputy, Stewart was his closest confidant and the non-operational linchpin of the Royal Marines Boom Patrol Detachment.

But his contribution was much more than that. Although his duties were largely administrative, Stewart insisted on taking part in all the physical activities of the RMBPD and for this, together with his easy manner, natural command, and, above all, his care for Hasler's men, he was much respected and admired. Hasler's Marines knew him as 'the old man', despite the fact he was only a little older than Hasler himself. One of those Hasler was to recruit in the weeks ahead, Colour Sergeant W.J. (Bungy) King, RMBPD's sergeant-major, was to say of Stewart, 'he got a brand of loyalty that was reserved for him alone'.[1]

Having secured the services of Stewart, Hasler turned his attention to the two junior officers he would need as his Section leaders. On 25 June, he rode his motorcycle to the Royal Marines Small Arms School at Browndown near Lee-on-Solent, which at this stage of the war also served as a training establishment for young Royal Marines officers. Here his diary records, he 'interviewed 10 volunteer 2nd Lieuts ... Selected MacKinnon and Pritchard-Gordon'.

In fact, it transpires, MacKinnon and Pritchard-Gordon were not so much 'volunteers' as 'volunteered'. According to William Pritchard-Gordon, speaking after the war, his young officers were assembled to hear Hasler explaining what he was looking for, after which he asked for volunteers. Pritchard-Gordon discussed this over a drink in the bar afterwards with his closest friend, Jack MacKinnon, and the two men decided this was not for them.

I was *not* selected as one of Hasler's two Lieutenants. In fact, MacKinnon and I were in the bar congratulating ourselves on *not* being selected when our names were called on the CO's tannoy. The CO had over-ruled Hasler's selection and suggested that MacKinnon and I were the two people he was looking for. We joined Hasler in Southsea seven days later ...[2]

Whatever the circumstances of their recruitment, none of this diminished the two young men's subsequent commitment to Hasler, his unit or the training and operations they undertook together.

Five days later, on 1 July, Hasler began selecting his Marines and NCOs. His diary for that day notes: '0900 train from Portsmouth arriving Plymouth 1530. Interviewed all NCOs and Mne volunteers. Evening run around the town [Royal Naval and Royal Marine parlance for going on a pub crawl, or having a good time]. Slept in [Officers'] Mess bedroom.'

The Marines offered to Hasler for interview were, not as originally stipulated in the Admiralty order, volunteers drawn from the much larger pool of the Royal Marines as a whole, but from the considerably smaller cohort of the Plymouth Division.[3] Some, moreover, were chosen, according to the RMBPD War Diary, 'at the discretion of the Adjutant', leading to the suspicion that here, too, for at least some, the well-known service practice of being 'volunteered' may have applied.

The RMBPD War Diary records that Hasler interviewed two sergeants, three corporals and twenty-eight Marines, from which he selected in total twenty-nine NCOs and men. Given that, having started at 1530, he had time for a night on the town, he must have finished his selection in three hours or so – fast going by any standard.

Few of those chosen had any experience in small boats and some could not even swim. Perhaps even more remarkably, contrary to the explicit requirement that volunteers should be 'free of strong family ties', two were actually married (one with two children). Hasler, who was recognised by contemporaries as a good judge of men, seems to have made his selection based on the person standing to attention in front of him and was prepared to overlook any inconvenient facts written on his service record.

It seems that he asked them all at least one common question: 'Why did you volunteer for hazardous service in my unit?'

Marine Bill Sparks, whose brother had recently been killed in the Royal Navy, answered: 'To avenge my brother, Sir.'[4]

Norman Colley says that, in addition to this question, Hasler warned him: 'Do you realise that your expectation of a long life is very remote if you join this unit?'

Colley replied, 'I never think of it like that, Sir.'[5]

A number of post-war chroniclers have commented that Hasler deliberately avoided seeking men of exceptional strength, boastful attitude, overt toughness or demonstrable aptitude for commando work, and that he sought, on the contrary, ordinary men, of a certain quiet modesty supported by self-discipline, resilience of mind and the ability to think independently. If so, his approach had the benefit of being not only, in his eyes, the right one, but also the only possible one. At this stage of the war, most of the best men had already volunteered for the Commandos. Hasler had to take what he got, as he himself later admitted, commenting that his men were 'just a good cross section of average young fellows and we had to do the best with what was offered to us'.[6]

On 3 July, Hasler was joined on Eastney front by Jock Stewart. The following day, MacKinnon and Pritchard-Gordon arrived. The next two days were spent drawing stores, moving the pair of experts Montanaro had lent him and their equipment from HMS *Vernon* to Lumps Fort and setting up the two Nissen huts which had by now been built on the seafront, and were to double as instruction rooms and storerooms. Despite these preparations, Hasler still found time to sail, test and make yet more alterations to the Mark II Cockle.

In the afternoon of 6 July the Marines and NCOs started to arrive from Plymouth. At 2100 that evening they were all put through a medical examination, after which Hasler briefly addressed them – chiefly about the need for secrecy – on the rugby pitch of the nearby Royal Marines barracks.

The Royal Marines Boom Patrol Detachment (RMBPD), which came into official existence on 6 July 1942, consisted of Hasler as CO, Stewart as second-in-command and two operational units – No. 1 Section under Jack MacKinnon and No. 2 Section under William Pritchard-Gordon – each being made up of one sergeant, two corporals and ten Marines. These operational elements were supported by an Administration Section consisting of a colour sergeant (who acted as the unit sergeant-major), an orderly (who looked after Hasler), a driver, 'Flash' Phelps[7] (whose proud boast, according to Lucas Phillips, was that he was never late for a rendezvous) and a storeman. Their technical needs were catered for by a Maintenance Section supplied by the Royal Navy and consisting of an engineer sub-lieutenant RN, six mechanics and artificers, a shipwright and two others. In total Hasler's RMBPD numbered forty-six men.

Although Hasler's Marines were not termed 'Commandos' and did not wear the coveted green beret, he managed to negotiate 'Commando status' for them. This meant that they received a supplement to their pay of six shillings and eightpence per day and were entitled to live, not in service barracks, but in privately rented accommodation. Two local guest houses were chosen for this purpose. No. 2 Section were accommodated at 35 St Rownan's Road, Southsea; the ten Marines of

No. 1 Section were accommodated not far away at the White Heather Guest House, a modest Victorian terraced house at 27 Worthing Road[8] run by Mrs Leonora Powell with the support of her sixteen-year-old daughter Heather. MacKinnon, Stewart and Hasler, together with the unit mascot, a cocker spaniel called Titch,[9] took up lodgings nearby at another private house at 9 Spencer Road.

The day after their arrival, the Marines began training in earnest, with Hasler throwing them in, literally, at the deep end by putting them to sea in canoes. The results were predictably disastrous: all of them capsized and had to drag themselves and their canoes back to the beach where he told them to try again. And then again. And again ... until they could do it.

And so it continued. On 24 July, when some new recruits arrived (probably to replace those who had been RTU'd – 'Returned to Unit' – because of injury or failure to meet Hasler's standards), Hasler's diary entry gives a flavour of his approach: '0825–0900 addressing new tps. A.m. new tps almost drowned themselves. P.m salvaging boats & continue training.' Another entry on 10 August notes: 'rescuing 6 of No 1 Section from watery death'. Now Hasler was fully and fiercely engaged on the job in hand. Mention of parties and recreational sailing trips with girlfriends vanish almost completely from his diary.

A vivid impression of what it was like for those in Hasler's unit at this time is conveyed in a post-war interview given by Bill Sparks of No. 1 Section:

> Training involved pretty near everything. Assault courses ... we did every day. They were self-made assault courses which resulted in many, many men being taken into [the local Royal Naval] Hospital. They got fed up with us there I think. This is [sic] a way of whittling us down, I suppose.
>
> We used to do exercises where we were dropped somewhere by lorry out in the country, and told to make our own way back with no money in our pockets and be sure we evaded capture from police et cetera ...
>
> I suppose these were the sort of exercises we were doing all the time, but in the main canoeing. [Then] once out in the sea, you

were alone, just two of you. It was a great thrill when we were doing exercises.

We used to attack aerodromes. We used to penetrate our naval defences, harbours, et cetera and it was a great thrill and a lot of pride to us to get in and out undiscovered ...

[Even in winter] Major Hasler would run us up and down the beach at Southsea barefoot on the pebbles and then finish up with a swim ...

Nobody grumbled. We were afraid that if we grumbled we would be sent back to unit, and nobody wanted this ... I think it was a matter of pride. The unit was a very select crowd and we were so proud that we had been chosen for it out of hundreds that he must have interviewed [sic] that to be sent back would have been a sort of disgrace. It's like saying that you couldn't make the grade.

Morale was terrific. The men worked very, very closely together and it was just a little unit that we were wrapped up in one another. Everybody helped each other. Many a time when we first started training, someone would tip over in the canoe, and immediately all hands were there to help them back to shore. Morale was very, very high ...

Quite a few ... couldn't make the grade. After a time the Major used to call them along and say 'Well I don't think you're the sort of material for this unit' and they were sent back. Some were sent back through injuries ... There was nobody that volunteered to go back.[10]

At first, Hasler himself had to give all the instruction, as he was the only member of the unit who had practised the techniques his men had to learn. But gradually he was able to train his core staff to take over much of the basic training, leaving him increasingly free to develop the Mark II Cockle and to deal with problems from higher up the chain at Combined Operations (including, in August, a determined attempt by Combined Operations HQ to combine his unit with those of Courtney and Montanaro, which Hasler managed to beat off only with difficulty). But there was never any doubt who was the driving spirit behind every detail of how his men were trained and prepared.

Hasler's training diaries give meticulous and detailed notes on every lesson taught.[11] The Marines received instruction on navigation and the handling of a wide variety of small vessels from explosive motor boats, through collapsible assault craft, to canoes. There were lessons in reading charts and tide tables, calculating tidal triangles, working out the variation to be applied to magnetic compasses to give a True North reading, taking soundings with a plumb line and sounding reel, terrestrial map reading and underwater diving. There were exercises in how to make a clandestine approach on foot and in a canoe and even training in the writing of farewell letters to next-of-kin. They learnt rope work, knots and splicing, the stripping down and stowing of the Mark II canoe, the operation of limpet mines, the setting of chemical time fuses and the layout of dockyards. They were taught how to use the special code employed by MI9 for secret communication with British prisoners in enemy prisoner-of-war camps and how to employ silent hand signals in canoes and on foot patrols. They practised living off the land, the use of water sterilising tablets, how to use condoms to waterproof watches and other items, how to calculate the times of the rising and setting of the sun and moon and how to use the specialist clothing Hasler had designed for them. They did basic sketching, learnt how to use magnets, practised writing on underwater writing tablets, exercised in reading with a specially dimmed torch and even received instruction on the proper use of the pencil.

On 26 August Hasler's diary notes that a 'Cockle Rally' was held on Eastney beach. Apart from the RMBPD, this also included 'representatives' paddling canoes from the Small Scale Raiding Force and No. 2 SBS. After a photographic session on Eastney beach they all paddled to the Isle of Wight. Given that it was done in the fast time of an hour and a half, this was probably a race – or at least highly competitive; the return journey took two hours.

On top of all this there were regular parade ground drill sessions. Hasler believed in the discipline of the parade ground in training his men. He insisted his unit was always smartly dressed and marched around in a properly formed body. No. 1 Section's sergeant, 'Sam' Wallace, even invented a special rapid march for them all which they christened the 'Southsea Stroll'. When living in hard conditions on exercises, Hasler required his men to shave and attend to bodily hygiene as best they could (a practice he would also insist on continuing even during active operations). Yet the discipline he really valued was the lonely self-discipline that drives a person to accomplish their duty even when no one is watching.

Hasler demanded that his Marines were, at all times and in all circumstances, the smartest of the smart, the fastest of the fast, the best of the best. And it worked. It was not long before 'Hasler's party' were looked upon by their fellow Marines in Eastney barracks, and by the population of Southsea in general, as 'something special'.

Hasler himself showed little emotion and rarely lost his temper, always giving the outward appearance of calm, confidence and certainty. Bill Sparks after the war described him as 'a compassionate disciplinarian',[12] so perfectly juxtaposing two opposite aspects of his personality. Norman Colley makes much the same point in a different way:

Blondie didn't mix much. But everybody loved him and respected him. You never messed with Blondie. He did most of the instruction and never asked anybody else to do anything that he hadn't done first. He did everything with us. He was not a disciplinarian in the sense that he punished many people. Indeed I never saw him punish anybody. And if he did, the word was that he tore you off a strip and then announced your punishment but almost never carried it out. With Blondie you were required to do your duty and if you did it you were fine. If you failed in your duty then you would simply do it all over again and you would go on doing it until you got it right.[13]

Despite the emphasis on discipline, the atmosphere inside Hasler's unit was relaxed. Hasler – known by all as 'The Major', or 'The Guv'nor'[14] – kept himself somewhat apart and addressed all his men by their rank and surname, or in the case of the ordinary Marines just their surname. The other officers were always referred to as 'Sir', though they frequently fell back on the first names or nicknames of their Marine canoe partners, especially when on exercises and at sea.[15] Hasler only joined their social events on very special occasions, but the rest – officers, NCOs and ordinary Marines alike – mixed freely, often drinking together at their 'local', the Grenada pub,[16] just round the corner from the White Heather Guest House in Worthing Road.

Hasler did not inspire love among those he led – he was too distant for that. But he did inspire respect and more importantly, absolute trust. However difficult the mission, his men knew, quite simply, that he would see them through.

By late July, Hasler must have felt that things were going reasonably well, for his diary shows him increasingly away from Southsea as the month progressed. On 20 July, carrying a five-foot model of the Cockle Mark II which Goatley had made specially for him, he took a train to Glasgow to pay his first visit to the submarine depot ship HMS *Forth*. Here, together with 'Jumbo' Courtney and others, he attended a meeting with Captain 'Tinsides' Ionides RN, Commander of the 3rd Submarine Flotilla, to discuss canoe operations from submarines.

The meticulous development of the Cockle Mark II continued throughout July. In late July a capsize exercise revealed that it was not always sufficiently easy for the crew to exit the canoe underwater because of the stiffness of the quick release catches on the cockpit cover. The problem was solved by using standard spring-loaded 'bulldog' clips obtained from His Majesty's Stationery Office. Finally, on 28 July, after a morning spent with Goatley on further testing and capsizing of the Mark II, Hasler noted in his diary, 'The end is about in sight I think.'

While Hasler continued in August 1942 to develop his chosen weapon of war and train his little force, Lord Selborne in London sent a complaint to the Deputy Prime Minister, Clement Attlee, about Britain's failure to act against German blockade runners:

In a Note dated 9th May I drew the Prime Minister's attention, to the development of blockade running between German Europe and the Far East. In a Minute dated 22nd June I brought the matter to your notice, emphasising particularly the scale of traffic between Germany and Japan planned for the next twelve months and the effect that such an exchange of goods and services would have upon the war potentials of both countries. Hardly a day passes without my seeing convincing proof of the determination of both countries to execute their programme ... The importance of this traffic is no less today than when I wrote my previous minutes. If immediate action could be taken it should not be too late.

PART II

Assembling the Forces

7

The Die is Cast

On 7 August, two days after Lord Selborne's letter to Attlee about the 'Bordeaux problem', the Chiefs of Staff Committee of the War Cabinet met at the Deputy Prime Minister's request.[1] Although no record of the conclusions reached at this meeting can be found in the National Archives at Kew, there is an intriguing passage in one of the papers presented to the Chiefs of Staff. An undated and unsourced extract from an Admiralty 'docket'[2] listing available options for tackling the blockade runner problem, it reads:

> It is possible to achieve a very considerable degree of unseen approach with canoes carrying small limpet charges and each canoe can carry at the time enough charges to sink an 8,000 ton ship. Canoes, if disembarked at the entrance to the Gironde from a submarine could make their way in stages to Bordeaux, deliver an attack and return to the submarine … however … it would be much more economical of effort if the whole expedition, together with a stock of limpets, could be moved from the submarine to a hideout within striking distance of Bordeaux and kept there long enough to enable the canoes to deliver a series of attacks with limpets timed to explode after the last attack had been delivered and the expedition had withdrawn.

A month later, on 7 September, Selborne sent yet another letter to add to his growing list of acerbic admonitions. This one was to the Admiralty and ended with the tart comment: 'I am … anxious to know whether …

the Admiralty regard as satisfactory, arrangements for dealing with surface vessels in the Bay of Biscay, and if not whether they have yet defined what is needed to make them satisfactory.'[3] The following day the Examination Committee of Combined Operations met at Richmond Terrace and having considered Selborne's demands, concluded that 'This project is to be referred to Major Hasler.'[4]

On the face of it, this seems rather premature, since RMBPD had only been in existence a mere eight weeks. But Hasler had been pushing his men hard. As the Marines reached full fitness and grew ever more confident in their skills, the number of injuries and rejections dropped, though this did not always mean that their exercises ended in success. On 10 August an attempt to reach the Isle of Wight in strong winds and heavy seas resulted in three of No. 1 Section's canoes being swamped and their occupants forced to climb onto the Portsmouth harbour boom they were supposed to be protecting, from where they were, in the words of Hasler's diary, 'saved from a watery grave'. By now the blisters and sores caused by the rubbing of paddles and the chafing of hard wooden seats, had turned into thick calluses on thumbs and backsides (the Marines called them 'hooves'), which, in the case of some, would last for years.[5]

In September the training moved up another gear, shifting from basic techniques like boatmanship and cooking in the field to more offensive skills, such as the priming and throwing of hand grenades, conducting ambushes, route memorisation, prisoner drills, the silent killing of sentries, canoeing in rough weather, overnight movement, shallow water diving, signalling, navigation, use of the compass, stripping down weapons and a lot of night work. Although Hasler was now able to transfer some of his more routine training burdens to his subordinates, his diary shows that he still did most of the instruction on new and more complex subjects himself.

On 10 September RMBPD's diary notes: 'Night training. No 2 Section left Southsea to attack Thorney Island in canoes. No boats reached objective.' Three days later, No. 1 Section repeated the exercise on a very dark night, with the result that '5 out of 7 boats made a successful landing'. A clear difference in capability was opening up between the two sections.

On 18 September, Hasler called in at Combined Operations headquarters on his way back to Portsmouth from a meeting in

Cambridge and spent an hour in the office of Colonel Neville, the Royal Marines Advisor and Chief Planning Co-ordinator at Richmond Terrace discussing, 'on prospective schemes'.[6] According to Lucas Phillips, the conversation between the two men went as follows.

Hasler: 'We ought to be thinking of a live operation soon, Sir. Have you got anything on the plate that we could tackle?'

Neville: 'Already? You have only been going a couple of months.'

Hasler: 'They're shaping up, Sir. Providing it's not a job needing very good navigation or seamanship, I think they'll soon be ready. Besides we must put the equipment and the tactics to a live test as soon as we can.'[7]

According to Lucas Phillips, Neville then called for some target files. Hasler looked through these for an hour or so; not finding anything he considered suitable, he continued his journey back to Portsmouth. Sometime over the next two days, Hasler received either a letter or a phone call from Colonel Cyril Horton, one of Combined Operations' Royal Marines planners: 'I think we have got something that might interest you; it might be worth your while to come up.'[8]

It is difficult to reconcile this account with the decision made by the Examination Committee ten days before Hasler's fruitless visit to look for targets, that the blockade-runner question should be 'referred to Major Hasler'. Perhaps Neville simply forgot and only remembered what he had been asked to do after Hasler had left. Or perhaps more likely, in retelling the story Lucas Phillips and Hasler simply muddled the true sequence of events. Whatever the explanation, Hasler responded to Horton's call without delay.

On 21 September he caught the train to Waterloo and spent the day studying the Frankton file, which outlined the parameters of the 'Bordeaux problem'. Hasler spent that night at the Royal Ocean Racing Club, in St James's Place, just behind the Ritz Hotel. Here he drew up his outline plan for using canoes and the RMBPD to attack the blockade runners lying alongside the quay at Bordeaux.

The following morning Hasler wrote up his plans at Richmond Terrace, adding a covering letter which stated:

Before proceeding with planning, it is requested that I may be informed whether the proposal made in the outline plan, that a carrying vessel should drop three Cockles not more than five miles from the mouth of the river, in the dark, is practicable.

At first examination, the Cockle side of the operation appears to have a good chance of success, and it is hoped that RMBPD may be allowed to carry it out.

That afternoon at 1500, Hasler saw Neville, who later described his proposal as 'the quickest outline plan of its kind on record'.[9]

That evening Hasler was sitting in a train carriage waiting to depart for Portsmouth when he was urgently hauled out and rushed back to Richmond Terrace to give his thoughts on what kind of parent vessel should be used if his proposed plan was accepted. He made it clear that, given the distance to be travelled from a UK port to the drop-off point through waters controlled by the enemy, the best – indeed the only – suitable carrying vessel would be a submarine.

Looking at his personal diary and the war diary of the RMBPD, it seems clear that when Hasler left London that night he did so with the presumption in his mind that his proposals would be accepted. Starting from this date, 22 September 1942, there is a further marked increase both in the intensity of the RMBPD's training and in Hasler's efforts to perfect the Cockle Mark II canoe.

What neither Hasler nor, it seems, anyone at Richmond Terrace knew, however, was that there was already a team, led by a British officer and directed from London, on the quayside in Bordeaux, no more than a hundred yards from the targets he had just been given – with orders to prepare an attack as soon as possible.

8

Scientist

On 19 September 1942, two days before Hasler was given the Frankton docket, a coded radio message arrived at SOE's Baker Street headquarters. Sent from a café on the Bordeaux quayside by the head of SOE's newly established *Scientist* network in the city, it was a report on the progress he had made in carrying out his mission to attack the Bordeaux blockade runners. On reaching Bordeaux just a few days previously, the new arrival had linked up with, first Robert Leroy (now returned from London), and then Jean Duboué. The message read:

> At first sight Louis [Leroy] did not seem to me to have a cut and dried organisation. He had only got in touch with a few people who seemed willing to follow him. His one aim is to attack the targets.
>
> Louis is only waiting for the necessary material [i.e. explosives] in order to get on with the job. He can then work on the painting of the ships down in the hold. He has already informed you how he needed the goods (small packages which could easily go into a workman's haversack).[1]

The 'targets' referred to were the Bordeaux blockade runners.

Four months before this secret message was sent, Lord Selborne's letter to Churchill of 9 May 1942 establishing the 'urgent need' to tackle the Bordeaux blockade runner problem, must have been especially welcome to the leaders of SOE – and not just because Selborne was head of SOE, as well as Minister for Economic Warfare.

The years 1941 and 1942 were difficult for SOE. Although Baker Street's training schools were quickly in operation,[2] SOE's F Section had, by mid-1941, achieved very little. Indeed there seems to have been confusion as to what SOE's role actually was, for there is a record in July of that year of Brigadier Colin Gubbins complaining that 'we are still awaiting final orders as to what our activities are to be'.[3] Underperforming, under-regarded and under attack from all quarters, the very existence of SOE was at this time being called into question right up to Downing Street itself.

Suddenly – improbably – Leroy's information from the dockside in Bordeaux had become a matter of vital national importance. That importance became even greater when, at 0450 on 10 June 1942, there was a sudden furious knocking on the door of the Paris apartment of Ange-Marie Gaudin, the Gironde river pilot who passed information on shipping and maritime matters in the Bordeaux area back to MI6. When he opened the door, Gaudin was confronted by Wilhelm von Schramm, head of the *Geheime Feldpolizei* (Secret Military Police) in Paris, accompanied by four or five armed men.[4] A search of his apartment revealed a mass of incriminating papers and other evidence, including wireless crystals. Gaudin and his fellow Gironde pilot Jean Fleuret had been betrayed by one of their own network, a young man named Pierre Cartaud.[5] SIS had, at a stroke, lost a source of vital maritime intelligence from the very heart of Bordeaux.

To SOE, Duboué, Leroy and the Bordeaux connection now had a double importance – first to Britain's war effort; second to SOE's own battle to maintain its credibility in Whitehall. SOE did not have to ponder how to meet Selborne's challenge. With their agent Leroy already in place – and another under training to be sent to Bordeaux – they had their own independent means to respond to their chief's demands.

On 12 May 1942, a young Frenchman with dual British nationality had started at SOE's initial training school at Wanborough Manor near Guildford in Surrey. Intractable, difficult, opinionated and one of the key characters of our story, Claude Marie Boucherville de Baissac was for SOE what Blondie Hasler was for Combined Operations, their home-grown answer to the 'Bordeaux problem'.

Although SOE told no one exactly what they were up to, their overall intentions were stated clearly enough in a resumé of SOE activities sent to the Cabinet on 26 June: 'As far as possible SOE is concentrating its sabotage activities on U-boat, blockade-running and communications targets. These activities are carried out not only from within, but are also supplemented by occasional "coup de main" parties from this country.'[6] In fact, even before this report was written, the 'coup de main' party they intended for Bordeaux was already being assembled. Its code name, taken from the SOE code name of its leader Claude de Baissac, was to be *Scientist*.

De Baissac was born on 28 February 1907 in Curepipe, Mauritius, to a well-to-do, property-owning French family with dual British citizenship.[7] He was sent to Paris at the age of twelve, living there with his mother in an apartment in the Avenue Mozart while attending the Lycée Henry IV, arguably the most rigorous and demanding public school in France. From here, having passed his 'Bachot',[8] he went on to study law and in 1927 started his military service.[9] This included a spell in the *Deuxième Bureau* – the French intelligence service – and then a period in an infantry regiment. Having completed his *service militaire*, de Baissac did not return to the law as might have been expected, but instead joined his father's firm, Les Minéraux de la Grande Île, mining mica in Madagascar. Things seem not to have gone particularly well here either, for in 1931 he returned to France and took a job as a publicity agent in a small film company based in Paris. The earliest existing photographs of him, probably taken not long after this, show a rather swarthy man whose slicked-back hair and neatly trimmed moustache have something of Errol Flynn about them; including – judging by the plumpness of his face – a similar attachment to good living.

At the outbreak of war, de Baissac was called up and sent to Mulhouse at the southern end of the Maginot line.[10] The fall of France found him in hospital in Metz recuperating from a bad dose of bronchitis. From here he was evacuated south ahead of the advancing German troops, arriving in Marseille in October 1940.

In February 1941, playing on his dual citizenship, de Baissac made contact with an Englishman called Captain Garo who, through a facilitator in Toulouse, arranged a guide, the papers necessary for leaving France and a certificate of 'safe conduct' through Spain. He picked up his younger sister Lise, who had been staying with their mother at the family country home in the Dordogne, and headed for Bañolas in Spain, crossing the Spanish frontier at the Col de Las Illas (known in French as

Les Illes) on 19 May 1941. Here his guide furnished the couple with tickets for the train to Barcelona. Despite his 'safe conduct', de Baissac was arrested by the Spanish police and thrown into the infamous internment camp at Miranda. Lise was allowed to continue her journey to Lisbon, from where she launched a tireless and eventually successful campaign for her brother's release.[11] In Lisbon, the two of them, now almost penniless, joined a vast crowd fleeing to Britain on a Polish boat, the *Batory*, which arrived in Gourock in the second week of January 1942. From Glasgow, brother and sister made their way to London where they took up residence with family friends.[12]

Three days after de Baissac's thirty-fourth birthday, a letter arrived at his London address. Signed by a Major L.E. Gielgud, it said: 'Since we spoke on the telephone yesterday, a point has arisen which I would like to discuss with you. Would you please telephone me as soon as possible so that we may fix a time for a short talk?'[13]

We do not know for certain what happened at the interview at which de Baissac was formally recruited into the SOE. But there are two accounts of how these interviews were conducted, given by Roger Landes and Harry Peulevé,[14] two of de Baissac's colleagues who were recruited at the same time. The would-be SOE agent was directed into a small, sparsely furnished room, to be greeted by a tall, elegantly dressed man in his forties who introduced himself as Major Lewis Gielgud.[15] Formal introductions over, Gielgud's recruiting technique was a brusque, no-nonsense affair:

> ... you have lived in France for so long, you are the perfect man to send [there], should you be willing to go. There are three ways to send you to France; by parachute, by motor boat, or by fishing boat from Gibraltar. The danger is you may be caught, in which case you will probably be tortured and sent to certain death. Will you accept? Yes or no? You have five minutes to think about it.

De Baissac accepted.

On 4 March 1942 de Baissac was formally taken on by SOE with a salary of five guineas a week and, very shortly afterwards, began to move through the SOE training system with a number of other newly recruited agents, including Roger Landes and Harry Peulevé. Their training, which lasted until early July, took place at SOE's numerous training establishments from Scotland through to Beaulieu on the south coast, where they learnt all the techniques necessary to be a successful SOE agent, from weapons skills, through survival, parachuting and Morse code, to silent killing.

By the end of the war, Claude de Baissac would become one of SOE's most successful and most decorated agents. But he was neither a congenial colleague nor an easy man to deal with. Colonel Maurice Buckmaster, the head of SOE F Section, later summed de Baissac up as:

A difficult character, but if properly handled, he produces results. He is spurred by vanity and very great ambition. He will grumble at every decision, but always grumbles courteously and ends up by accepting the situation and making the best of it ...

He is very loyal and I have a very high opinion of him, but he is the most difficult of all my officers without any exception. He is occasionally brilliant, occasionally brutally lazy and always charming.[16]

It seems probable that de Baissac shared with Hasler a diffidence – even coolness – which set them apart from their fellows.

On 27 July 1942, after two weeks' post-training leave, de Baissac reported to Baker Street to receive his orders. He was to make his way to Tarbes, where Gaston Hèches would assist him to cross the Demarcation Line into Bordeaux. There he was to take over the Leroy/Duboué organisation (to be known in future as the *Scientist* network), build up the access they had obtained to the blockade runners, identify landing sites for receiving further materiel and reinforcements and prepare sabotage attacks on a number of targets in the Bordeaux area, of which his first priority should be:

Rubber and other cargoes from Far East entering the Port of Bordeaux

    Attack 1 The ships.
             2 Cargo in ships.
             3 Cargo on wharf or in warehouse.
             4 Cargo on rail.

He was to be accompanied on this trip by Harry Peulevé, who would act as his radio operator.

De Baissac and Peulevé[17] parachuted into France[18] on the night of 30–31 July 1942, which was clear with a full moon and flying clouds driven by a boisterous mistral wind.[19] The original plan had been to drop the two agents at low altitude on a disused airfield[20] close to a small canal, five miles south of Nîmes. But despite making several passes, the pilot of the Halifax was unable to see any lights from the Resistance reception committee below. The two agents quickly decided that, rather than return to Britain, they would drop 'blind', finally making their jump just before 2 a.m., accompanied by two containers in which were arms and Peulevé's radio set. Almost immediately they found themselves in trouble. Investigations afterwards speculated that they may have been dropped too low, or the wind might have been too strong for safe parachuting – or maybe their parachutes had malfunctioned. Peulevé badly broke his leg on landing. De Baissac, who got away with only a sprained ankle, buried their 'chutes, hid Peulevé's radio in a ditch and, instructing his partner to lie low until dawn to give him time to get away, hobbled off to Nîmes station where he caught an early morning train to Cannes and then another to Tarbes.[21]

While de Baissac and Peulevé were wrestling with their parachutes, a striking-looking grandmother of forty-five with a direct gaze and a hairstyle whose cultivated untidiness told you she did not care much for convention, was being landed in choppy seas from the 'felucca'[22] *Sea Dog* on a rocky headland just outside the town, between Bijou-sur-Mer and Pointe Fourcade.

Yvonne Claire Rudellat[23] had come to London in the 1920s where, after several jobs and a failed marriage which produced a daughter (who now had her own child), she ended up as the receptionist of the Ebury Court Hotel[24] near Victoria station. Here one of the guests, an SOE agent, discovered her and passed her name on to F Section. On the same night as de Baissac landed near Nîmes, Rudellat,[25] carrying false papers in the name of Jacqueline Gautier, was landed from *Sea Dog* with two other SOE agents. The following morning she caught a train from Cannes heading, by way of Lyon and Paris, for the city of Tours, 170 miles north of Bordeaux.

De Baissac arrived in Tarbes sometime during the first week of August 1942 and made his way to Gaston Hèches' restaurant. Here he was provided with the identity documents necessary to cross the Demarcation Line and, after meeting up with Leroy, set off for Bordeaux. The pair arrived in the city and made contact with Jean Duboué in the third week of August 1942.

De Baissac immediately set about establishing his own operational headquarters and 'mail box' on the Bordeaux quayside, in the Café des Chartrons, run by two of Duboué's Resistance colleagues, Guy and Marie Bertrand.[26] The next two weeks de Baissac spent taking over the main elements of Duboué's network, reconnoitring parachute landing grounds and assessing his targets. On 11 September, he sent a message to London asking for a parachute drop of explosives to be made during the forthcoming 'moon period' in the third week of September. The site he proposed was adjacent to an old mill called the Moulin de Saquet[27] between the villages of Targon and Sauveterre-de-Guyenne, ten miles east of Bordeaux and six from Duboué's house at Lestiac-sur-Garonne, whose cellars and outbuildings were already being used to store arms and explosives.[28]

Yvonne Rudellat arrived in Tours on 8 August to take up the post of courier to Raymond Flower,[29] the head of SOE's Monkeypuzzle circuit in the Loire valley. Flower, a nervous and suspicious man, disliked her from the start and gave her a variety of tricky jobs to do. One was transporting packets of explosive to Resistance groups in the Tours area in her voluminous bloomers as she rode round the city on her bicycle. Another was carrying messages to and from de Baissac, who because of Peulevé's jump injury now depended on Monkeypuzzle's radio in Tours to communicate with London. It was by this method that de Baissac's report of 19 September 1942 had been sent to London.

The copy of this message held in de Baissac's personal file in the National Archives in Kew indicates that it was seen by a wide variety of SOE's key people. These included David Keswick, the Regional Controller of North West European operations (who, as Buckmaster's immediate superior, reported directly to the second most senior man in SOE, Colin Gubbins), Leslie Humphries (in charge of DF Section) and Colonel Robert Bourne-Paterson, Buckmaster's second-in-command.[30] The work of the Scientist circuit and its preparations to attack the blockade runners was being closely followed by SOE's most senior leaders.

Despite this, on 1 September, Gubbins attended a meeting of Combined Operations' Examination Committee[31] in order to encourage them to consider the possibilities of mounting their own raid on the blockade runners – without mentioning that his own SOE agents were already conducting an operation on exactly the same targets.

Meanwhile information (probably again carried to Tours by Yvonne Rudellat) continued to come in from Claude de Baissac. As a result, F Section was able to report up the SOE chain that:

> Only two or three Blockade runners have come into Bordeaux since August. He [de Baissac] thinks that two of these contained rubber and a third discharged a complete cargo of oil of all kinds, including vegetable oil as well as fuel oil. No-one has any idea where this vessel came from. He hadn't seen a tanker – all the oil is transported in barrels ... He reported the name of one ship, the Katanga of 8–10,000 tons [and that] all the crews were Germans. He gave us information a week or two ago that the Portland was ready to sail. The ship was loaded with machine tools and spare parts ... Six [other] ships were loaded and ready to sail. In addition there were three or four fair sized ships and very many small ones carrying food to Spain and bringing back pyrites. He believed that mercury was part of the blockade runner's trade.[32]

At 0035 on 25 September, a bright moonlit night with broken clouds, Claude de Baissac's sister Lise[33] (equipped with identity documents in the name of Irene Brisse and a cover story saying she was a widow seeking refuge from Paris) parachuted in to a site manned by a reception committee from Raymond Flower's *Monkeypuzzle* circuit at Boisrenard in the Loire valley, 200 miles north of Bordeaux.[34] Lise, a slight woman of thirty-seven with black hair, piercingly blue eyes, a strong but courteous personality and determined opinions, joined SOE soon after her brother and had volunteered, on finishing her training, to join him in southwest France.[35] She spent the night of 24 September at a nearby farm and the following day set off for

Poitiers, where her task was to form a new circuit (subsequently known as *Artist* – after Lise's code name – or *Scientist II*) which would assist her brother in Bordeaux by providing 'a centre where agents could go with complete security for material help and information on details'.[36]

With Harry Peulevé holed up on the Côte d'Azur nursing a broken leg, de Baissac was still having to rely on Jean Duboué's daughter, Suzanne, to courier messages to Gaston Hèches in Tarbes for onward passage over the Pyrenees to London, or on Yvonne Rudellat to smuggle them to Flowers' radio in Tours. Providing de Baissac with a replacement radio operator now became an urgent SOE priority. Baker Street quickly decided that the answer to their problem was the 26-year-old ex-architect Roger Landes, who after training with de Baissac had gone on to qualify as a radio operator from the SOE wireless school at Thame, near Aylesbury, in July.[37]

The first attempt to drop Landes[38] (travelling under the identity of René Pol) to the Moulin de Saquet site was made on the night of 20–21 September. But, as with de Baissac's drop at Nîmes, no lights from the reception committee were seen. Landes, no doubt conscious of what had happened when Peulevé and de Baissac dropped blind, declined to do the same and returned with the aircraft to Tempsford.

In fact Landes would have to endure a cancelled sea insertion by felucca and three further failed attempts to parachute him into France before finally, on 31 October, being dropped[39] to a *Monkeypuzzle* drop site[40] in the Loire valley. The two new arrivals were taken to a house owned by the local mayor, where they met up with Lise de Baissac and Yvonne Rudellat.[41]

On 2 November, Landes set off on foot for the nearby railway station, with Lise de Baissac and Yvonne Rudellat following separately on bicycles, each with their personal luggage in a suitcase strapped onto their bicycle carrier racks. Concealed in Yvonne's suitcase were Landes' radio and revolver, which she was to take, along with Landes himself, to Bordeaux. The three travelled by train to Tours, from where Lise went south to the little Charente town of Ruffec where she intended to establish the southern base for her *Scientist II* network, while the other two continued their journey to Bordeaux.

When Landes eventually arrived in the *Port de la Lune* on 3 November he had some difficulty finding a suitable site for his radio. But this problem was solved when Marcel Bertrand, the proprietor of the Café des Chartrons, lent him an empty house in the Bordeaux suburb of Cenon, on the east bank of the Garonne. This proved ideal for Landes' purposes. It was in a middle-class neighbourhood and on a prominence overlooking the city, with a good view of the Quai des Chartrons and the blockade runners below. The small, secluded villa, with four spacious rooms, had two entrances each leading onto a different street; its garden was fenced in such a way as to make it impossible to see the interior of the building from the road outside; very close to the headquarters of the German anti-aircraft batteries in the Bordeaux area, it was unlikely to be subject to constant searches. Best of all, it was adjacent to a powerful medium-wave German radio transmitter which gave Landes' short-wave radio excellent 'cover' from German detector vehicles.[42] To add to the building's informal security advantages, the front door lock was badly constructed and could only be opened from the outside in a certain way, meaning that Landes would be able to tell if anyone had tried to enter in his absence.[43]

Landes moved into the villa, spreading the word among his neighbours that he needed an airy house because he was recuperating from tuberculosis (an impression ironically reinforced by his smoker's cough). This had the additional advantage of explaining why he lived by himself, while at the same time discouraging neighbourly inquisitiveness. He transmitted to London from the kitchen table and kept his radio set, when not in use, under his bed. His transmission work plan and ciphers were kept in the garden shed, while his spare radio set was buried in his *potager* (kitchen garden).

On 15 November, after some minor adjustments to his aerial, Landes succeeded in getting through to SOE headquarters. *Scientist* was, at long last, in direct touch with Baker Street.[44]

On 31 October, the same night that Landes was parachuting into the Loire valley, a slim, wispy-haired, fragile-looking girl was landing from the felucca *Sea Dog* at the little inlet harbour of Port-Miou, on the outskirts of Cassis, some nine miles east of Marseille.[45] Mary Herbert[46] had strong Catholic beliefs, a degree from the Slade School of Art and could speak French, Italian, Spanish, German and Arabic.[47] She had joined SOE as a secretary but someone spotted her potential as an agent and sent her to Beaulieu for training. Afterwards she was assigned to join de Baissac as his courier in Bordeaux. Tonight, travelling with identity papers in the name of Marie-Louise Vernier and a cover story saying she was a young divorcee from Alexandria, she was on her way to Cannes with instructions to meet up with the head of the local SOE organisation, Peter Churchill.[48] He would give her further instructions for her onward passage to Bordeaux.

The reinforcement of *Scientist* to enable it to attack the blockade runners in Bordeaux was now well advanced. In the unofficial race to which Lord Selborne had fired the starting gun with his letter to Churchill of May 1942, SOE were now, unknown to everyone else, far ahead of the field.

And so it was that all the ingredients for a tragic duplication of effort were coming into place. SOE would soon have a team of five British agents, backed by upwards of maybe fifty French ones, on the quayside at Bordeaux. More manpower would soon be on its way, together with the materials necessary to attack the blockade runners. Meanwhile, across London, Combined Operations were actively engaged in planning to send in their own men, at great hazard, to do exactly the same thing.

It is worth pausing for a moment to examine further the origins of this fatal confusion. In February 1941, Major David Wyatt, Royal Engineers, an SOE officer, had been sent as Baker Street's liaison officer to Combined Operations headquarters. He had no formal position and was left, in the words of SOE's historian Professor Michael Foot, to 'wander the corridors picking up what he could'.[49] Despite this, Wyatt produced some ninety-three reports for SOE, detailing what was happening at Combined Operations.[50] In SOE's view, however, this liaison was a strictly one-way affair. SOE would receive information from Wyatt on what Combined Operations were doing, but Wyatt was instructed that there would be strictly no reciprocal flow of information.

On 14 August, Wyatt confirmed that, though Richmond Terrace may have known nothing of Baker Street's plans, Baker Street were fully informed of what was being planned at Richmond Terrace:

No difficulties are being experienced in keeping in touch with plans and operations at COHQ [Combined Operations headquarters]. D/CCO [Deputy Chief of Combined Operations – at the time Major General Charles Haydon] is a member of the Search and Examination Committee by which practically all plans are considered. D/CCO keeps the Country Sections [of SOE] in touch with any developments which may affect them.[51]

Five days after writing this report Wyatt was tragically killed in the catastrophic Dieppe raid of 19 August 1942.

With Wyatt gone, the one-way, fragile and serendipitous liaison between Baker Street and Richmond Terrace was abruptly ended. What was more, the leaders of Combined Operations and SOE failed to replace him until mid-December, four months later, by which time the main action of our story would be over.[52]

SOE is not alone to be blamed for this culture of secrecy. They were, after all – unlike Combined Operations – specifically excluded from attending the Chiefs of Staff (CoS) Committee, where they would have heard officially about Frankton. From Baker Street's point of view it was perhaps not unreasonable to conclude that, if everyone else was going to keep things secret from them, they would keep things secret from everyone else.

9

Approval and Preparation

The word 'Frankton' first appears in RMBPD's war diary on 12 October, when Hasler and Stewart are recorded as going to London for planning meetings.[1] But the acutely tuned ear and ever-sharp eye of the ordinary Royal Marine must have told those in the RMBPD that something was afoot long before that.

In fact, Hasler had briefed Jock Stewart about Frankton immediately after he returned to Southsea on 22 September. He then took seven days' leave. No one other than Stewart was officially told anything. Ostensibly everything in the Nissen huts on Eastney front was supposed to be continuing as normal.

But it wasn't. On 27 September, in Hasler's absence (but obviously at his instigation), the pace of the training, especially for No. 1 Section, suddenly increased in tempo and the unit's operating hours were altered to allow time for more night exercises. From now on there were exercises every other night, usually involving clandestine entries into Portsmouth and other harbours in the area. There were long-distance canoe paddles, more exercises in making silent approaches, more training in how to attack and kill sentries, more instruction on the layout of dockyards and, as ever, more and yet more boat-work.

RMBPD's war diary and Hasler's own personal diary show an increasing divergence between what 1 and 2 Section were doing at Eastney and Hasler's own activities at the time. The Marines' training was now mostly supervised by Stewart, while Hasler was ever busier with discussions and planning for Frankton – though he still found time to make final refinements to the Mark II Cockle.

There were two new areas of training, however, in both of which Hasler continued to be personally engaged: practice in landing and launching canoes from a beach in heavy sea (but no formal training in how to handle actual surf) and instruction on escape and evasion techniques, including how to use the tiny, 'button-sized' escape compass developed by MI9.[2] This latter instruction was reinforced by exercises in which the Marines, in full combat uniform, were taken, often some hundred miles or so away from Portsmouth, dropped off and required to make their way back to their base with an alerted police force and Home Guard looking out for them.

The emphasis on this latter area of instruction was not accidental. For at a planning meeting in London on 12 October, Captain S.M. Raw RN, the chief staff officer of the admiral in charge of Britain's submarine fleet, made it clear to Hasler that, though he would be allocated a submarine to take him to the Gironde – it would come from 3rd Submarine Flotilla in the Clyde – there could be no question of it returning to pick up his raiders after the operation. With the Battle of the Atlantic at a critical point, the Admiralty could neither dedicate a submarine to this operation for that length of time, nor risk one in a second approach to hostile waters once the enemy had been alerted.[3] Hasler and his men would have to make their own way back to Britain overland. For the first time in any Combined Operations mission, escape and evasion was to be, not just a fallback option if things went wrong, but an integral part of the operation itself.

After this meeting, Hasler and Stewart met for the first time the Combined Operations planner assigned to Operation Frankton, Lieutenant-Commander G.P. L'Estrange RNVR.[4] Over the next week L'Estrange and three assistant planners[5] put together the tidal and hydrographic information on the Gironde which Hasler would need to make his final plan.

On 18 October Hasler and L'Estrange met again in London and the two men wrote out their first outline plan for Frankton. Knowing that, to give Hasler and his team the best chance of moving undetected to Bordeaux, the operation should be carried out over a no moon period, they chose the next one, which would begin at the end of the first week of December. They proposed that only three canoes should carry out the operation, believing this to be the best compromise between a force large enough to carry sufficient explosive to do real damage, and one small enough to move undetected through heavily populated, enemy-occupied territory.

Submitted to the Examination Committee at Richmond Terrace on 21 October, the plan was approved for submission to Mountbatten, subject to two stipulations: first that, consistent with Combined Operations policy at the time,[6] Hasler, as the planner and commander of RMBPD, and because of 'his value to the experimental staff, particularly with regard to shallow water diving technique',[7] was not to lead the raid; and second that 'the question of taking spare cockles [canoes] on the submarine should be examined'.[8] There is no record of why it was eventually decided not to take a spare canoe on the parent submarine – a decision which was to have a profound effect on what would follow.

Hasler's outline plan was, it appears, discussed with Mountbatten, who according to Lucas Phillips approved it and confirmed the Examination Committee's view that Hasler himself could not go on the raid (Richmond Terrace were indeed already actively 'discussing whether, at this stage, it would be possible for this Operation to be carried out by another officer'[9]). Hasler immediately appealed to Neville to intercede with Mountbatten on his behalf and wrote a hurried and uncharacteristically impassioned minute to back this up:

1 Operation is an important one and appears to have a good chance of success. Main difficulty is a question of small-boat seamanship and navigation on the part of the force commander.[10] My 2nd in command has only been using small boats for about four months and chances of success would be materially reduced if the most experienced officer available were not sent.
2 A failure would prejudice all future operations of this type.
3 In a new unit, the OC can hardly gain respect if he avoids going on the first operation.
4 I am supposed to be no longer a member of the Development Organisation in general but simply OC of an operational unit.
5 If I am not allowed to go on this operation, what type of operation will be permissible for me? The case of Major Stirling[11] in Egypt is thought to be similar.[12]

Hasler met L'Estrange again on 21 and 24 October to finalise details of the plan to be put, after approval by Mountbatten, to the Chiefs of Staff Committee. During these meetings they also drew up the list of the stores they would require for the operation (see Appendix A). Even in these few hurried days, however, Hasler still found time to put the final touches to the Mark II Cockle and perfect his system for launching fully laden canoes from a T class submarine using slings and a girder bolted onto the barrel of the submarine's four-inch gun, so as to turn it into a makeshift crane.

Hasler's plea that he should be allowed to lead Frankton appears to have had the desired effect. When, on 27 October, the Examination Committee sat again, they 'agreed, on reconsideration, to recommend [to Mountbatten] that Major Hasler should, himself, lead the party'.[13]

On 29 October Hasler returned to London for the crucial meeting at which the final plan was put to Mountbatten. The conversation between the two men as recorded by Lucas Phillips (which once again appears to be somewhat contradictory to the facts; i.e. that the Examination Committee had already accepted that Hasler should lead) went as follows:

'I gather you want to lead this raid yourself?' Mountbatten asked Hasler at the end of the meeting.

'Yes, Sir.'

'Why?'

'Because it's an important operation, Sir. And I think we should put our best team into it. MacKinnon and his men have been doing intensive boat training for a few months, but I have been using small boats all my life and it's only natural that I'm better at it than they are.'

According to Lucas Phillips, Mountbatten then went round the table seeking the views of his senior advisors. All except Neville were against Hasler going. At the end, Mountbatten smiled and, turning to Hasler, gave his decision: 'Well, much against my better judgment, I am going to let you go.'[14]

Mountbatten submitted Hasler and L'Estrange's plan to the Chiefs of Staff Committee the following day, with only one change: he increased the strength of Hasler's force from three canoes to six 'in case of accidents'. It was to prove a mission-saver. Mountbatten's covering minute is revealing, for it seems to confirm that he had no idea of SOE's parallel *Scientist* operation:

Operation Frankton has been planned to meet Lord Selborne's requirement, referred to in COS (42) 223 (O) and subsequent papers, that steps should be taken to attack Axis ships which are known to be running the blockade between France and the Far East. Both seaborne and airborne methods of attacking the ships have been carefully examined and the plan now proposed *is the only one which offers a good chance of success.*[15] (author's emphasis)

The Chiefs of Staff duly approved Operation Frankton on 3 November.[16]

The crucial meeting with Mountbatten over, Hasler took the night train for Glasgow, where he was to meet No. 1 Section for a period of high-intensity training and preparation in the Clyde. He arrived on board HMS *Forth*, the depot ship of the 3rd Submarine Flotilla, a little after midday on 30 October.

On the following day, 31 October, the same day that Mary Herbert was landed in France, Jack MacKinnon arrived at HMS *Forth* with six canoes and the twelve Royal Marines of No. 1 Section. They spent the day stowing their canoes and equipment before a late-night session of instruction.

Hasler now had exactly a month to prepare them for the operation.

10

Hasler's Men

The twelve men of No. 1 Section, led by Lieutenant Jack MacKinnon, who Hasler took to Scotland for the final phase of their training, meant that these were the men he had chosen for Operation Frankton.

There is nothing in Hasler's personal diary or the RMBPD war diary to indicate either why, or when, Hasler made this choice. It seems likely, however, that the final decision would have been made about halfway through October and would have been based on Hasler's assessment of the two units' relative abilities, particularly when it came to seamanship and navigation. Hasler also encouraged competitions between the two sections in everything from football and rugby matches, and races over the assault courses, to tests in theoretical and practical seamanship – and in these, too No. 1 Section were nearly always dominant.

Having made his decision, Hasler effectively took over command of No. 1 Section from MacKinnon and began to weld them into an instrument he could take deep into enemy territory on one of the most hazardous enterprises of the Second World War. As part of these preparations he and Stewart probably spent some time allocating crews to each canoe and deciding who would be the canoe commanders. In the Cockle Mark II, the canoe commander was the Number One who sat in the forward seat with the compass and was responsible for navigation, while the Number Two sat in the back.[1]

The relationship between two men who paddle a canoe over long distances on operations is a very special one. It is not determined by rank, convention, or even by the relative backgrounds of the people involved. All the more so when the mission involves not just long and arduous paddling, but also living, sleeping and moving, often for many days and nights, in enemy territory, where the life of each man will depend on the other's ability to react to sudden peril with instant judgement, guile and professionalism.

The sense of teamwork that has to prevail between the Number One and the Number Two in a canoe is not about friendship – though it will probably break down if the two men actively hate each other. It is about trust. After wordless hours paddling through the darkness with only a low smudge of land ahead to break the monotony, or up an estuary where the mud banks, islands and trees take on fantastic shapes, the mind easily becomes deceived into conjuring up dangers that don't exist accompanied by unworthy thoughts about your partner: he isn't paddling as hard as you are; he's steering the wrong course (you know this to be so, because that star shouldn't be where it is in the sky); he took more than his fair share of the meal you cooked last evening, and it wasn't your turn to cook anyway. What's more, you spent more hours on watch than he did when you were lying up yesterday, and in any case his end of the canoe is more comfortable to sleep in than yours. And – just to annoy you – he deliberately farts in the sleeping bag you share just before you take it over, snores loudly, talks in his sleep and shits too close to the canoe. Worst of all, you caught him chatting up your girlfriend while you were getting the pints in at the pub the other night.

There would thus have been nothing haphazard about the canoe partnerships formed by the time Jack MacKinnon and No. 1 Section arrived in Glasgow. They would have been tried, tested and probably frequently changed during the many night exercises and long paddles over the previous two months.

Hasler gave each of his canoes the name of a fish beginning with 'C', which was stencilled in light blue letters on their starboard bows. He disposed of his crews – 'just a good cross section of average young fellows' – as follows.[2]

Catfish was the name Hasler chose for his canoe, in which, as commander, he took the Number One's position. But this created a problem – there were now thirteen men for six canoes. Someone would have to drop out.

The problem resolved itself when Jack MacKinnon's Number Two, Norman Colley, fractured a metatarsal bone in his foot in a rugby match.[3] This gave Hasler the opportunity to address the one remaining dysfunctional canoe partnership: that between Bill Sparks and Eric Fisher. Hasler took on Sparks as his Number Two and Eric Fisher was reassigned to become the Number Two to Bill Ellery.

Sparks,[4] the 'cheerful Cockney' from Shoreditch, known as 'Ned' to his comrades, was just twenty years old when he joined RMBPD in 1942. Having left school at fourteen, he worked briefly as a cobbler before enlisting in the Royal Marines on 5 September 1939 – four days after the outbreak of war.[5] In March 1942, Sparks, then on leave after a posting in HMS *Renown*, heard that his sailor brother Benny had been killed when the destroyer HMS *Naiad* was torpedoed off Crete.

Curly-haired with a thin, almost cadaverous frame, an infectious laugh and a face enlivened by a huge grin revealing bad teeth, Sparks is often portrayed as an eternal spring of Cockney humour in adversity. The truth is a little more modulated, for he was also capable of great blackness and gloom at moments of difficulty, not infrequently expressing critical views when he considered things were not going as they should; 'making disparaging comments in an audible undertone', Hasler described it.[6] This sometimes made him a difficult companion in a canoe. We know he did not get on with Eric Fisher, which was why Hasler took Sparks on as his own Number Two. But his occasional spikiness may have led to trouble with others too, for there is some suggestion that Sparks was popular only among a select few of Hasler's team (one of whom was his fellow Cockney, Bill Ellery).

Tough, with a capacity for aggression in battle and bar alike; never short of a moan ('dripping' in the parlance of the Corps), or of a joke in adversity; indomitable and utterly reliable when the chips were really down, there have always been plenty of 'Bill Sparks' in the Royal Marines, for they are the backbone of the Corps.

Known as 'Jack' or 'Mac' to all in RMBPD and 'Jacky' to his family, Lt. John Withers MacKinnon,[7] *Cuttlefish*'s Number One and Hasler's second-in-command, was twenty-one when he joined Hasler's team. As with so many of those whom Hasler valued, MacKinnon, who had worked as a coal merchant's clerk in Glasgow before the war, had come up through the ranks. He enlisted in the Royal Marines for 'hostilities only' (i.e. for the duration of the war) three months before his twentieth birthday in April 1941. After initial training at Exton in Devon he was quickly promoted to the rank of acting temporary lance corporal and posted to HMS *Atherstone* in early 1942, distinguishing himself by helping to shoot down an enemy aircraft during his first active engagement. His abilities must have been swiftly recognised, however, because by May 1942 he had been selected for officer training and was at the Royal Marines Officer Training Unit at Thurlestone in Devon, passing out top of his class. From here he was transferred to the RM Small Arms Training School in Browndown in Hampshire to finish his training, and it was here that Hasler found him on 25 June 1942.

MacKinnon, a non-smoker who drank only sparingly and played jazz drums (endearing him to Hasler who played jazz clarinet), was what was referred to at the time as a 'clean living young man'. He was five foot seven inches tall with dark brown hair, blue eyes, a fresh complexion and a dapper appearance, reinforced by a premature moustache. The eldest of four children, MacKinnon came from a close and (judging by his letters home) loving lower middle-class Presbyterian family who lived in a cramped tenement block at 22 Clarendon Street, Glasgow. His father had been a Piper in the Argyll and Sutherland Highlanders; one of his sisters was later to join the WRNS, while the other worked for the Glasgow optical equipment manufacturers Barr & Stroud. As a young boy MacKinnon, a devotee of cycling, camping, hill walking and other outdoor pursuits, had joined first the Cubs and then the Scouts, rising eventually to be a scoutmaster before the war.

One of the curiosities of this story is that, while Hasler clearly liked MacKinnon (later describing him as a 'close friend')[8] and often used him as a fellow officer to help plan some of No 1 Section's exercises, he never confided in him (as he did Stewart) about Frankton until after the operation had begun. It may be that Hasler looked on MacKinnon as still a young officer under training who was not yet ready for the full burdens of command. Hasler was particularly aware of one of MacKinnon's few deficiencies – his notorious inability to master the arts of night navigation in tidal waters.

MacKinnon's new partner in *Cuttlefish*, James Conway, was a former Co-operative milkman from Edgeley in Stockport. His closest confidant before joining the Royal Marines had been his horse, Freddie.[9] The youngest of five children, Jim, whose father died when he was six, was quiet and unassuming. He left school at fourteen and started his working life in a drawing office, but, being a keen cyclist and swimmer, disliked being indoors and gave up the position to work for the Co-op Dairy in Stockport. With a brother in the Royal Marines, James enlisted into the Corps at Plymouth on 13 January 1942, aged nineteen years and five months. A modest and self-effacing man, Conway was very much one of Hasler's 'average young fellows' when he volunteered for special service with the RMBPD.

Coalfish's Number One, Sergeant 'Sailor' Wallace,[10] was, at twenty-nine, the oldest man after Hasler on the Frankton team. Born and brought up in a tough quarter of Dublin, he spoke with a thick Dublin accent, which was – but only behind his back – much mimicked by his men.

Tall, dark and good-looking with a strong physique, Wallace had what Lucas Phillips called an 'engaging Irish personality'. Indeed he was at first refused when he applied to join the Royal Marines in 1930 and told that, as a citizen of the Irish Free State, he was not allowed to join a British unit unless his application was accompanied by two references 'from persons of high standing'.[11] He eventually succeeded in joining the Corps in January 1931, making him one of only four among Hasler's men – apart from Hasler himself – who had signed on as a 'regular'.

His strong physique, inexhaustible energy and ability to find humour even in the most difficult circumstances made him much respected among the Marines of No. 1 Section and valued by his superior, but much younger officer, Jack MacKinnon. Described by one of his Marines[12] as a man who was 'never known to show fear' and an excellent teacher and trainer, Wallace nevertheless had a habit of being impulsive[13] and tended to believe that physical strength, natural charm and mental quick-wittedness were all he needed to overcome life's most difficult challenges. Those same traits were to become evident during Operation Frankton.

Sitting astern of Wallace was Marine 'Bobby' Ewart,[14] known to his family as 'Bert' but in the RMBPD chiefly as 'Jock' or sometimes just 'Bob'.[15] Described by his best friend Norman Colley as a 'gentle giant',[16] Ewart, born on 4 December 1921, was one of the four sons of a farm labourer from Scone on the east coast of Scotland. His family moved to Springburn in Glasgow sometime around 1920, where, like his fellow Glaswegian Jack MacKinnon, he joined one of the local uniformed youth movements of his time – in his case the Glasgow Boys' Brigade.

Ewart, strongly built and at six foot the tallest of Hasler's men, was serious-minded, inclined to get things wrong from time to time and, because of this, often became the butt of good-natured jokes. But his qualities of steadfastness and dependability in times of crisis made him a valued member of the team. Norman Colley describes Bobby Ewart as 'a gentle person, not at all the kind who you think of as a killer, or someone much interested in hurting people'.[17]

Corporal Albert (Bert) Laver,[18] the commander of *Crayfish*, was, with 'Sailor' Wallace, George Sheard and Bill Ellery, one of the four members of Hasler's team who had joined the Royal Marines as a 'regular'. Before enlisting in March 1939 at the age of eighteen, he had been a butcher's assistant and lived in Hind Street in Birkenhead, Cheshire.* Laver was promoted to lance corporal in March 1942 and was on board HMS *Rodney* with Wallace during her engagement with the *Bismarck* in May 1942, serving as an ammunition handler in one of the Royal Marine manned turrets of the great battleship.[19]

Fair-haired, fresh-complexioned, round-faced and, in the words of Lucas Phillips, 'square rigged', Laver was moderate in his habits and one of the brightest of Hasler's team (with a particular penchant for navigation and seamanship). He was also endowed with considerable powers of endurance[20] and a marked ability to operate on his own initiative.

In almost every service unit, large or small, someone becomes the unit 'joker' – always fooling around; always good for a laugh; always the one with the witty comment at times of difficulty. Among the men of No. 1 Section, this was *Crayfish*'s Number Two, Marine 'Bill' Mills,[21] who provided the perfect foil to his quieter and more serious-minded canoe partner Laver. He was well-liked by his colleagues, who knew not only that he could always be relied on to make them laugh but also that he would go out of his way to help a 'mate' in need. After the war, a close family friend would say that he 'was a boy of an extremely lovable character, full of life and always ready to do someone a good turn'.[22] Stocky, with brown wavy hair, Mills was brought up with his two brothers in Kettering, where he had worked in the town's Rubber and Sports Stores before the war. An excellent swimmer and the treasurer of

---

* This street, which was behind the town's main railway station, has now been demolished.

the local football club, Bill and his fiancée Kitty Faulkner planned to get married in December 1942.[23] Just shy of his twenty-first birthday when he went north with No. 1 Section, he was fit, full of energy and, along with Bert Laver, one of the most educated of Hasler's Marines. His closest friends in No. 1 Section were 'Ned' Sparks and Bill Ellery (all three of whom shared a Christian name).

We do not know how West Countryman George Sheard,[24] *Conger*'s Number One, known as 'Jan'[25] and the third regular Marine in Hasler's team, managed to avoid the clear stipulation in Hasler's call for volunteers in May that he only wanted men who were 'free of strong family ties'. For the records at Plymouth Reference Library show that Sheard was married to his wife Renee in the second quarter of 1942[26] (i.e. between 1 April and 30 June). Given that Hasler recruited his Marines on 1 July, Sheard must have been married (perhaps just married) when Hasler chose him.

Sheard came, as his middle name Jellicoe suggests, from a Plymouth family with strong naval connections, who lived at 3 East Cornwall Street, Devonport. His father, who had served in the Royal Navy, had sired twelve children, of whom George was the seventh. He was, in consequence, brought up largely by his sisters – indeed, the fact that he joined the Royal Marines came as something of a surprise to his parents and siblings, for George had been a sickly child who attended a 'special' outdoor school for asthmatic children. Short, tough, witty and with a strong Devon accent, Sheard had, despite his early weakness, a frame which was as wide as it was tall. Though he too found difficulty with the complexities of navigation, he had a marked ability to command, immense reserves of strength and endurance and a strong sense of humour.

Marine David Moffatt,[27] Sheard's partner and *Conger*'s Number Two, was by all accounts a brilliant mimic who specialised in taking off notable personalities at the Royal Marines Barracks in Eastney, particularly among the non-commissioned officers – for which he got into trouble more than once.[28] His party trick at the White Heather Guest House consisted of turning his shirt collar back to front and, with mock solemnity and appropriate incantations, taking off to perfection one of the local parsons.

Moffatt was born in Belfast of a Roman Catholic family who emigrated and settled at 62 Whitley Lane, Lee Mount in Halifax. His best friend was the other member of No. 1 Section with a Northern Irish background, Eric Fisher. Moffatt, five feet nine inches tall, with a strong frame and a thin face of fresh complexion topped off with a mop of dark brown hair, had worked in the dyeing trade before the war. He was, like many of his colleagues, active in a uniformed youth organisation (in his case the Church Scout Troop), from which he enlisted in the Royal Marines at the age of twenty-two in 1941 for 'hostilities only'.

At twenty-seven, Marine 'Bill' Ellery[29] – known by some as 'The Crafty Cockney'[30] – was one of the oldest members of No. 1 Section and, at just an inch and a half short of six foot, also one of the tallest. As Number One of *Cachalot* he was the only canoe commander who did not have a rank to go with the job. He was born in Rampyne Street in Pimlico in 1915, an only child who never knew his father. Street-wise and quick on his feet, he learnt to fend for himself at a very early age, sharing both these qualities and his Cockney background with 'Ned' Sparks, with whom he was 'best mates'. A Watney's drayman before the war, Ellery too somehow bypassed Hasler's prohibition on having married men in his unit, for he had married before the war and already had two sons by the time the conflict started. Sparks in his autobiography describes Ellery as 'fearless in a typical Cockney sort of way', someone who 'knew how to con his way through life'; according to Sparks, Ellery on one occasion raided the local NAAFI in Eastney Barracks and came out with some pilfered bars of chocolate, saying 'I've got a rule in life. Everything you *can't* have, I *will* have.'[31] Physically very strong with broad shoulders and black hair, Ellery was a first-class footballer who was rumoured to have had a trial for Chelsea Football Club before the war,[32] and played occasionally for Portsmouth during the war years. He was a strong swimmer but suffered severely from claustrophobia and was most uncomfortable underwater.

Marine Eric Fisher,[33] a round-faced young man with light brown hair and blue eyes, was just a year younger than his canoe commander. Stoutly built, he often had his leg pulled by the others for being podgy and overweight, which he apparently took in good heart. When he joined the RMBPD Fisher could not swim, but this was soon put right by Jack MacKinnon, who taught him by the simple but brutal procedure of shouting 'Over the side, Fisher!' at random moments when they were out in the unit's boats. Despite this he became a proficient underwater swimmer, perhaps one of the best in the unit. According to Sparks, who objected to sharing a canoe with him, Fisher should not have been in No. 1 Section at all, as he was accident-prone and not up to the standards of the others in the team.[34]

Hasler had decided, probably fairly early on, that he should take a spare – or 'twelfth man' in cricket parlance – on Frankton, in case of accident or illness (this person was in fact the thirteenth man – but Royal Marines, like their Royal Naval counterparts, are superstitious creatures). Marine Norman Colley[35] had been Jack MacKinnon's Number Two until his rugby accident put him in hospital.[36]

On a visit to his bedside before the start of Frankton, MacKinnon presented Colley with an option: 'You can come with us if you are prepared to do without sick leave. On the other hand, you can stay in hospital.'

For Colley the choice was simple. He opted to join his 'mates' on what he was later to describe as 'Hasler's great adventure'.[37]

Colley, born in Pontefract, Yorkshire on 22 November 1920, was probably the strongest swimmer in RMBPD. Before the war he had worked first as a delivery boy in a local grocer's shop and then for a wholesale confectioner. He was called up for wartime service on 16 April 1941 and was persuaded (like Sparks) by an alert recruiting sergeant to join the Royal Marines, rather than the Royal Navy. His first posting, like that of his closest friend Bobby Ewart, was to the Orkneys where he helped build accommodation units on Scapa Flow. Bored and fed up, he had no hesitation in volunteering in May 1942 when he saw Hasler's notice calling for those prepared to participate in hazardous service: 'I would have volunteered for the Girl Guides if it meant getting away from Scapa.'[38]

11

Marie-Claire

In one crucial sense Operation Frankton was a new departure for Combined Operations. After each of their previous ventures, the extraction of the raiding party had been accomplished by Combined Operations units as part of the plan. But in Frankton, once the raid was finished, the participants would have to make their way back through enemy-occupied territory alone.

But there was an organisation that might be able to assist – MI9, the London-based clandestine network established in 1939 to help escaped prisoners of war and downed airmen make their way home.[1]

One of MI9's key organisers was Lieutenant Airey Neave, Royal Artillery, who would one day be a Member of Parliament and a favourite of Mrs Thatcher's, until he was killed in the courtyard of the House of Commons by an IRA car bomb. Having made one of the first ever 'home runs' (in his case from Colditz) back to England, he had been assigned to MI9, where he became notorious for doing much of his business from his favourite restaurant, Rules in Covent Garden. In his book *Saturday at MI9*, written after the war, Neave describes how he and the little Charente town of Ruffec first became involved in Frankton:

> Before the raid began, MI9 discussed with Combined Operations [almost certainly L'Estrange] the possibility of putting the crews in touch with an underground escape organisation to find their way to neutral territory ... Until this time no aircrew or Commando, even on a special mission, had ever been given the location in occupied territory, let alone a contact address, or an escape line ...

It was decided that Major Hasler and his Commandos should be told that on completion of their mission, they should make for the town of Ruffec, where they would find an organisation equipped to get them back ... This decision seemed to me to be the worst of both worlds: I did not see how those of the party who escaped could be certain of making contact with Mary in the Ruffec area. Nor had she been warned that the Commando raid in the river Gironde was taking place ...[2]

The Mary referred to here is Mary Lindell, who, in a story with more than its fair share of unusual characters, was arguably the most unusual.

Mary Ghita Lindell, the Comtesse de Milleville, alias Comtesse de Moncy and later and more famously, 'Marie-Claire', was petite and what the French call *très distinguée*. But she was also an Englishwoman from the top of her perfectly coiffured head to the bottom of her exquisitely fashionable shoes.[3]

She was born in 1897 to well-to-do parents in Sutton, then a small Surrey town outside London. Her mother, true to the traditions of her day, was big in 'good works', paying special attention to the Young Men's Christian Association (YMCA).[4] Mary's second name may hint at some connection with the Indian subcontinent in her family background, perhaps even Indian blood. She was, notwithstanding, fiercely and imperiously British. Mary Lindell may not have been high-born, but she behaved as though she ruled the world and, being of British blood, considered it inappropriate that she should be required to put up with impudence from those of less fortunate races, such as the Germans.

Her slightness of figure and feminine fragility concealed extraordinary physical toughness, courage which often tipped over into foolhardiness and a will so strong that even Blondie Hasler would, in due course, have to submit to it. A cross between the fearsome headmistress of a girls' school of the time and one of those dotty maiden aunts who inhabit the pages of P.G. Wodehouse, she was idiosyncratic, demanding and determined to have her own way in all things.

At the outbreak of the First World War, aged nineteen, Mary joined the Voluntary Aid Detachment (VAD) but soon fell foul of her matron; charged with challenging the authority of a superior, she either left voluntarily or was required to do so. Undeterred, she immediately (and as far as one can tell without being able to speak any French) went to France and joined the French nursing unit, *Secours Blessés Militaires*, nursing the wounded and dying from all sides at dressing stations within sound of the guns. For her dedication to caring for French and Russian soldiers she was awarded first the Croix de Guerre with Star in 1917, and later the Russian Order of St Anne, as well as being entitled to a number of British campaign medals. All of these she took pains to display prominently on the Red Cross uniform which – washed, pressed and immaculately starched – she insisted on wearing whenever on 'business' in German-occupied France during the Second World War.

The outbreak of conflict in 1939 found the Comtesse in Paris with her children: two sons and a daughter (her long-suffering husband was at the time in South America). With the Germans at the outskirts of the city, she donned her Red Cross uniform, pinned on her medals and jumped in the family car, on which she mounted a Red Cross flag. Placing herself at the head of a convoy of lorries bearing the wounded, she headed out of the city, pushing her way through the columns of refugees, waving imperiously and shouting 'Make way for the Red Cross!', while German aircraft strafed them and enemy armoured columns pressed all round. Over the following days she journeyed south, finally dropping her charges at Pau on the other side of the Demarcation Line. Here she left the convoy and returned north to collect her children and take them to Paris, arriving to find the city occupied and under German control.

In mid-1940 Mary set about creating an amateur escape line, which she operated with her children as a sort of small family business. Her first trip was with an escaping British officer, the dashing Captain James Windsor. Through a Russian prince of her acquaintance, she obtained an interview with the German military commander in France, General Otto von Stülpnagel. She told him that, in her Red Cross capacity, she was required to take two French children south to rejoin their family and demanded that he should provide her with instructions to issue a pass for her journey. Armed with this she went to see the impressively named *Hauptmann* von Bismarck, head of documentation for Paris, and ordered him to give her an *Ausweis*, adding that, in view of the length of the journey, the unreliability of the roads and the fact that she was a lone woman, she would require to be accompanied on her journey by a 'mechanic'.

A day or so later she left Paris in the family Peugeot (now redecorated with large German Red Crosses on each side) with Captain Windsor installed in the front seat alongside his 'mistress', dressed as her 'mechanic' in some of the Comte de Milleville's cast-offs and headed for the town of Ruffec, close to the Demarcation Line, begging, borrowing, and conning petrol from Germans on the way. In Ruffec she met up with Marthe Rullier, a First World War nursing friend and president of the local Red Cross. Here, despite the fact that the Rullier house was being used to billet German officers, the party stayed the night. On the following morning Mary presented her *Ausweis* to the local German *Kommandantur*, who, impressed by the Bismarck signature, agreed to instruct the guards on the Demarcation Line to let her pass.

After her first successful sortie using this impromptu escape line, she decided to set up something more permanent. She arranged through the Resistance for all escaping British pilots and POWs in the Paris area to be collected and brought to her flat where, after a short ceremony requiring them to swear an oath on British soil (acquired when the Germans weren't looking from the garden of the British Embassy), they were inserted into a 'pipeline' which delivered them into the hands of the organisation Mary had established in Ruffec with the help of Marthe Rullier and the local 'squire',[5] Gaston Denivelle. This comprised a courier network, manned by local smugglers (*passeurs*) who took escapers across the Demarcation Line and onwards to Spain.

The key local points on this route were two farms in the Ruffec area. The first, known as 'Farm A', was close to the line in the occupied sector, while the other, 'Farm B' (Marvaud Farm), owned by Armand Dubreuille, was on the other side of the Demarcation Line in the *Zone Non-Occupée*. From Marvaud Farm, escapers were passed on south, usually through Lyon and thence onwards to a seamen's home in Marseille run by a Scottish Presbyterian minister, the Reverend Donald Caskie.[6] From here passage was arranged over the Pyrenees to the British Embassy in Madrid. Several successful 'runs' of Allied escapers were made down this escape route in the last months of 1940.

Not satisfied with conning travel passes out of the Germans, obtaining petrol from them by false pretences and smuggling Allied escapers to safety (the penalty for which, according to a notice promulgated early in the German occupation by her 'friend' Otto von Stülpnagel, was summary execution by firing squad), Mary Lindell turned her attention to even more dangerous pastimes. She set up a small group of impromptu 'thieves' who specialised in stealing weapons from the Germans – and especially side-arms from officers dining at Paris restaurants. These were then spirited away into the hands of the local Resistance.

Of course it couldn't last. Early in 1941 she was arrested and, in the absence of any information which would have supported a more serious charge, was sentenced to nine months in Fresnes prison for 'insulting the German Army'.

Released from prison on 1 November 1941, the Comtesse de Milleville, weak and ill, was instructed by her captors – on pain of death – not to leave the city. She duly caught the first train south the following morning, ending up in Ruffec. Here she inserted herself into her own escape line, was smuggled across the Demarcation Line and spent some time recuperating at Marvaud Farm, where she was nursed back to health by Armand Dubreuille and his wife Amélie.

It appears that Mary, undeterred by her spell in Fresnes, then briefly returned to the escape business in Ruffec. There is a description of a meeting in March 1942 between her, Gaston Denivelle, 'Colonel' Ernst-Henri Gua, the 'Commandant' of the local Ruffec Resistance, and a new agent, the gendarme Lieutenant Henri Péyraud.[7] Péyraud relates what happened:

I arrived in [the Gendarmerie in] Ruffec in March 1942 ... When I entered the room I saluted a retired Colonel who we all thought was involved in the Resistance [i.e. Gua] and was presented to M. Denivelle ... [suddenly] 'Marie Claire' [Mary Lindell] appeared. She spoke our language with a pronunciation which was unquestionably English and was, moreover, wearing the uniform of the French Red Cross. But that accent![8]

It was probably during this period that Mary was introduced to François and Germaine Rouillon, the proprietors of the Hôtel de France in Ruffec.[9] A large rambling building with numerous entrances, an archway which had been used for carriages but now led to a convenient space for parking cars and vans out of sight at the back, and which always had a room or two to spare, it was just what the Comtesse was looking for. Despite the fact that it prominently flew the swastika alongside the French tricolour and housed German officers, she promptly declared it her escape headquarters.

We do not know how long Mary Lindell stayed in Ruffec before moving to Lyon. Here she was advised by the US Consul that the Gestapo were searching for her and that she should get out of France before her Vichy passport expired on 1 August 1942. She crossed into Spain disguised, somewhat improbably, as a governess and made her way to Lisbon, where the British Consul arranged for her passage to Britain in an RAF flying boat.

On arrival in London on 29 July 1942, Lindell was immediately picked up by MI9 and asked to report to one of its 'safe houses' above Overton's Restaurant at 6 St James's Street. Here she was taken into a well-furnished lounge on the first floor and introduced to Airey Neave and his MI9 colleague, Jimmy Langley, who had already heard from escapees about the Comtesse's exploits. They questioned her briefly before asking her to return to see them on the following morning, 30 July, for formal recruitment into MI9.

Mary Lindell spent the first two weeks of August 1942 at MI9's training establishment.[10] In the course of her training, Airey Neave proposed that, since 'Marie' was such a common French name, it would be better to use the code name *Marie-Claire* for her future escape line.

Commenting after the war on Mary as a student and potential member of MI9, Langley said that she was 'difficult … alright in very small doses',[11] 'a lady who was used to having her own way'[12] and someone who did not find it easy to accept instruction. Her post-war biography claims that, though she 'took some weeks' to learn coding, 'a radio set was not forthcoming'. The truth appears to be slightly different. According to SOE historian Michael Foot,[13] she was assigned a radio operator, an Australian called Tom Groome,[14] but took against him. Later she turned personal preference into an operational principle, claiming that she didn't much trust radios and had been determined from the outset, not to have one – a decision which was later to have important, even tragic consequences.

Mary's training ended in mid-October, after which she left on ten days' holiday in Cornwall with instructions to return to London to be briefed about her re-entry into France, which was planned for 26 October.

The timing here is interesting. Given that L'Estrange knew as early as 12 October that the Frankton team would have to escape overland from Bordeaux, it seems quite possible that he was discussing the possibility of using the *Marie-Claire* escape line with Neave while Mary Lindell was still in England. Yet, although she would be going into France without a wireless, no word about this was said to her before she left.

It seems likely that the reason for withholding this information was security. Trusting a returning agent well known to the Gestapo who had acknowledged vulnerabilities through her family with information about a forthcoming commando raid would have been foolhardy in the extreme. But MI9 might at least have used the opportunity of Lindell's presence in England to put in place some contingency for contacting her. It was, as Airey Neave later frankly admitted, not MI9's finest hour.[15]

On 26 October, Mary Lindell (travelling under false papers in the name of Madame de Milleville) was driven to Tempsford to be briefed for her return to France. After a farewell handshake with Airey Neave, she and a fellow agent clambered on board a Lysander and strapped themselves in. A few moments later, on a cold night lit by an occasional moon darting through flying clouds, the little single-engine aircraft climbed above the fields of England and swung south for the coast. Their destination was a small disused airfield in the Corrèze region, some fifteen miles east of Ussel and a mile northeast of the little town of Thalamy.[16] Here they were landed in the early hours of the morning and were handed over to the local Resistance.

The following morning the two new arrivals made their way into Ussel, entering the town half an hour after the curfew at 5 a.m. From there, Mary caught a train to Limoges, thence to Toulouse and onward to Monte Carlo where she met up with her eldest son, Maurice. The next day the pair headed for Ruffec, where, in early November 1942, they made contact with M. and Mme Rouillon and re-established their headquarters in the Hôtel de France.

Mary Lindell's escape organisation, now rechristened the *Marie-Claire* line, was back in business and looking for customers. And London, in the form of Captain Airey Neave and Commander L'Estrange, were just about to send her some rather important ones …

A Thickening of Plots

Both Combined Operations and SOE now started to quicken the pace of preparation for their parallel operations against the blockade runners of Bordeaux. These often involved events which, though up to a thousand and more miles away from each other, were only days, or even hours apart.

The first week of November

The Firth of Clyde, Scotland

The Scots word *dreich* describes to perfection the dull grey morning which greeted Hasler and No. 1 Section as they gathered on the deck of HMS *Forth* on Sunday 1 November 1942. The light nor'easterly that blew was not strong enough to stir the low cloud hanging over the leaden waters of the Clyde, or disperse the misty rain which dampened *Forth*'s wooden decks, made her superstructure glisten and insinuated itself into every crack and crevice of clothes, machinery and equipment.[1]

Hasler spent that morning lecturing, but in the afternoon No. 1 Section were in their canoes practising limpet mine attacks on a Dutch minesweeper,[2] the *Jan Van Gelder*, which Hasler had arranged as both training facility and base for their work in Scotland (she was soon rechristened by No. 1 Section's Marines as 'The Old Scranbag'[3]). During this exercise (repeated many times in the weeks ahead), the Marines were required to plant their mines on the *Jan Van Gelder* while she steamed on a steady course at two knots, so as to simulate the tidal flow the raiders would experience when attacking ships lying at harbour.

The morning of 2 November was spent hoisting out canoes from HMS *Forth* and in the afternoon there were more practice limpet attacks on the *Jan Van Gelder*. On 3 November there was a full day's paddle up Loch Long.*

The Marines spent the whole of the following day on board the *Jan Van Gelder* with additional practice hoisting out canoes (this time from the *Gelder*'s davits) and carrying out more mock limpet attacks.

On 5 November the freshening nor'easterly began to blow away the calm, misty, grey weather. Hasler set his men to camouflaging their canoes and equipment (according to Colley, this was the moment when some of the Marines of No. 1 Section began to suspect this was more than just training[4]). Blondie meanwhile spent the day planning Frankton with Jock Stewart, who had come up from London the previous night.

The following day, with a gusty Force 5 blowing from the west, was spent on HM/s *Taurus* sheltering under the eastern lee of the Isle of

Figure 1

---

* This remains a classic training paddle in the SBS. In a heavily laden canoe it can be quite arduous, especially when there is a stiff northerly blowing down the loch. The Marines of No. 1 Section were lucky this day, however. On 2 November 1942, the wind was westerly and very light, so the waters of the loch would have been relatively placid.

Arran while testing the crane Hasler had invented, which used a girder bolted to the submarine's four-inch gun to hoist out their canoes. It worked acceptably 'except for bending of girder', as Hasler's diary mournfully notes. The squalls this day were boisterous enough to keep the *Jan Van Gelder* in port in Rothesay.

Overnight the crew of the *Taurus* fitted a strengthened girder and on the morning of 7 November, with No. 1 Section on board, she made a rendezvous with the *Jan Van Gelder* off Rothesay. Here they successfully ran through the process of launching all six canoes, this time fully manned and loaded. Satisfied that they had a workable system, Hasler left MacKinnon to oversee the packing up of stores and canoes for No. 1 Section's return south and, accompanied by Stewart, took the train from Glasgow, arriving in London on 8 November for more planning meetings at Combined Operations.

Tarbes, southeast France

On 1 November Egbert Rizzo, SOE's man in charge of the *Édouard* line in Tarbes, penned one of his verbose reports to his bosses in London:

> Thomas [Gaston Hèches] informs me that L [Robert Leroy] came to town on 12 Oct to wait for a friend whose name is not given. After waiting for him [sic] for a whole week, he left for Bordeaux as the expected friend had not turned up. He asked me to inform you.

In fact the 'him' was a her – Mary Herbert.

It was about this time that Rizzo also informed London that he had recruited a new *Édouard* line agent in Bordeaux. Her name was Juliette Latour[5] and she was the concierge at 49 Rue de la Denise, just yards behind de Baissac's headquarters in the Café des Chartrons. Rizzo hoped she would act as both courier and as the Bordeaux entry point for his escape line smuggling fugitives over the Pyrenees.

Ruffec, the Charente, southwest France

When Mary Lindell arrived back in Ruffec sometime during the first week in November she immediately made contact with Gaston Denivelle, who told her that there were already six downed airmen scattered in safe houses around the Charente waiting to be smuggled down the *Marie-Claire* line to freedom. What Denivelle appears not to have told Mary was that he either had been, or was just about to be, recruited by another completely different London based secret organisation.

Denivelle's personal file in the French military archives shows that SOE's Lise de Baissac recruited him into the *Scientist II réseau* sometime in early November 1942.[6] Nor was he the only member of Mary Lindell's organisation who ended up working simultaneously for both MI9's *Marie-Claire* line and SOE's *Scientist* network in Ruffec. On 22 November 1942, George Flower's radio operator in Tours reported to London that Lise de Baissac had recruited the 'Commander' of the local Resistance, Ernst-Henri Gua,[7] whom Lindell had used as her key contact since at least March of that year (see Chapter 11). The French military archives show that, of the ten key members of the *Marie-Claire* line named in the history of the Resistance in the Ruffec area, six were also members of *Scientist II*.[8] One of these was Germaine Rouillon, who ran the Hôtel de France and is listed as providing '*hébergement*', or lodging and accommodation. It is therefore possible that, at the same time that Mary Lindell was hiding escapees in the Hôtel de France on behalf of MI9, Lise de Baissac was smuggling her agents in and out of the building on behalf of SOE.[9]

Did the two women meet? It is impossible to say. But given that they were both involved in helping escapees, shared a number of agents and were both shuffling their charges up and down the corridors of the Hôtel de France at strange hours of the day and night, they must at least have known of each other's existence.

Did London know? Almost certainly not.[10] Even if those on the ground found it sensible to cooperate against a common enemy, in Whitehall the principle of maintaining a separation bordering on enmity continued to apply.

Hitler's Chancellery, Berlin

In early October an event took place in the Channel which was, indirectly, to make Operation Frankton much more dangerous for its participants. On the night of 3–4 October, Combined Operations launched Operation Basalt, a classic 'butcher and bolt' raid on Sark in the Channel Islands. The aim was to carry out an 'offensive reconnaissance' on the island and capture German prisoners at the same time. According to the Combined Operations account, four prisoners taken early in the raid were being escorted to the beach, their hands tied behind their backs, when one made a break for it and was shot.[11] The Germans immediately accused the British of shooting prisoners with their hands tied behind their backs, giving Hitler the pretext for issuing his infamous *Kommandobefehl* (Commando Order) two weeks later:

> From now on all men operating against German troops in so-called Commando raids ... are to be annihilated to the last man. This is to be carried out whether they be soldiers in uniform, or saboteurs, with or without arms; and whether fighting or seeking to escape ... Even if these individuals on discovery make obvious their intention of giving themselves up as prisoners, no pardon is on any account to be given.
>
> ... Should individual members of these Commandos, such as agents, saboteurs etc., fall into the hands of the Armed Forces through any means – as, for example, through the Police in one of the Occupied Territories – they are to be instantly handed over to the SD [*Sicherheitsdienst*, the German security service]. To hold them in military custody – for example in POW Camps, etc., even if only as a temporary measure, is strictly forbidden.
>
> ... I will hold all Commanders and Officers responsible under Military Law for any omission to carry out this order, whether by failure in their duty to instruct their units accordingly, or if they themselves act contrary to it.[12]

Although the written, detailed version of this order had very limited distribution and was seen only by senior German officers – only twelve copies were ever issued – there were hints on German radio that in future all captured commandos would be shot.[13] The existence of this infamous – and illegal – order was widely discussed by those involved in special operations at the time, including the Marines of RMBPD.[14]

The second week of November

Tours, central France

Four days after Hitler issued his infamous order, a second event occurred which would further increase the risks to those about to take part in Operation Frankton. On 8 November, Lise de Baissac was back in Tours where she stayed the night with Yvonne Rudellat in her little flat. That evening the two women turned on the radio to hear the BBC news and 'messages for France'. They were puzzled to hear a single phrase repeated continuously for several hours: '*Attention! Robert arrive.*'[15]

They found out only later that this was the secret BBC signal telling resistance groups in North Africa that the Anglo-American landings on the North African coast – Operation Torch – had begun. Three days later on 11 November, fearing that what Churchill called 'the soft underbelly of Europe' – its southern coastline – was now exposed to Allied invasion, German columns stormed across the Demarcation Line and took control of the whole of Vichy France.

Up to now, SOE been relatively restrained in their use of sabotage for fear of giving the Germans the pretext to invade the *Zone Non-Occupée*. Now the gloves were off.[16] From this moment onwards, SOE agents in France would become much more active and their lives would be at much greater risk.

And so would those of the Royal Marines of No. 1 Section. Under the plan drawn up by L'Estrange and MI9, Hasler's men had a seventy-mile walk across enemy-occupied territory to reach Ruffec, after which, having crossed the Demarcation Line, they would be in the comparative safety of Vichy France all the way to Spain. Now, with the whole of France occupied, the entire journey to the Spanish border would have to be conducted under watchful German eyes.

Tarbes, southeast France

Mary Herbert, *Scientist*'s courier, arrived in Tarbes some time between 5 and 10 November,[17] having cycled most of the way from the south of France. She went, as instructed, to Gaston Hèches' restaurant in the Rue Avezac Macaya, asked for 'David' and identified herself using the appropriate code phrases. Hèches put her up while he made contact with de Baissac. When Leroy arrived to collect her, she left, travelling with him by train along the little single-track railway from Tarbes to La Réole. From here, she was taken across the Demarcation Line by the *Édouard* line's agents in the town (she must have crossed just a day or so before the German armoured columns came storming over in the opposite direction). She and Leroy made their way to Bordeaux where she was met by Yvonne Rudellat, who found her a small flat in the city. This eventually became a rendezvous point for new arrivals and a safe house in which de Baissac could hold meetings.[18]

With three agents, a radio operator and a courier in place, and one of Britain's most important strategic targets tied up to the quayside less than a hundred yards from their headquarters, *Scientist* was almost ready to strike. All they needed now was a demolitions expert and some explosive.

Margate, Kent

Hasler, however, was still in the process of training and preparing his men for the ordeal ahead. He arrived in Chatham dockyard on 9 November to arrange accommodation for No. 1 Section, who were about to take part in an exercise – in effect a full dress rehearsal of Frankton – which would replicate the conditions, the obstacles and the distances they would have to cover to reach their targets in Bordeaux.

Called Exercise Blanket, the plan was for No. 1 Section to put their fully laden canoes into the sea at Margate and paddle the ten or fifteen miles of open water along the coast to reach the entrance of the Swale (an estuarial passage separating the Isle of Sheppey from Kent). Here they would cross the Swale boom before continuing past Sheerness, then enter the Thames estuary and on to Deptford where they would carry out a mock ship attack before catching the ebb tide back down the Thames to Chatham dockyard and 'EndEx' – the end of the exercise. The journey, which was to take five days, would cover seventy miles and would be made by night with the canoes 'lying up' in camouflaged positions by day. To add to the realism, the local harbour defences and coastguards were alerted to look out for canoes. And they carried loaded rifles.

For most of 11 November – the day the Germans stormed into Vichy France – Hasler was in conference with L'Estrange, who had come down to Margate to bring him up to date with planning for Operation Frankton. Meanwhile, according to Bill Sparks, some of No. 1 Section spent the early evening in a pub, being bought drinks by the locals. But their enjoyment must have been short-lived, for at 2055, with the weather calm and misty, Hasler led his men out to sea from Margate beach and, swinging the bows of *Catfish* onto a westerly bearing, began to paddle towards London with the others strung out in echelon behind him.

Hasler's planned dress rehearsal for Frankton was an almost complete disaster. Leaving the enclosed waters of the Swale for the more open waters of the Thames estuary, George Sheard made the cardinal error of trying to follow the canoe in front without bothering to check his compass. He only realised that what he was following in the darkness was a seagull and not, as he thought, Hasler's canoe, when the bird took off.* By this time he and Moffatt were hopelessly lost and heading down the Thames estuary towards the open sea.

Meanwhile Jack MacKinnon's navigation gremlin struck again when, after running aground on a sandbank, he set his compass, not on the correct course for Deptford, but on its reciprocal, only realising his mistake when he paddled under a railway bridge he had already passed earlier that same night.[19] One canoe was holed on the Swale boom. Others were separated on the first night and had to paddle by day to catch up. And all, without exception, were spotted by the defences and challenged at least twice. When the exercise was called off at 0800 on 14 November, the whole unit were suffering from exhaustion and none of them had reached their objective. Hasler and Sparks had come closest, reaching Blackwall Point close to the southern end of what is now the Thames Barrier by 0600 that morning. The rest were strung out behind him as far back as Greenhithe and Gravesend.

It was not a good omen for an operation which was now little more than two weeks away. On the following day (a Sunday), Hasler caught the train to London for a day's planning with L'Estrange. He was in the canteen at Combined Operations headquarters taking a lunch of sandwiches and a glass of beer when Mountbatten approached him.

---

* This kind of thing is much easier to do at night than might be imagined. One very dark night I managed to waste a crucial hour waiting for the canoe in front of me to move off – only to discover it was a log!

'Well, how did the rehearsal go?'

'I am afraid it was a complete failure, Sir.'

'Splendid!' beamed Mountbatten. 'In that case you must have learned a great deal and you'll be able to avoid making the same mistakes in the operation.'[20]

This may seem a rather casual way to treat serious deficiencies in the operational abilities of a team which would soon be undertaking a highly hazardous and difficult mission. But this is to judge the decisions of 1942 by the standards of today. The concept of 'duty of care' did not exist then. These were, moreover, desperate times. Mountbatten knew, as did Hasler, that if they missed the no moon period in December, they would have to wait another month. Moreover, the longer they waited the shorter the nights would be. No. 1 Section would have to go, ready or not.

The chief lesson Hasler learnt from Exercise Blanket – beyond the fact that his men were not ready, especially when it came to navigation – was that six was too large a number of canoes to have in a single body. He would have to split No. 1 Section into two groups when the time came to do things in earnest.

On 17 November, the Combined Operations Examination Committee considered the near total disaster of Exercise Blanket and, in a masterpiece of the Panglossian art, pronounced it 'satisfactory'. More helpfully, they also agreed to commission three special photo reconnaissance missions to be flown over Bordeaux and the Gironde, the first to be carried out on the day planned for Hasler's launch, the second two days after that and the third two days after the intended date for Hasler's attack.[21]

SOE headquarters, London

SOE F Section's history, written after the war by Colonel Maurice Buckmaster, contains the following passage covering mid-November 1942: 'Upon the total occupation of France by the Germans it was decided to call for sabotage immediately and on as large a scale as possible … Scientist [was] ordered [into] action against all shipping which used the port of Bordeaux.'[22]

Scientist now had the people and the access to carry out Buckmaster's instructions. But they still had neither an explosives expert nor the materials necessary to do the job. Accordingly, Baker Street now started to move with some urgency to supply the Bordeaux area with both expertise and explosives.

On the night of 17–18 November, the first day of the moon period, an attempt was made to drop explosives and stores to de Baissac at the Moulin de Saquet site.[23] But, once more, no reception committee lights were seen and the aircraft returned to Tempsford with the containers still on board. A further attempt the following night was again abandoned, this time due to engine trouble.

However, 150 miles to the north in the Loire valley, at 2330 on 18 November, a Whitley bomber of No. 138 Squadron made a successful drop of two passengers, two packages and four containers to a parachute site three and a half miles west of the little village of Doué la Fontaine, near Tours. One of the passengers was 34-year-old ex-dental mechanic Charles Victor Hayes.[24] Travelling under the identity of Victor Charles and with the *nom de guerre* of Yves, he was bound for Bordeaux, where he was soon to earn the soubriquet among his French Resistance colleagues[25] of '*Charles le Démolisseur*' – literally 'Demolition Charlie'.

Charles Hayes – short, sturdy, bald-headed and with a fresh complexion, small moustache, blue eyes and the air of a provincial bank manager – had returned to Britain at the outbreak of the war and joined the RAMC in Liverpool, where SOE found him as a lance corporal in July 1941. Hayes had left his young French wife and child behind in France[26] with instructions to follow him later. In August 1941, at the end of his first month's SOE training, his report commented that, though 'promising', Hayes was distracted by worries about 'the long time it is taking to get his wife from Lisbon to England'.[27] This is followed by a brutally succinct note, dated 7 November: 'This officer is no longer married as his wife [and presumably his child as well] has recently been drowned.' Nevertheless, Hayes passed his SOE training as 'the only one of the [training] party who can be recommended without reserve'.

Bordeaux was, in fact, Charles Hayes' second clandestine visit to France. In May he had been landed from a felucca in the south of France with orders to blow up power stations in the Lyon area. But two months later he was forced to flee over the Pyrenees (probably through Tarbes),[28] the Gestapo hard on his heels after a rash reconnaissance of a German aluminium plant near Grenoble. Having arrived in London on 13 August, after a full debriefing and some well-deserved leave he volunteered to return to France and was tasked to join *Scientist* as their explosives expert.

Finally, at 1730 on 20 November, de Baissac heard the BBC coded signal that meant there would be a further attempt to drop 'stores' that night. Right on time, at 2240, de Baissac's parachute reception party at Moulin de Saquet heard the noise of the approaching Whitley and turned on their upturned torches. The big bomber took a little time to find them, but then in two low passes dropped four containers, containing 60 lb of plastic explosive, twelve Sten guns, twelve revolvers, sixty-six hand grenades and fifteen 'clam' mines. After the containers were unpacked, their contents were hidden until the end of curfew – probably in the ruins of the old mill – before being taken the following day by horse and cart, most likely to the cellars under Jean Duboué's house in Lestiac-sur-Garonne.[29] They could then be moved to Bordeaux at a later date.

Some have argued that the explosive from this parachute drop was insufficient for de Baissac to mount an effective attack on his targets immediately and that he would therefore have had to delay, perhaps for several months. But this is to misunderstand the different means of attack the two sabotage teams would have used. Even discounting the 'clam' mines, 60 lb of explosive, almost as much as Hasler had for his attack, would, if distributed internally in relatively small amounts (3 lb or so) on propeller shafts, rudder control mechanisms and other vital machinery, have been more than enough to do serious damage. Hasler could only attack the blockade runners from the outside, using the 8 lb explosive charge in his limpet mines to breach the steel sides of the ship. De Baissac, attacking from within the hull, could have done far more damage with much smaller amounts – as Baker Street recommended, when they instructed him to plan on the basis of using relatively small amounts of explosive to damage the ship when she was under way.*[30]

---

*   When I was taught demolitions the approved method for damaging a ship (almost certainly inherited from the SOE techniques taught to Charles Hayes) was not to try and sink it with large charges in the shallow water alongside the quay where it could be easily refloated, but to set smaller charges designed to cripple its control mechanisms and timed to go off when the ship was under way in the confined waters of the harbour. In this way the effect of a relatively small amount of explosive could be multiplied many times over: the damage being done by the ship's uncontrolled kinetic force as it crashed into other ships, harbour walls and installations.

De Baissac himself, in a later report, hints at this approach and makes it clear that the amount of explosive he had available was not an inhibition to him mounting an attack 'against all shipping which used the port of Bordeaux', as he had been urgently instructed to do: 'In spite of the comparative lack of material, SCIENTIST was well on the way to organising an attack on his shipping targets by the introduction of ... explosives through the dockers and the paint sealers working on the vessels.'

Whitehall, London

Hasler spent 18 November with Stewart and L'Estrange at Combined Operations headquarters on final detailed planning for Frankton. In the afternoon, he and MacKinnon (who was still unaware of the operation ahead) went to the War Office to be briefed on the No. 3 'Prisoner of War' Code which Hasler and his men would use to communicate with MI9 on their escape across France.[31] The two men then had supper at the Royal Ocean Racing Club and caught the night train to Glasgow.

On the morning of 18 November, No. 1 Section left Eastney for Scotland. Officially they knew nothing of the operation ahead, but the little unit was abuzz with rumours that this was 'it'. The prevailing view was that their target was to be the German pocket-battleship *Tirpitz*.[32]

As Bobby Ewart left the White Heather, he turned to sixteen-year-old Heather Powell, the landlady's daughter, with whom he had fallen in love, and said: 'Look after our things, we will be back soon.' As the lorry, with 'Flash' Phelps at the wheel, carried No. 1 Section away, Heather turned to her mother and said, through tears: 'Oh Mother, they'll never come back. I know they'll never come back.'[33]

The Firth of Clyde, Glasgow, Scotland

After breakfast and a haircut at the Central Hotel, Hasler and MacKinnon met up with No. 1 Section at Glasgow station on 19 November and took the train to Gourock, followed by the ferry to HMS *Forth*. On arrival they were told that there was no more accommodation on *Forth* and No. 1 Section would have to stay on a nearby merchantman called the *Al Rowdah*, where the accommodation was considered by the Marines to be 'rather luxurious compared to our usual sleeping quarters'.[34]

The same day, Her Majesty's Submarine *Tuna*, under her captain, Lieutenant Dick Raikes RN, returned from a patrol around the Orkneys and docked in the outside berth alongside a number of other submarines by their mother ship, HMS *Forth*. On arrival Raikes found a message ordering him to report immediately to his superior, the Commander of the Third Submarine Flotilla, Captain 'Tinsides' Ionides.

Raikes, thirty years old and thus Hasler's senior by two years, had joined the Royal Navy in 1925 and was already one of its most experienced submariners. As 'Jimmy' (or first lieutenant) on the submarine *Talisman* he had landed agents on the coast south of the Gironde in August 1940.[35] In September 1941 he took over his first command, the submarine *Sea Wolf*. In June 1942, Raikes was awarded the DSO for 'daring, enterprise and devotion to duty' while on patrols north of the Arctic Circle.

Small of stature, with a thin face enlivened by eyes which had a permanent look of mischief about them and a mouth around which a smile seemed always to be hovering, Raikes like Horatio Nelson suffered from a weak constitution and frequent bouts of seasickness.[36] He was, however, a formidable and determined submarine commander who ran an efficient and happy 'boat'. His strong sense of humour and even stronger dislike of bureaucratic hurdles made him a man with whom the likes of Hasler found it easy to do business.

Judging by Raikes' account, his meeting with Ionides was short and to the point. He was to prepare to take on board Hasler and No. 1 Section for an operation in which 'A small party of approximately twelve officers and men will be disembarked from the submarine in the vicinity of the mouth of the Gironde estuary. The party will paddle up to the Bassens-Bordeaux area in Cockles Mark II where they will carry out a limpet attack on blockade runners in the port. The party will escape overland to Spain.'[37]

HM/s *Tuna*'s role was 'To disembark the military party in a position from which they can proceed in their Cockles to the mouth of the Gironde estuary approaching from the Southwestward. The whole operation is to be so conducted that the disembarkation is undetected by the enemy.'[38]

The fourth week of November

The Firth of Clyde, Scotland

The last week before the launch of Operation Frankton was an exceptionally busy one for Hasler and his men.

The morning of 20 November, David Moffatt's twenty-second birthday, was spent checking and packing their kit on the deck of *Forth*. In the afternoon, No. 1 Section carried out a mock raid on the commando base at Ardnadam, followed by a forced march across the Argyll hills, with interludes for practice firing of their .45 automatic pistols and silent Sten guns. In the evening they were given instruction on their new 'Cockle suits' and on the 'escape box' each of them would carry.

The morning of Saturday 21 November was spent on another cross-country march, followed in the afternoon by practice in setting the chemical fuses on limpet mines and instructions on how to fit the holsters for their pistols and commando fighting knives. That evening until half past midnight was spent updating their 'farewell' letters to next-of-kin.

The following day there was more fusing of limpets. This time, however, they were allowed to drop live mines onto the seabed of Holy Loch so they could experience the time delay and witness the size of the ensuing explosion.

On 23 November they once again practised placing limpet mines on the *Jan Van Gelder*, this time steaming a little faster at 2.5 knots to simulate a strong tide. In the afternoon they practised stealthy approaches by canoe, once again using the *Jan Van Gelder* as their target.

On 24 November Jock Stewart arrived from Combined Operations headquarters with additional stores and some final changes to the plan. For No. 1 Section, the early part of the day was spent on more fusing practice and on navigation lectures. But at 1615 Hasler gave his men the rest of the day off. He stayed on board, while his Marines went ashore for a brief tour of Glasgow, no doubt not excluding the city's bars.

The next day, with the first target date for Operation Frankton now only ten days away, Mountbatten, writing from Combined Operations headquarters, signed off a letter to Air Marshal Bottomley in the Air Ministry, requesting that 'all mine laying in the Gironde Estuary and its approaches should cease from 5th to 15th December inclusive'. Back in the Clyde, Raikes received his final written orders while, for No. 1 Section, who were still officially ignorant that this was anything other than more training, there was yet more practice fusing limpets in the morning and more packing of bags and navigation instruction in the afternoon.

L'Estrange arrived in *Forth* on the following day, 26 November, bringing with him the final version of their escape plan[39] (such as it was) and the latest planning changes, together with the most up-to-date aerial photographs. No. 1 Section spent the day carrying out trial packing of the canoe bags in which they would carry their equipment for the raid, while in the late afternoon each canoe crew began to 'swing' (i.e. adjust for accuracy) their canoe compasses, a process that had to be stopped because of failing light. It was continued the following morning.

The rest of the morning of 27 November was spent packing and repacking their canoes and sewing up their waterproof cargo bags. Hasler again gave them the afternoon off, this time going ashore himself for a couple of hours with Jock Stewart. That evening the pair got into a drinking match with some Poles on the *Al Rowdah*, with, as Hasler's diary laconically puts it, 'disastrous results'.

Whether Hasler was any the worse for his previous night's excesses when he paraded his Marines on *Forth* the following morning, his diary does not relate. But Dick Raikes commented later that, this morning, Hasler had 'probably the worst hangover he'd ever had in his life'.[40] This seems to have been a fairly easy day: the Marines camouflaged their canoes and cockle suits with special paint (it was at this time that the names of the canoes were overpainted), while Hasler spent much of the day discussing the operation ahead with Raikes.

Sunday 29 November was spent in final packing of stores and operational clothing and more 'swinging' of canoe compasses to iron out the errors caused by the magnets on the eight limpet mines carried by each canoe. At 2330, Hasler finished packing the operational papers he would not need to take with him and handed them over to Jock Stewart for safe keeping.

Bordeaux, France

On the night of 29–30 November, at about the same time that Hasler was packing up his papers, Flight Lieutenant Sutton RAF, the pilot of

Halifax 9618W from 138 Squadron, carrying another four containers of arms and explosive for *Scientist*, was circling over the landing site at Moulin de Saquet. Peering through the ground fog, he tried to identify the lights of the reception committee he had been promised. After thirty minutes circling in vain he decided the fog was too thick to see anything and, turning his aircraft north, headed back to Tempsford.

For de Baissac in Bordeaux, this failure was not critical. For by now Charles Hayes was well installed in the city. De Baissac had his demolitions expert, he had his orders and he had enough explosive to carry them out. All he needed to do now was draw up a plan of attack and set up the charges.

So, that night, as the hours ticked away to the start of Operation Frankton, Hasler and his twelve Royal Marines were preparing to set out on an 800-mile journey of great hazard to attack ships on the Bordeaux quayside. Meanwhile, a stone's throw from Hasler's targets was an SOE team consisting of six British officers, with reliable wireless communication with London, an extensive network of local Resistance fighters, regular access to the blockade runners and a full suite of equipment from explosives to light weapons with which to carry out exactly the same task. If, against all odds, Hasler and his men were to make it through to their objective, their lives would depend upon escaping undetected across nearly 700 miles of enemy-occupied territory, relying on help from a local population whose language only one of them – Hasler himself – could speak, and an MI9 escape organisation who had no idea they were coming. Yet 300 yards from the Bordeaux quayside was the start of an established SOE escape line through Tarbes and over the Pyrenees into Spain, which had already been reliably used to pass dozens of fugitives to safety.

Confusion, duplication, personality squabbles and petty rivalries in London were about to put at unnecessary risk the effectiveness of a vital operation against a key national strategic target – to say nothing of a lot of brave young lives.

13

Fortress Gironde

When the Germans overran southwest France in 1940, they lost no time in securing Bordeaux and the Gironde. The first heavy guns arrived in Royan on the east side of the estuary entrance on 22 June,[1] the day that France fell. Four days later the occupiers were in full control of the Pointe de Grave and Soulac. At Le Verdon on the western side of the Gironde they took over the seventeenth-century 'Vauban'[2] fort and quickly replaced the superannuated cannons with modern heavy coastal artillery. The massive programme to construct the Atlantic Wall was begun in the autumn of 1941.

Although nominal overall command was exercised from his headquarters in Nantes by the Kriegsmarine (German navy) flag officer in control of western France, Admiral Johannes Bachmann, effective operational control of each unit was exercised on individual service lines. Bachmann is described by those who knew him as:

> A man of weak character. To take a quick decision when there was no answer 'in the book' was beyond his powers. When, on the other hand, he felt sure of his grounds, as for example when backed by standing orders or superior instructions, he chose to play the strong man and to express himself in the arrogant manner so fashionable in the Third Reich … He wished his strong stands [in favour of the execution of higher orders] … to be noted in high places. He was anxious to join the … SS when he retired from the Navy,[3] and perhaps these facts were not unconnected.[4]

In May 1942, after several changes of command and units, the German
1st Army under Senior General Johannes Blaskowitz was charged with
the defence of the Atlantic coast between Pornic, just east of Nantes, and
the Spanish border. Blaskowitz set up his headquarters in the Hôtel de
Ville in Bordeaux[5] and deployed one of his units, the 708th Infantry
Division, under Lieutenant-General Hermann Wilck, to defend the area
between Seudre, fifteen miles north of Royan, and Montalivet-les-Bains,
about the same distance south of the Pointe de Grave on the southern
side of the Gironde estuary.

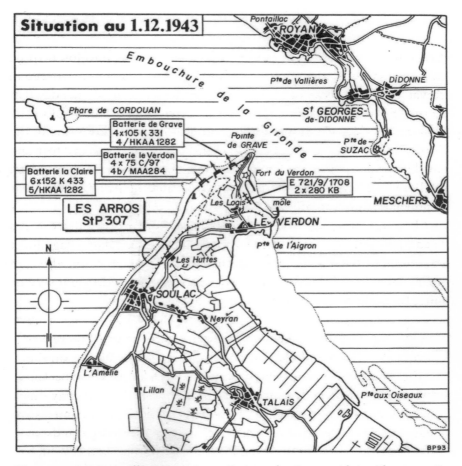

Figure 2 Main artillery positions, Pointe de Grave. Alain Chazette, *La
Forteresse de Royan-Pointe de Grave* (Editions Heimdal, n.d.)

Wilck's 708th Division, which numbered 16,000 troops in all, was heavily concentrated around the Gironde entrance, with its headquarters in the 'Vauban' Fort de Chay at Royan.[6] It consisted of two infantry regiments, one of which, the 748th, was headquartered at Soulac just three miles south of the mouth of the Gironde. To assist in his task, Wilck was also given significant elements of heavy artillery, including Coastal Artillery Group 754 which deployed two batteries each consisting of heavy coastal guns in massive concrete casemates around the Pointe de Grave area itself.

In addition to regular Wehrmacht units, the defence of the Bordeaux area was further supplemented by two SS motorised divisions (10,000 men each) – the SS-Panzer-Grenadier Division *Gotz Berlingen* and the 2nd SS-Panzer Division, both of which reported directly to the Führer in Berlin.

The Luftwaffe also had a considerable presence in the area amounting to some 10,000 men and 150 aircraft (including the much-feared four-engine C200 Condor anti-ship bombers). These were stationed at Bordeaux's Mérignac airport,[7] as well as at Royan, Hourtin and other smaller airfields, including on the Pointe de Grave itself. In addition, in the Pointe de Grave area, there were two sections of the Luftwaffe's 999 Light Flak Anti-Aircraft Division consisting of thirty or so light and medium anti-aircraft guns and four large searchlights each supported by their own radar stations, which included one long-range radar – the 'Mammoth' – capable of providing early warning of enemy aircraft. One of the sub-units of this division, Flak Unit 595, was accommodated in some requisitioned French fishermen's cottages at the tip of the Pointe de Grave, close to the terminal for the small ferry unit – the *Fahren Flotilla* – which provided a regular service across the estuary mouth between Le Verdon and Royan.

The Kriegsmarine was strongly represented in the area, too: a further two batteries of heavy coastal guns from Marine Artillery Division 284, supported by searchlights, were positioned around the Pointe de Grave and a coastal radar station at Arros. This latter was tasked with keeping track of all shipping around the Gironde entrance. In addition the Kriegsmarine had a number of small river patrol boats based around the Môle d'Éscale, a long concrete pier which protruded almost a quarter of a mile into the Gironde estuary just south of Le Verdon.

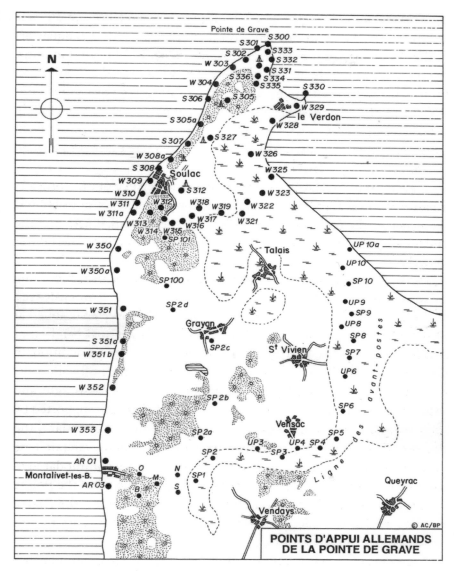

Figure 3 Pointe de Grave strongpoints (marked W, S, SP and UP). Alain Chazette, *La Forteresse de Royan-Pointe de Grave* (Editions Heimdal, n.d.)

While the concentration of German forces around the entrance of the Gironde was formidable (with a total troop strength in the Pointe de Grave area alone of close to 10,000), their lines of command and control were fractured and muddled. In the area from the Pointe de Grave to

Montalivet, there were thirty-nine different gun and radar installations. Of these, four were under navy control, nine were under Luftwaffe control and the remaining twenty-six were controlled by the army. There was a provision that, in the case of an invasion, the Kriegsmarine (commanded by Bachmann) would take command of all units – to the considerable distaste of the Wehrmacht, since, in terms of size, they were by far the most numerous. But in normal times, each of the separate service units responded only to its own chain of command.

The Wehrmacht organised their defence of the Pointe de Grave area in depth, with fighting and reserve units occupying positions based around strongpoints and spread out in a line six miles deep stretching from the beach south of Soulac, along a line of trenches which ended at the Pointe aux Oiseaux on the edge of the Gironde, just east of St Vivien en Médoc.

All of this meant that the Pointe de Grave area was, by mid-1942, one huge and varied military camp, much of it housed in hastily thrown-up wooden and concrete huts on either side of the Bordeaux–Pointe de Grave railway which ran through the wooded area behind the town of Le Verdon. Here each of the separate services had its own fenced-off areas, including canteens, medical facilities and headquarters elements. There was even a small German military graveyard for those who died on duty in the area.

Although many of the German troops posted to the Pointe de Grave at this stage in the war were raw conscripts (including Hitler Youth units),[8] by 1942, when the Russian campaign was in full swing, the area, with its outstanding beaches, surf and sun, also served as a 'rest and recuperation' posting for veterans from the Russian front, including a number of Cossack 'white Russians'.

Altogether, including the German and Italian submarine crews and their administrative staff based in Bordeaux, the overall strength of Axis forces in the Gironde area in the winter of 1942 has been estimated as well in excess of 60,000 men.[9] Little wonder that, when Mountbatten sent Hasler and his eleven Royal Marines through the front gates of this 'impregnable fortress'[10] and tasked them to paddle seventy miles[11] through the middle of such a massive concentration of enemy troops in order to deliver their attack, he did not expect any of them to return.

14

Planning, Tides and Escape

Apart from finalising the training and preparation of No. 1 Section for the operation ahead, Hasler, assisted by L'Estrange and his three Combined Operations planners, spent much of November putting flesh on the outline plan for Operation Frankton.

It is remarkable how little the final plan for Frankton altered from the initial outline drawn up by Hasler on 21 September 1942. But there was one area Hasler would have been unable to cover in detail as he assembled his first rough proposal: the tides and the other hydrographic conditions his team would encounter in the open sea and in the mouth of the Gironde.

Tides and hydrography play an important role in the planning of all but the most deep-water of naval engagements. But they are especially important for amphibious operations since, by definition, these take place at the interface between sea and land. So the height and flow of the tides and what lies beneath the surface of the sea is of vital consequence. This importance is multiplied several times over when small craft such as canoes are involved, since their lightness of construction and shallowness of draught makes them especially susceptible to wind, waves and tides. This hydrographical information is drawn today, as in 1942, from three primary sources: the charts, the Admiralty 'Pilot' for the area (also known as 'The Sailing Directions' this is a book of navigational notes which supplement the information given on the chart) and the relevant tide tables.

While Hasler's initial plan covered the main elements of *how* he would approach his target in Bordeaux, he would not have been in possession at that time of the astronomical and hydrographic information which would determine *when* the operation could be mounted; though his impatience to carry out the Frankton operation may be indicated by the fact that he claimed that his men could be ready as early as 7 November.

In choosing the final dates, Hasler needed to find a precise combination of three factors. First, he needed long nights in order to give him sufficient hours of darkness to cover the seventy miles to Bordeaux. This meant that the operation had to take place over the midwinter period.

Second, he needed to launch the operation at the beginning of a no moon period (which lasts for no more than five nights) in order to give his men the advantage of maximum darkness during their approach. Having to choose a no moon period (normally defined as the period when the moon sets before midnight) created advantages but also problems. This is also the period of 'springs', when the tides have the greatest range and strength, creating the highest high water, the lowest low water and the strongest tidal flows.[1] From one point of view, this was what Hasler needed: a stronger flow behind him meant greater speed and more distance covered. But the increased flow also meant increased tidal turbulence, especially in the confined waters of the mouth of the Gironde.

Third, with tides in the Gironde running, when at full flow, at between four and five knots, Hasler knew that his canoes could only make progress when the tide was behind him (i.e. flooding on the way down to Bordeaux and ebbing on his way back) or when it was 'slack' water (which occurs between changing tides and for Hasler's purposes meant either still water, or a contrary flow of less than 1.5 knots[2]). This was especially important on the first night when he had more than twenty miles to paddle to get past the main area of German defences at the mouth of the estuary.

So he needed to find a date during midwinter in which the no moon period began with a night when the flood tide would start shortly after nightfall, giving him a full six hours of flow to carry his canoes in darkness through the mouth of the Gironde and far enough into the estuary to be past the main line of German defences before daylight.

Such a combination of factors normally occurs only once a month. Having rejected the no moon period beginning on 7 November as too early, he was left with the next no moon period, which fell between 6 and 12 December.

The final condition Hasler needed was fine weather and a calm sea, for his canoes were unable to cope with a wind greater than Force 4 – and probably less in waters exposed to a combination of Atlantic rollers and very strong tidal currents. He was extremely fortunate that, this December, the beginning of the no moon period coincided with a large high pressure zone whose centre was positioned precisely over the Gironde estuary.[3]

The Combined Operations officer responsible for planning the more predictable hydrographic aspects of amphibious operations, Lieutenant-Commander L'Estrange, prepared the charts and tide tables. Indeed Hasler valued L'Estrange's work so highly that he was to recommend him for an award, saying that L'Estrange 'did the bulk of the detailed planning and personally prepared, with great thoroughness and accuracy, the actual charts, tide tables etc used by the attacking force'.[4]

L'Estrange's calculations took as their base, the times of high and low water in the port of Brest on the Brittany coast, to which a coefficient was added to give tide times at the mouth of the Gironde.[5] To make matters even more complicated, the times of high and low water vary at different points on the Gironde as progress is made down the estuary towards Bordeaux. For example, at the point where Hasler planned to make his first landfall, about a quarter of the way down the estuary, high water occurs twenty minutes, and low water thirty-five minutes, later than at the Pointe de Grave. At Bordeaux, the delays are much larger – three and four hours respectively.

The importance of L'Estrange's tidal calculations for the tides, moon and sun can be judged by the fact that each of Hasler's canoes carried a set of tide tables, which he no doubt produced (but unquestionably, Hasler, meticulous planner that he was, would have double checked).

The second document Hasler and L'Estrange studied carefully would have been the Gironde chart. Copies of the portion covering the route they were to take, marked up in colour to show the proximity of German positions and French centres of habitation, were carried in each canoe.[6]

Hasler's first plan was for the submarine to drop his force 'not more than five miles from the mouth of the river'.[7] But it was presumably decided that being so close inshore would place the submarine at too great a hazard, for the drop-off point was finally fixed, just before the night of the launch, at 9.5 nautical miles southwest of Pointe de Grave and around two nautical miles due west of the little coastal town of Montalivet-les-Bains. This significantly increased the distance Hasler's men would have to paddle before reaching the shelter of the estuary.

Hasler's hope was to make the eastern (far) side of the Gironde on the first night, so as to avoid the patrol boats and concentration of German forces – especially naval vessels – around Le Verdon and a substantial oiling and dockyard facility further down the Gironde's west shore at Trompeloup. He established a Decision Point one mile due north of the Pointe de Grave light (Point 'X' in his plan – see Appendix A) which he had to reach by, at the latest, two hours before High Water Brest (HWB in Hasler's plan – this equated to 0100 on the night). If he was later than this, he would have to abandon any attempt to make the east bank of the Gironde and canoe instead down the western side to find a lying-up position for the next day.[8]

The coastline from the Pointe de Grave, through the seaside resorts of Soulac and L'Amélie to Montalivet, runs pretty well north–south at 90 degrees to the Atlantic swell, the next landfall to the west being the West Indies. Any experienced sailor would immediately know on looking at the line of this coast that there would be big 'dumping' surf on its shoreline,[9] and that this would be very dangerous to Hasler's canoes.

In view of this hazard, it is perhaps surprising that, though Hasler's men had some training in landing on shore in moderately rough conditions,[10] they were given no formal training in how to handle canoes in proper surf.[11] According to Norman Colley, Hasler's team was taken down to Cornwall to experience surf once, but they used surf boards, not canoes.[12] Colley adds that the danger of surf, whose thunder could be heard only a little over a mile to their east as they paddled in that night, was never mentioned to them in their briefing.

Hasler's planned route took him on a course around 035 degrees magnetic,[13] parallel to the shore and a mile and a half or so out from it. This meant canoeing past the Pointe de Negade (the word is a corruption of the French word *noyer*, meaning to be drowned) and over a number of offshore sandbanks and shoals, the most significant of which were the Banc des Olives and a rocky underwater shoal called the Rochers de St

Nicholas, which were, respectively, four miles southwest and two miles west of Pointe de Grave.

In planning this, the most hydrographically dangerous part of the whole paddle, Hasler and L'Estrange would have been aware that they were dealing with Europe's greatest estuary, famous for its constantly shifting sandbanks caused by the huge flows of water in and out of the narrow mouth at Pointe de Grave.[14] These ebb flows, moreover, would have been significantly augmented at this time of year by the increased winter volumes of the two great rivers which feed the Gironde, the Dordogne and the Garonne.

Here Hasler and L'Estrange were, in one sense, unlucky. The two people who would have been in an unparalleled position to pass on advice from Bordeaux to London on the local conditions and hazards were Jean Fleuret and Ange-Marie Gaudin, both of them Gironde pilots. But, as we have seen, Fleuret and Gaudin were arrested by the Germans in June 1942, just ten weeks before the detailed planning for Operation Frankton began.[15] This meant that L'Estrange and Hasler had to fall back on conventional sources: the tide tables, the chart and the Admiralty's Bay of Biscay Pilot. It was here – perhaps because of the speed at which Frankton had to be put together – that the planners made a mistake which was to have profound implications for both the operation and those who took part in it.

They missed – or at least seriously underestimated – the severity of the tidal disturbance around the mouth of the Gironde and specifically the tidal rips, or overfalls, which occur at this point. Hasler was later to say that these were 'comparable with those at Start Point and St Alban's Head on the South Coast of England' and 'came as an unpleasant surprise, not having been apparent from the chart or the Sailing Directions'.[16] Tidal rips or tidal overfalls are the result of turbulence caused by a tidal stream sweeping round a headland or over underwater sandbanks (such as the Banc des Olives) lying across the tidal flow. This has the effect of forcing the tidal stream to the surface, causing standing waves and even tidal whirlpools. Because the direction of the flow is different, these tidal eddies frequently occur in different places during the flood and the ebb tides. This area of turbulence is, moreover, often greatest when the tide changes from flood to ebb or vice versa – precisely the circumstance which would apply at the time Hasler intended to paddle into the mouth of the Gironde. Hasler's plan had him leaving

HM/s *Tuna* with the tide on the ebb (i.e. running against him) at a little less than two knots. By the time he reached the Banc des Olives, it would be on the flood at the same speed. And increasing.

This 'tidal overfall' phenomenon occurs at three key points on the south coast of England – at St Albans Head* near Poole,[17] at Start Point on the Devon coast and at the 'man eating'[18] tidal rips off Portland Bill. Hasler himself had sailed through, or close to, each of these on his many sailing expeditions along the south coast – hence the references in his later comments.

One of the characteristics of tidal rips is that they produce waves which are steep, of short interval and come from all directions. This makes it very difficult indeed to keep the bows of a canoe, especially a keel-less one, into the waves in order to prevent 'broaching'.

Hasler's assertion that there was nothing on the 1942 chart to indicate these tidal hazards was correct. This absence of warnings might be explained by the fact that the tidal rips off the south coast of Britain, being in relatively deep water, generally occur in a fixed place which can be marked on a chart; whereas the position of those at the entrance to the Gironde, which occur over shallow water, alter depending on whether they are caused by the flood or the ebb tide. It stands to reason, however, that tidal turbulence would be very likely at the exit point of such a large body of water. Indeed, in a minute of 20 April 1943 – after Frankton – one of the hydrographic planners acknowledges just this point: 'Although the Charts and Sailing Directions do not mention the existence of a tidal race, it seems reasonable to expect that water disturbances would occur over the shoals off the Pt. de Graves at springs and I feel somewhat to blame for not having pointed this out.'[19]

Hasler, too, should have been familiar with the dangers which can occur at the mouth of such an enclosed body of water since the same phenomenon occurs, although in smaller proportions, at the entrance to the Solent and, especially, Langstone Harbour, where he had sailed and paddled all his life. Indeed he had himself experienced tide rips when paddling in a canoe in this area in the months before Operation Frankton was launched.[20]

---

*   I have paddled a laden canoe through these overfalls, they are indeed most uncomfortable.

Although it is true that there are no markings on the charts of the time which might indicate these dangers (and none on the modern ones either, for that matter), it is *not* the case, as Hasler asserts (along with every other chronicler since), that there are no hints in the contemporary Pilot of severe hazards of this kind occurring in the area through which Hasler intended taking his men.

The Bay of Biscay Pilot (to which Hasler and L'Estrange's attention was specifically drawn in the ISTD report prepared in advance of the raid)[21] was the second edition of 1931. It warns that, when taking the southern passage into the Gironde (roughly the line Hasler was following) in bad weather 'and especially during the ebb stream', turbulence or 'breaking' white water was likely to be encountered across the whole channel approaching the Pointe de Grave.[22] White or 'breaking' water chiefly occurs where waves cross over banks, or shoals, where the water is shallow. White water occurring in a deep channel can only be caused by one thing: tidal turbulence. The Pilot continues: 'Under these conditions [i.e. when the white water is breaking], a vessel should wait until the flood stream is well established, the best time to enter being two hours before high water, *but a small vessel should not attempt to enter*' (author's emphasis).[23] Commenting on the Pointe de Grave itself, the 1931 Pilot says that in this area 'caution should be exercised ... as the tidal streams cause dangerous eddies'.[24]

The Gironde estuary has, in fact, been famous for its dangerous tides for centuries. In 1813 the British Rear-Admiral Charles Penrose, ordered to enter the Gironde in support of Wellington's invading army, made a detailed study of the estuary's hydrography. The chart he subsequently produced is littered with warnings about the hydrographical dangers around the mouth of the Gironde: a box marking the area around the Cordouan light contains the stern injunction 'currents are so strong [in this area] that no ship can enter it without being lost', while the illegible writing in an elliptically shaped area marked about 150 yards north of the line of Hasler's approach seems to indicate that this was an area of severe tidal disturbance.[25]

The later French chart of the Gironde produced in 1874[26] clearly shows major tidal turbulence and dangerous eddies and whirlpools occurring during the flood tide (and in different places, during the ebb) in the three places (just north of the Banc des Olives, 5–700 yards southwest of the Pointe de Grave and 200 yards east of it) through which Hasler and his men would have to pass to gain entry to the estuary on the first night of Operation Frankton.

But indications of dangerous and turbulent white water around the mouth of the Gironde were not confined to historical reports or recent warnings in the Biscay Pilot. A previous ISTD report dated 3 March 1942,[27] on which the report prepared for Frankton drew heavily, contains aerial photographs which show very clearly three large areas of turbulent white water at just the locations indicated on the Pilot.

Later in his life, Hasler was to express 'concern verging on anger'[28] that the hydrographers had not warned him of these dangers.[29] It is tempting to speculate that, if Frankton had been put together with less haste, these warning signs might have been heeded. It may be that these were hazards which Hasler's team just had to confront to get into the estuary. But they should not have come, to use Hasler's words, as an 'unpleasant surprise'.

The other area in which Hasler's initial plan had to be expanded was, as we have seen, how his men were to get back home after the operation. From the middle of October, when Hasler was informed that there could be no question of a submarine pick-up, it must have been clear that the raiders would have to be prepared for a long and dangerous journey home. The march to Ruffec through enemy-occupied territory would test the endurance and determination of Hasler's men to the limit.

But, as we now know, even when – or if – Hasler's men reached Ruffec, the chances of them connecting with Mary Lindell and slotting into the *Marie-Claire* escape line depended much more on serendipity than MI9 was willing to admit. The undertaking made by MI9 to Hasler and L'Estrange that the *Marie-Claire* line would be 'looking out' for his men in Ruffec, was more to do with hope than deliberative planning.

But now, seventy years after the event, we know something else, too. That even without a radio, the London secret organisations *did* have a line of communication to Mary Lindell in Ruffec; through Roger Landes' radio in Bordeaux by courier to Lise de Baissac in Poitiers and thence to her *Scientist II* agents in Ruffec – Commandant Gua, Gaston Denivelle and others – who also 'doubled' as Mary Lindell's *Marie-Claire* agents in the town.

Given the thought and planning which went into enabling Hasler's team to reach their targets, it is surprising how little, by modern standards, went into how they got away afterwards. Apart from Hasler, none of the Marines could speak any French.[30] Their escape equipment consisted of enough 'composite' rations to last for three days and a small 'escape box',[31] made of light pressed metal about the size and shape of a small cigar box, which contained a button compass (in view of the vulnerability of these to damp, they carried three spares), some fishing line, some hooks, a box of Bryant and May 'Victory' matches, a torch bulb, a bar of soap, lavatory paper, water purification tablets, Horlicks tablets (said to aid the digestion of raw vegetables), Benzedrine to keep them awake,[32] a pack of fifty cigarettes, several hundred French francs supplied by MI9,[33] an RAF pilot's silk escape map showing the southern half of France on which the Demarcation Line and the German forbidden zones near the coast were marked and a second, more detailed escape map of the same area.

Hasler's Marines received no interrogation training or preparation – though they were all well aware that, if captured they should reveal no more than required under the Geneva Convention – that is name, rank, number and date of birth.[34] In this they were not alone: no Combined Operations raiders received interrogation training in this period of the war.[35]

The reasons why MI9 were not prepared to risk giving details of the Marie-Claire line to the escaping raiders were perfectly understandable – Airey Neave ran an appreciable risk with one of his most important escape networks by even going so far as to tell Hasler's men that Ruffec was a Resistance centre. But this necessary secrecy does not explain why so little else was done to help Hasler's Royal Marines prepare for the ordeal of escaping across a vast expanse of enemy-occupied territory.

There had, in fact, been discussion in Combined Operations headquarters as to whether the raiders should be dressed in civilian clothes. It was argued that Hitler's Commando Order would result in all captured personnel being shot anyway, so they might as well have the advantage of wearing clothes in which they could escape.[36] Hasler rejected this as 'defeatist' and insisted that his team would not only conduct the operational phase of Frankton as Royal Marines, but would be properly identified as such by the uniform badges which were sewn onto their canoeing smocks just before they left. In this judgement he was almost certainly right. Although there was a high likelihood that, even if found in uniform,

Hasler's Marines would be shot, some German officers were reluctant to commit an act they knew to be against the laws of war; they often simply ignored or delayed carrying out Hitler's order, perhaps in the hope that this could be avoided.[37] Moreover, where the Germans did execute captured commandos, they took some pains to cover up the fact.

Wearing uniforms on the raid would not, therefore, have given Hasler's men much protection from execution; wearing civilian clothes on the other hand would have meant that their execution would have been certain – and legal, according to the Geneva Convention, which defines enemy personnel on active service in civilian clothes as 'spies' who can be executed.

But Hasler's insistence on wearing uniform during the raid did not apply to the escape phase, as Hasler himself made clear when he told his team at their initial briefing: their first act after beginning the escape phase should be to beg, borrow or steal civilian clothes and bury their uniforms.

At that time both SOE and MI9 were well used to supplying authentic French clothes and identity cards for their agents in France. A spare set of clothes was carried by each of Hasler's team in their canoes. But these too were British service issue garments, not ones which would enable them to pass visual inspection as French. This omission – about which the Germans, too, later expressed their surprise – was to put both Hasler's men and the French from whom they had to beg clothes, at real risk. Nor were any of the escapees equipped with identity cards, which might have enabled them to pass routine German checks.

Perhaps the most glaring indication of the different approach taken by the planners to the raid itself and to the escape phase afterwards lies in the comprehensive list of stores (See Appendix A) which Hasler laid out for each Marine to carry. Everything needed for the operation is listed here, down to the very last detail (e.g. 'pencils *half-sized*, sharpened'). But the only item included for the escape phase was the individual escape kit carried by each man. Their equipment did not even include a bag or rucksack in which they could carry their kit once their canoes had been disposed of.

Norman Colley, commenting on this afterwards, volunteered the view that, in comparison to the raid itself, the planning of their escape was 'haphazard', perhaps, he suggests, because this was seen as a 'suicide mission' and they were regarded as 'expendable'.[38] Given what we know now, it is difficult not to have sympathy with that view.

PART III

The Operation

15

The Start of the 'Little Adventure'

30 November 1942[1]

A strengthening south-southwesterly wind blew down between the shoulders of the Argyll and Ayrshire hills, picking up into rufflets the placid waters of the Clyde, stirring the white ensigns of warships crowded round the naval base and streaming ribbons of smoke from the funnels of those waiting to leave on the tide for the Battle of the Atlantic, far out to the west. The sky was leaden[2] and the barometer steady at just under a thousand millibars.[3] Settled weather was on the way.

At 0815 in the still murky first light of this morning, a sharp-eyed observer would have spotted a scurrying of unusual activity around Her Majesty's Submarine *Tuna*, pennant number N94, lying in the outside berth of three submarines moored alongside their mother ship, HMS *Forth*. Six long black shapes, which could have been mistaken for torpedoes in the early morning light, were slipped down into the submarine's black hull through its forward torpedo-loading hatch. Other stores followed, all carefully handled. Finally, as the light became stronger, twelve dark figures, definitely not sailors, crossed the narrow gangplanks from *Forth*, made their way to *Tuna* and descended into the cramped space below through the boat's forward loading hatch, which closed behind them.[4] As they went below, the Marines' names and those of their next-of-kin were taken by *Tuna*'s chief coxswain, William Stabb, who entered them in the submarine's next-of-kin record book.

Two hours later, at 1030, a small farewell party gathered on *Forth*'s deck. It consisted of Captain Ionides, *Tuna*'s captain, Dick Raikes,

Blondie Hasler, Lieutenant-Commander L'Estrange and Captain Jock Stewart, Royal Marines. Ionides handed over *Tuna*'s sailing orders to her captain, who returned a salute to his commander and then, with Hasler, made his way across the gangplanks to *Tuna*. There Coxswain Stabb saluted and reported that the next-of-kin book had been returned to *Forth*'s submarine office, all hands were at their stations and *Tuna* was ready for sea. Up on the bridge, Raikes leaned over the lip of the conning tower for a final check that everyone was in their allotted place on *Tuna*'s casing. Then: 'Let go for'ard – let go aft ... Slow ahead together.'

As the thin black shape of *Tuna* slid silently away, a bugler sounded the 'Still' and those on *Forth*'s deck – Captain Ionides' white hair standing out against the ship's newly painted superstructure – stood to attention and saluted her departure.[5] Someone, probably Ionides, shouted: 'Good luck – good hunting.'[6] Jock Stewart, who knew better than any of them the dangers that lay ahead, thought of the six small craft, each named after a fish, neatly stowed away in *Tuna*'s bowels and wondered about friends he might never see again.

Operation Frankton had begun. Although Hasler's Marines would not launch their canoes for the best part of a week, this was the moment that they began to close with their enemy. In operations such as this the long approach through a hostile sea to the target area can be as dangerous, difficult and fraught with the possibility of failure as the last leg to the target itself.

Ranged on *Tuna*'s casing as she slipped silently down the Firth of Clyde were members of her crew, together with an incongruous collection of twelve Royal Marines wearing strange new camouflaged, smock-like uniforms. As she passed down the line of warships, all hands on deck snapped to attention as each in turn paid their respects, the shrill sound of bo'suns' pipes ringing out across the water. To each *Tuna* responded in kind, dipping her ensign and returning the piped acknowledgement.[7]

Soon *Tuna* was in open water and heading for her next stop, the degaussing range at Helensburgh, further down the Clyde.[8] It took an hour and a half to get there, swing her magnetic compasses for the last time and, using the facilities at Helensburgh, remove as best she could the last remnants of her magnetic signature: in a few days' time she would be running close to a known magnetic minefield where a mistake could instantly blow her, her crew and Operation Frankton into eternity.

Hasler spent the first part of *Tuna's* journey discussing the passage ahead with Dick Raikes, poring over the chart table in the control room. At around 1130, he left Raikes and passed down the submarine to the forward torpedo compartment (known in a submarine as the 'fore-ends') to brief his men,[9] including Jack MacKinnon, who like the rest of them still did not know what lay ahead. The space in the fore-ends had been divided into two 'floors' separated by a false deck which rested on the racks that normally carried *Tuna's* forward torpedoes. The Marines' six canoes, each folded flat, were stacked one against the other in their reverse order of unloading, on the upper and lower floors of this makeshift division. The larger bags containing their equipment were stacked on the top floor on the starboard side of the compartment, while the space directly below doubled as the Marines' sleeping quarters and extra stowage space for smaller bags. All this unaccustomed equipment made the fore-ends extremely crowded. There was little space for Hasler's briefing.

Hasler called his men around him and told them to sit on the bare deck. When they were settled he started to brief them, first leaning against a bulkhead and then sitting on a small stool which he had brought in with him.[10] According to Lucas Phillips he began: 'This time it's the real thing. I haven't been able to tell you before, but we have started to carry out an actual operation against the enemy. We are going to do the sort of job we have been training for these past four months and I have chosen you chaps because I feel confident you can do it.'[11] But, he continued, their target was not, as they had imagined, the *Tirpitz* in Norway. It was enemy blockade runners in Bordeaux.

There were smiles all round. Getting back from France would be a lot easier than from Norway – and the water would be warmer, too.[12]

A blackboard was produced on which Hasler drew a rough map of the Gironde estuary. Using this, he ran through the outline of the operation beginning with the launch from *Tuna* some nine miles from the mouth of the Gironde. He then marked their course from the point where *Tuna* would drop them off to the entrance of the great estuary. He warned them of the powerful tides and sketched in the strength of the German defences in the area, including two armed trawlers on permanent patrol, six minesweepers and perhaps twenty-four torpedo boats and numerous river patrol craft. He showed them the location of the batteries of heavy and medium guns on both sides of the estuary mouth, a radar station on Pointe de Grave, the location of several squadrons of bombers, fighters and specialised maritime patrol aircraft, searchlight batteries and numerous interlocking anti-aircraft gun positions and machine-gun posts.

Next he plotted their planned course and daytime 'lying up' positions down the Gironde. As soon as they entered the estuary proper, the six canoes would split into two groups, or 'divisions' – one under Hasler himself and the other under MacKinnon. They would move separately along the east bank of the estuary, converging on Bordeaux on the fourth night after their launch when they would carry out separate attacks. MacKinnon's group would attack the ships on the east bank of the river and Hasler's group those on the west. Then they would catch the ebb tide for their escape.

Here Hasler stopped: 'Any questions so far?'

'Yes Sir. How do we get back?' 'Sailor' Wallace asked in his broad Dublin brogue, voicing the question in everybody's mind.[13]

Hasler explained that the submarine could not return for them. It would be too hazardous. They would have to split up into pairs and escape overland through France, linking up with a French escape organisation and making their own way to Spain. The earlier smiles were replaced by gasps. But there were no complaints.[14] They trusted Blondie. If he said it could be done, then he would do it and they would follow just as when they were under training.

'If I get caught, I'm going to declare myself neutral, because I'm Irish,' said Wallace, to a round of nervous laughter.[15]

Hasler continued: after they had planted their limpet mines, they would catch the ebb tide to the area of Blaye,* some twenty miles from Bordeaux on the east bank of the estuary. Here they would sink their canoes, split up into twos and head, not southwest for Spain as the Germans would expect, but for the little town of Ruffec 100 miles to the northeast. There the Resistance had been warned to look out for them and would escort them on their onward passage back to Britain. He appreciated that none of them spoke French, so he would teach

---

* Pronounced 'Bligh'.

them some phrases and also how to master the special No. 3 Code used by prisoners of war to communicate with MI9 in London.

At the end of his briefing Hasler handed round aerial photographs, telling them to study these carefully over the next few days so they could memorise the layout of the estuary, the positions of the German defences and their planned routes in and out. He finished: 'If there is anyone who feels that this operation is too much for him, I want him to say so now. No one will think any the worse of him.'

No one said anything.

This is a scene much beloved of war movies. The commander says: 'This mission is only for volunteers. Any man who wishes to withdraw at this moment should step forward.' And of course no one does.

Of course no one does! Contrary to what our Leaders tell us, few soldiers fight for their country – they fight for their mates. It is the man alongside them whose opinion matters most; they will never let him down and they know he will never let them down. That principle applies with particular intensity to Special Forces, where camaraderie and spirit among the members of the unit matters above all else. Such men would, quite literally, rather die than back out in front of their mates. Everyone is frightened at this point: if they aren't, they have failed to grasp what is going on and should be left behind as a menace to their comrades.* It is not courage that sees a soldier through this critical moment, it is the shame of letting down his mates.

It must have been after this briefing that Jack MacKinnon, no doubt hoping to post a last letter home before *Tuna* left the Clyde, sat down, probably at the wardroom table in the submarine's midships, and wrote to his mother:

This is just one of my well-known short notes, which everybody thinks are just a waste of time. However, it's just to let you know that I am still in the best of health and enjoying life to the full …

Well, I just want to confirm that you will not hear from me for a number of weeks, so don't on any account worry over the fact that

---

* An SBS friend of mine used to say, 'A hero is just a man who's too afraid to say no in front of his mates.' My personal rule when going on operations was never to take anyone who was not at least as frightened as I was.

you get no letters. Would you please tell Margaret this, as I have not had time to do so myself.

Remember, dear, look after yourself and Dad, and the children, and I will carry on 'watching crossing the road'.

Your loving son,

Jacky

At 1250 *Tuna* was on her way again, this time for the shelter and seclusion of Scalpsie Bay near the southern tip of the Isle of Bute.[16] Here, for two or three hours, Hasler's men and a team from *Tuna*'s crew under their first lieutenant, 'Johnny' Bull, did one daylight and one night-time practice of the launch procedure they would use. Each exercise began with the submarine surfacing from the dived position, followed by Raikes giving the order 'Up canoes.' The canoes were then brought up in the prescribed order (Hasler's *Catfish* last so he could be the first to disembark) and laid out on *Tuna*'s casing. *Catfish* was then placed over the lifting slings attached to *Tuna*'s makeshift 'gun crane' and, with Hasler and Sparks and all their stores embarked, was hoisted up and swung out over the side.

Figure 4

Raikes gently vented his buoyancy tanks, trimming *Tuna* down so as to decrease the distance to the water, the gun barrel was depressed and *Catfish* was gently lowered into the sea.[17] The operation was repeated for each of the other canoes until all six were lined up in two arrowheads, one behind Hasler and the other behind MacKinnon.

Hasler and Bull carefully timed the length of the operation. Their fastest, from the moment Raikes gave the order 'Up canoes' to the second the last canoe was launched and *Tuna*'s gun swung back into position, was thirty-one minutes. Too long for comfort, given that, on the night, they would be close to a shore bristling with the enemy. Equally worrying, one canoe, *Coalfish*, was damaged in the process, as was *Cuttlefish*'s compass. But both were quickly repaired.

At 2000, with the night now firmly set in, *Tuna*'s casing was cleared and she headed down the Clyde for a rendezvous at Garroch Head with HMS *White Bear*, an armed yacht which was to be her escort down the Irish Sea. At 2235, setting a course of 175 degrees, *Tuna* left the shelter of the Clyde for the open sea with the *White Bear* in attendance. Down below in the fore-ends, Hasler's men were inspecting, repairing and drying out their canoes, after which each craft was collapsed for stowing and carefully re-stacked for the long passage ahead. That night, as in the nights which followed, the two officers 'hot bunked',[18] Hasler in Raikes' bunk in the captain's cabin and MacKinnon in the wardroom. Sergeant Wallace did the same in the petty officers' mess.[19] The rest of Hasler's party bedded down as best they could in the little space that remained in the forward torpedo compartment. They had no mattresses to cushion the hard metal deck on which they lay, and only a blanket to pull over them. Norman Colley regarded himself as especially fortunate in managing to take possession of a half-empty sack of potatoes which he used as a pillow.[20] It was cramped, uncomfortable and claustrophobic – sleep did not come easily to any of them.[21]

The next few days on *Tuna* as she made her way south were almost as unpleasant as the days which would follow on the operation itself. The need to conserve electrical power meant *Tuna*'s stoves could not be used when she was dived, so her chef 'Joe' Lawrence (the only gypsy chef in the Navy, according to Raikes) could serve nothing but cold fare during the day. Seasickness when *Tuna* was on the surface and diesel-laden fug to breathe when she was dived would be their constant companions. Sleep would be fitful, broken and uncomfortable. They even had to be careful with their bodily functions. Because of the external water pressure, flushing a submarine's 'heads', or toilet the wrong way, results in a 'blow back' which empties the bowl, not out into the sea, but back into the submarine; a mistake not calculated to make the perpetrator popular among his ship-mates.

Tuna's crew did all they could to ease conditions for the Marines. But their kindnesses could not prevent the high-tuned fitness of Hasler's men from deteriorating little by little over the next few days.

1 December[22]

At 0030 HM/s *Tuna* altered course to 203 degrees and, remaining on the surface, began her long transit down the Irish Sea. By dawn the following morning she was passing Chicken Rock Light at the southern tip of the Isle of Man and by dusk, Bardsey Light at the north end of Cardigan Bay.

By now the wind had freshened to a southwesterly Force 5. This was not by any means rough, but with the sea now on *Tuna*'s starboard bow, she rolled, wallowed and yawed like some great beast in travail. Hasler noted in his diary for that day: '2115–0045. Turned hands to. Re-stowing bags, paddles etc and boats. Everyone except NCOs pretty useless (seasickness). Self continued planning until 0145.' It seems that the Marines' initial attempts to secure their canoes and equipment had not withstood the rigours of *Tuna*'s first day's sailing and they had to completely un-stow and re-secure their precious and fragile craft and equipment.

Meanwhile, on the chart table in Tuna's control room below, Raikes' pilot, Sub-Lieutenant Gordon Rowe, plotted her journey south to the mouth of the Bristol Channel.

2 December

By 0345, *Tuna*'s log records, she was abeam St Govan's light vessel off the western extremity of the Pembrokeshire coast. First light found her some fifteen nautical miles west off Hartland Point and the rugged cliffs of the north Devon coastline. By now the wind had swung to the south and decreased slightly to Force 4, which meant that *Tuna* was butting, bow on, into the sea, lessening her pitching and yawing and giving some respite to Hasler's seasick men in the cramped conditions of the forward torpedo compartment. According to Hasler's diary: 'Slept most of the day. 1500 turned out the troops to go through bags, re-stowing and sewing them up again ... Lecturing troops, who have by now recovered.'

At least, on this stage of the passage, with *Tuna* on the surface, the Marines were able to enjoy the draught of fresh cold air blowing through the submarine from the open hatch leading to the conning tower above; and they could smoke.

Soon however, they would no longer enjoy even these small luxuries. For at 1500, half an hour after she had passed the Longships Light at Land's End, *Tuna* entered the 'operational zone' for enemy activity and started to follow a zigzag course. Two hours later, at 1720, with the light on Wolf Rock off the Isles of Scilly beginning to glow in the gloom on her port beam, she parted company with *White Bear* and slipped beneath the waves, levelling out at seventy feet as daylight faded into darkness. She surfaced again and recommenced her zigzag course when it was fully dark, at 1900 hours.[23] For the rest of her passage south, *Tuna* would remain dived and on electrical power during the day and run on the surface only during the hours of darkness when she could recharge her batteries.

For Hasler's Marines in the fore-ends, this new routine had some advantages, but also new discomforts. Dived, *Tuna*'s sickening rolling, pitching, corkscrew motion mercifully ceased. But now the air in the confined space of the submarine became humid, close and pervaded with the stomach-churning smell of bilge water mixed with diesel. Almost as bad, with *Tuna*'s banks of batteries venting as they discharged, smoking was now forbidden. For some, claustrophobia took the place of seasickness.[24] When she surfaced after dark and the conning tower hatch was thrown open, a cloud of dense condensation swept through the submarine as the cold, fresh December night air met the humid and foetid atmosphere accumulated over the hours when she was dived[25] – then they could smoke again. But then the pitching and rolling began again, too.

During these night passages on the surface, *Tuna*'s survival depended on her lookouts straining hour after hour into the dark wilderness of the sea, watching for an enemy they had to see before they were seen.[26] Coming down below, bitterly cold and exhausted after a two-hour watch, the lookouts were rewarded with a meal of baked potatoes, peppered, salted and buttered (and often used as a hand-warmer before being eaten) and a steaming hot mug of *kye* – the all-purpose Royal Navy comforter of thick cocoa, stiffened with custard powder and, as often as not, laced with a tot of rum.[27]

3 December

Tuna's log for this day is almost empty apart from recording that she dived at dawn sixty nautical miles southwest of Finisterre, surfacing at dusk about a quarter of the way down the Bay of Biscay and around eighty nautical miles due west of the great enemy naval base of St Nazaire. With the barometer steady at almost 1000 millibars and the wind constant at Force 4 from the southeast, it was clear that they were running into a high pressure zone. This meant settled, if cold weather and calm seas – just the conditions they needed for disembarkation and a long paddle into treacherous waters.

Hasler's diary, too, indicates a quiet day: 'Tuna dived all day. Lecturing Troops all day – examining photos of approach, instructions for escape.'

It was probably on this occasion that Hasler took them through the detail of the MI9 briefing L'Estrange had brought up to Glasgow the day before they sailed. An extract from this instructs: 'When starting on the overland escape, get well clear of the river (say 10 miles), moving by night in uniform. Then try to contact friendly farmers, or peasants, borrow civilian clothes, hide uniform and weapons and proceed by day'[28] to Ruffec. There the Resistance, Hasler repeated, would be expecting them and would smuggle them across the Demarcation Line and back home by way of Spain.

4 December

In the early hours of this morning *Tuna* had to alter course to avoid tuna fishing boats under sail. These would, in their hundreds,[29] be regular companions for the remainder of her journey as she made her way south, parallel to the French coast and past the fishing communities of Les Sables d'Olonne and Talmont Saint-Hilaire. *Tuna* dived at dawn sixty nautical miles due west of La Rochelle, surfacing again at dusk a similar distance west of her target, the mouth of the Gironde estuary. By now the wind had dropped completely and the sea was flat calm, save for a long rolling Atlantic swell. Sub-Lieutenant Rowe noticed that the water here was full of phosphorescence which, at night, formed little arrows of light around *Tuna's* bows, rippled in glistening rivulets down her sides and left a brief trail of luminescence behind her as she passed through the dark water.[30]

Today was 'Bobby' Ewart's twenty-first birthday. But there is no record of how it was celebrated by his fellow Marines in the cramped conditions of the fore-ends.

For Hasler in the wardroom, it was a quiet day. His diary records: 'Lecturing Troops all day. Subjects – the attack. Resumé of complete orders. Evening working out detailed timetable for the attack and first night's passage. As a result asked Tuna to make night of 6 Dec the first possible night [for the launch].'

The initial plan drawn up by Hasler and Raikes had been for *Tuna* to surface and bring up the canoes fifteen nautical miles southwest of the mouth of the Gironde. Once the canoes and their occupants were on the casing, the submarine would trim down and, with her profile now much lower, run in on the surface to the dropping point where the canoes would be launched. Judging from Hasler's diary, this must have been the day when it was decided that Raikes would instead make the passage to the drop-off point submerged and only then surface to launch Hasler's canoes. There are two possible reasons for this change. First, Raikes was nervous about running on the surface in an area known to be covered by the German radar station at the Pointe de Grave. But more likely, Hasler, reviewing his timings, decided that he would need as many hours of night as possible, along with a flood tide, to paddle the twenty-four miles necessary to get beyond the line of German defences around the mouth of the estuary before dawn. He could not therefore afford to lose the hour or so of darkness that *Tuna* would need for her surface run-in to the drop-off point. So the last daylight hours would have to be used to get them all the way, submerged, to the launch point. Raikes hinted at this thinking when he later commented that he had agreed Hasler's request to the change of plan because it meant that 'the boats would have a fair tide for an extra hour'.[31]

5 December

Now *Tuna* was deep into enemy territory. At half past midnight the alarm was sounded and the crew took up diving stations after her lookouts on the conning tower heard engine noises closing astern. At 0135 an aircraft was heard, but not seen, passing overhead. Then all went quiet, enabling Raikes to give the order to stand down fifteen minutes later. But the submarine continued to zigzag until 0400, when she returned to a steady course of 250 degrees until dawn, submerging around eighty nautical miles southwest of the Pointe de Grave. The day was filled with constant changes of course to avoid fishing fleets and minor alarms for aircraft. Once submerged, *Tuna* began to describe a long arc to the east, surfacing after dark at a position only thirty nautical miles from the Bordeaux coast and sixty south of the Pointe de Grave.

The tempo of life for Hasler and MacKinnon began to quicken too:

A.M. troops off. Self + MacKinnon continue working out attack time table & study photos. P.M. lecture troops on timing of first night and of attack. Evening MacKinnon lectures troops on coastal features around 2nd lying up place. Then spending evening writing fair copy of orders and studying advanced bases.

One of Hasler's key points in these briefings, according to Lucas Phillips, was the importance of pressing home their attack:

Nothing must be done to prevent us, or at least some of us, from getting through. Any boat that gets separated from the rest must continue alone ... Any boat that gets into difficulties and gives the SOS will be aided by the boats of its own division. Any canoe that gets swamped and cannot be bailed out will be scuttled and its crew left to swim for it with their No. 5 bags [containing dry clothes] ... Never take offensive action unless compelled. Your job is to get through. If you are challenged or fired upon, adopt the lowest position and let the tide carry you. Never return fire. If you have to kill, kill silently with your fighting knife, conceal the bodies and get away as soon as it's dark.[32]

As Norman Colley[33] recalls, it was this morning that Hasler distributed pens and paper to those who wished to write additional farewell letters to their relatives and loved ones in the event that they did not return. Some declined the offer. Those who took it up wrote their last letters home on their knees, or leaning against the remaining torpedoes on *Tuna*'s racks. Despite the evidence of 'common phrases' – presumably the product of their training writing these last letters – these remain poignant and articulate and are worth quoting at length for the insight they offer into both the courage and maturity of these very ordinary young men.

Bill Mills wrote to his parents in Kettering:

Dear Mother and Dad,

At last I have found the time to write a few letters, although they must only be short ones.

It will be a few days before I am again able to write but will do so as soon as possible. There is just one little thing I wish to make clear. There is little chance of it ever happening, but should by some bad luck I don't come back, I want Kitty to have any of my personal belongings she wants. Although I have stacks of interesting news, I am afraid that it will have to wait until the end of the war. In my opinion this is not far off and I am looking forward to getting back home for good ... forgive the short note but I must rattle off a few lines to other people.

Thanks for all you have done for me. I always appreciated it. You are the finest parents a bloke could wish for.

Bill[34]

James Conway's letter was addressed to his mother and sister in Stockport:

Dear Mother and Mary,

I'm taking this opportunity to write a few lines though I hope they won't be necessary.

As you know I volunteered for a certain job which I trust you will learn about at a later period. Being very secret I cannot enclose in my letter the work I do. However, I hope you won't think hard of me. I know it looks foolish to you that I had to do this but I've enjoyed it and I know that what we have done helps to end the mess we are in and make a decent and better world.

You will know by recovery note whether I am a prisoner or otherwise, which at present doesn't worry me in the least, only don't give up hope, there is always a chance, because I've a feeling I'll be like the bad penny, so don't upset yourself over my safety.

I would like to tell you how much I love you but I can't compose a suitable phrase but my heart will be with you always. Think not only of me but the thousands already over there, many of them worse off than me, who have left wives and daughters behind. I have done my best so what more can be expected? After all, we only live once and so far I've always been on my own two feet, so please for my sake don't worry.

I hardly think it necessary to write my autobiography as you know me better than I do. Don't think of this as a suicide note, but think of it just as I want you to.

I can't thank you. You are the best mother and sister anyone can have had and although I have let you down sometimes you always knew how I felt about it. Anyhow mother, you can always say you had a son in the senior service and although I say it myself, 'one of twelve heroes'.

I'm leaving this note with one of the boys who fortunately isn't coming with us. Maybe he's lucky but I wouldn't take his place if asked. As you know, I've always wanted a crack at the other side and this is it.

I can't thank you enough for all you have done for me but I will take it with me wherever I go, so trusting we will meet again I'll say goodbye to you both, thanking God for the two who have been so kind and given me courage as you have done.

God bless you and keep you both.

I know this will hurt you both but I think it is the best way.

Jim[35]

Bobby Ewart, just twenty-one and a day, wrote two letters. The first was to his family in Cowlairs Road, Springburn, Glasgow:

Dear Mum and Brothers

I'm taking this opportunity to write you these few lines, although I hope they won't be necessary. As you know I volunteered for a certain job which I trust you will learn about at a later period. I've enjoyed every minute of it and hope that what we have done helps to end the mess we are in and make a decent and better world. You will see by recovery note whether I am prisoner or otherwise, which at present isn't worrying me at least. I have a feeling I'll be like a bad penny, so please don't upset yourself over my safety. My heart will be with you always, you are the best parents one could wish to have. Anyway Mum you can always say you had a son in the most senior service and, though I say it myself, one of 'twelve heroes'.

Bobby[36]

Ewart's second letter was all his own words. It was given to Colley personally to take back and was to his girlfriend, Heather, in Southsea:

Dear Heather,

I trust it won't be necessary to have this sent to you, but since I don't know the outcome of this little adventure, I thought I'd leave this note behind in the care of Norman who will forward it to you should anything happen.

During my stay at Southsea, as you well know, [you] made me realise what the good things in life are and I'm glad I have this opportunity to help bring back the pleasant times which I am sure you always had and what you were made for. I couldn't help but love you Heather although you were so young. I will always love you as I know you do me. That should get me through with this. But one never knows the turns of fate. One thing I ask of you, Heather, is not to take it too hard. You have yet your life to live. Think of me as a good friend and keep your chin up. Some lucky fellow will find you who has more sense than I had and who can get you what you deserve. You are young yet for this sort of thing but I had to do it, so please don't worry yourself about me. With your future in front of me, I feel confident that I shall pull through and get back to you someday. I won't have you read more Heather, but I will thank you for all you have done. I pray that God will spare me and save you from this misery. So hoping for a speedy reunion, I'll say cheerio and God be with you and your Mother, from the bottom of my heart, at present in your care.

God bless you all

Yours for ever

Bob

PS. Chin up sweetheart[37]

The SOE progress report to the Cabinet for the period ending this day, 5 December commented: 'In spite of the difficulties caused by the [German] occupation of the ZNO, good progress has been made, especially by our groups at Tours, Poitiers and Bordeaux. Personnel sent out last moon have now safely joined their groups ...'

The report continued by noting, with regret, the 'failure ... with the consequent loss of life' of Operation Freshman,[38] a joint SOE/Combined Operations raid in Norway: 'It is hoped, as a result of a conference recently held at COHQ,* that the closest possible co-operation will be maintained both on planning and operational sides in Norway.'[39] It did not add that, thanks to SOE, such cooperation had been conspicuously absent in the operation on which Hasler and *Tuna* were now embarked.

6 December

Now *Tuna* began to work her way gingerly east towards the coast. At 0300 an aircraft was spotted. At a little past 0500 her lookouts, spotting a darkened ship on their port quarter, initiated a second alarm that called the crew to diving stations. But the danger passed and Raikes was able to stand them down again at 0624. An hour later, with the first light of a bright, sunny day beginning to redden the eastern sky and a mist lying low over the coast in front of them, *Tuna* slipped below the waves again. She was now just twenty nautical miles from the shore and forty south of the entrance to the Gironde. From here she slowly worked her way further in, constantly having to change course to avoid fishing vessels, her crew holding their breath when aircraft, including some maritime patrol seaplanes, flew overhead.

According to Lucas Phillips, Raikes told Hasler during the morning, 'We ought to be able to take a look at the land this afternoon. But last night's star sights were not good and so I will have to get a decent fix[40] before we approach that infernal [RAF laid] minefield. Unfortunately there is precious little on the chart that will help us.'[41]

At 1340 Raikes sighted land through the periscope, but the morning's thin layer of mist – a by-product of the still weather from which they were otherwise benefiting – had not yet dispersed. This made it very difficult to pick out reliable features on what is anyway a notoriously featureless and flat piece of coastline. They could see houses and churches clearly enough –

---

* Combined Operations Headquarters.

but none they could confidently identify with those shown on the chart.[42] 'Landmarks do not exist or have been moved by the Germans and the charts are as much use as a midwifery course to a rabbit,'[43] Raikes was later to write in his Night Order book. To add to his problems, *Tuna* encountered 'inexplicable density layers changing our buoyancy' – almost certainly caused by running through pockets of fresh water. 'You could be in perfect trim at 30 feet one minute and the next – wham! – you'd gone down deep and hit the bottom.'[44]

Hasler took a turn at the periscope in order to assess the lie of the land, but like Raikes could identify nothing of interest. At one point Raikes saw 'feverish activity ... constructing coastal defences and building a railway', including 'at least one new big gun emplacement' which 'it was not possible to fix' due to the hazy conditions and the lack of identifiable coastal features.[45] Acutely aware of the RAF minefield at the approach to the estuary mouth and deeply suspicious that the pilots who dropped the mines had not positioned them with any great accuracy,[46] Raikes did not want to risk his crew, his passengers and the operation by beginning the very hazardous journey up the coast without first getting an accurate and reliable 'fix'. Indeed, this minefield was the main worry for both Raikes and Hasler at this stage of the operation, though they took pains not to show it.[47]

During the afternoon, with tension rising in the forward compartment, Hasler's team began to prepare for disembarkation; un-stowing their stacked canoes and rebuilding them, inflating the canoe buoyancy bags, loading most of their equipment bags, unpacking and checking compasses and greasing the forward hatch so that it would open easily and noiselessly.[48] But as the afternoon wore on it became clear that Raikes would not get a sufficiently accurate fix to enable him to begin his run-in to the drop-off point. Hasler's diary tells the story:

Tuna dived all day approaching coast a.m. P.M. commenced preparations for disembarking – flat calm. Slight swell. Tuna picked up land at 1340, but was unable get a fix in spite of closing in all afternoon. Start was therefore postponed. Slight reaction on all sides.

It is not difficult to imagine the deflation of nerves and expectations among the Marines in the forward compartment when they heard the news. In typical Marine fashion, one wag lightened the atmosphere: 'Oh well. Decent breakfast tomorrow instead of compo rations.'[49] They spent the next hours undoing all they had done that afternoon and re-stowing their canoes.

That night, when *Tuna* surfaced, Hasler joined Raikes on the bridge to find a flat calm sea disturbed only by a long gentle swell under a black moonless night with stars blazing down and a smudge of coastline partially obscured by a low mist – just the conditions they needed to give Hasler's Marines the best chance of slipping past the German positions around the Pointe de Grave.

'Terribly sorry,' Raikes sighed. 'Hope we'll be able to do something better tomorrow. We'll see if we can get a decent astral fix in the morning.'[50]

16

Black-Faced Villains

7 December 1942

> Tuna right inshore. Trying to obtain a fix. Succeeded about lunch time. Self slept most of the morning and afternoon. 1700 final talk to troops. 1745 supper. All set for disembarkation.

Hasler's terse diary summary gives no hint of what was to be one of the most dramatic days of Operation Frankton and, arguably, of all small-scale raiding in the Second World War.

Tuna spent the night lying silent and motionless, save for the slow rocking of the Atlantic swell, under a pitch-black sky spangled with winter stars. Just before dawn Dick Raikes was at last able to get a good star fix.[1]

He dived *Tuna* before first light at 0700, retraced his steps to the point where the shore was plainly visible again, turned *Tuna* onto a course of 360 degrees and began 'tiptoeing' (Raikes' phrase) up the coastline. Raikes got his first good land fix at 1345 when he finally caught sight of the slim finger of the Cordouan lighthouse,[2] positioned in the middle of the mouth of the Gironde. Raikes was still unable to get a second fix on a recognised object on the shoreline, so he had to use another method to establish his exact position. He knew from the Bay of Biscay Pilot that the height of the Cordouan light was 223 feet. So, measuring the angle subtended by the lighthouse on his high-powered periscope, he used trigonometry to calculate the distance from his point of observation on *Tuna* to the top of the Cordouan stack. The point where the distance line

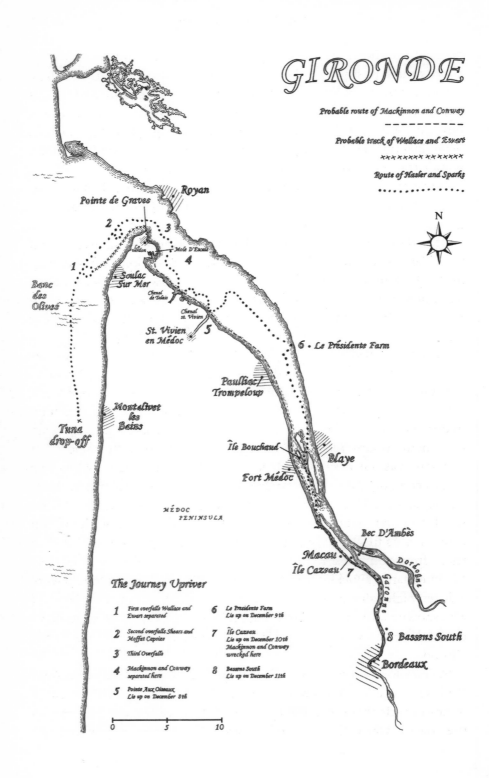

GIRONDE

Probable route of Mackinnon and Conway
– – – – – – – – – –

Probable track of Wallace and Ewart
×× ××××× ×× ×××××

Route of Hasler and Sparks
• • • • • • • • • • • •

N

Royan

Pointe de Graves

2

3

Le
Verdon

Mole D'Exail

4

1

Banc
des
Olives

Soulac
Sur Mer

Chenal
de Talais

Chenal
st. Vivien

St. Vivien
en Médoc

5

6 • Le Présidents Farm

Pauliac/
Trompeloup

Île Bouchaud

Blaye

Fort Médoc

Montalivet
les
Bains

Tuna
drop-off

MÉDOC
PENINSULA

Bec D'Ambès

Macau

Île Cazeau

7

Dordogne

Garonne

8 Bassens South

Bordeaux

The Journey Upriver

1 First overfalls Wallace and
   Ewart separated

2 Second overfalls Shears and
   Moffat Capsizes

3 Third Overfalls

4 Mackinnon and Conway
   separated here

5 Pointe Aux Oiseaux
   Lie up on December 8th

6 Le Presidents Farm
   Lie up on December 9th

7 Île Cazeau
   Lie up on December 10th
   Mackinnon and Conway
   wrecked here

8 Bassens South
   Lie up on December 11th

0   5   10

crossed the line of the bearing of the lighthouse indicated *Tuna*'s approximate position. As he worked his way up the coast, the angle subtended by the lighthouse increased as the distance shortened. *Tuna*'s position was calculated using this method every half-hour from 1345 onwards. Sometime in late afternoon Raikes managed to get a second fix on an identifiable physical object, a prominent water tower in the little seaside resort of Montalivet-les-Bains.[3]

It was around this time, according to Chief Coxswain Bill Stabb, that Hasler came into *Tuna*'s control room to find out how things were going.

'It's all OK now,' Raikes said. 'I'll put you ashore tonight at 1930, if these damn patrol boats keep out of the way and we don't get blown up by the RAF mines.'[4] During the hours that followed, Hasler grabbed what opportunities he could to use *Tuna*'s high-powered periscope to investigate the coast to the north along which he would be paddling that night.

Tuna's crew had other matters than navigation to worry about on her passage north. Those 'damned' RAF magnetic mines were, of course, constantly at the back of their minds – but now there were enemy aircraft to contend with as well. An entry made in *Tuna*'s log at around midday notes, laconically, 'intense air activity' and lists the aircraft flying over them: Arados, Ju88s, Me109s, Me110s, and Dornier flying boats.

There was one aircraft, high above *Tuna* that afternoon, which she almost certainly did not see – and need not have worried about. At 1315, a lone, unarmed blue-painted Spitfire flying at 25,000 feet passed from south to north over Bordeaux and the Gironde, the high-definition camera in its fuselage whirring busily. The aerial photographs it took that afternoon were rushed to the air interpretation unit at RAF Medmenham in Buckinghamshire, where they revealed that there were a dozen high-value targets in the Bordeaux docks, waiting for Hasler. It also showed four or five of the small minesweeper-type vessels used to patrol the estuary, heading north for Le Verdon and the mouth of the Gironde ...[5]

Seven more enemy aircraft were sighted by *Tuna* that afternoon. With sea conditions reported as 'oily calm with a long swell',[6] it seems a minor miracle that none of these spotted the dark shadow creeping up the coast towards the gates of the great German maritime fortress.

Raikes must have been thankful that he was not in the gin-clear waters of the Clyde but in the murky sea at the mouth of the Gironde. But this had its downsides, too. The mud and silt that provided cover from the air also caused constantly shifting sandbanks, and even created uncharted new ones from time to time.

High water springs reached the full twenty-four feet above chart datum* at this point on the French coast at 1453 that afternoon. This gave *Tuna* the maximum depth for the first part of her approach, but then left Raikes with progressively shallower water, as well as occasional buoyancy-changing pockets of fresh water exiting from the Gironde, to contend with as the afternoon wore on.

Throughout these tense, blind hours as *Tuna* slipped north through the local fishing fleet and past the RAF minefield, hearing was her crew's most important sense – their sole means of detecting danger. There was absolute silence on board. Raikes gave his orders by hand signals and the eyes of every man in the control room were either on him or the dials in front of them. Robbie, *Tuna*'s hydrophone operator, sat hunched over the Asdic cabinet, his hands clasped over his headphones; listening, assessing, sieving every tiny vibration of sound. Sifting each for the first tiny 'dub dub dub' of propellers; or the rhythmic thumping of a diesel engine; or – most feared of all – the 'ping – ping – ping' of a warship's sonar beam probing for them through the dark layers of the ocean. At one point something metallic bumped down their port side and everyone's back ran cold as they held their breath for the explosion that would blow them all to kingdom come. But it never came and they relaxed again – for the moment.[7]

At about 1500, Hasler's team in the fore-ends began to repeat the process they had gone through the previous afternoon. By 1730, with the canoes prepared, packed and laid out in the order they would go up onto the casing, they broke for an evening meal. Afterwards they dressed, each man ticking off the other against a checklist of equipment. First they hung their identity tags round their necks and donned their

---

* Chart datum is the point from which the depth of water on a chart is measured. It is usually set at the level of mean low water springs (i.e. the average of the lowest low water). Thus 3 fathoms (18 feet) on a chart indicates that, at low water springs, there is still a depth of around 18 feet of water at this point.

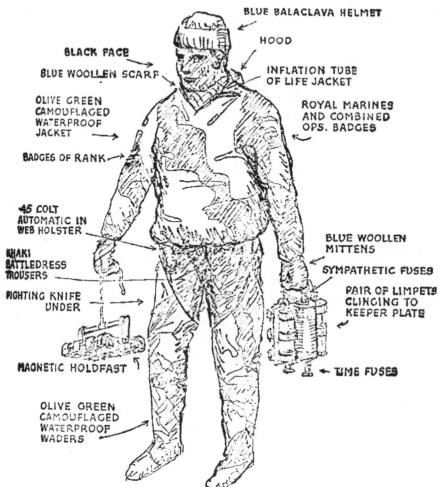

BLUE BALACLAVA HELMET

HOOD

BLACK FACE

BLUE WOOLLEN SCARF

INFLATION TUBE
OF LIFE JACKET

OLIVE GREEN
CAMOUFLAGED
WATERPROOF
JACKET

ROYAL MARINES
AND COMBINED
OPS. BADGES

BADGES OF RANK

.45 COLT
AUTOMATIC IN
WEB HOLSTER

BLUE WOOLLEN
MITTENS

KHAKI
BATTLEDRESS
TROUSERS

SYMPATHETIC FUSES

FIGHTING KNIFE
UNDER

PAIR OF LIMPETS
CLINGING TO
KEEPER PLATE

MAGNETIC HOLDFAST

TIME FUSES

OLIVE GREEN
CAMOUFLAGED
WATERPROOF
WADERS

Figure 5

long woollen pants, over which went stockings and battledress trousers. On their feet, they wore first rubber-soled 'commando boots' and then camouflaged thigh-length waders made of light rubberised material with very thin soles. Under the waders, their commando daggers were strapped in sheaths to their left thighs. On the top half of their bodies they wore woollen vests, a service khaki woollen shirt, a roll-neck blue sweater, a blue woollen scarf, a .45 Colt automatic in a holster and a lightweight inflatable life jacket. Over all this they put their 'Cockle suits', which were made of the same rubberised camouflaged material as their waders. An elasticated skirt sewn on the suits could be hitched over the edges of the canopy openings of their canoes to make a waterproof seal. Before they left the Clyde they had carefully sewn onto the suits their Royal Marines and Combined Operations flashes and badges of rank. Their hands were protected by first silk and, on top, woollen gloves. Finally, each man hung around his neck a lanyard to which was attached a seagull bird-call which they would use to communicate with each other.[8]

Once they were dressed and checked, *Tuna*'s fore-ends were cleared of all clutter which might impede the unloading of canoes and the hatch clips were once again greased for easy and silent opening.

Sunset that afternoon was at 1622, with the moon a ghostly silver daylight orb sinking into the sea on *Tuna*'s port stern quarter just three minutes later. After darkness fell at 1755 Raikes continued squeezing his way north in the narrowing channel between the RAF mines to port and the shore to starboard, using as his reference point the constant white light now visible from the top of the Cordouan tower.[9]

On *Tuna* they switched to red lighting to enable eyes to grow accustomed to the dark, while Raikes himself donned red-tinted goggles so his night vision would not be blinded by any white light he saw through the periscope. He must have felt some relief now that, with the advent of darkness, he could forget the problem of aircraft and concentrate solely on getting his boat the last few miles to the drop-off point.

Bill Stabb describes what happened next.

Suddenly, at around 1800, Robbie from the Asdic station whispered urgently. 'H.E.[10] contact – propellers!'

'Silent routine. Stop all machinery. Shut off for depth charging.' Raikes' calm voice echoed softly from the intercom throughout the boat.

'Range eight miles. Diesels,' Robbie reported.

'Periscope depth.'

Tuna tipped upwards, levelling out at forty feet. Looking through the periscope, Raikes saw a small patrol boat moving from the mouth of the Gironde on their port bow.

'Down periscope – seventy feet.'

Tuna sank silently back down again. Now they could all hear the methodic, probing *ping* of the patrol boat's sonar raking the seabed around them. Five minutes dragged by. The patrol boat was two miles away – not close enough to detect *Tuna*, but too close for comfort.

'H.E. fading away,' Robbie reported to quiet relief. Raikes made another sweep with the periscope.

At 1952, he was satisfied that *Tuna* was in the right position – 45° 22' 1" N, 1° 14' W – some two nautical miles due west of Montalivet. Making a last check through his periscope, Raikes saw exactly what he had hoped *not* to see – the armed German trawler was now patrolling backwards and forwards across the estuary on a line which cut precisely across his point of disembarkation. If he was to avoid the enemy patrol boat, he would have to change the drop-off point. But that would mean a new approach and new, unknown hazards.

Raikes decided he had to take the risk. Positioning *Tuna* as close to the coast as he dared so that her black shape would be hidden against the land behind her, he turned her stern towards the trawler (which at this stage was 5000 yards away) so as to present the smallest visible target to her (but the largest electronic target to the German radar at the mouth of the Gironde, which was now five miles away on *Tuna*'s port beam). Then he gave the order: 'Blow main ballast – stand by to surface,' followed two minutes later by: 'Stop main engines.'

Raikes, *Tuna*'s pilot Gordon Rowe and two lookouts raced up to the bridge even before the submarine had fully broken surface. Their eyes were already adapted to night vision, for they too had been wearing dark red goggles for the last hour or so. The surface of the sea was flat calm over a long rolling swell and the night was very clear and very cold. Raikes sent Rowe up the small iron ladder on the after periscope housing[11] to give him an extra fifteen feet of height. From here he could clearly see the enemy trawler and reported that otherwise, the horizon was clear.[12] One lookout trained his powerful binoculars on the trawler, which was now off *Tuna*'s stern and only two and a half miles to seaward. His job was to keep a constant watch on her, while the other lookout scanned the horizon and the shoreline for any other dangers.

'Major Hasler to the bridge.' Raikes' voice came quietly down the bridge voice-pipe into the control room below. According to Lucas Phillips, Hasler was standing on the bridge beside *Tuna*'s captain a few moments later. 'Beastly clear night,' commented Raikes. 'But looks alright for your launching. We can see the patrol boat there, but I don't think he can see us. Do you want to start?'[13]

Hasler paused to look at the thin line of the French coast and listen to the sound of the surf thundering on the beach some two miles away.

'Yes.'

'Up canoes,' Raikes called softly down the voice-pipe. The time was 1936.[14] The attack stage of Operation Frankton had begun.

As the two men stood watching the preparation on the casing below, Hasler suggested that when he got back home in, he estimated, three months' time, they should meet for dinner in London. 'Book a table at the Savoy on April 1st,' he instructed Raikes.

'No I won't! Not April 1st! I'll book a table on March 31st or April 2nd,' Raikes replied.[15]

'Well, I'd better get along and look after my own canoe. Thanks for everything you've done on our behalf.'

'Well cheerio, old boy. See you before long,' Raikes replied, as the two men shook hands.[16]

The first person on *Tuna*'s casing that night was Lieutenant Johnny Bull, who – as they had practised – swiftly set about turning *Tuna*'s four-inch gun into a makeshift crane. Meanwhile, Jack MacKinnon was down below supervising the passage of canoes, equipment and crews onto the casing in the right order: *Coalfish* (Wallace and Ewart), *Conger* (Sheard and Moffatt), *Cachalot* (Ellery and Fisher), *Crayfish* (Laver and Mills), *Catfish* (Hasler and Sparks), *Cuttlefish* (MacKinnon and Conway). The first items up were the slings which would be used to lift the canoes; next the canoes themselves, each followed by its crew – faces blackened now – then their remaining equipment bags which, kneeling on the casing, they immediately began stowing into their little craft. What Hasler didn't know was that, contrary to his orders, some of the Marines had smuggled into their jackets certain items which were not on his very precise list of stores for the raid: bars of chocolate and small bottles of Royal Navy rum which *Tuna*'s crew, who had developed a high regard for their passengers during the journey south,[17] had saved from their daily 'tot' (rum ration) to give to Hasler's men before they left.

The canoes were laid out on *Tuna*'s casing in precise order, with Hasler's *Catfish* closest to the four-inch gun, followed by MacKinnon's *Cuttlefish*, and then the others arranged on the submarine's bows beyond them. Somehow, as Ellery and Fisher's canoe, *Cachalot*, was being brought up onto the deck, it was damaged, apparently on the jagged edge of one of the fastenings on the locking clasp of the forward hatch (known by *Tuna*'s crew as the 'hatch claws'[18]). Hasler was called down from the bridge, took a look at the tear in her side and instructed the two Marines to return their stricken craft below and follow it themselves;[19] they could not take part in the operation. Despite pleading from both men – and even tears from Fisher – Hasler insisted. Before going below Fisher shouted softly to his best mate, David Moffatt: 'Hurry up back, I'll have a pint waiting for you at the Granada.'[20] Apart from the crews, only Norman Colley was allowed to stand on *Tuna*'s casing, watching as Hasler and Sparks, after packing and checking *Catfish*, jumped in and were hoisted up and lowered into the Atlantic swell.

As *Catfish* was being lowered towards the sea, the German searchlights on the Pointe de Grave suddenly burst into life and probed out across the estuary mouth, paying particular attention to the area around *Tuna*. At the same time, the submarine's lookouts reported that the armed trawler to their northeast had turned and was heading towards them.[21] Raikes speculated inwardly that he had probably been spotted by the German radar four miles to his north.[22] There was no time to waste. On *Tuna*'s casing, Johnny Bull swiftly hoisted out the other canoes, which then, one by one, gathered in predetermined order behind Hasler and MacKinnon, riding the black swell until their numbers were complete. While he was waiting, Hasler checked his compass against the North Star, sparkling brightly in the winter night. Below it lay the Great Bear low on the horizon and, on the other side of the North Star, the 'W' shape of Cassiopeia, almost directly overhead.[23] Hasler was shocked to find that, despite all the checking and 'swinging' he had done to iron out the distortion of the sixteen magnets on the limpets he was carrying, the P8 Spitfire compass on the canopy in front of him was off by a full twenty degrees.[24] He adjusted it and noted to himself that he would need to keep a constant check on his course with the positions of the stars as the night wore on.

When Corporal George Sheard and Marine David Moffatt in the final canoe, *Conger*, had joined the group, Hasler set his compass to a bearing of 035 degrees,[25] gave the hand signal to move off and the group started to paddle away from *Tuna* in a lopsided arrowhead with its '*Cachalot* barb' missing and Hasler in the lead. Norman Colley's last view was of five dark shadows under a starry sky, already moving purposefully towards the mouth of the Gironde ten miles away to the north.[26]

It had taken *Tuna*'s crew, under Johnny Bull, forty-six minutes to launch them all – fifteen minutes longer than their best time at Scalpsie Bay; perhaps a consequence of the time spent dealing with the damaged *Cachalot*. At 2022, *Tuna* turned on her main engines, swung her bows to the southwest and, after waving 'au revoir' to what Raikes later referred to as 'a magnificent bunch of black faced villains with whom it has been a real pleasure to work', slipped away into the night.[27]

German signals

At 1950, Major Beyer of Flak Unit 999 signalled his Luftwaffe Chief of Operations that his *Luft-Nachrichten Gerät* (radar) at W310 had located a ship 4 km southwest of Pointe de Grave. There were no further details.[28]

Five minutes later came an order from the Chief of Operations to Battalion Headquarters at Soulac to adopt 'heightened awareness'.

Then at 2000 the Chief of Operations sent an urgent enquiry to Captain Panzel of Naval Artillery Unit 284: 'What's going on? illuminate the area.' This signal was taken directly to Panzel, who was dining at Kriegsmarine headquarters in the Fort de Chay in Royan with Admiral Johannes Bachmann, the flag officer in command of western France, who happened to be on an inspection visit to the area from his headquarters in Nancy.[29]

Twenty minutes later the Chief of Operations contacted Panzel again: 'What's going on?'

Panzel checked with his searchlight batteries and ordered a reply to be sent back: 'Nothing to see. Searchlights illuminate approx. 8 km. Probably a fishing boat which has got lost.'

The Chief of Operations noted in his log, 'Division decides against any further action. Nothing further observed.'

17

The Pointe de Grave

For the first two hours, Hasler's canoes – five darker shadows on the dark surface of the Atlantic swell – made good progress. The only sounds to break the night silence were the soft, rhythmic rise and dip of their paddles and the distant muffled thunder of the surf to starboard. Soon muscles settled into the swing of the paddles and lungs filled with clean sea air after the fug of the submarine. The exertion kept the Marines warm despite the deep chill of the night. Behind and to their left the dimmed lights of the armed trawler scurried around the space vacated by *Tuna*, finding nothing. To their right lay the coast, a low grey smudge sprinkled with pinpricks of light,[1] with here and there a flash of white where a big breaker crashed onto the shoreline. Ahead and slightly to the left, just under the three stars that sketched out the handle of the Plough, the fixed light atop the Cordouan stack marked the entrance of the Gironde, now six miles ahead. At some moment during this first stage of the journey, Sam Wallace was heard being sick – but otherwise things were going well.

As time wore on, they began to see, first as a tiny point of light then growing into a flashing beacon, the little lighthouse of St Nicholas, perched on the sand dunes above the dangerous Rochers de St Nicholas reef. There, in the next hour or so, they would swing to the east, and onto a new course which would take them through the passage between the light and the rocks and straight on, past the lighthouse at the Pointe de Grave, into the Gironde itself.

Every now and then as the hours ticked by, Hasler would raise his hand for the other canoes to 'raft up' around him. As each canoe joined the raft, its crew laid their paddles across their own canoe and the canopies of their neighbours so as to make a structure stable enough for them to stand up and change places, if they had needed to. Then, while his men chatted in low voices, Hasler took out the short stub of a fishing rod on which was mounted a reel with a substantial fisherman's lead weight attached. This he used as a plumb-line which he lowered over the side to measure the depth below, checking it against his chart with the light of a dimmed torch held out of sight below the canopy of the canoe.[2] He had taught them to let the lead weight rest on the bottom for a minute so as to assess the strength of the tide, and occasionally to tip the weight with beeswax so that it would bring up traces of material from the seabed as an aid to navigation. But here, where the composition of the seabed never varied from mud and sand, this technique was of little use.

For the first forty-five minutes of paddling the Marines found themselves pushing against an ebb tide of around two knots which held down their speed and nudged them in towards the shore.[3] But at a little after 2115, the ebb diminished to still water and by 2130 the flood tide started pushing behind them, sweeping them down the curve of the coast at increasing speed. At around 2350, Hasler's plumb-line told him that they were passing over the shallow water of the Banc des Olives, and the Marines had to work hard to keep their canoes' bows into the sea as the tidal flow began to boil under them and the waves shortened into rollers and turbulence.[4] Hasler was too seasoned a sailor not to have known what they were experiencing – the beginnings of tidal overfalls. He hadn't expected these. If they were occurring at a point so far down the coast, he must have wondered, what would it be like nearer the mouth of the great estuary where the tidal flows would be so much stronger?

In fact Hasler's men may have been lucky here. Local fishermen recognise the Banc des Olives as an area of dangerous tidal disturbance. Hasler passed over the Banc des Olives at near slack water, before the flood tide started to run at full force. If he had been even half an hour later at this point, he might have found this passage far more difficult.

Once over the Banc des Olives, the water calmed again and the tide swept them on. Thirty minutes later, they paddled past the St Nicholas light and over the Rochers de St Nicholas. Here Hasler altered course to the east so as to follow parallel with the new line of the coast. By this time the Plough had swung, its handle now pointing down, almost touching the horizon just three fingers' width to the right of Hasler's course, which was now in alignment with the middle stars of the constellation of Leo Minor. Ahead they could see the dark expanse of the coast leading up to the Pointe de Grave lighthouse that marked the entrance to the Gironde itself. Soon, with luck, they would be past the German defences and into the protected waters of the estuary.

But now they began to hear a new, unfamiliar – and unexpected – sound. It began as no more than a whisper, then grew into a murmur and finally, as the tide bundled them onwards, built up in a crescendo like the angry roar of a great waterfall not far ahead. It must have dawned on Hasler that his earlier fears at the Banc des Olives were about to be realised. Ahead there were strong tidal disturbances that both he and the Frankton planners had failed to anticipate. He called the other canoes in to raft up and explained in a low voice that the noise they could hear was a tide rip; the tide behind them was so strong they couldn't avoid it. He hadn't expected it. But it wasn't a problem. He had been through them many times before. The waves would be short and steep-sided, much as in rough weather. But they would come from all directions. The trick was to paddle in fast, keep their canoe bows always into the sea and concentrate on getting through the area of turbulence as quickly as possible. He would go first and they should all meet up on the other side.

Hasler and Sparks tightened their canoe canopies and paddled furiously into the maelstrom, pushing their canoe as fast as they could so as to maintain headway among the jumble of waves and crests – some of them three or four feet high. They were tossed around like flotsam and had constantly to rebalance their canoes with their bodies, like two tightrope walkers on a violently swaying rope. In a few seconds they were through and into the calmer water on the other side. Hasler swung *Catfish* round to watch the others come through. A moment or so later, Laver and Mills in *Crayfish* shot out of the turbulent water to join them, followed by *Conger* with Sheard and Moffatt and then *Cuttlefish* carrying MacKinnon and Conway. They peered into the darkness for Wallace and Ewart in *Coalfish* to follow. They watched and watched. No sign. Hasler tried calling on his seagull bird-call. No answering cry.

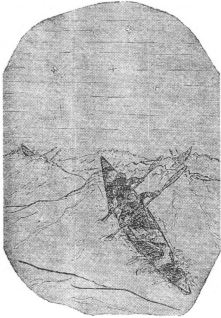

Figure 6

It was now about 0015, and Hasler had only forty-five minutes to reach his 'Point X' in time to make the other side of the estuary before dawn. They could afford no more delay. Confident that, if they had not capsized, Wallace and Ewart would press on with the attack even if they were alone, Hasler turned *Catfish* and began paddling again towards the mouth of the estuary.[5]

But they had not gone far before they heard the same noise again and were soon being borne by the tide into another patch of boiling white water. Once again *Catfish* went first and waited on the other side, Hasler and Sparks panting for breath from the exertion of paddling through waves which, at some five feet high, were even bigger and more turbulent than those of the first overfalls. They were swiftly joined by *Cuttlefish* and *Crayfish*. Then they heard a sudden cry and a splash. *Conger* had capsized. The next thing they saw was Sheard and Moffatt being swept out of the maelstrom, clinging to their canoe, coughing and spluttering as they cleared their lungs of seawater. Hasler pulled *Catfish* alongside. Sparks tried to bail out the stricken craft. But, with the waves now lapping over the brim of *Conger's* cockpit, it was impossible. The only way to empty the canoe would be to beach it, but that was out of the question, given that they were in the middle of the most densely defended area in the Pointe de Grave. By now it was 0200 on 8 December. With the night more than half gone, they still had the most delicate part of their journey to negotiate and ten miles to paddle before they could reach a safe area to lie up.

As they struggled with *Conger* and the two men in the water, the tide swept them round the Pointe de Grave and past the small jetty which sticks out from its point. Now they were within a few hundred yards of the German guns guarding the mouth of the estuary. At this moment the Pointe de Grave lighthouse suddenly snapped on at its full 25,000 candlepower, lighting up the area as its beam swept over the Marines' heads, making them feel very exposed and vulnerable. Hasler realised that if he did not act fast, the whole enterprise might founder.

'Try to scuttle her,' he ordered Sparks, who used his knife to slash the canoe's sides and puncture her buoyancy bags.[6] But even weighed down by her limpets and some 300 lb of stores, *Conger* refused to sink. Her cockpit now fully awash, Sparks released the stricken canoe and she was soon carried away into the darkness on the tide.

'Corporal Sheard, hang on to the stern of my boat. Moffatt, hang on to Mr MacKinnon's. We will tow you as far into the beach as we can. Then you must swim ashore and try to escape overland.'

They began to paddle again, their speed now reduced to one knot because of the deadweight, sea-anchor drag of the two men in the water. Then, almost immediately, they heard that dreaded sound once more. A moment later the tide swept the three remaining canoes and the two men desperately clinging to their sterns through a further tide rip a few hundred yards past the Pointe de Grave – this one, with waves only three feet high, mercifully less violent.[7]

Sheard and Moffatt had now been in the icy water for almost an hour and were beginning to suffer badly from the cold – Sheard, according to later reports, being in a worse state than his partner. Hypothermia, the silent killer of even strong men in cold water, was tightening its icy grip.

By now they had lost so much time that Hasler knew there was no chance of making the other side of the estuary before daybreak. Besides which, the tide had now pushed them too close to the beach at Le Verdon, and they had no choice but to hazard a passage around the end of the Môle d'Éscale sticking out into the estuary beyond. Hasler had hoped to avoid this obstacle, whose constant blue light he could now see ahead,[8] he knew it was the base for the fast *Chasseur*-type light patrol boats used by the Germans to police the estuary (several of which the previous day's aerial photographs had shown heading towards the Môle). He had thought there might be one of these boats moored at the end of the jetty – but to his horror, he now saw three or four of them moored in line ahead, some distance from the end of the Môle.[9]

Hasler would doubtless have preferred to give the patrol boats the widest berth possible by canoeing down the middle of the estuary. But the tide had now swept him and his comrades in so close to the shore that paddling across the estuary to gain deep water would have taken too much time – indeed, with such a strong tidal flow, would almost certainly have been impossible. He had no option but to risk passing down the channel between the line of patrol boats and the end of the Môle.

There could be no question of attempting this risky passage with Sheard and Moffatt hanging on to the back of their canoes. Besides, the two men's condition was deteriorating by the minute and they were becoming increasingly unable to swim.

When the little convoy was about a mile from the Le Verdon beach (known as La Chambrette at this point), Hasler rafted up his three remaining canoes and said quietly to George Sheard: 'I am sorry, but we have to leave you here. You must swim for it. I am terribly sorry.'

Sheard, grey and trembling with cold, replied: 'That's alright Sir. I understand. Thanks for bringing us so far.'

They all shook hands: sodden woollen glove on sodden woollen glove. Laver pulled out the flask of 'pusser's'[10] rum he had been given by *Tuna*'s crew and stuffed it under Sheard's life jacket. Hasler realised with a shock that, contrary to orders, his men had brought these flasks with them. But this was not the time to make an issue of it.

'God bless you both,' he said, as he turned his canoe and, with the others following, paddled off into the darkness.

There are those who see Hasler as a ruthless professional prepared to sacrifice his men in a suicide mission for glory. Among the many ways of illustrating that this is a false judgement, one of the most powerful is Hasler's handling of George Sheard and David Moffatt's plight in the terrible hour after their capsize. By taking his stricken colleagues so close in to the coast, Hasler knew that there would be a chance, albeit in that icy water a slim one, that they would make it to the beach and would as a result be captured, thus alerting the Germans to his presence.[11] By giving them this slim chance of survival, he was therefore not only placing his operation in jeopardy but also breaking his own very specific orders, given just two days ago: orders which made it clear that, in all circumstances, the operation must come first. Hasler opted to risk his operation in order to give his men a better chance of surviving. In the end, his humanity proved more powerful than his professionalism. If fault that be, there are worse.

In his autobiography, Sparks claims that, as they paddled away from their two colleagues, he saw Hasler's shoulders heave with suppressed sobs. This seems unlikely. Whatever his inner turmoil, Hasler came from a generation that did not show their emotions.[12] There is, moreover, plenty of evidence from other witnesses that the most striking feature about Hasler's demeanour throughout the operation was that it *never changed*. He never appeared tired to his men; or depressed when things were going badly (as they clearly now were); or despairing when hope appeared to have gone. His style of leadership was like that of Shackleton; whatever he felt internally, the leader should only ever show confidence and unshakeable determination to those under his command.

With his force now reduced to half its original size, Hasler had to concentrate fiercely on what lay ahead rather than upon the human tragedy drifting away astern into the darkness. And what lay ahead was the Môle d'Éscale.

Built in 1933 on concrete piles, this ran on a curve some 400 yards[13] out into the estuary. It was originally used by transatlantic liners, especially those carrying passengers on pilgrimage to Lourdes. The structure was served along its length by a double-track railway line linked to the main French rail system. The German patrol boats were moored one behind the other some 1000 yards[14] off the end of the Môle in a line parallel to the coast and at ninety degrees to the Môle itself. This presented Hasler with a corridor more than half a mile wide, bounded on his left by the line of boats and to his right by the end of the Môle, which he had to assume would be closely guarded by sentries. Given the darkness of the night, this should not have been a difficult passage to negotiate without being seen, provided that he could follow a course down the centre of the defile. But it seems probable from Hasler's description of this passage and from Lucas Phillips' account that, with the tide having swept him in so close to the shore, Hasler and his men had no alternative but to pass much closer to the end of the Môle and its sentries than was prudent.

'We shall have to go through one at a time,' whispered Hasler. 'Single paddle, lowest position. I shall go first. Corporal [Laver], you will follow when you see that I have passed. Mac, you will follow when Crayfish is through. I shall wait for you in the clear water beyond.'

'Very good, Sir.'

'Take it quietly.'

'Yes, Sir.'

Lying low and stock still, their bodies bent over the front of their canoe, Hasler and Sparks began their journey. They made only the tiny movements with their single paddles necessary to keep direction, and let the tide carry them through the pool of light cast by the lamps on the end of the Môle and out into the darkness beyond, their nerves tingling with anticipation for the shout above them, spines braced for the shot that would follow. Suddenly, halfway through their passage, a signal light on one of the German patrol boats started flashing at the shore. They prayed they hadn't been spotted.

Back into the safety of the night, Hasler again swung Catfish round to watch for the others. First Laver and Mills came drifting slowly, like a large log on the tide, through the patch of light and into the darkness to join them. The two canoes rafted up and watched for MacKinnon and Conway, eyes straining for movement in the circle of light and the dark sea around it. They heard a sudden shout and saw the signalling light begin to flash again. Then more shouting. Hearts in their mouths, they waited, watched and listened for the shot which would tell them MacKinnon and Conway had been spotted. But nothing. No sound, no shouts, no shots – but no MacKinnon and Conway either. They waited and waited, their fingers freezing in their woollen gloves. Hasler used his bird-call again. But there was neither sight nor returning seagull's cry.

There has been much speculation about what exactly happened to MacKinnon and Conway at this point. One possible explanation for their disappearance may lie in the fact that the Môle is constructed on piers.

Since the tide had been constantly pushing them towards the Môle, it may be that MacKinnon and Conway, the last through, were pushed too far towards the piers by the time it was their turn to attempt the passage. To have followed Hasler's line from this position would have necessitated paddling parallel to the line of the Môle before they could reach its end, with the tide pushing them ever closer to both the structure and the sentries guarding it. MacKinnon may have opted instead to pass *under* the Môle between the piers, rather than round its end. This would explain why Hasler and the others, watching the gap between the end of the Môle and the moored patrol craft, saw nothing and why MacKinnon, emerging from under the Môle, was unable to find his colleagues further out in the darkness of the estuary.

Worried now about finding a hiding place before dawn, Hasler finally turned *Catfish* and, with only *Crayfish* to accompany him, set a course of 135 degrees on his compass and started to paddle down the Gironde. The tide was now pushing them at a speed of around three knots past the low flat land of the Médoc peninsula to starboard, lightly veiled under a morning mist. Low on the horizon, just a finger to the right of *Catfish*'s bow as it sliced through the mirror-calm waters of the estuary, the six bright stars of Orion's belt blazed out in the night sky.

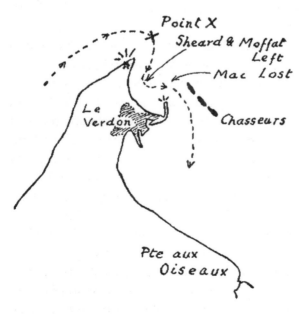

Figure 7

One can only imagine what Hasler must have felt at this point. In the first ten hours of his mission he had lost two-thirds of his attacking force. Lesser men would have faltered after such a disastrous start. Hasler dug deep, and paddled on.

Hasler's original plan, if he were forced onto this side of the estuary, had been to land somewhere close to the outfall of a small but navigable river, the Chenal de Tallais, which took its name from a village in its upper reaches. But when he got there, he found it was impossible to land at this point without risking damage to the canoes because of a line of fishing stakes just offshore. He decided to push further down the estuary. By now the time would have been about 0630 and already soft grey smudges of light would have been appearing in the eastern sky.

They had no time to lose if they were to find a hiding place before dawn. High water at this point in the Gironde that morning was at 0400, so by now, to add to their difficulties, Hasler and his exhausted team would have been pushing into an ebb tide that was strengthening against them every minute.

Eventually, Hasler found a spot for a safe landfall at the mouth of a second small river called the Chenal de St Vivien, just by a promontory which he at first mistook as an island.[15] Exhausted, he brought the remnants of his force ashore. They had paddled twenty-three nautical miles, negotiated three deadly tidal overfalls, abandoned two comrades to their fate in the icy sea and lost contact with four more.

Hasler knew from his study of the maps that this place was called Le Pointe aux Oiseaux. What he did not know was that this was precisely the point where the main German defensive line of strongpoints marking the southern end of the Le Verdon pocket met the estuary. He had landed right in the middle of one of the key concentrations of German troops on the whole Médoc peninsula.

18

The Pointe aux Oiseaux

8–9 December 1942

For the fishermen of St Vivien en Médoc, there was nothing in the way the morning of 8 December 1942 began to distinguish it from any other since the Germans had come to the region. It had been a clear, moonless, star-spangled night, somewhat colder than usual for this time of year. A light frost lay on the flat fields leading down to the Gironde and a low, thin winter mist hung over land and water alike.

These fishermen lived their lives by the rhythm of the tides. This was the time of the month when the spring tides ran – so today's low water would expose the maximum of sand and mud bank on which they could gather the oysters that gave them their living. This morning, the ebb tide, which would carry their sturdy little *chaloupes*[1] down the narrow Chenal de St Vivien, began to run at around 0400. But there was no hurry. There was no point in reaching the shellfish beds before first light, which this winter morning would not be until 0730. A bustle of lanterns and quiet activity began at 0600, as the men and women of St Vivien's principal fishing families, the Ardouins and the Chaussats among them, loaded their food and prepared their boats for the day's work.

These were hard times for many in France, in this, the third year of the German occupation. Indeed, there were more than 200 German troops billeted in St Vivien itself and still more in the German strongpoints dotted along the banks of the Chenal. But mostly, the Germans left the fishermen alone. Unlike many in France at this time, food was not a great problem for the fishing families of the Gironde. Life was not easy, of course. But then it never had been for these tough men and women who wrestled their living from the dangerous waters of Europe's greatest estuary.

At about 0630, the little flotilla of boats, perhaps thirty in all, each carrying a lamp, cast off and started to row and chug on small engines quietly down the narrow channel, the ebb tide carrying them swiftly past occasional banks of high reeds and between flat pasture on both sides. They rounded the last bend in the Chenal de St Vivien at around 0730, just as the sky was light enough to see the wide grey expanse of the estuary stretching out ahead of them.

At this moment, they saw something else as well. Something that would change this ordinary morning into an extraordinary one and put at risk the lives of everyone in the little flotilla. Something that would give them a place in the history of the Gironde estuary.

For there, between them and the sea – lying silently in the water alongside the stakes which marked the edge of the channel – were two camouflaged canoes each carrying two men whose blackened faces did not mask the fatigue and terrors of the night through which they had just passed. There must have been a moment of surprised silence as both sides wondered what to do next. It was broken by one of the British soldiers, an imposing man with a prominent blond moustache, who spoke atrocious French with a German accent: 'We are British commandos,' he said. 'We ask for your help as loyal Frenchmen. Above all we ask that you do not say anything of what you have seen to the Germans.'

Yves Ardouin, who was accepted by the fishermen as their informal leader, replied rather gruffly that they should not under any circumstances stay where they were. The Germans carried out regular armed patrols – often several times a day – along the banks of the Chenal de St Vivien and the edges of the estuary. They would have to move. He pointed to a nearby prominence some 200 yards away – the Pointe aux Oiseaux – and told them they would be safer there among the reeds, stunted trees and tamarisk bushes which crowned the sandy feature. Two fishermen left their boats and walked along the dyke to show the visitors their hiding place, while the Marines paddled parallel with them, meeting them on the sandy shore at the base of the point. After the canoes were dragged into cover, the fishermen helped erase the tracks they had made in the dry sand and mud at the water's edge. Hasler must have realised his extreme good fortune that the first people down to the mouth of the Chenal de St Vivien that morning were the fishermen of the town and not the regular early morning German patrol.

After the fishermen left, Hasler supervised the concealment of the canoes, first throwing a camouflage net over each and then covering them with foliage and branches. When he was satisfied he took the first watch himself, telling his Marines to brew up tea and get some sleep. Sparks pulled out his flask of rum. When Hasler spotted the flask, Sparks thought he was about to be in trouble. But Hasler's only words were: 'After you.'

Meanwhile, the St Vivien fishermen and women went about their day's work gathering oysters on the exposed sandbanks of the estuary.

Five miles north of the shellfish gatherers, Mlle Jeanette Lhermet and her cousin, Mano Etinette, arrived for work at the German camp just behind the Pointe de Grave at around dawn, as they did most mornings. Conscripted by the Germans to work at the camp soon after the occupation of Le Verdon, Jeanette was the camp commandant's cook and her cousin a cleaner.

The camp was one of many in the area among the pine forests and the sand dunes. Next door, across the railway line, was the naval camp. Further towards the Pointe de Grave, near the ferry terminal, were the commandeered houses of local fishermen which now housed the personnel and offices of the flak battery and the crews of the German ferry service which crossed to and from Royan. Back towards Le Verdon, on the Soulac road, there were larger infantry cantonments, tank parks, a small airstrip, an ammunition dump and a firing range.

This morning, when the two cousins arrived, they found the area abuzz with activity and the canteen full of soldiers, including an early morning patrol which had just returned and was tucking into breakfast. Outside, laid out on a trestle table, was the body of a young man in a strange camouflage uniform who the patrol had found dead at the water's edge on La Chambrette beach, only three hundred yards or so from the point at which Hasler had said his goodbyes to Sheard and Moffatt. His face was grey and his hands were white. Water still dripped from his sodden clothing.

A few moments later another man was brought in, wearing the same kind of uniform. He was in a bad way with the cold – but he was alive.

They gave him something warm to drink and took him away – to the first aid centre close by, Jeanette thought.[2] She heard afterwards that he was one of two men who had walked into one of the old French fishermen's houses at the end of the Pointe, thinking it was occupied by locals. But they had bumped instead into one of the German anti-aircraft batteries and had been arrested. Later that morning they were taken across the water to German naval headquarters in the Fort de Chay in Royan.

In the very early hours of this morning, Admiral Johannes Bachmann, staying in the guest house reserved for VIPs in Royan, was woken to be told that 'two English seamen' had been captured by a Luftwaffe flak unit (Flak Unit 595) stationed near the tip of the Pointe de Grave. 'The doctor of the Flak unit declared that the prisoners arrived soaked to the bone, their faces mottled with green. Footsteps confirmed that the men had arrived at the shore at the same level as the Le Verdon battery, which is currently not occupied. A folding canoe has been spotted at low tide near the Pointe de Grave.'[3]

At 0915 that morning Bachmann crossed the estuary from Royan to Le Verdon to inspect the little flotilla of harbour defence vessels at the Môle d'Escale which had caused Hasler such difficulty the night before. After the inspection he was led to the two 'shipwrecked' men, who were paraded for him, shivering in the morning cold, on the road nearby.[4]

During the day, further discoveries were made, including 'foot-prints as far as the lighthouse, magnetic limpet mines, maps of the Gironde estuary, aerial photos of the Bordeaux port installation, camouflage material, food and drinking water for several days'.[5] In a report written that afternoon explaining his actions to his superiors in Berlin, Bachmann complained that at first the counter-intelligence services in Bordeaux refused to interrogate the two men on the grounds that they were naval personnel and should be sent initially to the naval intelligence interrogation centre at Fallingbostel in Lower Saxony.[6]

However, Bachmann claimed, he had insisted. Although the two men had 'declared that they were shipwrecked English sailors'[7] it was clear from the equipment discovered that they were in fact saboteurs. He ordered that an interrogator be sent up from Bordeaux immediately.

Lieutenant Harstick[8] of Bordeaux counter-espionage arrived later that morning and was briefed by Bachmann: 'I drew [his] attention to the importance of the following points: from where were the prisoners disembarked and from what vessel? what was their mission? what was the number of men involved in the sabotage operation? I told him of my intention to execute the prisoners after their interrogation for attempted sabotage.'[9]

Outside the mouth of the Chenal de St Vivien, the tide turned that morning at 1030. Laden with the day's harvest of shellfish, the Ardouins, Chaussats and other fishing families caught the flood back up the Chenal to their tiny port outside St Vivien en Médoc. But not before passing the Pointe aux Oiseaux, where they left the Marines the remains of their food – some pâté, some bread and a half-empty bottle or two of wine.

By the time they were back in St Vivien, all on the boats that day knew that they had committed acts which, if the Germans were to find out about them, would lead some to the firing squad and place the remainder at risk of transportation to German concentration camps. They swore among themselves never to talk of the matter again and to tell no one what they had seen: neither their dearest, nor their friends, nor their families. And this secret they kept for the rest of the war, until the armistice in 1945.

There was only one exception to this iron rule of silence. Jean Baudray ran the Café de Progrès in St Vivien and it was here that the fishermen would go for a drink after they returned each day. Regarded as wise and utterly trustworthy, Baudray was often sought out for advice on matters of importance. They would, the fishermen decided, let him into their secret and ask for his advice. Baudray listened and was clear. They had done the right thing. They should now gather more food and take it out to the foreigners. Baudray himself, however, had a heart condition, so it was agreed that Yves Ardouin and Baudray's sixteen-year-old daughter, Jeanne, would cycle out with food to the Pointe aux Oiseaux after dark that night.

At about the same time as the fishermen of St Vivien were telling their story to Jean Baudray, a dispatch rider delivered a telegram to Richmond Terrace in London. It was addressed to Mountbatten from Admiral Sir Max Horton, Commander-in-Chief Submarines. 'The following signal has been received from Tuna: Operation Frankton completed at 21h00 7 December.'

That evening, five hundred miles to the south, Admiral Bachmann wrote up his journal in his small, precise, spindly hand. Taking care to concentrate on what he had done (and what others had not done) after the capture of the two raiders, he ended his day's entry:

> I have ordered that at the end of the interrogation, if the statements made until now are confirmed, the prisoners are to be executed for attempted sabotage.

> The disembarkation of the prisoners is probably linked to the investigations we carried out on 7/12, around 22h00 at the mouth of the Gironde. The searches, carried out with searchlights, were without result.

Hasler and his team at the Pointe aux Oiseaux spent a nervous day fearing that the St Vivien fishermen had reported their presence to the Germans. They saw a number of spotter aircraft flying up and down the banks of the estuary, clearly looking for something. This probably meant that the fishermen had not talked, as that would have resulted, not in aircraft overhead, but in German troops storming their position. Perhaps all this activity was because Wallace and Ewart – or Sheard and Moffatt – had been captured? Perhaps the Germans had been alerted to their presence?

But air activity aside, the day was uneventful, enabling the Marines to lie down, head to toe, inside their canoes and catch up on much-needed sleep. The canoes gave them some protection from the chill, although without sleeping bags or any kind of covering, the cold was still intense.

They also managed to make several brews of tea in the billy-cans carried in each canoe, which were heated over solid paraffin-block 'Tommy cookers'. This had to be done discreetly, for although the little cookers had almost no visible flame, their distinctive smell could carry a long way downwind.

Their rations consisted of a tube of condensed milk, some meat mixture resembling Spam, a small tin of cheese, a hard oatmeal block from which they could make porridge (but which was more usually eaten cold as a biscuit), a packet of dried fruit, some hard tack biscuits, a tin of rather stodgy fruit pudding (known by the Marines as 'figgy duff'), a few bars of chocolate and some sweets. Fresh water was a problem, as they had sweated heavily during the night and there was none available on the Pointe aux Oiseaux. Each canoe carried five half-gallon cans of water, but this had to be carefully rationed as it was never possible to know when they would get access to fresh water again.

During the day there were weapons to clean and canoes to repair, inspect and repack. Sparks was able to use the time to mend a small leak in *Catfish* which had caused trouble the previous night, using the little repair kit carried in each canoe.[10]

They had their only real scare as dusk was drawing in, when their sentry suddenly whispered urgently to Hasler: 'Look! Jerries!' All eyes turned in the direction of his pointed finger and saw a line of some fifty shapes advancing towards them through the gathering dusk. Every man reached for his weapon and fighting knife as they tensed themselves for battle. Then, according to Lucas Phillips, Hasler raised his binoculars – and relaxed.

'You can stand easy. They're not Jerries – just the same line of stakes that we've been looking at all day!'

'But they were moving!' said Mills.

'Just our imagination. Shows we're a bit on edge. We must shake it off.'

'Glad we didn't have to shake them off,' quipped Laver, dryly. 'Bit too many for us they'd have been!'

'That's true. Now better get some sleep while you can. We can't start for some hours yet.'[11]

At about this time, two unlit bicycles carrying large packages quietly left St Vivien. In her package, Jeanne Baudray had included the last of her precious chocolate as a gift for the foreign raiders. The two cyclists left their bicycles at the halfway point and continued their journey on foot. When they reached the British major's camp, they found two men sleeping and one on guard with the major. The others were very cold and fatigued, but the major seemed completely unaffected. He chatted with them for a while in his broken French, frequently stressing that they should say nothing to the Germans. Yves Ardouin told him not to worry – they wouldn't.

Then it was time to say goodbye. Yves Ardouin said, 'I suppose you're on your way to Bordeaux?' The major denied it firmly. He offered to light the way for the two locals through the trees with a torch, for the night was very dark. But Ardouin refused, saying it was too dangerous: German eyes were everywhere. The major's last words, as they shook hands in the darkness, were: 'Merci. Merci beaucoup.'[12]

Later, Jeanne Baudray asked Yves Ardouin if the raiders could have reached Bordeaux. He replied that it was – perhaps – just possible, but very unlikely. All the fishermen were of the same view: it would have been near impossible to make the journey in such frail craft. They would almost certainly have drowned or, more likely, been shot by the Germans.

Sunset that evening was at 1622, with moonset about an hour later at 1717. Hasler would no doubt have liked to leave as soon as it was dark and the moon was down, for he planned to cover some twenty-five miles that night. But high tide in the Pointe aux Oiseaux area occurred at around sunset (1646), meaning that if he left now he would be paddling against the ebb tide. In order to have the flood behind him, he had to wait until the tide turned at 2250.

A little before 2300, the Marines pulled the camouflage nets, branches and grass off Catfish and Crayfish and hauled them out of their hides among the tamarisk bushes. Since it was now low water, they had to drag their heavily laden canoes across more than half a mile of sandy mud, into which they sank up to their knees with every step. It was hard work and they sweated profusely. But at least the rising tide would erase their tracks in the next few hours.

They reached the water's edge at about 2330, launched their canoes into the flood tide and set off for the other side of the estuary on a southeasterly course. Hasler's actual compass setting may well have been closer to east than southeast, for he had to lay off for the strong southward push of the flood which would reach three or even four knots by the mid-point of his crossing.

One of the puzzles of this night is why Hasler decided to stick to his plan of trying to reach the eastern shore of the Gironde instead of continuing to head down its west bank, a shorter route which would have enabled him to catch up on lost time. However, the ISTD report produced for the Frankton planners shows that there were substantial port installations – and therefore, it had to be presumed, German troops

– at two points on the western bank of the Gironde between Le Verdon and Bordeaux: Trompeloup and Pauillac. These included two large dry docks, an oil refinery and cracking plant, oil jetties and a railway wharf at the former, and a copper blast furnace, together with small fishing port and facilities for loading and offloading smaller merchantmen (especially those in the wine trade) at the latter. Both of these were, like Le Verdon, centres of population and activity to be avoided.

The first hazards the two canoes encountered on launching that night were submerged sandbanks and areas of shallow water swept by rollers. These they had to cross head-on in order to reach the main shipping channel, which was marked down its length by buoys and flashing blue lights. Although it is not mentioned in any account, there may have been a low mist lying over the water at this stage of their crossing, because, in the middle of the navigation channel, Hasler's men were suddenly surprised by a convoy of six or seven large merchantmen heading for Bordeaux which suddenly loomed up out of the night behind them. They had to paddle hard to avoid being ploughed under and were then nearly swamped by the ships' wakes. Once clear, they froze to avoid being seen by anyone standing on deck and then relaxed, watching the great black shapes continue upstream, the reflection of their port lights dancing in the ripples left behind.[13]

'More targets for us, Sir,' quipped Sparks.[14]

Having crossed the shipping lane, Hasler set a bearing of 135 degrees on his compass and led the two canoes down the middle of the estuary, following a course parallel with the shipping channel. This positioned him in the middle of the maximum flow of the flood tide, which helped push him down the estuary and ever closer to its eastern shore. The two canoes reached a point close to the eastern bank just above the Porte de Collonges at about 0500. Here Hasler turned south, following a line about a mile offshore until the time came for them to find a suitable lying-up place before dawn. As the last hours of night ebbed away, the weather suddenly turned even colder and Hasler noted that the salt spray from their paddles froze on their canoe canopies and their woollen gloves. As they paddled, their tunics, stiff with ice, crackled like starched shirts. Now tiredness was beginning to take hold. Hasler spotted that *Catfish* was no longer holding a steady course. He looked round, saw Sparks beginning to flag and passed him some Benzedrine tablets. A little later he gave some to Laver and Mills as well.[15] He was afterwards to comment that this was the moment when he began to realise the quiet authority and leadership of Corporal Laver, who had not shone during training but whose steadiness and capacity for endurance was now increasingly in evidence.[16]

With the eastern sky beginning to show faint streaks of light, Hasler was now looking urgently for a place to lie up. This time, luck was on their side. Hasler, who had exceptional night vision,[17] spotted, coming down at right angles to the bank, lines of double hedges, each enclosing a drainage ditch (these features are known locally as *esteys*). He paddled into one of these and stepped out straight onto a field. It was a near perfect place for lying up. When the tide dropped, their canoes would rest on the bottom of the ditch and would be invisible from the river. Hasler carried out his usual reconnaissance of the area to make sure that they had not landed near a German position and then told the others to camouflage their canoes, brew up some tea and get some sleep. Here they could be secure and comfortable all day.

They had covered another twenty-five miles that night – only this time in six hours rather than eleven. They were now more than halfway to their target.

But Hasler and his Marines were not the only ones busy driving that day. Having ordered the two 'shipwrecked sailors' to be taken to Royan, Bachmann now ordered that they should be transferred back across the estuary to Le Verdon in order to be interrogated by the special interrogation officer, *Kapitän-Leutnant* Harstick, who finally arrived from the counter-espionage office at Bordeaux in the late morning and swiftly identified the two prisoners as Wallace and Ewart.

At 1600 the intelligence officer of the Wehrmacht's 708th Division, Captain Rosenberger, reported what had been found so far:

1 A dinghy at W 301,[18] anchored, some 100 meters in the water, not yet recovered due to the surf.
2 2 aerial photographs of Bordeaux submarine bunker and other small objects.
3 A map of the Gironde estuary at W 302 with military bases marked in colour.

Now the sound of German stable doors being slammed shut began to be heard from every corner of the Gironde.

At 2105, the 708th Divisional Headquarters in Royan sent a coded signal to Supreme Headquarters in Berlin giving a full resumé of events – including the initial belief that Wallace and Ewart were 'Anglo-American Marines' (caused no doubt by Wallace's thick Irish accent) and the fact that the two men had mistakenly blundered into the Luftwaffe sick-bay unit, believing it to have been occupied by French civilians. Most of this long message, which is instructive for its revelations about the confusions in the local German command structure, was dedicated to pointing out that it was Luftwaffe and naval units who had discovered Wallace and Ewart (and by inference been slow to react), while Wehrmacht units had led the response by initiating searches of the area. The divisional report included an explanation from the officer on the ground, *Oberleutnant* Pirkel, blaming the Luftwaffe for the delay in reporting the capture of the Marines:

> The Commander of the FLAK unit thought that they were shipwrecked. Only after the boat was discovered, flooded by the high tide (which is to be brought in tonight at low tide by the Navy) and when other equipment was found, did he realise that it must be a sabotage unit and informed the Battalion Soulac.

Pirkel went on to explain that he, as an army man, couldn't be blamed: after all, the incidents had taken place in areas controlled by the Luftwaffe or the Kriegsmarine, who had either not informed him of what happened, or failed to provide the appropriate documentation 'because it was the lunch hour'. He finished his report by listing for his superiors the instructions which had been sent – 'in the strongest possible terms' – to the Kriegsmarine and Luftwaffe demanding that they improve their performance in the future.

Meanwhile, Johannes Bachmann was also carefully listing in his diary (which, again, has the flavour of a description written for consumption by his superiors after the event) the actions he had taken during the day, ending with a report on the interrogation of Wallace and Ewart:

Towards 21h30 I received a telephone communication from Lt. Harstick informing me that the interrogations have resulted in some important information. One of the prisoners, a native of Glasgow, has refused to say anything at all. The second, an Irishman, has given some information. Bordeaux Counter Espionage requested I delay the execution order. I insisted they stick to my decision that the prisoners should be executed. But immediately afterwards I received a phone call from Capt. Krenig[19] in Paris to say that postponement of the execution is considered more important.

An hour and a half later, Bachmann received his reply from Berlin:

You are ordered to obtain from the prisoners, before execution and by all means necessary – including the promise of pardon and an undertaking to treat them well – the following information considered important by this Headquarters:

1 Were there other men disembarked, where and for what reason?
2 How were they delivered: from a surface vessel, a submarine or airplane?

Bachmann responded immediately:

Execution provisionally postponed. Interrogation will recommence 9.12.

Declaration already made by the older of the prisoners, an Irishman from Dublin:

a His comrade and he were the only men to be disembarked by a submarine, which had left England two weeks before.
b Their mission, according to him, consisted of sinking ships in the Gironde.

It was no doubt because of Berlin's insistence that 'all necessary means' should be used – a phrase that can only mean that extreme duress and torture were sanctioned – that, as we now know, a further telephone call took place that evening. It was made to *Fregattenkapitän* Dr Erich Feiffer of the Kriegsmarine Counter-Intelligence Section at Dulag North,[20] Wilhelmshaven, near Bremen, who described it after the war:

In the evening ... I was rung up by Commander Lange of the staff of Admiral Bachmann. He told me that the interrogation of the prisoners captured at the Pointe de Grave had to be carried out at all events and with no methods barred that same night, since the results had to be ready early the next morning. He said he was asking whether we had special means to extort a 'confession'... such as laughing pills or light projectors or drugs ... he said that he had been told that if we did not do this, then we would just have to hand them over to the Sicherheitsdienst to do it.[21]

Whatever means were used on Wallace and Ewart, they seem to have worked. At 0150 the following morning, at about the same time as Hasler was crossing the main shipping channels, *Kapitän-Leutnant* Harstick made a phone call from Wehrmacht Divisional Headquarters to Berlin, reporting the results of the interrogation so far:

The two Englishmen set sail from Portsmouth on a submarine about 14 days ago. The submarine had been cruising until yesterday evening due to bad weather and had launched the two men in a kayak in the Bay of Biscay, probably in front of the Gironde estuary, at the beginning of the night.

They had been given a course which they followed. After a while they saw a fire and headed towards it. Probably around 02:00 hours their boat capsized in the surf at Pointe de Grave. They alleged that they were only able to save their lives. They landed, supposedly, to get arrested. They are wearing an English uniform, consisting of drill trousers and a blouse, similar to a camouflage shirt. On the sleeves there are insignia inscribed 'Royal Navy' and badges for combined operations (Army, Navy, Air Force). No headgear.

Their alleged mission was to paddle at night, to hide on land during the day, to travel up the Gironde and to attach magnetic explosives to a German ship and to sink it by blowing a hole into the hull. They were carrying detailed maps of the Gironde up to Bordeaux and 2 aerial photographs from November 1942. On the maps, occupied and unoccupied areas were clearly marked. A magnet and some ammunition, a camouflage net and other equipment was found. It has not yet been possible to recover the capsized boat.

They were only informed about their mission on board the submarine, after they had been at sea for a week, by the Commander of submarine P 49.

The men were part of a group of 14 men which had been assembled in Portsmouth by the Navy. Assembly of the group had started approx. 9 months ago. In addition to these two men, the submarine was to drop off a further two men. This failed because the second kayak was damaged when it was launched.

After completing their mission the two prisoners were to try and reach unoccupied territory. They allege that they had not been given any French identity cards or addresses, nor any money.

The leader of the mission [Wallace] willingly provides information whereas the other man [Ewart] is very reluctant to tell the truth and claims not to know the purpose of their mission.[22]

Although we know that Harstick was assisted during his interrogation by a *Hauptmann* Glatzel (who penned the above report) and an English-speaking officer, *Oberleutnant* Weidemann, we do not know the precise means the interrogators used (though Glatzel reports that Wallace gave his information 'willingly'). If torture was used, however, then it is probable that it would have concentrated on Wallace. He was, as far as the Germans were concerned, the leader of the operation; it would not have been so open to him, as it was to Ewart, to claim ignorance.

Nowadays all Special Forces troops have to pass a realistic interrogation test on a regular basis. But in 1942, no such training was given, beyond the instruction to give only name, rank and service number.

There is good reason for this stipulation, apart from the fact that it is the minimum required by the Geneva Convention – for once an interrogator has any further information, he has a thread upon which he can pull until the truth is unravelled. The interrogator's most difficult task is to 'break a door' through his subject's initial barrier of silence. Once that is done, the rest becomes much easier. Breaking the barrier is frequently achieved by using some sort of duress – sleeplessness, uncomfortable restraint, torture – in order to induce a form of temporary mental breakdown in the prisoner so that he abandons his values and, for a period at least, accepts those proposed by the interrogator. Once this is achieved the prisoner has no further reason to withhold information and the interrogator's job is essentially done.

But sometimes a prisoner will make the fatal error of believing he is cleverer than his interrogator and therefore, capable of making his own judgements about what information he can safely give. In this case, the prisoner is himself giving the interrogator the open door he needs. Indeed – rather in the manner of TV detective Lieutenant Columbo – an interrogator will sometimes encourage his prisoners to believe that they are cleverer than he is, precisely in order to get the talking started.

Some have suggested that Wallace deliberately gave the Germans enough information on the operation to fool them into believing that it was all over, thus hiding from them the fact that Hasler and his men were still on the water. This is of course possible – though there is no supporting evidence and it is clear that Bobby Ewart took a different view of the wisdom of this approach. Even if this was Wallace's intention, it was a dangerous line to take: although Hasler's existence may have remained hidden, almost every other fact about the operation was now known by the Germans, leaving them open if they chose to take precautions which would have led almost certainly to Hasler's discovery.

There is however another possibility. Wallace may have been tempted into making revelations he never intended to make, believing that he could use his native wit to create a relationship with his interrogator different from the obdurate silence which may have been his best protection. If this was Wallace's strategy then it was misjudged, because it gave Harstick a cornucopia of information on Frankton which he should not have had.

Whatever happened, and however Harstick obtained his report, the Germans now knew, less than thirty hours after Frankton had begun, almost everything about its method, its means and its target. Only two crucial pieces of information had been withheld: that Hasler's men were still on the water and that Operation Frankton was still in progress.

At this point, however, Bachmann and the Germans made a classic tactical error. Keen to avoid blame from Hitler's headquarters for what had happened, they became fixated on satisfying Berlin rather than protecting Bordeaux. Perhaps it was overconfidence in their own superiority, or an excessive belief in the impregnability of their naval fortress; perhaps, like the fishermen of St Vivien, they simply thought it impossible for canoes to make it all the way to Bordeaux. These factors, more than any attempt by Wallace to deceive, led Bachmann to believe what he wanted to believe: that he was dealing with an operation which was over, rather than one which had only just begun. Because of this, he ordered his troops to take only half-hearted and inadequate measures to look for further raiders. As a senior German officer on Bachmann's staff was later to put it, they judged that this operation 'was a failure, as at first appeared the case, when the first two men were taken prisoner'.[23]

This error of judgement gave Blondie Hasler and his men the chance they needed to get through.

19

La Présidente Farm

Hasler and his little force had landed 150 yards from a secondary road running parallel to the shoreline, some 300 yards from a farmhouse called La Présidente[1] and near the little town of Braud et Saint Louis. They were in fact not very far south of the spot Hasler had chosen as his initial landing point if all had gone to plan on the first night. Instead, Hasler was now almost twenty-four hours behind schedule. It already looked likely that he would have to mount his attack a day later than planned – that is, on the fifth, rather than the fourth night after disembarking from HM/s *Tuna*.

There were other complications, too: from now on, the times of high and low water would become progressively more awkward for long nights of paddling, as the flood tide they needed to push them towards Bordeaux began to run over into the hours of daylight.

High tide at this point of the Gironde on the morning of 9 December was at 0737, with the sun rising twenty minutes later and, an hour after that, the moon climbing into a clear blue sky just over the eastern shoulder of the medieval citadel at Blaye, squatting on its rocky riverside bluff five miles to their south. The weather, though cold, was clear with a light, steady easterly wind and a slight morning haze lying over a flat, calm sea.

Soon after it was fully light and the Marines settled down for the day, they were interrupted by the furious barking of a small dog which suddenly appeared, hackles raised, outside their hide.[2] It was followed by a farmer whose look of curiosity turned quickly to shock when he saw what his dog had discovered. The Marines curled fingers over triggers, while Hasler made his now familiar pitch in bad French, explaining that they were British commandos on a mission and asking the intruder not to give them away.

Despite Hasler's German accent, Alibert Decombes, the tenant farmer of La Présidente who had been out on his morning round of his fields, accepted his story without hesitation and said, in the best traditions of French hospitality: 'Come up to the house and have a glass of wine. It'll do you all good!'

'We're very sorry, but we have to be going soon and so we can't accept your invitation.'

'Do you think the war will be over soon?'

'I have no idea. But in any case,' Hasler added, with perhaps more optimism than his situation warranted: 'I promise to come back after the war.'

'I'll count on it! My door will be wide open for you ... And I promise to say nothing to anyone about you.'[3]

The rest of the day was a quiet one for Hasler and his raiders. But, following the revelations obtained by the Germans from Wallace, there was a good deal of air activity during the day, chiefly from light spotter planes scouring the banks of the Gironde, one of which flew so low over the Marines' lying-up position that they could clearly see the pilot in the cockpit.[4]

German aircraft, however, were not the only ones busy above the Gironde that day. At 1400 an aerial reconnaissance Spitfire flying at 30,000 feet made a pass over the Gironde. When the photographs were analysed by the experts at RAF Medmenham, they showed that Sparks had been right: there were plenty of targets awaiting them. The RAF photo interpreters identified the following ships alongside in Bordeaux:

A tanker, probably the Italian *Todaro*.
A German ship, the *Usaramo*.
A German ship, the *Dresden*.
A German ship, the *Tannenfels*.
An ex-French ship, the *Alabama*.
A German ship, the *Portland*.
Six further merchant ships of over 200 feet in length lying alongside the quays of the port.

Their report also revealed that the German naval patrols in and around the estuary were unusually busy – the five small patrol vessels which had barred Hasler's way at Le Verdon two nights previously had been reinforced by a destroyer and were now escorting ships in and out of the Gironde and actively patrolling the estuary's waters.[5]

The information about the number and type of target ships in Bordeaux could not, of course, have been sent to Hasler and his team hiding at La Présidente Farm. But it could very easily have been sent to Claude de Baissac through Roger Landes, who was by now in regular Morse contact with London from his villa on the Cenon escarpment.

The Marines' only other visitors that day were a herd of cows who came to take a look at them before ambling off to graze elsewhere in the field. Hasler spent much of the day using his binoculars to study a dry dock at Trompeloup on the opposite bank, about five miles away. He noted in his later intelligence report that it contained a merchant vessel so big that its bows and stern stuck out from the dock at both ends. He also took the opportunity to discard some of the heavier stores they would no longer need, including his Thompson sub-machine gun.[6]

The German commanders, meanwhile, again spent the day doing their best to protect themselves from thunderbolts emanating from Berlin. Artillery General Gallenkamp sent a furious signal to Lieutenant-General Wilck, the Commander of 708th Infantry Division: 'I demand that Divisional Commanders exact the greatest punishment for the delay of the information concerning the capture of two English Marines arriving at General Command Headquarters.'

Meanwhile, Bachmann, his mind still concentrated on what to do with Wallace and Ewart, was also carefully recording his every action: '[I received orders at 1100] that the prisoners should be questioned by Corssen, an officer charged with special missions, and that their execution should be delayed until the completion of these interrogations.'[7]

That same afternoon, the stop press column in a London evening paper printed a report (repeated in a Portsmouth paper the following day and spotted by those who knew its significance in RMBPD), quoting a German High Command wireless statement: 'On 8 December a small British sabotage squad was engaged at the mouth of the Gironde River and finished off in combat.'

Mountbatten decided it would be best to pre-empt one of Churchill's famously querulous memos demanding to know what was going on and, indulging in more speculation than may have been wise, wrote a memo to the Prime Minister:

> It seems possible that the Germans may only have intercepted one section of the raiding party. The Commander of the party ... would probably have been with the leading section. The capture by the Germans of one section would not necessarily have compromised the other section, since no papers were carried, other than charts.[8]

This memo contained two convenient misrepresentations. First, Mountbatten claimed the raiders had only been captured, while the German report was clear that they had been 'finished off in combat'. And second, Mountbatten's reassurance to Churchill that the operation had 'not necessarily been compromised ... since no papers were carried' overlooked the fact that aerial reconnaissance photographs of Bordeaux harbour were carried in all canoes. He must have realised therefore that the Germans almost certainly knew (as indeed they did) the target of the raid.

Hasler knew that the tide would reach its lowest mark at this point of the Gironde at 1531 that day, after which, following a short period of slack water, the flood would begin to run down the estuary once more. He needed to make up time, but had to wait for darkness and moonset. With sunset at 1622 and a moon which would not set until 1845, Hasler had to waste three hours of flood tide before launching his canoes. This would leave only a short period of flood to assist his journey south before the tide turned. He would have to break his journey into two stages that night.

Just before dark, according to Sparks' account, Alibert Decombes paid a second visit to the strangers to wish them good luck:

'*Bonne chance*. I hate the Nazis. Your secret is safe with me.'

A reconstruction of the tides that night indicates that, by the time Hasler finally launched at a little after 1830, he had only 0.1 knot of tide behind him. He and his team were paddling in slack water and soon the tide would begin to turn against them with increasing force.

As they passed down the Île Patiras, the first of the small archipelago of islands which reach from this point down to the junction of the Dordogne and the Garonne, the Marines suddenly heard the throb of a motor-boat engine. They took swift refuge in a patch of tall reeds at the water's edge and watched a German patrol boat go by, its crew chattering away as they probed the banks with high-powered torches. Hasler noticed that the boat had no lights, confirming his suspicion that it was probably looking for intruders. They listened to the sound of the engine fading away, their canoes bobbing up and down in the boat's wake as it washed through the reeds. When Hasler deemed the coast clear, they slipped out of their cover and continued on single paddles, hugging close in under the overhanging trees and bushes on the riverbank.

In fact, Hasler and his team were only able to make some four miles south before the tide forced them ashore at 2000 on a small island called Île de Bouchaud[9] between the town of Blaye immediately to their east, and, to their west, moored on the opposite bank of the Gironde, the black, silent bulk of the French liner *De Grasse*.[10] The tide was still relatively high at this point, so it was not too difficult for them to get their canoes ashore. Now they could only wait and snatch a little sleep until the tide once again turned in their favour.

At Fort Médoc, on the west bank of the Gironde about a mile away, and almost exactly opposite where Hasler and the remnants of his force were lying up, Jean Raymond and his father were indulging in a little night fishing. This was strictly illegal, because it meant breaking the curfew. It was also boring and, on such a night, very cold. Still, the risk and the discomfort was worth it, with food so scarce and the price of fresh fish high.

Suddenly the two men heard a strange rhythmic splashing sound bearing down on them. Soon they could hear urgent voices whispering in a foreign tongue. Germans!

'Lie down in the boat and they'll pass without seeing us.'

Crouching as low as they could in the bottom of their boat, the two fishermen, hearts pounding, watched as *Cuttlefish*, carrying Jack MacKinnon and James Conway, paddled furiously by twenty yards away.[11]

We do not know exactly where MacKinnon and Conway spent the previous day, but given the location and time of this encounter and the disposition of the tides, it seems probable that the pair did not follow Hasler across to the eastern bank of the Gironde but found a lying-up position on the western bank somewhere between Le Verdon and Fort Médoc.

While Hasler and his men were waiting for the tide to turn, Bachmann received orders to transfer Wallace and Ewart to the SD headquarters at Place Tourny in Bordeaux.[12] When they arrived there at a little after 2 a.m.,[13] they were immediately incarcerated in the underground cells beneath the building.[14]

Wallace and Ewart had thus effectively passed out of the hands of German military security and into the hands of the Gestapo, for Place Tourny was the headquarters of the *Kommandeur der Sicherheitspolizei und des SD* (KdS),[15] the regional German police structure which coordinated all counter-espionage and security activity across southwest France – including the *Abwehr*, the *Feldpolizei*, the *Geheime Staatspolizei* (or Gestapo) and the *Sicherheitsdienst* (SD). The senior officer at Place Tourny at the time was, nominally, SS *Sturmbannführer* Dr Hans Luther. But in practical terms it was the Gestapo element,[16] under the command of Bordeaux's Gestapo chief, 29-year-old *Hauptscharführer* Friedrich Wilhelm Dohse,[17] which called the shots (often literally).

Dohse was by all accounts a most unusual Gestapo officer. Smart, well dressed, sophisticated and highly intelligent, especially when it came to human psychology, he spoke near perfect French[18] and enjoyed the wary respect even of many in the Resistance for his observance of the codes of war and his reasonable treatment of suspects. The same could not be said for his assistants, the most senior being his three SS lieutenants, Künesch (a dyed-in-the-wool Nazi who was infamous for his use of torture[19]), Küdell and Scheuder.

It seems likely that, given their importance, Wallace and Ewart would have been dealt with by senior members of Dohse's team, if not by him personally. (According to Hans Luther's orders, all prisoners entering Place Tourny had to be interrogated by Dohse before being passed on to others.[20]) Only one member of Dohse's staff could speak good English: the head of the political department in Place Tourny, Gunther Buckmann, who was described as thin faced with a sallow complexion and a fondness for torturing prisoners.[21] While supervision of the interrogation of Wallace and Ewart would have been Dohse's responsibility, the interrogators would probably have been Buckmann and Künesch, especially if torture was to be used.

Meanwhile, on the Île de Bouchaud, low water that night occurred at a little after 0235. Hasler and his Marines started to lower their canoes carefully down the now fully exposed six-foot almost vertical bank of the island onto the bed of ooze at the bottom and haul them across the mud to the water, avoiding the logs and debris thrown up by the winter floods. Like their launch from the Pointe des Oiseaux, it was hard, sweltering, painstaking work. A single moment of lost concentration might result in a broken, damaged or catastrophically torn canoe.

Hasler records that, conscious of the need to make up time, they tried to launch their canoes at 0200, well before low tide. But they found the ebb flow still too strong for them and had to wait, sitting in their canoes, for forty-five minutes before finally getting away at 0245, heading for the western bank.

Catfish and Crayfish were soon in the narrow channel which runs between the long slim shape of the Île Cazeau (also known as Île Verte) and the Médoc peninsula on the Gironde's western shore. Here they were in confined waters and Hasler, concerned about the noise of double-bladed paddling, ordered them to use single paddles, relying on the surging flood to carry them through the narrows. They were now past the junction of the Dordogne and the Garonne and only fifteen miles from their targets.

At 0630, with an hour of darkness left, Hasler decided it was time to look for a lying-up position on the Île Cazeau. He saw the dim outlines of a small jetty sticking out from the shore. Though this could mean that people frequented the place, the thick woods surrounding the area would make excellent cover. Deciding to take the risk and go ashore for a reconnaissance, he quickly found a small path running through the woods and cautiously followed it, coming after about 100 yards to a small clearing in the middle of which was what appeared to be a wall. Creeping closer, he saw that it was in fact a sandbagged German gun position. Remembering the intelligence reports that had warned him of anti-aircraft positions on the Île Cazeau, he quickly withdrew and rejoined the others.

They paddled a little further downstream. But by now, as the tide swept them towards Bordeaux at nearly two knots, they were in danger of being carried past the island altogether. They had no choice but to go ashore very close to its pointed southern end. Dawn was breaking and they could hear the sound of traffic and human movement from the opposite shore. Hasler carried out another swift reconnaissance and then ordered his men to drag their canoes ashore and camouflage them as best they could in the only place available – some long grass in rough marshy ground in the middle of a field inhabited by a herd of cows.

It was going to be a long, uncomfortable and very exposed day.

At first light that morning a party of farm hands from Blaye landed on the Île Cazeau at a point some four miles north of Hasler's position. According to evidence collected after the war, they stumbled across two British soldiers and a canoe hidden in the undergrowth on the east side of the island. Though they did not know it at the time, MacKinnon and Conway had chosen the same island as Hasler, Sparks, Laver and Mills.[22]

The success of a deep-penetration Special Forces operation depends on the raiders' ability to approach the enemy without being seen. But moving invisibly through densely populated countryside such as the banks of the Gironde is extremely difficult. By the second day of Frankton, Hasler and his team had been spotted by all those on the *chaloupes* at the Pointe aux Oiseaux; by Jeanne Baudray (and by inference her father); by farmer Alibert Decombes and his dog at La Présidente Farm; by Jean Raymond and his son, the two night fishermen; and, this morning, by the woodmen from Blaye. From this moment on, Frankton hung, not only on the skills of the Marines, but also on the hope that none of those who had seen them would betray them to the Germans.

20

Approach and Execution

10–11 December 1942

The fine settled weather of the last few days began to break during 10 December as patchy cloud blew in on a rising southeasterly breeze. Late in the day there were scurries of light drizzle, with heavier rain towards evening.

None of this improved the comfort of Hasler and his three Marines, who felt extremely exposed sitting in their canoes, hidden in their boggy lying-up position only by hastily thrown camouflage nets and the long grass. As dawn broke they could see, through a thin screen of bare trees, the dim outline of the German gun position they had nearly stumbled upon just an hour ago. They could even hear the clanking of cooking vessels and the occasional voices of the gun crew.

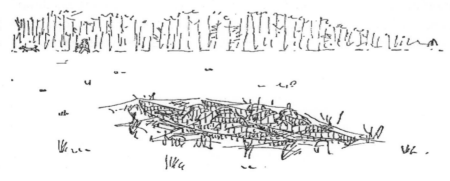

Figure 8

The need to stay absolutely still and to respond immediately to the danger of discovery meant they could not lie down in their canoes but had to sit upright, a position in which it was very difficult to get much sleep. Soon limbs became stiff and cold. But there could be no question of moving around to loosen them, or to cook, or to smoke or brew tea; they had to make do with cramped limbs, plain water and cold rations. Even leaving their canoes to urinate or defecate was out of the question. These bodily functions had to be accomplished using small slow movements and the single bailer attached by a string to the bottom of their boats.

But their day on the Île Cazeau was not just extremely uncomfortable; it was also nerve-racking.

In mid-morning some cattle were let into the field to the north and wandered down to inspect this strange new object hidden in the long grass of their grazing area. For some minutes the cows stood around them in an inquisitive circle, unaffected by the Marines' attempts to shoo the animals away with hissed imprecations. While the cows were carrying out their inspection, a spotter plane flew low over the strange gathering, clearly searching the island. Eventually the cows moved off to graze further down the field. Some time later a man and his dog walked along the edge of the wood at the corner of the field, about a hundred yards away. But this time the dog did not catch their scent – probably, Hasler later speculated, because the smell of the cows had masked their odour.[1] According to Bill Sparks' account, two German soldiers from the nearby anti-aircraft position wandered to the edge of the wood and stood looking out into the field, talking and smoking, before rejoining their colleagues.

Hasler's original plan had set the ambitious target of the next night – the fourth after their launch from *Tuna* – as the night for their attack. But he knew that to have the best chance of planting their limpet mines undetected, they would need to catch the tide on the turn so that they could drift silently on the last of the flood up the line of ships to be attacked and then drift back down again on the beginning of the ebb, so giving them a double opportunity to place their limpets before making good their escape downstream with the ebb gathering pace behind them. The moon, however, would not set tonight until 1925. In such confined waters and with an increasing density of habitation on the western bank, Hasler knew he could not afford to leave before the moon was low on the horizon; perhaps around 1845. With high water at Bordeaux occurring at around 2030, this would leave him less than two hours to cover the remaining twelve nautical miles and plant his limpets. There was no chance they could make the *Port de la Lune* in time. Indeed, with no more than ninety minutes after high tide when there would be either slack water or an ebb sufficiently weak for them to be able to paddle against it,[2] he had to reach his next lying-up position no later than 2330. He therefore had no option but to delay his attack until the following night, 11–12 December. Not knowing that MacKinnon and Conway in *Cuttlefish* were actually behind him, he must have speculated that they might, just possibly, be close enough to mount their own attack that night, so pre-empting any possibility of him launching his own on the following one. But that was a risk he had to take.

This night's paddle would therefore be a short one, enabling them, he hoped, to establish a forward base close enough to their targets to be able to reach them at the turn of the tide the following night.

It is all too easy, simply recounting the catalogue of events since their launch from HM/s *Tuna*, to overlook how Hasler himself must have felt during this day. Hasler never indicated, whether in his demeanour to his colleagues, in his subsequent report, or in anything he said afterwards, that he had a single low moment or crisis of confidence either during the period of Operation Frankton itself, or the subsequent escape phase. But this day must have been, if not the lowest point of his journey, then very close to it.

He must have been approaching the limits even of his formidable powers of endurance. Cold, wet, cramped, stiff, exposed, sleepless, living every moment within a hair's breadth of discovery, his decimated team lost somewhere behind him, the daylight hours of 10 December must have felt like an eternity as he waited for friendly darkness to hide them once more.

For Hasler as leader, however, there were more than physical challenges to endure. Without MacKinnon, he carried the burden of leadership entirely alone. He had suffered blow after blow and lost two-thirds of his force. He was now in the very bowels of enemy territory – an enemy moreover who, judging by the air- and water-borne patrols, were now almost certainly fully alerted to the nature of his target. Hasler would not have been human if he had not, during this cold, damp, dangerous day, wondered at the futility of what he was attempting.

Even if they succeeded, what difference could they possibly make with such a tiny force; such a small amount of explosive? And after the mission was over – what then awaited them? It was a question that suggested its own bleak answer: the high probability of capture, torture and death before a firing squad.

Although Hasler never showed it and Lucas Phillips never mentions it, we know that he did experience fear. As will be recalled, he had confided to a friend after the Norway campaign that he had been plagued by doubts as to whether his courage would hold up enough not to let his men down at the crucial moment. This was the crucial moment and Hasler was altogether too human not to have had fear and despair, accompanying doubt and exhaustion, gnawing at his spirit.

The truth was that the other three Marines sharing the day's discomforts with him were, at this point, little more than explosive carriers. Whether now, so close, they could drive their attack home against an alerted enemy, rested upon the singular pillar of Hasler's will, courage and determination.

Operation Frankton depended upon a very special kind of courage. Not the brief 'bubble' courage bolstered by the speed and violence of a 'butcher and bolt' raid; but the slow, sustained, cold-blooded nerve that endured hour after hour over long days and nights, as Hasler's raiders worked their way cautiously, ever closer to their targets.

At last, dusk drew its cloak around them. Just before night fell, the cows returned to take a final look at the intruders before ambling off into the night with a final swish of their tails.

At 0845 this morning, according to Johannes Bachmann's diary:

The ADC to the Chief of the SD in Paris SS Obersturmführer Dr Schmidt, telephoned the ADC to the Commandant-in-Chief of the Navy and demanded a deferment of the execution of the prisoners because their interrogation had still not been completed and they had already furnished a lot of very important information on the organisation and formation of their unit.

After a conversation with the Chief of Staff [in Supreme Headquarters in Berlin], the SD in Bordeaux received an order that they were to take no further instructions on this matter, unless they came directly from the Führer's Supreme Headquarters.

We do not know whether any such instructions arrived. Nor, if they did arrive, what they said. Nor do we know whether, when the naval officer in command of Bordeaux Port, Commander Ernst Kühnemann, told his secretary Theodore Prahm at the end of his day's work that he would be out of contact for the evening, he did so because he thought nothing more would happen that night – or because he knew something would, and wanted to be as far away as possible when it did.

We do know however that, not long after Kühnemann left, Lieutenant Prahm received a telephone call at the Kriegsmarine harbour headquarters in Bordeaux from the duty chief petty officer: the SD at Place Tourny had asked for an execution detail to be available for that night. What should he do? Prahm recalled that he had seen the reports of the two 'Englishmen' who had been captured at the Pointe de Grave and had read Admiral Bachmann's orders that they should be executed. The request to provide an execution detail seemed to him, therefore, perfectly in order. He agreed that the detail should be provided.

At 1845 that night, *Catfish* and *Crayfish* launched into a two-knot flood tide from the Île Cazeau, where they had the same difficulty as the previous night getting their canoes down the steep banks and across the exposed mudflats to the water's edge. They were glad to be moving again. The night was perfect for the next stage of their passage. The moderate breeze had shifted round to the south, ruffling the water as it funnelled up the river, blowing a refreshing chill into their faces and carrying their small sounds away behind them. The sky was largely overcast with occasional scurries of rain, which meant that, after the moon had dipped below the wooded skyline on their right at 1925, the night was unusually dark.

Hasler led them first down the centre of the river and then, as the banks began to close in, told them to change to single paddles and move closer to the western bank. By now most of their speed was due to the tide carrying them up the river towards the great port, the dim glow of whose lights began to illuminate the dark shore ahead. Rounding the last left-hand bend at 2230, they suddenly saw the lights of the sub-port of Bassens South on the east bank of the river and, some two miles further upstream, the glow from the main port itself. Soon they could hear the clank of cranes loading and unloading the ships lying alongside and see, beyond them, the lights of Bordeaux spreading out into the distance. Suddenly all tiredness fell away, to be replaced by excitement and anticipation. At last their quarry was in sight.

Somewhere behind them, MacKinnon and Conway had also launched from their daytime hiding place. But they cannot have gone far when disaster struck. *Cuttlefish* collided with a submerged obstacle – perhaps a fishing stake or an underwater post – which neither MacKinnon nor Conway had been able to see in the darkness. The damage was sudden, catastrophic and irreparable. *Cuttlefish* sank so quickly, weighed down with gear and limpet mines, that though MacKinnon was able to grab his escape bag before he got clear, Conway found himself trapped by the leg and dragged down by the doomed craft, only managing to struggle free – again with nothing but his escape bag – at the very last moment. There was by now a strong flood tide running, so in the time it took Conway to get clear of the boat, the two men became separated. They must have been close to the bank of the Île Cazeau, however, because both were able to make it back to the island – though neither knew at the time where the other was, or even if they had made it safely to shore.[3]

There has been speculation that disaster struck *Cuttlefish* and her crew at Bec d'Ambès, the name given to the point at the junction of the Gironde and the Garonne. But later reports make it clear that they were actually wrecked close to the southern end of the east side of the Île Cazeau, possibly on the opposite side of the narrow point of the island from which Hasler and his team had left perhaps only minutes before.

At about the same time as MacKinnon and Conway were struggling to get clear of the sinking *Cuttlefish*, a car arrived to take Theodore Prahm from the Bordeaux Kriegsmarine headquarters to Place Tourny. In a later report to a War Crimes investigation, Prahm (described as a 'colourless bank clerk'[4]) takes up the story:

> [When I arrived] the Naval execution detail was already outside the Place Tourny in a truck. The two prisoners were waiting in a big car under the guard of SD men. The head of SD would not accept my repeated refusal [to carry out the execution] and my demand that he should have the execution carried out by his men, pointing out that execution by the Navy had been expressly ordered. He explained that, as he was in charge of the operation, he bore the responsibility. He insisted on haste, as he had to report to one of the highest Headquarters by 2300 or 2400 hrs. I had no option but to comply with his request as ... the head of the SD had the necessary authority and, in addition, bore responsibility for the action.
>
> I joined the head of SD[5] in his car and the column moved off (one truck with the execution squad consisting of 16 ratings and a Chief Petty Officer, one big car with the two prisoners and 3 or 4 members of the SD as guard, a further car with the head of the SD, his driver and me). We drove first to the submarine base where we fetched a naval surgeon, as the harbour surgeon had not been available ... When I asked whether a priest was coming with us, the head of the SD replied that a priest had been with the two prisoners for the whole of the afternoon. He also said that the death sentence had been read out to the prisoners before their departure.
>
> The column then drove into a wood, which, as I recollect (and it was difficult to see where we were going at night) was to the north-east of the town, approximately five to ten km outside the town.
>
> So far as I can recollect, the SD had already had two coffins put ready at the edge of the wood. These coffins were taken along by the lorry to the place of execution.
>
> The place of execution itself was a sand-pit, the far side of which served to stop the bullets. The SD men dug in two posts, which were lying there. The prisoners were tied to the posts; this was the first time that I saw the prisoners. The two cars were then placed in such a position that the beams of their headlights shone on the prisoners.

I placed the sixteen men into two rows, the front row kneeling, gave each group its target and gave the order to fire. Immediately after, I ordered the squad to turn about and march off. The surgeon went to the men who had been shot, while at the same time, two SD men, who had already drawn their pistols, fired several shots into the back of the heads of the victims. The surgeon then established that death had taken place. The time was 2330 hours.

The SD men placed the dead bodies in the coffins and loaded these onto the truck. As it appeared to me – and to my men too – as irreverent to get into the lorry with the coffins we therefore went up to the road at the edge of the wood. The truck also came up there, after the two coffins had been placed in a building, which was also at the edge of the wood ...

I then drove back into town with my men.[6]

21

Priming the Weapon

11 December 1942

When, the following morning, Johannes Bachmann read Prahm's report of the execution of Wallace and Ewart, he added in pencil at the bottom: 'Security Services should have done this. Phone the naval Officer in Command in future cases. The Operation was particularly favoured by the weather conditions and the dark night.'[1]

That same dark night also favoured Hasler and his tiny band of hunters. As their two comrades stood before the firing squad, four miles away, the crews of *Catfish* and *Crayfish* arrived opposite the merchant ships which, even at this late hour, were being worked by the cranes of Bassens South. The whole river was illuminated by the lights on the quayside opposite the cranes. But the two canoes creeping down the dark reed-lined bank were invisible to those working in the pools of light on the far side of the river. At this point Hasler encountered, sticking out into the river, a small pontoon pier at the end of which a coaling lighter was moored. *Catfish* and *Crayfish* slipped between the pontoons and under the pier. Emerging from the other side they found the river bank bordered by high reeds into which small water channels ran at right angles. They pushed their way down one of these and secured the canoes side by side so that they were well hidden. It was a piece of real luck to have found such an ideal hiding place.

Indeed, it seems that this was the moment when Hasler's luck changed. Until now Operation Frankton had been dogged by bad luck at almost every turn. From now on, fortune never left Hasler; though the same could not be said for all his companions.

After his night of absence, Commander Kühnemann arrived at the Kriegsmarine harbour headquarters early this morning, noting in his diary:

> As a result of a telephone message informing of the interception at the mouth of the Gironde of a rubber canoe [sic] and the capture of its occupants (suspected saboteurs), the captains and first officers of cargo ships have been instructed to increase their vigilance and watch keeping.[2]

Kühnemann, as port commander, was responsible for some twenty-five ships, most of them cargo vessels, lying alongside the quays of the port of Bordeaux. Among those at Bassens South were the *Portland* (7100 tons) and ex-French merchantman the *Alabama* (5600 tons). In the main port were two separate clutches of ships, lying 100 yards or so apart along the Quai des Chartrons. We do not know the names of the second group, which seems to have numbered around ten. The group closest to Hasler lay just beyond the entrance of the lock gate which gave access to the inner basin of Bordeaux harbour, where the newly constructed concrete submarine pens were located.

Of this group of seven ships, the first in line was a tanker. The second was a passenger/cargo ship. Then came a freighter, the *Dresden* (5567 tons), alongside which was moored another, smaller tanker, the *Cap Hadid*.[3] Next in line was another merchantman, the *Tannenfels* (7840 tons). She had only just slipped into Bordeaux under a false name – *Taronga* from the Norwegian port of Tønsberg – in an attempt to fool the British blockade. And finally, at the end of the line, was a ship whose identity we do not know,[4] alongside which was moored a German naval patrol vessel, *Sperrbrecher 5* (roughly the equivalent of a small frigate).[5]

Hasler and his men were not the only ones closing in on their prey that night. A little upstream from the *Tannenfels* and no more than seventy yards beyond the cranes and warehouses at the dockside, lay the Café des Chartrons, the headquarters of de Baissac's *Scientist* network.

On this day, 11 December 1942, SOE submitted its regular activity report to the Cabinet Office in Whitehall. Speaking of *Scientist*, it reported that in Bordeaux 'A very considerable organisation has now been built up.'[6]

Meanwhile, on the ground in Bordeaux, responding to the message sent from Baker Street two weeks previously instructing *Scientist* to begin 'sabotage [operations] immediately and on as large a scale as possible ... against all shipping which used the port of Bordeaux',[7] Captain de Baissac (he had been promoted two weeks previously) was preparing to carry out *his* attack on the ships alongside the Quai des Chartrons. But de Baissac, with his contacts on the docks, almost certainly knew something Hasler didn't – the ships were empty; they were due to be loaded over the next few days.

It seems reasonable to speculate that de Baissac's plan was to mount his attack from the Café des Chartrons itself and that those involved would have included Guy and Marie Bertrand, the proprietors of the café, Jean Duboué, *Scientist*'s chief French agent, its courier Mary Herbert and Charles Hayes; '*Charles le Démolisseur*'. Despite de Baissac's concerns about Robert Leroy, it seems likely that he too would have been involved, for he was the chief contact with the painters and sealers upon whom they would rely for access to the holds of the target ships.

The Café des Chartrons is a rather cramped two-storey building without any cellars (none of these Bordeaux quayside properties have cellars due to the danger of water seepage from the nearby river). It is probable therefore that the explosive de Baissac would use was stored in one of his nearby safe houses – perhaps at 43 Cours Portal, a handsome two-storey building 300 yards or so back from the waterfront which was owned by one of de Baissac's other key accomplices, Paul Mansuy, and used by *Scientist* as their second 'letterbox' in the city.[8]

Hasler's lying-up position on the river bank two miles away was near perfect for his purposes. The bed of nine-foot-tall reeds in which *Catfish* and *Crayfish* were hidden was dense and about twenty feet wide. The channels that ran into it gave them an easy way in and left no trace of their passage; it would give them an easy way out when the tide started to flood that evening. Behind them, as they knew from aerial photographs, the built-up area of Bordeaux came down almost to the water's edge. All around them they could hear the hum of the great city: dogs barking in the distance; the rumble of a road close by; the hooting of cars and the grumble of lorries grinding up a nearby hill. Three hundred yards away, on the opposite side of the river, they could hear the rattle of chains, the clank of the cranes and the whirring of winches working the ships that would be their prey that night.

Once the tide had gone out, their flat-bottomed canoes rested on the mud. They could stand up now and, provided they were careful, inspect their quarry and the river traffic ploughing up and down the Garonne without risk of being seen. Thanks to the background noise, they could talk in low voices, even risk a brew of tea, a hot meal and a discreet cigarette. And with daylight temperatures of around six degrees centigrade and only an occasional scurry of rain out of a sky of patchy clouds floating by on a light southwesterly breeze, they could, at last, stretch out in their canoes and get some blessed sleep. The terrible weight of fatigue of the last few days had been replaced by rising anticipation and the excitement of being, at last, in the heart of the enemy's citadel and only a metaphorical stone's throw from their quarry.

During the day, Hasler made his final plan of attack. The tides and the moon were again in awkward juxtaposition, given that he had to place his limpets close to the time when the flood turned to ebb – or at least in the slack water before the ebb started to flow. High water in Bordeaux

Figure 9

Blondie Hasler *Imperial War Museum*

First tidal overfalls

Second tidal overfalls

Third tidal overfalls

Pointe de Grave (c. 1946) *delcampe.net*

Quai des Chartrons, Bordeaux (c. 1938), looking east. Hasler's approximate track.

BORDEAUX. — Vue d'ensemble prise du Transbordeur. - B. R.

Café des Chartrons

Bert Laver (above)

Bill Mills (above right)

"Ned" Sparks (right)

Jack MacKinnon
(left)
James Conway
(right)

Bobby Ewart
(far left)
"Sailor" Wallace
(left)

"Jan" Sheard
(left)
David Moffat
(right)

Hasler and Stewart in Cockle Mark Two

Trustees of The Royal Marines Museum

Hasler and Stewart pushing off Southsea beach

Trustees of The Royal Marines Museum

No. 1 Section leaving Southsea beach

Trustees of The Royal Marines Museum

Lise
de Baissac

Claude
de Baissac

*The National
Archives UK*

Marie-Louise, Jean and Suzanne Duboué (c. 1946).
Note Jean's false leg. *M. and Mme Leglise*

Charles Hayes (left) and Jean Duboué in Marseilles,
Summer 1943. *M. and Mme Leglise*

Gaston Hèches (top left) and Mimi Hèches (top right) *Dr Pierre and Denise Hèches*
Charles "Le Démolisseur" Hayes (centre) *The National Archives UK*
Yvonne Rudellat (bottom left) and Mary Herbert (bottom right) *The National Archives UK*

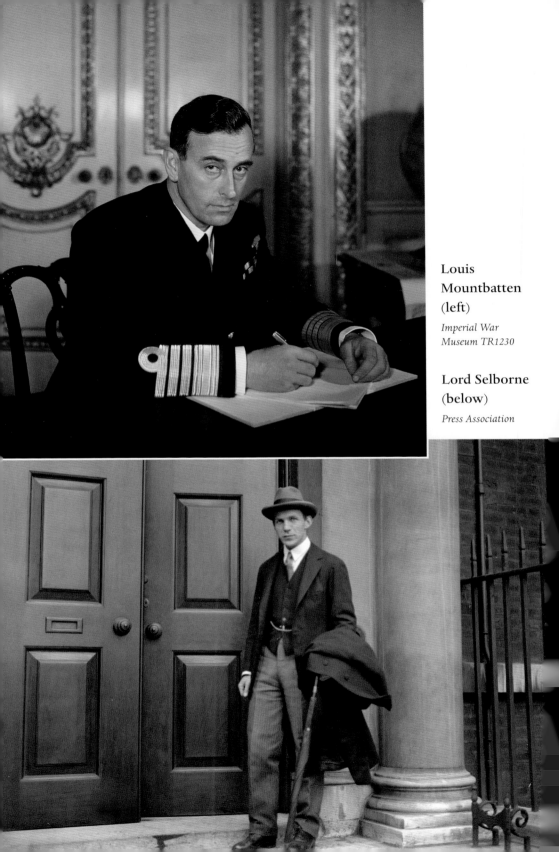

Louis Mountbatten (left)
Imperial War Museum TR1230

Lord Selborne (below)
Press Association

Dear Heather,

I trust it won't be necessary to have this sent you but since I don't know the out come of this little adventure, I thought I'd leave this note behind in the care of chorman who will forward it to you should any thing ~~expectit~~ happen.

During my stay at South Sea as you well know made me rea- lise what the good things in life are and I'm glad I have this opportunity to help bring back the pleasant times which I'm sure you always had and what you were made for. I couldn't help but love you Heather although you were so young, I will always love you

Dick Raikes (above)
Imperial War Museum A14400

**HM/S *Tuna*, Clyde
(c. 1942)**
Imperial War Museum A18930

**Yves Ardouin and his wife.
Pointe aux Oiseaux, 1961**
Trustees of The Royal Marines Museum

Schnöppe's photos of the scenes on Quai des Chartrons after Hasler's attack: (top) Cap Hadid, (left) *Tannenfels* officers on listing deck, (right) Kühnemann interrogates a docker, (bottom) *Tannenfels*

German U-Boat Museum, Cuxhaven

Clodomir
and Irène
Pasqueraud,
1940s

David Devigne

Rene Flaud
and the van in
which Hasler
and Sparks
travelled

Marvaud Farm (left), mid-1990s

Lucien Gody, pre-war (below left) *David Devigne*

The Barn at Beaunac, today (below)

Louise and
Louis Jaubert
(1940s)

Toque Blanche,
Ruffec, today

Chez Ouvrard,
today

Mary Lindell, post-war (below left)

The Mandinaud Sisters, 1960 (below right)

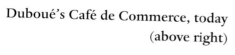

Duboué's Café de Commerce, today
(above right)

Chez Jaubert, today (right)

Hasler and José Ferrer during the making of *Cockleshell Heroes*

Alamy

"Ned" Sparks c. 1990 (top right)

Press Association

Hasler trying out a junk rig, Solent (right)

Press Association

Hasler on his farm in Argyll in the early 1980s

The Hasler Family

Jean Mandinaud, early 2000 (above left) *David Devigne*
Amélie and Armand Dubreuille, early 2000 (above centre) *David Devigne*
Roger Landes, early 2000 (above right) *Mark Bentinck*

Norman
Colley, 2012
Norman Colley

Memorials
at Pointe de
Grave (right
and below)

Blondie Hasler in
the early 1960s

Press Association

Hasler on his
trusty Ferguson
tractor in the
late 1970s

The Hasler Family

that night occurred a little after 2100.[9] But the moon would not set until half an hour later at 2132. What was more, the setting moon would be, like the previous night, at 245 degrees – that is, behind the glow of the city's lights, on their starboard bow as they paddled up the Garonne and almost dead ahead after they turned the last bend for their final run-in to their targets. With the moon low on the horizon, a canoe paddling along the western bank of the river would be exposed in the moon's reflection on the water's surface to any observer either behind them or on the eastern side of the river. To add to Hasler's difficulties, the weather would also be less helpful to them than the previous night. It was going to be a fine starlit night with no rain, few clouds and little wind.

Hasler would doubtless have liked to launch the attack at 2000 so as to capitalise on the tides. But he could not afford to start before the moon was down. He chose 2110 as the best possible compromise, hoping that by that time the moon would be low enough on the horizon to be hidden behind the city and the hills beyond.

His second decision was to split his force. Two canoes working together in the same area doubled their chances of discovery. He therefore decided to send *Crayfish* with Laver and Mills to attack the shipping on the eastern bank of the Garonne, ordering them first to investigate shipping lying on that side, further upstream of Bassens South. If they found no alternative targets they were to return to Bassens South and place their limpets on the *Alabama* and the *Portland*. Having done so, Laver and Mills were to take the ebb tide back down the Gironde, paddling as fast as they could with the aim of reaching Blaye, twenty-five miles away, before dawn. Here they were to land, scuttle their canoe and begin their escape overland to Ruffec.

Hasler and Sparks, meanwhile, would paddle *Catfish* the two miles to the Quai des Chartrons and attack the shipping they found there before, like Laver and Mills, catching the ebb to Blaye and making good their escape.

If only Combined Operations had been cooperating with SOE, there would have been on offer a much easier and more secure escape route for Hasler and his team. Rather than retracing their steps to Blaye, they could, with the right tides, have continued through Bordeaux and been picked up by de Baissac's team on the far side of the city – or even paddled on up the Garonne for ten more miles to Jean Duboué's safe house at Lestiac-sur-Garonne, which they could have reached well before dawn. Then it would only have been a question of destroying their canoes and plugging themselves into the *Scientist* escape route through Tarbes, over the Pyrenees to Spain – and home.

During the day the Royal Marines repacked their canoes, ditching the items they no longer required. They stowed their canoe compasses away so that the luminous dials would not be visible to a sentry above and packed the things they would need after completing their mission into two escape bags which could be readily grabbed if they were in a hurry. In the late afternoon they ate their last meal before Hasler took them painstakingly through the process of arming their limpets.

The limpet mines Hasler used were shaped like a brick with a convex top and six magnets on the bottom which held them to the ship. Each was fitted with two different fuses; an AC (acetone-celluloid) Delay time fuse and what was referred to at the time as a 'sympathetic' fuse.[10] These 'sympathetic' fuses were required because the time fuses were very unreliable and inaccurate. They depended on a chemical (acetone) to dissolve a celluloid disc, thereby ultimately releasing a spring-loaded firing mechanism and detonating the mine. The speed at which the process occurred could be greatly affected by temperature and minute variances in the thickness and composition of the celluloid disc – meaning that the timing of the subsequent detonation might vary by an hour or more. The danger was that if one limpet placed on a target went off early, the detonation could displace the other limpets further down the ship. The 'sympathetic' fuse was supposed to cope with this possibility by detonating automatically if subjected to a strong jolt, shock or abrupt change in the water pressure. This double detonation system no doubt increased the effectiveness of the limpets, but it also greatly increased the delicacy – not to say anxiety – with which the little mines had to be stored between the Marines' legs in the bottom of their canoes and handled alongside an enemy ship in the heat of an operation.

Among the equipment carried in the canoes was a small wooden box for each pair of limpets. These contained sets of glass ampoules, each the size of a thimble, in which were liquids of different colour denoting different time delays. Hasler ordered them to use the orange ampoules, which would give them a delay of approximately nine hours from the time the limpets were armed. This was a procedure they had practised many times in all conditions, day and night, wet and dry, fingers warm and frozen. Nevertheless, Hasler now closely and meticulously supervised Bert Laver, *Crayfish*'s Number One, as he took one of his limpets and, placing it between his knees, unscrewed the cap, revealing a recess into which the time fuses were inserted. Then, taking an orange ampoule, he inserted this into the recess and, after smearing grease on the threads of the fuse cap, lightly screwed it back a few turns, taking care not to let it touch the glass ampoule inside, for breaking this would immediately arm the limpet. After scratching a cross on the top of the fuse cap with the marlin-spike of his jack-knife to indicate the limpet was ready to be armed, Laver followed the same procedure for his remaining seven limpets. Then the limpets were turned over so that their 'sympathetic' fuses could be fitted into recesses at the other end.

When Laver had finished fusing his limpets under his commander's watchful eye, Hasler followed the same procedure with *Catfish*'s eight limpets, probably with Laver checking his actions as he went.

Meanwhile, the Number Twos, Ned Sparks and Bill Mills, greased the clips and sleeves of the telescopic 'placing rod' carried by each canoe, which would be used to position the limpets six feet below the waterline of their targets. They checked that the rod would snap into its extended position as silently as possible and that each limpet would engage and disengage smoothly. Finally, each Number Two unpacked and made ready the magnetic 'holdfast' he would use to hold his craft tight against its targets while the limpets were placed by his colleague in front.

With sixteen limpets to be armed, it took Hasler and his men more than an hour to complete their task, the last part of which would almost certainly have taken place in the failing light of dusk. Finally at around 2100, after a cold meal and with faces and hands now blackened, Hasler gave them the order to arm their limpets. One by one the fuse caps were screwed down until there was a small audible 'crack', indicating that the glass ampoules had broken and the acetone had begun its work. The limpets were now armed. Nothing could stop the little mines from going off in around nine hours' time, just before dawn – when, Hasler fervently hoped, they would be well clear.

And so it was that the long tentacles of London, 700 miles away, had uncoiled to position two fully equipped teams, each led by a British officer, within striking distance of their common target. Two teams of brave men and women, perfectly placed to carry out the same strategic task – neither of whom knew the other was also poised, a hair-trigger away from striking, very close by.

22

Attack

12 December 1942

At 2110, with the moon sinking slowly into the glow of lights from Bordeaux, Hasler's men shook hands and wished each other good luck. Then they quietly pushed aside the reeds and slipped out onto the black water, *Catfish* turning south towards the Quai des Chartrons while *Crayfish* headed southeast for the far bank of the Garonne.

The attack had begun.

With the tide behind them at only a tenth of a knot, they were paddling now in slack water under a moonless, but uncomfortably starlit sky. The temperature, which dropped sharply after sunset, would have been hovering around freezing, so they needed their woollen gloves for the first part of the journey. But when it came to the delicate business of fitting limpets to placing rods, only the sensitivity of naked fingers, frozen or not, would do.

All now depended on the last two miles and the final approach to their targets; on maintaining maximum concentration and absolute stealth until the mission was completed.

It took Hasler and Sparks ninety minutes to cover the two miles to the Quai des Chartrons. With the heights of Cenon sweeping down to the left bank of the river and a low bank of scrub and reed marking the right, they paddled as silent as shadows, single paddles dipping in and out of the water, bodies bent low over their canoe like crouching hunters.

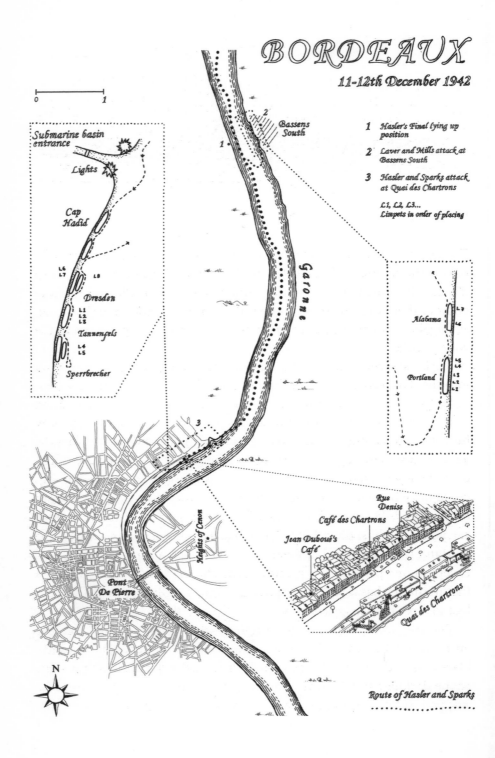

BORDEAUX

11-12th December 1942

0 1

Submarine basin entrance

Lights

Cap Hadid

L6
L7   L8

Dresden
L1
L2
L3

Tannenfels
L4
L5

Sperrbrecher

Bassens South

Garonne

1 Hasler's Final lying up position

2 Laver and Mills attack at Bassens South

3 Hasler and Sparks attack at Quai des Chartrons

L1, L2, L3...
Limpets in order of placing

Alabama
L7
L6

Portland
L8
L4
L3
L2
L1

Église of Cenon

Pont De Pierre

Rue Denise

Café des Chartrons

Jean Duboué's Café

Quai des Chartrons

N

Route of Hasler and Sparks

Figure 10

To start with at least, Hasler may have hoped to stay close to the reeds, risking the squawks of startled water birds in preference to exposure in the middle of the river. But as they rounded the first bend at the halfway point of their journey, they saw that Bordeaux was not under blackout, as they had anticipated, but instead blazed with light right down to the water's edge.

Hasler steered *Catfish* out some two hundred yards from the bank into the darkness of the river, hoping that any observer who saw their dark, low shape would think it no more than a log drifting up on the flood tide. With about four hundred yards to go and his targets now fully visible and brightly illuminated under arc lights, he decided that the lesser risk was to hug the shore again where he could make use of the deep shadows cast by the dockside. Hasler was not to know it, but things could have been much worse. From here onwards, running the length of the *Port de la Lune*, were a line of regularly spaced lamp posts, each carrying a bright sodium light. These had been broken at the start of the war and the Germans had been content to leave them unrepaired – except in one place: at the mouth of the channel which gave access to the submarine basin on the west bank. And it was this which Hasler now had to cross to reach his quarry.

The area was illuminated in a bright pool of light which covered the entrance to the submarine basin and extended in a wide arc into the blackness of the river. Hasler again pulled *Catfish* out, skirting the edge of the darkness until it was safe to close in to the quay again. Here he stopped to take a good look at his targets, knowing that he would be better able to assess their shape and suitability from a distance; when tucked tight under their flanks, all that would be visible would be a vertical iron-sided cliff towering high above them.

Now the pair went into the ship-attack routine they had practised so often.

Sparks reached into the canoe and drew out the placing rod. There was an audible crack as its spring-loaded joints clicked into position. He checked the rod, ensuring that each joint was fully locked, then, with Hasler's help, carefully secured it along the deck of the canoe with the paddle-retaining fastenings.

Hasler let *Catfish* drift gently back into the shelter of the darkness under the edge of the quay. Noting that there were arches let into the quayside at regular intervals, covering tunnels of darkness into which he could vanish if needed, they began to work their way towards the first ship. Finding it was a tanker and not one of the cargo-carrying blockade runners, he slid quietly down its side to look at the vessel beyond, a mixed passenger and cargo ship. It is testimony to Hasler's single-minded determination that, after so many days and hours of danger, hardship and tension, he did not take the first target that they reached. Instead, he pressed on.

The third ship was a large cargo-carrier. This would have been an excellent target, but there was a complication. Another smaller ship, a tanker, was secured alongside, exposing only the larger ship's stern and bows as suitable places for limpet mines to be attached. Hasler wanted to find a vessel on which he could do more damage than two stern-planted limpets were likely to achieve. He decided to return to this prey later if he could not find anything better, and again pressed on.

His next target was a large cargo vessel whose riverside flank was fully exposed. Perfect! He allowed *Catfish* to slide below the big ship's overhanging stern,[1] took off his gloves and reached below his cockpit cover for the first limpet while Sparks took out his holdfast and, careful to suppress any 'clang' as the magnets took hold, rolled it onto the ship's side. Having attached his limpet mine to the placing rod, Hasler lowered it slowly over the side to the full length of the rod and brought it in gently until he felt the small jolt which told him that the magnets had found the ship's steel plates. Pushing the rod down a few inches more to disengage it from the limpet, he then drew it up, secured it on the deck of the canoe and signalled Sparks to release the holdfast and move on.

The first blow had been struck.

Aided by a few small paddle strokes, they glided down until they were amidships where he planned to plant their next limpet. But the ebb tide was becoming stronger and there was a real danger that, with *Catfish* attached by Sparks' holdfast at the stern and Hasler busy placing his second limpet at the front, the flow against them would catch the canoe's bows and push her out, away from the ship's side. So Hasler signalled to Sparks to hand him the holdfast and passed his Number Two the placing rod; Hasler now held *Catfish* at the bows while Sparks planted the limpets behind him. They were by this time abreast of the great ship's engine room and could hear the hum of its auxiliary engines, even catch snatches of conversation and music coming from the crew's quarters.

As soon as the second limpet was planted they began to make their way towards the bow. Now they had to pass under the ship's water and sewage outfalls, drenching them from above. The main outfall from the ship's condensers was so large that Hasler feared it might swamp their canoe. He had to risk pushing *Catfish* out into more exposed water in order to avoid the danger. They then returned to hug the ship's side with its heavy rivets and waterline coating of sharp barnacles and weed and moved on to place their third mine under the overhang of their prey's stern.

The last ship in line was another cargo ship, but again there was a vessel lying alongside, tied up to her river-facing flank. This turned out to be the German *Sperrbrecher 5*, along whose side they placed two more limpets before edging past both ships to look at the second cluster of vessels lying further down the quay. But by now the ebb was gathering pace and Hasler realised he could not reach the second group in time.

The two of them exchanged the holdfast and placing rod again for the return journey and quietly began to swing *Catfish* round so they could make their way back down the line, where they would get rid of their remaining limpets on whatever suitable targets they could find. They were right in the middle of this delicate manoeuvre when there was a sudden clang from above. Looking up, they saw the outline of a sentry silhouetted against the arc lights. A moment later his torch snapped on, pointing directly down at them. The two Marines, bodies low, hoods up, had no option but to rely on stealth, camouflage and training. They took one swift, low paddle stroke which pushed *Catfish* close in to the

Figure 11

side of the *Sperrbrecher* and then stayed still as the tide floated them slowly down the side of the ship and on towards her bows. To their horror they could hear the clang of the sentry's iron-tipped boots as he followed them down the ship's side, never taking his torch off the dark shape drifting like an idle log, fifteen feet below. Hasler, waiting for the shout and the shot which would rip into them a moment afterwards, was later to say: 'I felt as though my back had been stripped naked.'[2]

After what seemed like an eternity, *Catfish* reached the overhanging bows of the warship. Here they were invisible, enabling Sparks to roll his holdfast gently onto the ship so that he could hold *Catfish* until the sentry, they hoped, lost interest. Minutes turned into what seemed like hours as they waited for the sound of his boots to move on. But all they could hear was movement above them as he shifted position, shining his torch into the empty black waters around them. Eventually Hasler gave the signal to Sparks to let go and they drifted out, the tide now carrying them downstream with increasing speed. Once again they waited for the shout and the shot. But none came and after a few minutes they found themselves back in the safety of darkness.

They allowed themselves to drift quietly past the ship they had already limpeted, intending to revisit the cargo ship and tanker they had passed over earlier. Hasler steered *Catfish* between the two ships and began to prepare his limpets. But at this moment he looked up and saw the two ships' huge iron sides above him yaw and begin to come together under the effect of the tide. There was a real danger the canoe would be crushed as the iron walls of the canyon began to close. The two men pushed *Catfish* violently out of the closing jaws just in time to avoid disaster and then back-paddled furiously against the tide in order to pass round the upstream end of the outward ship, so they could float on down its outer-side with the tide and plant their last three limpet mines, two on the stern of the *Dresden* and their last one on the stern of the tanker *Cap Hadid*, lying alongside her.

As soon as they were clear of the harbour's lights, Hasler silently lowered the placing rod for the last time and allowed it to drop into the deep water of the harbour. It no doubt lies there to this day.

Bombs planted. It was done. Mission accomplished!

Hasler turned in his cockpit and, grasping Sparks' hand, shook it warmly. Then the two men took *Catfish*, now much lighter and more lively, out into the middle and started to paddle hard downriver. The time would have been perhaps 2330. To reach the vicinity of Blaye and hide themselves before dawn, they had just six hours to cover the next twenty-plus nautical miles – but at least this time they would be assisted by a driving ebb of nearly three knots, canoes which were lighter and higher in the water and the elation of success to spur them on.

Now, after so much concentration and nervous energy, it was recklessness which took over. Hasler later told Lucas Phillips: 'I felt as though I owned the river and my respect for the enemy gave way to contempt. I took *Catfish* straight out into the middle of the river where the tide was strongest and we shot off downstream, paddling strongly in single [sic] paddles.[3] We must have been visible and audible to both banks, if anyone had been looking, but we just didn't seem to care.'[4]

Although an entirely understandable emotion, this was a dangerous one too. For, from the moment they planted their last limpet, there was an immediate and fundamental change in their circumstances. Soon they would have to realise this, if they were going to survive.

Before, there had been planning and preparation; now there was only luck. Before, everything they had done had been decided by them and the needs of the operation; now they would be wholly at the mercy of others. Before, they had been the hunters; now they were the hunted. Before, they had been soldiers; now they were merely fugitives.

Soon *Catfish* passed the two ships at Bassens South, where, Hasler hoped, Laver and Mills would have planted their limpets. Then on, down the gradually widening river to the Île Cazeau and the junction of the

Garonne and the Dordogne, past dark woods, sleeping villages and silent countryside. Here they again took the western channel, catching the surging ebb that swept them through the narrows past their uncongenial lying-up position of two days ago on one side of the river and the vineyards of Margaux on the other. Here, at around two in the morning, Hasler decided they could take a short break, allowing themselves to drift for a little on the tide. Suddenly the two men froze. Behind them they heard a furious, fast-approaching noise – like, said Hasler afterwards, 'a Mississippi stern-wheeler at full speed'.[5] Even before they could reach a hiding place on the bank, they saw *Crayfish* creaming towards them, with Laver and Mills spurring her on as though the devil drove them.

The two Marines were in high spirits. According to Lucas Phillips, Bert Laver said, 'We went down the east bank as far as we could, Sir, like you said, until the tide turned against us and we found no targets at all, so we came back and attacked the two ships at Bassens South.'[6]

'Well done. What did you give them?'

'Five limpets on the first ship, Sir, and three on the second.'

'Meet any trouble?'

'None at all, Sir.'

'Well done indeed, you two. You've all done wonderfully. I am really proud of you.'

The two canoes stayed together for a few minutes before Hasler said it was time to split up and make their way separately again.

'Couldn't we go along with you for a bit, Sir?' Laver asked. 'It would be nice to keep company as long as we can.'

'Alright. If you'd like to. But we shall have to separate again before we land.'[7]

Three hours later, at a little after 0500, just after they had crossed back over the main shipping channel and were approaching Blaye on the eastern shore, Hasler turned to look back. Suddenly he saw a searchlight snap on and begin sweeping the entrance of the Garonne at Bec d'Ambès, six miles astern.

It was now some three hours before dawn, which this morning would occur just before 0800. Time for *Catfish* and *Crayfish* to split up and their crews to take their separate paths to Ruffec on the first step of the long journey home.

To Hasler's left, across the Gironde, he could see the silent black hulk of the French liner *De Grasse*, lying at her mooring near Pauillac. To his right, the towering outline of the medieval fortress of Blaye, etched against a starlit sky, with the little town which took its name huddled, silent and sleeping under its right shoulder. For the last time, Hasler gave the signal to raft up.

As *Crayfish* slid alongside, he said to Laver: 'Well, Corporal, this is where we have to separate. You are about a mile north of Blaye. Go straight ashore here and carry out your escape instructions. I shall land about a quarter of a mile further north.'

'Very good, Sir. Best of luck to you.'

'Goodbye, both of you and thank you for everything you have done. Keep on as you have been doing and we'll be meeting again in Pompey in a few weeks' time.'

They reached across the gap between the canoes and shook each other's hands.

'See you in the Granada,' Sparks said. 'We'll keep a pint for you.'[8]

The two canoes parted, Laver and Mills heading for the shore. To Hasler and Sparks, *Crayfish* seemed suddenly small, fragile, insignificant. As she disappeared into the dark shadows of the shoreline, he remembered that so it had been when he had said goodbye to Jan Sheard and David Moffatt, on that terrible first night which now seemed so long ago.[9] Then he turned *Catfish* and began making his way a little further north – against the gathering tide now – to find a good landing point.

He found one just below the Château de Segonzac. Here *Catfish* turned towards the shore. Once again – and for the last time – Hasler and Sparks broke down to single paddles for a stealthy approach. The shore, dotted with fishing cabins festooned with nets and built on stakes sticking out into the estuary, seemed completely deserted. Hasler carried out a brief reconnaissance of the area and returned to tell Sparks that they could begin unpacking *Catfish* and prepare to abandon her. Again, with the tide now very low, they cannot have found it easy to carry their escape bags, spare clothes, boots, enough food for two days and a half-gallon can of water up the steep muddy banks strewn with rocks, rubbish and tree trunks washed down by the winter floods. This done, the two men made their way back across the mud to *Catfish*, their home and companion for the last five nights and four days. She was lying now empty and forlorn at the water's edge. Using their knives, they slashed her sides and buoyancy bags. Then, with Sparks looking on, Hasler waded out as far as he dared and pushed her off into deep water. They watched, hoping she would sink. But she stayed resolutely afloat, the tip of her cockpit still proudly showing, as she was swept south into the last of the darkness, down the Gironde and away from them for ever on the flooding tide.

PART IV

The Escape

23

Bangs and Blame-Dodging

12 December 1942

SS *Alabama*, Bassens South

At 0350 on 12 December, a full two hours before Laver and Mills' limpets were timed to explode, the night watchman on the *Portland* felt a slight juddering of the ship. Forty minutes later there was a more distinct explosion followed by a modest plume of water erupting up the side of the vessel. It came from somewhere below the waterline under *Portland*'s bows, beneath No. 1 hatch. An inspection revealed water pouring into *Portland*'s forward hold through a hole about two feet square. All attempts to plug the breach failed. Pumping seemed to make little headway against the rising water as the big ship began to settle in the water. Fortunately for the *Portland*, low tide occurred at Bassens South only forty-five minutes later at 0445, so she did not have far to settle before she came to rest on the mud.

At 0500, the same time Hasler saw the searchlight burst into life at the Bec d'Ambès, an explosion shook the *Alabama*, which was moored at the *Portland*'s stern. It too seemed to come from below the waterline, under No. 5 hatch. But no one had time to investigate: three minutes later, *Alabama* was rocked by another detonation, this time under her midships by Nos 3 and 4 hatches. Water immediately started to pour into both *Alabama*'s holds, which, like those of *Portland*, were empty at the time. She too started to settle on the river bed.

The 8.8 lb explosive charge of a Second World War Type 6 Mark I limpet, detonated six feet below the water, was capable of blasting an

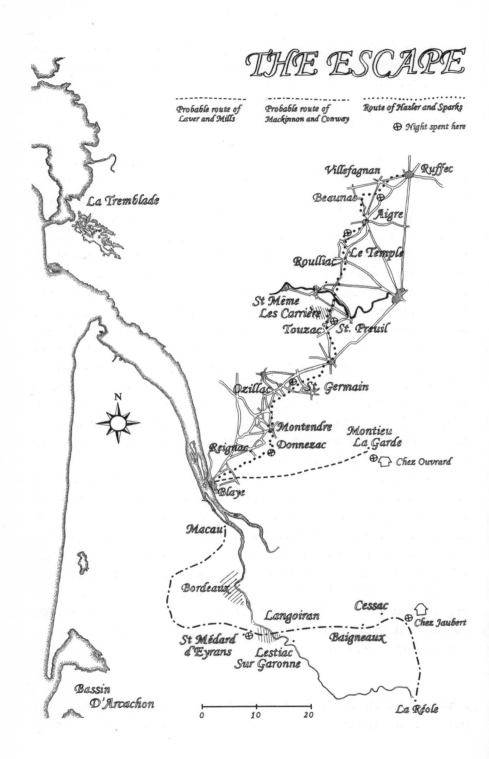

THE ESCAPE

Probable route of
Laver and Mills

Probable route of
Mackinnon and Conway

Route of Hasler and Sparks

⊕ Night spent here

La Tremblade

Villefagnan Ruffec

Beaunac
Aigre

St Même
Les Carrière
Touzac St. Preuil

Roulliac Le Temple

Ozillac St. Germain

N

Montendre
Donnezac

Montieu
La Garde

⊕ Chez Ouvrard

Reignac

Blaye

Macau

Bordeaux

Cessac

Langoiran

Chez Jaubert

Baigneaux

St Médard
d'Eyrans

Lestiac
Sur Garonne

Bassin
D'Arcachon

La Réole

0   10   20

oval-shaped hole some forty inches long and twelve inches wide in the steel of a typical Second World War merchantman.[1] Some contemporary reports describe great white plumes of water being sent skywards and the tiles of nearby houses rattling when the detonations occurred. This is unlikely. The limpet mines of World War Two (and today) were shaped so as to maximise what is called 'the Munroe effect'.[2] This establishes that, if a charge is so constructed that its exterior (the place from which it is detonated) is convex and its interior (closest to the target) is concave, then the force of the detonation will project away from the point of detonation so as to fill the void of the concave face, the full effect of the explosion being focused at a point 'in front' of the face of the charge, opposite to and at approximately the same distance as the deepest point of the concave. The main force of the explosion of Hasler's limpets would thus have been directed inwards onto the hull of their targets, not into the sea around. The pressure of the six-foot column of water against the outside of a limpet acts like 'tamping' on the charge, further intensifying the blast and concentrating it inwards rather than upwards. At the moment of detonation there *might* have been a column of water blown up the side of the ship, but this would have been relatively modest, and the sound of the blast that attended it would have been muffled and probably not especially noticeable more than two or three hundred yards away. Talk of these blasts – and those which were to follow – 'shaking the city' is fanciful.[3]

This is confirmed by at least one eye-witness on the quayside that early morning. At a little after 0500, twenty-year-old Jean Trocard arrived to begin his day's work at his post managing the double locks on the entrance passage from the Garonne to the submarine basin. He found the port in uproar and his friends full of rumours of an act of sabotage – but he had heard nothing. He watched as German troops occupied the port and the fire brigade rushed onto the dockside. He heard rumours of more mines going off on the ships just 200 yards down the quay. He even saw the ships beginning to list – but he neither heard nor saw any explosions.[4]

Johannes Bachmann, by this time back at his headquarters in Nantes, recorded the day's events in his diary, beginning with an early morning report from Kühnemann of 'substantial acts of sabotage' and emphasising, as always, the actions he had taken to ensure that the stable door was now firmly shut:

The following security measures have been instituted:

The port was immediately closed and all checkpoints and controls reinforced.

All units, including the various corps of the Wehrmacht, have been informed of the capture near Le Verdon on 8.12.42 of two English sailors [sic].

The coastal Mine Service at Bordeaux has also been warned. Its Commander has informed the Captains of various ships of the capture of two English seamen [sic] and has read to them the script of telex messages sent by the Commander, Naval Forces to all units. He told them to pay particular attention to the quayside-facing hulls of their ship.[5]

In fact, as the Germans were soon to find out, if they were looking at the side of the ships closest to the quay, they were looking in the wrong place.

Fifteen minutes after Admiral Bachmann wrote the above entry, a third mine went off on the river-side flank of the *Alabama* in Bassens South; then, at 0830, the first of Hasler's limpets exploded at the Quai des Chartrons in the main port, with two detonations thirty seconds apart under the *Tannenfels*, which almost immediately began to take on a pronounced list to port. At the same time, an explosion under *Sperrbrecher 5* sent up a brief spout of water, but did no damage (it later turned out that Hasler's limpet had exploded on the seabed, having presumably become detached from the warship). Fifteen minutes after this, the *Dresden* shuddered with an explosion, followed ten minutes later by another which tore open the tunnel containing her propeller shaft and flooded her rear four holds, causing her stern to sink gracefully onto the mud. Then an explosion under the stern of the tanker *Cap Hadid* started a fire in one of her fuel tanks. And so it continued all morning, the last mine to go off being, like the first seven hours previously, one of *Crayfish's* limpets on the Bassens South side of the river which exploded under the *Alabama* at 1105. This caused the underwater investigations that were by then in progress to be suspended for several hours.

As the port area was sealed off and German troops rushed in, rumours flew around the city. At first the Germans thought the explosions had been caused by floating mines. Some speculated that the Italians had carried out the attack as revenge for the Germans' insistence that only their submarines should be allowed in the shelter of the submarine pens, leaving the Italian submarines outside and vulnerable to British air raids.[6] 'It is just the sort of things the Italians would do, sinking merchant ships in the night', was the common word on the Bordeaux street.[7] One Italian submarine captain, Claude de Baissac later reported, even became the beneficiary of free drinks in local bars by conspicuously failing to deny this cheery piece of local gossip.

In fact the opposite was true. The Italian admiral in Bordeaux, Polacchini, immediately offered the services of his three divers who, assisted by Lieutenant Schulz-Höhenhaus of German Coastal Mine Defence Service[8] (and with some courage, given that there were limpets still going off all the time), quickly established from an underwater inspection that the blasts had come from *outside*, not inside, and that this was therefore not likely to be local sabotage.

Among others who were quickly on the scene was the local Bordeaux Port Fire Brigade, which deployed six pumps and the fire tender, MV *Stockling*. What the Germans did not know was that the man in charge of this fire-fighting machinery, Raymond Brard, was also head of the *Phidias-Phalanx* Resistance *réseau*. Brard later reported that, when the Germans' attention was elsewhere, he reversed the flow of his pumps so that, instead of pumping water out of the stricken vessels, they pumped it in[9] – though this did relatively little damage because, in the early hours of the emergency, the tide was low and the ships were already resting on the bottom. His assistant, Albert Juenbekdjian, was later to claim that he took sticks of plastic explosive on board the ships and set them off to add to the mayhem.[10] The fact that the fire brigade hindered rather than helped the Germans seems well authenticated, making the fulsome praise heaped on Brard's men afterwards in a letter of commendation from Commander Kühnemann, all the more ironic.[11] But it is difficult to believe that the Germans would not have noticed had extra explosive charges been set off in the ships. Moreover, the absence of supporting evidence of explosions beyond those of Hasler's limpets means that Juenbekdjian's claim must be treated with extreme caution.

By the time of the next high tide at 0923, the Germans, greatly assisted by the fact that the ships were empty and the tide was out, had begun to bring the situation under control. Balks of timber and a floating crane were used to help prop up listing ships; special cement was brought in to fill holes and extra pumps were deployed to pump out cargo holds. Divers were sent down with steel plates to cover the holes. Since these makeshift patches could not be welded in place underwater, they were held in position from the outside by a construction of timber and strops. A watertight seal was effected between the iron repair plates and the ships' hulls, using a novel form of sealant: rashers of bacon obtained from the crews' galley.[12]

By mid-morning the Quai des Chartrons was full of German troops and officials, while the fire brigade attended to the stricken ships, experts consulted one another urgently on what to do next, Kriegsmarine officers interrogated dockers and ships' crews unloaded their kit onto the quayside. Some curious locals were also no doubt present to enjoy their occupiers' discomfiture.

One of those on the quayside at about this time was Walter Schnöppe, a Kriegsmarine officer and war correspondent, who took photographs and wrote a piece describing what he saw – the only extant eyewitness photos and account of the damage done by Hasler's attack. Schnöppe was in Bordeaux specifically to write an article on the arrival of the *Tannenfels* – regarded as the 'Queen of Blockade Runners' – after another successful run through the British blockade. He began his piece, which was probably for publication, by setting out the historical context:[13]

On 19th April 1941 the German steamer Tannenfels broke through the British blockade under cover of the name Taronga. Safe and secure, she lay in Le Verdon roadstead of Bordeaux.

After being unloaded and reloaded, she left for Japan and on 12th May 1942 reached Yokohama. The ship left Japan on 8th August 1942 and reached Bordeaux safely again.

On 2nd November 1942, the ship, unbeaten at sea, was back in Bordeaux and crossed over from Bassens to the pier at the Quai des Chartrons in Bordeaux in order to be reloaded for a return journey to Japan. On the morning of 12 December, around 5 a.m., tiles rattled along the Quai and a powerful explosion tore through the silence of the waking harbour. A sailor stumbled into the headquarters of the 6th Navy to report what had happened. A further explosion then followed on the Tannenfels.

The ship starts taking in the water. She leans strongly to one side and threatens to capsize, but the heavy towropes, stretched like violin strings, are still able to hold her.

There followed much research: the result: British saboteurs during the night applied a magnetic mine with timer and then disappeared, just as they came.

The saboteurs had disappeared; only the damage remains.[14]

Also among the milling crowd that early morning were members of de Baissac's *Scientist* network who had 'reconnoitring parties actually on the quayside making their last recce before they attacked the following night, when they heard some quiet pops below the water and watched as their targets started to settle into the water under their noses'.[15] In a later report to the Cabinet Office, probably based on a message sent by de Baissac over Roger Landes' radio, Combined Operations said 'the operation was successful as far as can be deduced from reports. Explosions [from Hasler's limpets] were heard.'[16]

At 1245, an aerial reconnaissance Spitfire made another high-level pass over the Bordeaux docks and the Gironde. Although the photo interpretation experts at RAF Medmenham identified little that was unusual, they did note that two floating cranes and a dredger had been moved from other parts of the port and were now anchored alongside ships on the Quai des Chartrons.[17]

At about the same time, the German *Grenzenschützdienst* (border guard service) made a discovery confirming what the German authorities now strongly suspected – that the explosions were connected with the capture of Wallace and Ewart on 8 December. Searching the shoreline just above Blaye, the Germans found two half-submerged canoes which had clearly been deliberately scuttled. These contained various items of British equipment similar to those found at the time of Wallace and Ewart's arrest.

By the end of the day, the results of the sabotage had been compiled. The following day they were sent to Berlin by Ernst Kühnemann:[*]

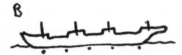

1. Steamer *Alabama*: 5 explosions (0700, 0703, 0800, 1005 and 1305 hours). All explosions on the waterside. 1. Explosion at hatch 5; 2. At hatch; 3 at hatch 4 (without any visible damage); 4. near to rudder stem (after peak); 5. at stem (fore peak). Explosion 1.5 m below waterline. Hatch 1 and 5 took in water. Ship is able to float; athwart lines have been attached for safety reasons.

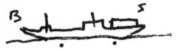

2. Steamer *Tannenfels*: 2 explosions; 1. approx. 0830, second one 30 seconds later (bigger explosion). Explosions on waterside between hatch 2 and 3 approx 2.5 m below the waterline, hatches filled with water, size of holes 10 m x 0.6 m. Leaks were sealed by divers. Boat still floats, but is listing by about 16 degrees.

3. Steamer *Dresden*. 2 explosions (0845 and 0855 hours), hatch 5 and hatch 4. Leaks approx 3.0 to 4.0 m below waterline. Hatch 5 and 4 filled with water due to tear in the shaft tunnel also hatches 6 and 7. Size of leaks 1.25 x 0.85 m. Stern of ship was immediately grounded, attempts to seal the leaks are being made.

4. Steamer *Portland* – watchman felt slight vibration of ship at about 0550 hours and at 0630 hours at hatch no 1 waterside, 1.0 to 1.5 m below waterline. Water jet was seen. Hatch 1 under water, leak approx. 0.5 x 0.4 m. Sealing sail has been attached, little reduction of water by pumping.

---

[*]   Curiously the damage to the *Cap Hadid* is not mentioned, perhaps because it was neither a naval ship nor a blockade runner.

5. *Sperrbrecher* 5: Explosion on waterside at about 1030 hours, no damage midships. It is assumed that the mine fell off due to previous searching of the boat wall and then exploded later on the sea-bed.[18]

It must have been with growing foreboding that the German authorities in Bordeaux realised they would have to account to Berlin for the fact that they had had four days' detailed warning of an enemy attack on a key German strategic facility – and had totally failed to stop it happening.

Throughout the afternoon and evening, signals flew between Commander Kühnemann's office in Bordeaux, Admiral Bachmann's headquarters in Nantes and German Supreme Headquarters in Berlin, the latter demanding to know, with an increasing note of menace, who was responsible. These angry missives culminated in a late-night signal which hinted strongly at the possibility of courts-martial.[19]

Bachmann tried with rising desperation to shift the blame elsewhere, pointing out that Kühnemann had responsibility for the port, the Coastal Mine Defence Service for security of the ships, the Wehrmacht for the guards on the locks and the shore, the SD in Bordeaux for counter-intelligence and for failing to get the full story out of Wallace and Ewart. He even blamed the ships' captains, all of whom had, he observed, been warned of the increased threat and told to strengthen their guards. It was *they* who, as Berlin knew, bore ultimate responsibility for the safety of their own vessels. Finally, he reminded Berlin that he had, on several previous occasions, asked for more resources to guard the harbour but had always been refused.[20]

In the late afternoon, in response to repeated Berlin requests to know what he was doing about the situation, Kühnemann issued urgent instructions for new defensive measures. These included strengthened land patrols and pickets, a constant boat patrol in the harbour at night, the illumination of the river-side flanks of all ships lying alongside the quays, the restoration of the peace-time lighting on the Quai des Chartrons, two sentries on all ships at all times, new booms across the river, continuous searchlight sweeps of the Gironde mouth and barbed wire protection for all important shore installations.[21] By the end of the day, the Germans had succeeded in minimising the damage, and had taken steps to prevent a repeat attack. But those responsible must have known that there would nevertheless be repercussions from Berlin – especially if they now failed to capture the perpetrators.

Hasler had hoped the Germans would anticipate that his escape route would be southwest towards Spain and would therefore not expect them to head east towards Ruffec. But the discovery of two canoes on the east bank of the Gironde, north of Bordeaux must have indicated that southwest was not their intended direction. The hunt was afoot. The hunters knew where the raiders had landed – and could make a fair guess which way they were headed. Hasler had, at best, a six-hour start on his vengeful pursuers.

24

The Start of the Long Walk

12 December 1942

It would have been about 0630, with an hour of darkness left before dawn, when Hasler and Sparks, having watched *Catfish* being swept away on the tide, made their way back up the mud bank, collected their kit and pushed themselves noisily through the high reeds along the river's edge. They soon broke out onto a bund topped by a track running parallel with the shore. Beyond this lay a flat grass field, intersected by deep drainage ditches; beyond again was a minor road.[1] They crossed the road and made their way up the slope on the other side, the square bulk of the eighteenth-century Château de Segonzac, with its prominent iron water tower, now beginning to stand out against the lightening eastern sky. Here they struck a bewildering problem. Shortly after crossing the road they met a three-foot-high fence running through what looked like a line of thin bushes. Clutching their escape bags, they climbed laboriously over the fence, only to encounter another a few yards later. 'Ah! A fenced cart track,' thought Hasler.[2] They clambered over that fence too, only to find yet another a few yards further on.

'Seem to have plenty of fences in this country, Sir,' Sparks commented dryly.

Finally, the penny dropped. They were in the middle of a vineyard. They would have to walk, not against the line of the vines, but with them.[3] The zigzagging this entailed cut down the straight-line distance they could cover and made navigation with their tiny 'button' escape compass very difficult.

Dawn was now coming on fast. It was time to find a place to hide. If their mission had been successful their bombs would soon go off, unleashing a hornets' nest around their heads. Finally, as colour began to seep into the greys and blacks of night, they found a place to lie up: an isolated wood with a stream running along its edge, midway between the little village of St Genès de Blaye and Fours, a small hamlet to its north. Here they were well hidden and far enough from habitation to be at little risk of discovery.[4]

For Hasler and Sparks, this was their quietest day since leaving *Tuna*. As the sun came up, each was able to see the other for the first time since they had left their hide in the reeds the night before – haggard faces streaked with sweat and brown camouflage cream; eyes sunk into sockets with the strain of the last few days; clothes caked with mud. All the triumph and euphoria of last night had drained away, leaving only exhaustion and the sudden realisation of their vulnerability.

They washed first in the little stream, which was deliciously cold and cleansing – their first proper wash in five days. Both men shaved, brewed tea and cooked a meagre meal. They cut grasses and gathered dried bracken, leaves and branches from the floor of the wood, piling them up to form a makeshift mattress and covering. Then they slept.

The weather was kind that first day: patchy cloud; a temperature of six degrees centigrade; light southwesterly winds and a few scurries of rain around midday.

Not long after first light, young Olivier Bernard took his catapult and left his house in the nearby hamlet of Fours to go hunting rabbits, as he often did during the wartime years. These were difficult times for ordinary families in France and a rabbit for the pot was a welcome addition to his mother's meagre larder. Moreover, now that the Germans had made the possession of firearms illegal, the rabbits had become daring in the presence of humans and vulnerable to anyone with a good eye and a strong catapult arm.

One of Olivier's favourite hunting spots was a derelict patch of scrub close to a coppice which was often flooded in winter. Here stood a small windowless hut built of concrete blocks with a tiled roof. Its name – *Cabane Fume Bas* – was carved into a rectangular stone set in the wall by its single door. This morning, for some reason, Olivier pushed open the door of the hut – and was startled to find two men with blackened faces and mud-caked clothing inside. They said something to him in a language he couldn't understand.[5]

Frightened, Olivier ran back to Fours and sought out a schoolteacher who lived in the village, Pierre Gacis. M. Gacis returned with the boy and attempted to communicate with the two men. Although neither could speak the other's language, the schoolteacher did understand one thing – they were hungry. He returned home and, without telling his wife Solange, a fellow schoolteacher, took a dish of rabbit pie she had made, carried it back and gave it to the two fugitives.

Pierre Gacis swore young Olivier to silence about the event; he never even told his wife. She was furious when she found that her precious rabbit pie was missing and blamed the two Gacis children for stealing it. It was only after the war that Solange Gacis discovered the truth about the pie and the lengths to which her husband had gone to help two strangers in need. Towards the end of her life she wrote a letter to her children and grandchildren telling them the story of the rabbit pie:

> The dish had been ceremoniously set aside, since I had carefully prepared with my own hands, a stuffed rabbit – a rabbit given us by old 'Mother Rachat' from Segonzac, who bred them. Papa had given her a little extra fuel for her lamp, which had been given to him by another neighbour who used very little …
>
> Surprised by the larder being empty I silently accused the two big children, Colette and Nanou, of having stolen the evening meal for their tea. (Nicole was also over 2 years old and could well have profited, too!) It was all most inexcusable! Without actually dying of hunger there were still many restrictions on food during this harsh period.
>
> It's a long time since I confessed it, but I want to renew to my dear daughters my apologies for having accused them of this theft. What an unfair suspicion![6]

Bert Laver and Bill Mills must have left the hut shortly after dark, for at 1700, Maurice Marchais and his wife Michelle were taking an evening walk from their home in the nearby village of Eyrans to collect milk from a local farm, when their dogs started barking furiously. Suddenly two men in camouflaged uniform emerged out of the gloom and engaged them in English. Neither side understood a word the other said, but later Maurice Marchais remembered that the two Englishmen repeatedly used the word 'Angoulême'.[7] Unable to make themselves understood, the two strangers left into the darkness, heading east.

Assessing his situation during the day, Hasler must have calculated that the Germans would concentrate their search near the banks of the Gironde; he and Sparks had to make their way further inland before taking the risk of begging for civilian clothes. They would continue their journey in uniform that night, hoping to throw themselves on the mercy of a local family the following day.

As soon as it was dark, Hasler and Sparks set off northeast, probably crossing what is now the D937 near its junction with the N137 between Le Pontet and Cartelègue. For this first part of their journey they would again have been heavily impeded by vines. But north of Cartelègue the ground opens up into sparse conifer woods with only occasional vineyards, isolated farmhouses and smallholdings dotted among the trees. This is ideal country for evaders: the terrain is flat, the cover good and the habitation sparse. And they could make use of the occasional roads and tracks running in the right direction, confident in the knowledge that if headlights approached, they would have plenty of time to dive into the bushes, bracken and heather which bordered the roadside. The weather this night was overcast and blustery with occasional squalls of rain, so it would have been very dark, especially in the woods. Their biggest problem would probably have been finding their way in the darkness with their tiny compasses, dimmed torches and an unwieldy expanse of escape map.

Printed on special waterproofed paper, these maps were cumbersome affairs, twenty-six inches from north to south and twenty-three from east to west. They were folded into two halves, each fold being reinforced by a band of transparent paper. Certain places on the maps carried their original French names, inviting the speculation that they were put together by the ISTD, based on an original French Michelin map of the 1930s overprinted with military symbols and letters, including some apparently designed for RAF navigators.[8]

Despite nearly twelve hours on the march, the two men covered only eight miles that night. They needed to make faster progress. It was time to beg for civilian clothes so that they could begin to move by day – and a sack so they could get rid of their cumbersome escape bags.

Meanwhile, Claude de Baissac was coming to terms with the consequences of Hasler's clandestine visit to the Bordeaux quayside. When it came to striking the Bordeaux blockade runners, the Combined Operations 'tortoise' had beaten the SOE 'hare'. At a stroke, de Baissac's orders had been made irrelevant and his primary mission rendered impossible. The surprise, frustration – even anger – that he felt at this moment is evident in his description of the event, given in a debriefing eight weeks later. He reported that he had been on the verge of mounting his attack when:

> At the critical moment ... the unfortunate (from Scientist's point of view) Commando attack took place. Scientist's information was that charges were laid on seven ships, but the only result was that the ships, which were empty, settled one meter into the water and were immediately raised. Only one had to go to dry dock ... As a result of this attack which must be considered abortive, the Bordeaux Docks are now in a state of continuous alert, constant *rafales* take place and the dock guards were increased to 200 men who were armed with grenades and automatic weapons. The guards operate both on the ships and on the quays and fire at sight. There are sounds of shots every night and any floating piece of wood is immediately fired at. Searchlights are ready and mine-sweepers and corvettes are available with steam up.
>
> As a result, Scientist has had to give up these targets.

The only good thing that had come out of Hasler's attack, de Baissac concluded, was that everyone presumed that it was *Scientist*'s work and this greatly increased their standing in the area. De Baissac was to capitalise on this meagre dividend to recruit more agents, strengthen his organisation and prepare for an extensive campaign of sabotage on other targets in the Bordeaux area.

25

Begging Clothes and
Braving Daylight

13 December 1942

No. 10 Downing Street, London, morning of 13 December 1942

Documents to be read by the British Prime Minister are always put in his 'red box' at the end of the working day. Churchill habitually woke early and read the contents of his 'box' sitting up in bed wearing a silk dressing gown emblazoned with dragons, surrounded by the day's newspapers, his official documents and the wreckage of his breakfast; the day's first cigar firmly clamped between his teeth, a glass of brandy and water on his bedside table and a favourite cat, 'Nelson' or 'Munich Mouser', curled up at his feet.[1] In a next-door office, the duty Downing Street secretary would sit waiting for his summons to take down the letters and minutes he fired off across Whitehall each day, the most urgent of which carried the label ACTION THIS DAY and caused a panic of scurrying activity wherever they landed.

Among the other important documents, Churchill's box always contained a summary of the highly secret ULTRA decrypts of enemy signals from Bletchley Park. This summary was always seen first by 'C', the head of SIS, and signed off by him in the green ink which, according to Whitehall convention, is reserved exclusively for his use. This morning, the summary of German naval decrypts contained a message sent from Bordeaux to Marseille, which had probably been received and decrypted by Bletchley Park the following evening: 'Following landing of the English sabotage party on southern bank of the Gironde on December 8, four ships in Bordeaux harbour were sabotaged on December 12.'[2]

Reignac, Charente, southwest France

The fine, settled weather which had dominated southwest France since Hasler and his team left HM/s *Tuna* began to break in earnest as successive frontal systems moved across the area, ushering in unsettled conditions dominated by bands of heavy cloud and showers carried on freshening winds. The bitter cold of the last few days had passed, but from now on the escapers would have to endure squalls of wind and driving rain during the day, and damp ground to lie on at night.

Judging by Hasler's account, dawn found him and Sparks 'about a mile south of Reignac' – that is somewhere between the village of Verdot and the small settlement of Petit Brignac. Now, Hasler decided, they had to risk begging for civilian clothes.

The countryside in this area is dominated by sparse conifer woods interspersed with patches of deciduous trees and bushes, with here and there small, single-storey stone-built farmhouses surrounded by small-holdings of poor quality rough pasture. The farming here would have provided, at best, a subsistence livelihood during the war, for it supports little more than that even now. These would have been people living at the very edge of their own sufficiency with little left over for strangers.

But the two vagabonds, however, had one advantage in this sparsely populated countryside. At this point of the war while opposition to the Germans in urban areas was weak both in terms of numbers and intensity; anti-German sentiment in country areas was much stronger.[3]

Almost as soon as it was light, Hasler chose a small isolated farmhouse (an unnamed farm just outside Petit Brignac which is attached to its own barns, set in the middle of rough pasture and flanked at the rear by a small wood of conifer trees and scrub fits the description well) and, leaving Sparks concealed nearby with instructions to come in only when signalled[4] – and leave the area as fast as he could if Hasler did not return in fifteen minutes – he cautiously approached the farm buildings over the open fields. There was a man working in the yard. He was small, wiry, dressed in a beret and shirtsleeves (despite the cold) and had a Gauloise cigarette screwed as a semi-permanent fixture to his lower lip.

'Good morning Monsieur. We are two English soldiers escaping from the Boches. Can you give us some old clothes?'[5]

The man looked up at this strange figure with no more surprise than he would his neighbour asking for a pail of milk, shrugged his shoulders and, returning to work, gave Hasler a nod of his head which indicated that he should go inside and see 'her indoors'.

Hasler went to the back door of the house and knocked. It was peremptorily opened by a stout, bustling, middle-aged woman, around whose frame billowed an aroma of something delicious cooking on the stove behind her. Hasler had clearly interrupted her in the midst of a frenzy of domestic chores, which no doubt also explained why her diminutive and underfed husband had been banished to wield a broom in the yard.

Hasler launched into his routine once more:

'*Bonjour Madame* …' But he got no further than the word 'English' before his formidable interlocutor interrupted.

'Impossible! You can't be English. I can't possibly help you!' This was followed by a swift, prolonged torrent of French, of which Hasler understood not a word. His only response was to do his best to look hurt and desperate, which in the circumstances required little acting ability.

She regarded him closely for a few moments and then wordlessly turned her back and went inside, leaving behind only the tempting aroma as proof that she had ever existed.

But she did not shut the door. So Hasler waited, peering inside for clues, conscious that the old man behind him, though not missing a sweep of his broom, was watching closely too. A few moments passed and then, out of the darkness of the passageway and again accompanied by a gust of delicious cooking smells, she swept up to the back door with a black beret and a cloth cap that looked barely more than rags.

'They are very old, but we have no good clothes left. It is the war. Now go away, please – and don't tell anyone you have been here.'

Hasler thanked her profusely and, having added a '*Merci, Monsieur*' to the back of the cadaverous brush-wielder without receiving either sign or sound in return, made his way back to Sparks, clutching his two tiny threadbare trophies.

They would have to try again.

Hasler used the same routine at the next suitable farmhouse. But here, despite more desperate pleading, the response of the lady in charge was swift, unbending and wholly negative.

'We have nothing. We cannot help you. Try the farm over the hill,' she said pointing.

By now, both men must have felt very nervous. They were failing – and much more importantly, too many people now knew of their presence. In the open. In broad daylight. And still in uniform. Hasler and Sparks' inability to find civilian clothes now posed a mortal threat to both.

The kitchen door of the farm to which they had been directed was opened by a kindly-looking woman. She heard Hasler's pitch in silence and then, after a long, searching look, said: 'I will see' – and vanished.

Hasler was left exposed at the door for what seemed an age before the woman returned with a bundle of clothes. Hasler signalled Sparks in from his hiding place and then asked the woman if she could spare any food, or 'un sac, pour porter les choses' ('a bag for carrying our things'). She disappeared again for a moment, returning not with food as they had hoped, but with an ancient sack with a hole in it.

The two men thanked their benefactor warmly and retired to a nearby wood where, having eaten, they exchanged their uniforms for the new clothes, being careful to keep their warm service woollen underwear. They filled the sack with their balaclavas, seaboot stockings, gloves and escape boxes, buried their discarded uniforms, their fighting knives and their Colt automatics and emerged – they hoped – looking like two French vagabonds, ready to join the rag-tag army tramping French roads looking for work and shelter at this time of the war. Sparks wore the cloth forage cap (known as a brodequin in this region), his blue naval sweater, an old pair of trousers and the jacket they had just been given. Not having a coat, Hasler had to be content with old trousers, his blue sweater and the beret (he was lucky to find one big enough for him, for he had an unusually large head), all incongruously adorned by his most un-French-looking, luxurious blond moustache. Both men wore their rubber-soled commando boots, but these, fortunately, were not especially conspicuous to the casual observer.

They left the shelter of their wood and took to the open road in broad daylight, taking it in turns to carry the sack over their shoulders.

During the two or three hours Hasler and Sparks spent in the area, it would have taken only one German vehicle to pass, one collaborator to have seen them, and it would all have been over. The pair were subsequently plagued by the thought that one of those on whose doors they had knocked might have gone to the police after they left, or even simply gossiped casually to a neighbour. But they must have known that this risk was small in comparison to that of having to continue their journey in uniform.

The most dangerous moment of their escape had passed. Now all they would need was absolute determination, unbreakable resilience and, above all, incredible luck.

Though they had slept not at all the previous night and must by now have been reeling with exhaustion, Hasler wanted to put some distance between him and the farms at which he had called. He insisted they press on.

The first place they had to pass through was Brignac, a small village of forty or fifty houses gathered around a confusing square of roads. Their hearts must have been in their mouths as they sauntered casually through the village. Would they attract any interest? Would anyone stop and ask where they were going? Would they run into a gendarme?

In fact no one paid them the slightest attention. After anxious minutes they were taking the first turn left out of the village at a farm called La Fenêtre. They continued their journey northeast towards Donnezac, two or three miles away. Somewhere on this road, quite close to Brignac,[6] they were able to obtain a second sack and a jacket large enough to fit over Hasler's frame. By now it was late afternoon. Close to Donnezac they found some thick woods – possibly around Fortuneau – and, after gathering dead ferns, leaves and branches for a bed and putting on all their warm clothing they settled down, bodies huddled close together for warmth, and tried to sleep on the damp, cold ground. Though they had done their best to eke out the food they had brought with them, this was now running out. From now on hunger would gnaw away at them. So too would exhaustion and fear.

Somewhere four miles or so to their south, Laver and Mills, who had been unable to find civilian clothes, were breaking out of their cover to continue their journey east. Still in uniform, they could move only under the cover of darkness.

Meanwhile, on the west bank of the Garonne, seven miles or so south of Bordeaux, sixteen-year-old Anne-Marie Bernadet was leading her father's six cows home in the gathering dusk from the little field her family owned on the outskirts of St Médard d'Eyrans. She remembers the date well because it was St Lucie's Day, when they held the annual fair at the neighbouring village of La Brède. Every night Anne-Marie collected the cows, ambling with them back through the centre of the village past the *mairie* and on to the modest one-storey, one-bedroomed house in which she lived with her mother and father – a *petit agriculteur* or smallholder who eked out a living with a few cattle, a clutch of hens and a small patch of land on which he grew vegetables. His main source of income these days was selling milk to the neighbours, who would come to his house every night after he had milked the cows to have their pails and jugs filled up.

These were not easy times for the inhabitants of St Médard. There was a German artillery unit billeted in the village, some of whose personnel lived in a large house little more than a hundred and fifty yards from Anne-Marie's. But, for people like the Bernadets, survival and getting enough to eat posed a bigger problem than the Germans, who mostly left the local inhabitants alone – unless they made themselves conspicuous by showing their opposition to the Nazi presence or helping the enemy. Then retribution was brutal and swift. Anne-Marie had seen the posters: 'It is forbidden to give shelter to or to aid in any way, persons who belong to enemy forces … Anyone who contravenes this instruction exposes themselves to being taken before a German military tribunal of war and punished in the severest manner, including death.'[7]

As Anne-Marie led her cows into the village, she saw a man sitting at the roadside. Such a sight was not particularly unusual; there were many vagabonds and travellers looking for work and shelter these days. But his dress looked odd – not very French, somehow out of place. As she drew closer he stood and hobbled towards her. At first she was a little frightened, thinking he must be an escaped prisoner: only a few days previously a black man who had escaped from prison had come to their door for help. She noticed now that he was wearing denim trousers and a thick military-style jacket under which was a dark blue sweater. He had a rucksack slung over one shoulder and – to her surprise – very new-looking shoes; local shoes.

'*Sauvez-moi! Sauvez-moi! Sauvez-moi!*' he said urgently.

She tried to speak to him, but he didn't seem to understand, so she signalled him to follow a few paces behind the cows. When she got home, her father said the stranger must be hidden immediately and she was to say nothing about him to anyone. They ushered him into the back of the house, out of sight, until the neighbours had collected their milk and it was dark. Then they all sat round the family table together. With no house allowed to show a light after dark – anyone that did so would be swiftly visited by the Germans and fined – the windows were heavily curtained. And her father had fitted a black hood around the single electric light bulb in the main family room so that its light shone down in a tight circle on the table around which they now sat: four dimly lit figures, like conspirators in the gloom.

The stranger had taken off his shoes to reveal terrible blisters. Anne-Marie's mother told her to fetch some soap and a bowl of warm water so that she could wash his feet. When she came back, the stranger looked at their rough brown wartime soap and immediately started rummaging in his rucksack, pulling out some fragrant pure white soap of the sort no one in France had seen since the start of the war.

They did not have much to eat in the house. But her mother brought a mug of milk, some bread and a pot of home-made jam, made with precious sugar. The stranger ate and drank voraciously.

'*Prisonnier evadé?*' asked her father.

'*Non! Non!*' the stranger answered: '*Capitaine Écossais. Bateaux Allemands.* Boom! Boom! Boom!' he shouted, laughing uproariously and throwing his hands up in the air, knocking the lamp violently.

They talked as best they could for a while, but neither side really understood the other. The stranger produced a large map which he spread out in the circle of light and, by pointing and sign language, explained that he had to get to the other side of the Garonne so that he could make for Spain, perhaps by catching a train at La Réole eighteen miles to the southwest. Her father told him that the only bridge was at nearby Langoiran, but they didn't know if it was guarded or not.

Then her father told Anne-Marie to take their guest to a little barn about a hundred yards down the road, in which he kept hay. It was dark, so none of her neighbours saw her accompany Jack MacKinnon down the street. She left him to sleep in the pile of hay and propped a balk of wood against the outside of the door to discourage anyone from entering.

Next morning, after she had taken him some milk and bread, the stranger left, heading for Langoiran just after first light. He seemed to be hobbling a little less. Half an hour after he left, another stranger dressed in the same fashion passed by, walking strongly in the same direction.

We can only speculate how Jack MacKinnon and James Conway reached St Médard d'Eyrans. But given that MacKinnon was wearing new shoes of a local type and carrying a proper rucksack which was not part of the Marines' escape kit, it seems clear that they had help. Moreover, MacKinnon would have had no way of knowing that Hasler's raid had been successful, unless this information had come from local sources.

We do know[8] that, on the morning following the wreck of their canoe, MacKinnon and Conway were each found by local people and taken separately to the western shore of the Garonne, where they were reunited, probably in or near the little town of Macau. It seems likely that it was now that MacKinnon got his new shoes, the rucksack and the civilian clothes he wore over his blue sweater (Anne-Marie is sure that his trousers and jacket were blue denim and not camouflaged). Moreover, given that Anne-Marie found MacKinnon immediately outside a timber yard, into and out of which lorries passed regularly all day long, it seems possible that MacKinnon and Conway's helpers were local woodmen who had found them while cutting wood on the east bank of the Île Cazeau. Taking them first to Macau, they had given them clothes, food and shelter and then smuggled them to the vicinity of St Médard, perhaps on a timber lorry.

But why were they separated? Here again we can only speculate. Perhaps they concluded that since the Germans would be looking for two men, they should travel singly. Conway – for it was clearly Conway that Anne-Marie saw the following morning – spent his night elsewhere, perhaps hidden in the timber yard itself.

The story about Langoiran is intriguing. Afterwards, when they talked about that night, Anne-Marie and her family thought perhaps the stranger had friends to contact on the other side. Perhaps MacKinnon's helpers had arranged for him to meet others there who would also assist them, but had felt that, with the countryside in hue and cry after the Bordeaux explosions, it would be too risky to take them across the iron suspension bridge[9] over the Garonne at Langoiran.

MacKinnon and Conway may therefore have decided to go separately through the most dangerous areas, such as the few miles on either side of the Garonne, meet up on the banks of the river – which is still tidal at this point – and swim the two hundred yards across at slack water. Or perhaps it had been arranged that they should be picked up and carried across the river by one of the many small fishing boats in the area.

The two evaders' decision to abandon Ruffec as a destination in favour of Spain was a natural one, forced on them by the fact that they had been wrecked on the western bank of the Garonne. To reach Ruffec, they would not only have had to travel much further, but would also have had to cross both the Garonne and the Dordogne at their very widest points. If only SOE had been talking to their colleagues in Combined Headquarters, however, MacKinnon and Conway would have known that when they reached the town of Langoiran, they were less than a mile from the safety of Jean Duboué's house in Lestiac-sur-Garonne.

While MacKinnon burrowed into the hay in farmer Bernadet's barn and Hasler and Sparks huddled together for another damp and uncomfortable night in the woods near Donnezac, Norman Colley, Eric Fisher and Bill Ellery were bedding down in the Royal Marines Barracks at Stonehouse, Plymouth.

HM/s *Tuna* had endured a difficult journey home after dropping Hasler's team off at the mouth of the Gironde. The weather had been atrocious and, in the latter days, so overcast that Raikes could get neither an accurate star sight nor a decent sun sight. As a result they had navigated the last leg of the journey by dead reckoning, estimating their position by calculating the distance from their last accurate position by plotting the estimated speed of their vessel through the water, taking into account the course steered and the effect of both wind and tide. It was one thing to rely on dead reckoning when navigating in a large expanse of water like the Atlantic; quite another to depend on it when approaching hazardous and confined waters like the Western Approaches of the English Channel. In fact, *Tuna*'s return home would almost certainly have ended in disaster had it not once again been for the sharp eyes of her lookouts and the alertness of Lieutenant 'Johnny' Bull, as an account he wrote after the war illustrates:

> Approaching the English coast without a single [star or sun] sight, I climbed to the top of the periscope standards [on the conning tower] and sat there with a sextant for about five hours and finally got a sun/moon fix on a poor horizon. I rushed below and worked this out and, as soon as I had finished, shouted to Dick Raikes to alter course to the westward or we would pile up on the rocks.[10]

Shortly after changing course they heard the sound of the Lizard foghorn and soon saw the light itself, from which they were able to get a fix to see them safely on past Falmouth. Finally, sometime in mid-afternoon of 13 December, *Tuna* rounded Penlee Point and began running up Plymouth Sound, leaving the breakwater on her starboard side and finally tying up to D Buoy in the safety of the harbour at around 1900 hours, 13 December.

Colley and his two fellow Marines had little to do on the journey home except brood on their departed colleagues. Ellery seemed to withdraw into himself and keep his own company. Fisher and Colley played cards, smoked, read and whiled away the days as best they could. But *Tuna*'s fore-ends suddenly felt bereft and ghostly, haunted by the spirits of their departed comrades. The three Marines had plenty of space now, but this only made things worse – the emptiness seemed to mock them after the crowded jumble, noise and clutter of the journey down. No part of a submarine can ever be silent. But somehow it seemed so to them now, empty as it was of the banter and chatter of their colleagues. It felt as if all that comradeship was now somewhere else: on the dark waters of the Gironde, or hiding with their colleagues in some wood, or tramping alongside them down a lonely country road in the falling dusk – or locked up in the same cell of a German prison, perhaps.

Throughout *Tuna*'s voyage home, Hasler's papers (among them those precious last letters) had been kept safely under lock and key in Dick Raikes' cabin. As soon as *Tuna* was securely tied up, the papers were put in a waterproof bag and handed to Colley with instructions to take the first boat ashore and deliver them to the Adjutant of Plymouth Division, Royal Marines, at Stonehouse Barracks – where they had all been tested and selected by Hasler only five months previously. A lifetime ago.

Norman Colley's arrival outside the barracks – dirty, dishevelled, unshaven and reeking of diesel oil – was not welcomed by the Royal Marines sentry on duty. He took some convincing that the scruffy creature before him belonged to the same bright-buttoned, razor-creased, sparkle-booted Corps of Her Majesty's Royal Marines as he did.

Eventually Colley managed to persuade the sentry of his identity and a runner was sent to the adjutant's office. When Colley was brought before the adjutant's desk he felt naked and uncomfortable appearing before this lofty figure in such a disreputable state. The adjutant took the package, opened it and started to read the contents. After a few moments he looked up and ordered: 'Marine Colley and his two colleagues are to be taken to the barracks, given a square meal, a good bath, a complete new set of uniform and a proper bed in that order. They can report for duty in the morning after a good night's sleep.'

But, when Colley tucked himself up in clean sheets for the first time since they had sailed from the Clyde two weeks previously, he found that he had become so accustomed to lying on the hard deck of *Tuna*'s fore-ends that sleep would not come. So he lay on the floor, finally dropping off to a fitful slumber full of ghosts and memories.[11]

26

Hunger, Betrayal and Refuge

14 December 1942

Raymond Furet's parents were angry when, at the age of fourteen, he told them he was not going to school any longer.[1] As punishment, they set him to work on a small plot of land they owned not far from the family home in the little hamlet of Clérac, five miles due east of the Donnezac woods where Sparks and Hasler had spent the night.

The plot contained an old derelict house called Chez Ouvrard – little more than a room, an open barn and a large tool shed.[2] Raymond always left some food for himself in the larder cupboard – usually just bread, cheese and a bottle of wine – and, in this isolated area, never bothered to lock the house. This morning, when he entered the little house to *casse croute* ('break bread') before starting the day's work, he immediately noticed that someone had been there overnight. He went to the wire-gauze-covered door of the cupboard in which he kept his food and was surprised to find that his breakfast had gone and the cupboard was bare.

Except for a brief note – in English: 'Thank you'.

Perplexed, Raymond showed the message to his parents that evening. His father took one look at it and immediately consigned it to the fire, telling his son to say nothing of it to anyone.

Late the previous afternoon, Laver and Mills, still only some ten miles from where they had landed near Blaye, had bumped into a local man, Joseph Gagnerot, on the road. They appealed to him for help and shelter. Gagnerot directed them to Chez Ouvrard and told them that they would 'be alright spending the night there'.[3]

Perhaps Gagnerot also told Laver and Mills to help themselves to the food in the house. Perhaps the two Marines, tired, hungry and wet, felt that, having been led to this shelter, it was acceptable to help themselves without being invited. Either way, good manners required that the two young Englishmen should leave a thank-you note. Why did they make the cardinal error of writing it in English? Perhaps because they felt secure; more likely, for more poignant reasons: they knew no French and, having had no proper escape and evasion training, knew no better.

In fact, Laver and Mills' luck had just run out. Gagnerot was one of the most notorious pro-German locals in the area. He went to the gendarmerie in nearby Montlieu-la-Garde at five o'clock that evening and reported the presence of the two English soldiers to the adjutant, Georges Rieupéyrout, adding that he was only doing his duty and that he expected Rieupéyrout now to do his.

Early the following morning, Rieupéyrout sent a civilian friend to warn the two Marines, but they had moved on. After the war the Nuremberg War Crimes Tribunal ordered a full examination into the events surrounding Frankton. This was conducted by a British investigator, Captain Nightingale of the War Crimes Investigation Unit, who took evidence from, among many others, Georges Rieupéyrout. In his deposition Rieupéyrout said of this incident that he had no option but to mount a search for Laver and Mills, since Gagnerot kept the gendarmerie under close observation to ensure that action was taken and would otherwise have reported the matter directly to the German unit stationed in Montlieu just two hundred yards away. The ensuing search party found the two Marines asleep in a hay barn at a nearby farm called Chez David.[4]

Laver and Mills were arrested and taken back to Montlieu for interrogation, where Rieupéyrout advised them, according to his post-war testimony, to 'get rid of the papers they were carrying'.[5] Unusually, no list of possessions found on the Marines when they arrived in Montlieu exists, as was normally required under the regulations – though in his later evidence, Rieupéyrout comments that the men carried arms and were in full uniform 'with a blouse bearing the words Royal Marines on the shoulder and two crossed rifles [sic]'.[6]

Later that morning, in Montlieu-la-Garde, young Jules Bergéon was told by his father – who had been told by the town barber – that two

British prisoners who had escaped from a POW camp were being held in the gendarmerie. On the pretext of going to the bakery to fetch bread, Bergéon walked past the police station and, looking in through the open front door, saw two bare-headed young men in khaki shirts and trousers standing in the main hall, awaiting interrogation.[7]

When Adjutant Rieupéyrout searched the two fugitives he found an escape map in one of their jacket pockets. Aware that this would be incriminating if found by the Germans, he handed it over to M. Gaujean, proprietor of the Hôtel du Commerce, whose wife prepared the meal for the two prisoners which was taken to their cell at 2000 that night.[8] The ensuing interrogation of the two men was hampered because no one could be found in the town who could speak English. Nevertheless, Rieupéyrout gained the impression, perhaps deliberately planted by Laver and Mills, that the two had been heading south for Spain.[9]

The suspicion that the local gendarmerie may not have been over-eager to catch the fugitive Marines is reinforced by the fact that Commander Joliot, the regional head of the Gironde Gendarmerie Squadron, did not report their arrest either to his superiors or to other units in the area – or indeed to the Germans – until five days later. Only at 1300 on 19 December did he finally send a message to all neighbouring units, copied to the SD in Bordeaux: 'From the interrogation of two English soldiers arrested in Montlieu it appears that 15 other English soldiers remain at large in the area. The [captured] soldiers were in uniform and armed. You are requested to carry out active searches for them.'

Commandant Joliot's tardiness in reporting the incident won him an instant reprimand from his superior, Lieutenant-Colonel Demougin, Commander of the 18th Legion of the Gendarmerie in southwest France. He complained angrily of not being informed earlier, adding: 'Report to me in detail your reasons for not believing you had a duty to warn the Commander of the Legion [about this incident], which appears to be an important one [and] ensure that the proper reports are sent in future.'[10]

By the time Laver and Mills were arrested, Hasler and Sparks were already three or four miles into their day's journey. They had spent an uncomfortable night with almost constant rain; sleep, except in brief snatches, had proved impossible. So they set off before dawn, marching as fast as they could to get warm and overcome the gnawing pangs of empty stomachs. It was still dark when they passed through Donnezac, with its imposing *mairie* and thin-steepled church. Here, through lit windows, they would have caught homely glimpses of families gathered round breakfast tables, of near-dead embers being blown into glowing fires, of wives preparing their husbands' haversacks for the day's work. And felt the full pain of the fugitive, excluded from such mundane comforts – perhaps for ever.

North of Donnezac, in the Landes du Terrier Pêle, the landscape of sparse woods interspersed with pasture and occasional vineyards gives way to flinty, bracken-covered heathland, dotted with coppices of silver birch and with heather crowding right down to the sides of the road. This is empty country, with a few meagre one-storey farmhouses and almost no cultivation beyond occasional asparagus beds; good country for fugitives, though, with plenty of cover to dive into at the sound of an approaching car.

Turning right onto what is now the D253, they headed for Montendre, little realising that they were passing within five hundred yards of the German airfield at Montendre-Marcillac. In his biography, Sparks comments that German troop-carrying lorries and cars passed them frequently. Though this was an ever-present and sudden hazard throughout their journey, it would have been especially apparent on this straight stretch of road.

In their attempt to capture the remaining fugitives, there is some evidence that the German authorities flooded the area east and south of Blaye with troops, including – according to a rumour still prevalent in the Pointe de Grave area – the horse-borne Cossack Regiments stationed at Le Verdon.[11] Against this formidable force, Hasler and Sparks had only one flimsy means of defence: camouflage – but not of the sort they had been taught. If there was insufficient time for them to dive for cover at the sound of an approaching lorry, Hasler would indulge in energetic Gallic hand movements while appearing to gabble away in French at the silent Sparks, who would nod in agreement and give occasional, if unconvincing, Gallic shrugs in return. It was their sole means of persuading the passing hunters that these two vagabonds were not the prey they sought. Every French person they met received the customary and, they hoped, suitably French-sounding *'Jour M'sieur'* or *'Jour Madame'* as appropriate. Surprisingly perhaps, their ruse worked. But there was still the best part of sixty miles to go before they could hope to reach safety.

At around midday, the two fugitives turned left at Gablezac in order to avoid the large town of Montendre with its gendarmerie and concentration of Germans and headed northwest towards Champouillac. Here the countryside begins to open up again, with occasional vineyards scattered among the fir woods and patches of rough ground. With a brief turn southeast along what is now the main D730 and then, swiftly, another turn left onto a little country road heading northeast towards Rouffignac, they were now travelling through much richer countryside: good grazing pasture, increasingly frequent vineyards, small orchards, substantial farmhouses and little prosperous villages perched on hill tops above verdant valleys. By the time they reached Rouffignac, with its imposing Romanesque church and octagonal tower, they had covered some eight miles and were approaching the halfway point of that day's journey.

Here they nearly made a fatal error. Rouffignac lies at the meeting point of five roads, each of which joins the road through the centre of the village at a different spot. To add to the confusion, there are also numerous smaller roads and tracks leading off in every direction. Inevitably, Hasler and Sparks got lost. Unable to pull out their map and compass in plain view, they were exposed as strangers in the area and spent nervous minutes casting about trying to find the right road out of the village.

After Rouffignac, they developed a routine for use whenever they passed through any but the smallest and simplest settlements: they would discreetly leave the road a short distance before the village and find some cover in which they could study their map, carefully memorising the route. Once confident they knew the way, they would saunter casually through the town, with plenty of French chatter from Hasler and *faux* Gallic shrugs from Sparks, trying to look as though they knew the place like the back of their hand. Whenever this failed and Hasler felt the need to consult his escape compass, he would ask Sparks to light a cigarette in his cupped hands and used these as cover to take a surreptitious glance at the little instrument.

They continued north from Rouffignac through Villexavier and then Ozillac, where the terrain changes again. This is lush country with an English look to it: chestnut and walnut and oak; substantial houses with trim gardens; well-watered pastures and prosperous vineyards growing now white, rather than red grapes. Outside Ozillac they would have walked down a fine 300-yard avenue of mature chestnuts before crossing a railway line and heading northeast again. As they passed north of the village of St Médard, they would have seen ahead an escarpment scattered with vineyards and crowned with two substantial old windmills – Les Anciens Moulins de Chaillot.

Darkness was falling now and they had covered, in all, eighteen foot-wearying, nerve-jangling, famished miles. It was time to find a place for the night, which would have to be spent once again out in the open and with nothing between them and a cloudy, wind-blown and increasingly rain-filled sky. Exhausted now, they were down to the very last scraps saved from their original escape rations, supplemented by whatever they could scavenge from the fields in this mid-winter season.

Lucas Phillips says they took shelter this night in woods near St-Germain de Vibrac. The only woods substantial enough to have given them cover lie south of the village, near the modest grounds and buildings of the little Château de Peublanc. They had covered perhaps a quarter of their journey to Ruffec and had a good seventy or more miles still to go. Soon they would have to beg food and find a roof waterproof enough for a good night's sleep.

Baigneux

Fifty miles south, a well-dressed young man who appeared to have just descended from a bus was standing in the street which runs between the church and the school in the little village of Baigneux.[12] He looked rather lost. If only Richmond Terrace and Baker Street had been cooperating with each other, he would already have been comfortably hidden in Claude de Baissac's safe house at the Moulin de Saquet, less than two miles away. Fortunately there were other friends at hand.

When James Conway, wearing a blue serge suit and rubber-soled shoes,[13] saw Edouard Pariente on the street and decided to approach him for help, he chose well. For Pariente, who worked at the nearby

Frontenac quarry and had emigrated from Spain with his parents in 1926, was no German sympathiser. The Frenchman recognised only one word the young man said – 'English'. But he knew instinctively that this was an escaping British soldier asking for help. Edouard lived locally with his wife Félicie and two children, all of whose lives he would place in mortal jeopardy by helping the fugitive. Nevertheless, he did not hesitate. The Pariente home was too small to accommodate a guest, so he led Conway to the home of a local lawyer, Maître Delorge-Guilhon, who spoke English. The Maître's door was opened by his nine-year-old son Jacques. He explained that his father was not at home and ran back into the house to fetch his mother.

Mme Delorge-Guilhon was at the time pregnant and, apart from Jacques, had in the house an 84-year-old uncle, her eight-year-old daughter Claudie and a nine-month-old baby. She explained to Pariente that, without the Maître, she simply could not take the risk of accommodating the Englishman. So Pariente turned to a workmate at the quarry, Robert Pouget, who lived with his wife Cécile in a house invitingly called Chez Loulou. Pouget, who was active in the black market, agreed without hesitation to put the stranger up until somewhere more secure could be found. But, before he entered the house, Conway insisted on leaving for a few moments. He returned a short time later accompanied by Jack MacKinnon who, Pouget noticed, walked with a pronounced limp from an injured knee.[14]

MacKinnon and Conway again appear to have accomplished this stretch of their journey by different routes,[15] meeting at a prearranged spot near the quarries at Frontenac and then making their way together to Baigneux. We do not know their detailed route, how they travelled, or how MacKinnon sustained the injury to his leg. But given that the two had left St Médard d'Eyrans – some twenty miles away – that morning, they must have had help, both to cross the Garonne and to travel (perhaps in timber lorries again) to the Baigneux/Frontenac area. Moreover, since Anne-Marie Bernadet is sure that MacKinnon did not have an injured knee when she saw him the previous night, he must have suffered this injury during the journey.

Ars en Ré, near La Rochelle

At 1600 hours, an unmanned camouflaged canoe containing military equipment was found, washed up on the Ars beach on the Île de Ré, forty miles due north of the mouth of the Gironde.

None of the locals were surprised. Quite often, the flotsam and jetsam – and sometimes even bodies – washed out of the Gironde estuary ended up being carried by the tides and deposited on the beach, lying as it does at right angles to the northerly tidal stream.

But the local German commander, Lieutenant Blumröder, was not so relaxed about the discovery. Conscious of what had happened in Bordeaux, he reported to his superiors:

> It is without doubt that English sabotage troops are now at liberty on the Île de Ré or in La Rochelle. Increased watchfulness is necessary. I have already instructed the General Command at La Rochelle to introduce a higher degree of watchfulness ... [all units] must ensure maximum measures are taken day and night.[16]

No. 10 Downing Street, London

Among the Bletchley decrypts of German signals in Prime Minister Churchill's box this morning was the following:

> German S.S. 'Tannenfels', S.S. 'Portland,' S.S 'Dresden' and French S.S 'Alabama' were damaged by underwater explosions in Bordeaux on the morning of December 12th, and it was therefore concluded [by the Germans] that members of the sabotage party landed on the south bank of the Gironde on 8 December had succeeded in reaching Bordeaux. All these ships were reported empty at the time of the damage.[17]

This report was the only one in that morning's naval summary against which an approving tick appears in the red pen used exclusively by Prime Minister Churchill to sign off, amend or add notations to his documents.[18]

27

The Fiery Woodman and the Quarry Workers

15 December 1942

An entry in the diary of the Gendarmerie, Gironde Department, for this day reads: 'Starting today a large number of searches and road blocks have been put in place for the purposes of finding the English saboteurs who placed mines [on the ships in Bordeaux].'[1]

Montlieu-la-Garde

Today, 15 December 1942, was Bill Mills' twenty-first birthday.

In the early hours of the morning a detachment of the German *Feldgendarmerie* arrived unannounced in a truck outside the gendarmerie at Montlieu-la-Garde and demanded Laver and Mills. There has been speculation since as to who informed the Germans of the presence of the two Marines. It was originally presumed that Gagnerot had passed on the information. But from depositions taken after the war we now know that Rieupéyrout had informed his gendarmerie superior, Captain Borie of Jonzac, of the Marines' capture earlier in the day. It was Borie, a well-known collaborator, who informed the Germans and accompanied them to Montlieu to make the arrests; he boasted of it afterwards to friends.[2]

Laver and Mills were seized, bundled into a truck and driven away. They were taken first to the Fort du Hâ, the main German military prison in Bordeaux, where they were interviewed by a German officer,

Kapitänleutnant Franz Drey. A tobacconist in England before the war, Drey spoke near perfect English and was brought in specially to question the two Marines. He later described finding the two still in full uniform with insignia and with their hands and feet bound: 'I refused an interrogation of the two soldiers ... as long as the soldiers were not freed from their bonds ... My request was granted,' he said to the War Crimes Tribunal after the war. During Drey's later questioning of the two men, 'one of the English soldiers [asked] if they would be looked upon [by the German authorities] as saboteurs and not as soldiers? I emphasized that I regarded them as soldiers by reason of their special uniform with rank and insignia on their arms.'[3]

Following this interrogation (which took place in the presence of *Sicherheitsdienst* officers) it seems that Laver and Mills were removed from the Fort du Hâ and transported to Place Tourny, where, like Wallace and Ewart five days previously, they were locked up in the cells under the building before being handed over to Friedrich Wilhelm Dohse and his interrogation team.

Jack MacKinnon and James Conway were, meanwhile, being taken by another of Edouard Pariente's quarry mates, M. Cheyrau, along a farm track which runs east out of Baigneux for 400 yards until it joins what was, in 1942, a small-gauge, single-track railway line.[4] At this point the lives of Jack MacKinnon and James Conway hung precisely in the balance. Had they turned right and travelled southeast on the railway track for 750 yards, they would have arrived at the edge of Claude de Baissac's parachute site at the Moulin de Saquet and found safety with the Eliautout family and the *Scientist* network, who could have smuggled them home through Gaston Hèches in Tarbes. But, not knowing this, their well-meaning guides instead turned left and took them 500 yards northwest along the little train track to the house of Louis and Louise Jaubert.

The Jauberts lived in an isolated area called Séguin. The house, though tumbledown, is still there. Its rear aspect looks over the edge of a steep bramble-covered bank leading down to a stream along the side of which ran the light railway between the quarry of Frontenac, a mile distant to the north, and the village of St Brice on the Bordeaux road, two miles away in the opposite direction. But it was not just the isolated nature of *chez Jaubert* which made this an ideal place to hide the two fugitives: the Jauberts themselves were committed patriots. Their son, Roland, had been evacuated by the British from Dunkirk and, according to his letters home, had been treated very well. His imprisonment by the Germans on his return to France had been a much less happy experience.

Louise Jaubert later described what she saw from her back window that morning: 'Looking out of the window of our little house we saw our neighbour [Cheyrau] coming along the railway line, with two strangers following him. M. Cheyrau explained to us that they were two Englishmen who had come from Bordeaux.'5

The Jauberts, whose livelihood came from raising a few sheep on their smallholding, were not wealthy people. But they welcomed the two fugitives with open arms, even offering them money for the journey ahead. This Jack MacKinnon turned down, saying they still had more than enough left from the money they had brought with them in their escape kit. But they did not refuse Louise Jaubert's offer to wash their clothes (she particularly remembered the blue shirts and seaman's sweaters, with their English labels) – or the attention she gave to cleaning and treating MacKinnon's injured and now abscessed left knee.

Sixty miles to the north, Hasler and Sparks had endured a much less comfortable night. These thirteen-hour periods in the dark and damp of the woods must have been like prison sentences – especially if, as last night, it rained most of the time. Lying on sodden bracken, with no protection from the elements and lacking even the comfort of an evening meal, the hours must have dragged interminably until the curfew was lifted. Then they could get back on the road and enjoy again the small luxuries of exercising stiff limbs and getting the blood circulating, before exhaustion and hunger began to weigh down on them once more.

Though Hasler never mentions it, the two men would certainly have lain tight against each other at night to share body warmth. Such close contact would have been uncomfortable to them both, given their difference in rank and class and the more formal social norms of the time. The two had, moreover, so little in common that long silences must have dominated both their hours on the march and the dark sleepless watches of the night. Hasler's natural shyness and habit of maintaining a certain distance between himself and his men would have made this forced closeness especially awkward. And it would have required the patience of a saint to cope with what was, by his own admission, Sparks' most annoying habit – incessant grumbling and complaint. Later on Hasler was to say, one suspects only half in jest, that if he had known before he started what it was like to have to live with Sparks, he would have given himself up to the Germans in preference.[6]

Sparks' son, Terry, himself an ex-Royal Marine, recalls in his childhood seeing a field diary – now lost – kept by his father during and after Frankton.[7] Terry Sparks remembers the almost daily entries during the journey to Ruffec which began with expressions of black despair, such as 'All hope gone' and 'We will never make it.' Yet there is no evidence that Hasler ever lost his patience with his travelling companion. In his autobiography Sparks himself touches on Hasler's saintly tolerance of his constant whingeing and depression, describing how he would let Sparks ramble on until he became exhausted and then say, simply, 'Finished now, Sparks? Feeling better? Then let's get on with getting home.'

One thing is certain, given these long, dark, silent nights spent so close to each other, there would have been little or nothing that each man did not know about the other's habits, opinions and bodily functions by the time the journey was over.

The two fugitives passed through St Germain-de-Vibrac with its squat white limestone church and medieval fishponds just as the light started to seep into a lowering, overcast sky. It had rained throughout the night and they were soaked through, their damp clothes chafing their legs as they walked. Before leaving they had eaten the last of their escape rations: half an oatmeal biscuit and some dry tack.[8] Now they would depend entirely on what they could beg from homes or scavenge from the fields. After eight days without a proper night's sleep, they were at their lowest ebb.

The rain, which had briefly stopped around dawn, began falling insistently again early in the morning. Passing through St-Ciers-Champagne they turned right onto what is now the D3. This would have been the most nerve-racking and exposed part of their journey: the road here, apart from being the most major highway they had travelled on so far, is long, straight and without cover on either side. They could see and be seen for at least a mile in either direction as they tramped along through open arable farmland, devoid of friendly woods or the smallest patch of scrub. There must have been a lot of German military traffic on this main road during the two hours it would have taken them to tramp the five miles to Champs des Doux.

Here they turned left to avoid the large town of Barbézieux-St-Hilaire and began to follow small, friendly country roads again. Given that the Germans were now searching every corner of the land for the fugitives, it seems almost unbelievable that no passing truck or car ever stopped to question them; and no checkpoints to pass through, either. Even the most casual enquiry at this stage would surely have unmasked them as two evading British raiders.

Famished though they were, Hasler decided that they should wait until after '*midi*' before taking the risk of begging for food, in the hope that there was a better chance of leftovers after lunch than before it. They were now tramping north on minor country roads past the village of Barret with its roadside stone cross and on through open countryside peppered with small well-tended farms, patches of woodland, occasional pasture and an increasing number of vineyards. They were working their way towards Cognac now, passing through the white grape vineyards from which the famous brandy is made.

It must have been around two o'clock, as they turned north up what is now the D1, that they decided to try their luck once more. Working on the assumption that plumpness is the sign of a generous spirit, they approached the back of a corpulent man working at a roadside garage at Maison Rouge. When he turned round the two fugitives saw that, though his frame was generous, his face and eyes were thin, mean and unappealing. To Hasler's now well-rehearsed appeal for help he gave the equally well-rehearsed response in these country areas – a Gallic shrug and a synchronised hand and head gesture whose meaning was universal in any language: 'Go and ask the missus. And much good may it do you!'

The lady of the house looked as famished as her husband looked well-fed. But her face was equally sour. And so too was her response.

'I have nothing to give you. We do not have enough for ourselves. Clear out!'[9]

On their way out the two beggars noticed that there were telephone lines coming into the garage – relatively unusual at the time in country areas. Worried that the woman of the house might call the police, they made a mental note not to call at houses with phones in the future and pressed on as fast as they could so as to put as much distance between them and the garage as possible.[10]

Three miles further on, as they were leaving Touzac with its fine church and prosperous houses, they saw a woman feeding chickens in her hen run at the front of one of several small, modern houses on the outskirts of the village.[11] The promise of generosity hinted at by her plump figure was in this case borne out by a homely and maternal face. According to Lucas Phillips, Hasler decided to try again.

'Are you really English, Monsieur?' she asked, suspicious no doubt of Hasler's German accent.

'Indeed, Madame.'

'And your friend?'

'He is English too. But he speaks no French.'

'You speak no French, Monsieur?' she questioned Sparks.

Not understanding a word, Sparks rubbed his stomach and replied, hopefully, *'Ver-y hun-gry.'* This seemed to convince her, for she turned, went into the house and re-emerged with a chicken leg and half a stale loaf.

The two fugitives chatted to their benefactor while they divided the chicken leg in two, sucking the bones dry. But it was the bread, with bulk enough to fill up yawningly empty stomachs, that gave them most comfort.

'There are Germans in Lignières-Sonneville,' she warned, pointing to the next village, a mile away to the west.

Their brief snack over, the two men doffed their battered caps and, giving Lignières-Sonneville a wide berth, turned east two miles further on, towards St Preuil. It still rained incessantly and Hasler discovered that the dampness of his clothing had caused moisture to seep into his button compass, making it useless. Fortunately they carried three spares.

The light was beginning to fade now.[12] They had covered eighteen miles. It was time to find a place for the night. Descending into the bowl which contains the village of St Preuil, Hasler decided to knock on the door of the first house they came to, a small farm called La Pitardie. But the owners, the Trouillet family, made it very clear that they did not want them, directing them instead to a nearby house called Maine-

Laurier, the home of the Malichiers, who were *vignerons*: wine makers. Madame Malichier took one look at the two vagabonds, their haggard eyes hung with dark bags of tiredness, their cheeks sunken, their clothes sodden – and called the son of one of her husband's labourers, a young man called Cadillon.[13]

Clearly herself very frightened by the presence of the two fugitives on her property, Mme Malichier told the young man that these were two escaping Englishmen whom he was to take immediately to a nearby, isolated farm called Napres, the home of Clodomir and Irène Pasqueraud. Hasler and Sparks followed their young guide wordlessly up the hill and out of the village, retracing their steps until they came to a wood. Here they turned left off the road and followed a track through the trees.[14] The two Marines began to suspect a trap. But presently they came to a clearing, in the middle of which sat a small, meagre-looking house with a comforting curl of smoke issuing from its chimney.[15]

It was fully dark now, bitterly cold and blowing hard. A dog barked furiously as they approached the back door, under which shone a chink of light. Cadillon knocked on the door. It was opened abruptly by a squat, fearsome-looking figure, whose wild countenance was reinforced by an unkempt red moustache, a barrel chest and eyes ferocious enough to be the envy of any self-respecting pirate. Behind him through the half-open door, the visitors could see a circle of light coming from two candles, a room of earthen floors and tumbledown furniture, a blazing fire and a homely-looking woman with an assortment of children of varying sizes, watching them closely.

Cadillon, stammering, explained the purpose of his visit and the identity of the night travellers. There was a moment's fierce examination of the three figures before the door was flung wide and they were ushered inside.

It took a moment for Hasler and Sparks to adjust their eyes to the scene as the door was bolted shut, closing out the night behind them. Against one wall was a large cast-iron cooking stove enclosing a roaring fire and surmounted by a clatter of pots and cooking utensils. From its every crack and orifice, smoke belched, mixing with the pungent odour of cooking and garlic, filling the room with a haze that made their eyes smart and their mouths water at the same time. Close to the door was a large rough-hewn table surrounded by benches. On the walls hung an assortment of battered cupboards, and scattered round the room were a collection of ancient chests to match. Filling the end of the room furthest from the door was a giant family bed which appeared to have mislaid its mattress elsewhere. The guard dog crouched, growling, spring-loaded, teeth bared and ready to launch all its massive shagginess at the strangers in an instant – if only its master would give the signal. And behind it, in silent, inquisitive array, the woman and children, eyes fixed on their fearsome host, the young man Cadillon and the two night strangers.

'Who are you? Why do you come here? Who the devil told you to come to *me*?' began Pasqueraud, according to Lucas Phillips.

Hasler ran through his routine. But it had no effect. It was Cadillon's turn next to weather the assault, which he vainly tried to turn away with soft answers. Then, to Hasler again:

'You are NOT English! It's not true! You cannot be! Where's the proof? Where are you from?'

Hasler and Sparks reached under their damp, malodorous clothes to pull out their identity discs. But these too were dismissed with anger.

'That means nothing! What have you been doing? Where did you escape from?'

'That's a secret,' Hasler replied. 'But it was a commando raid.'

The word 'commando' seemed to have some subterranean effect on this volcano of fury and interrogation. But not enough to stop the eruption.

'Show me some English things!' he demanded.

They pulled out their escape boxes and showed him their V for Victory matches, their British soap, their British toilet paper; their escape compasses.

But none of it was enough. The torrent of disbelief continued unabated. Suddenly the little bundle of muscular fury swung on Sparks and fired a salvo of quick questions. Sparks, understanding nothing, replied, pointing to himself and flashing his most disarming, gap-toothed Cockney grin: 'English – savvy?'

At about the same time, the two escapers heard the familiar voice of the BBC coming from behind the curtain in the corner of the room. It was the news from London and the voice was saying something about a great battle won in North Africa; the two men leaned forward, listening intently, and congratulated each other on the good news of the Eighth Army's desert progress.[16]

Suddenly convinced their host's interrogation was over and his welcome became as fierce as his hostility had been before.

'*Je suis Clodomir Pasqueraud. Communist moi!*' – raising his fist at this point – 'Drop me a gun! I will kill Nazis for you! I'll kill them behind! The Russians will kill them in front. Soon the war will be over! Have you eaten? Tell me, have you eaten?'

'If he's asking if we have eaten, tell him I could eat a horse,' Sparks said.

'My friend says he could eat a horse.'

Clodomir fired off some rapid orders to his wife, who trotted dutifully over to the stove while the children crowded round the two strangers, touching the maps, compasses and matches and saying wonderingly '*Anglais, anglais*' to each other, while Sparks ruffled their hair and started to play with them.

The ice was now well and truly broken. While Madame cooked, Clodomir the woodman became more and more animated.

'You are going back to England?'

'We hope so.'

'Good, tell the Air-Ah-Eff [RAF] to drop me some weapons – here!'

Dashing round the room, grabbing at imaginary items falling from the sky with the children in gay pursuit, he caught an imaginary pistol and fired it at an imaginary German. '*Paf!*' The German fell dead.

Then a rifle, which he put to his shoulder. '*BANG!! BANG!!*' – another Nazi bit the dust.

Next, a tommy gun. Crouching now, the weapon tucked into his hip to control the recoil – '*AT-TA-TA-TA-TA-TA-TAT!!*' – a whole platoon of Boche collapsed like falling cards.

'We'll fight! We'll kill plenty of Germans!'

Suddenly there was a knock at the door. In an instant, make-believe turned into the possibility of terrifying reality. From somewhere, Pasqueraud, with a single swift movement, pulled out a real weapon – an old 7.62 rifle – while at the same time unbolting the door and shouting: 'Come in!'

The door swung open, letting in a cold blast of the stormy night and with it the figure of a young man, who found himself with the muzzle of Pasqueraud's rifle planted firmly in the side of his neck.

In a moment it was over. The little woodman recognised their late-night visitor as Robert Patience, the seventeen-year-old apprentice of the local baker who often brought the Pasqueraud family leftover bread at the end of the day's work – risking, as tonight, both the wrath of his boss and punishment for breaking the curfew to do so.

'Dine with us,' Clodomir ordered the young man, who gratefully accepted.

By now Madame Pasqueraud had brought to the table a steaming casserole filled to the brim with the carcass of a fat chicken. The children had already laid out rough wooden bowls. When they all sat down to eat together, Madame made sure that Hasler and Sparks got the biggest share.

From behind the curtain the BBC kept up background chatter, with an unbroken stream of coded messages for France: 'Bébé, tell mother that all is well – Valentin is to go to the bakers and ask for a baguette – Lucie says hello to Amélie and Georges – the geese will cross the moon tonight …'

Suddenly Clodomir Pasqueraud banged the table.

'When you get home *you* must send us a message on the Bay-Bay-Say, so we know you are safe. But it must be … in code!' – drumming his fingers on the table – 'I have it!' he exclaimed, pointing at the steaming casserole: *Le poulet est bon – le poulet est bon* – that will be our code on the Bay-Bay-Say to tell us you are home!'

After dinner the little woodman took Robert Patience outside into the yard where the young man had hidden his bike and warned him not to say anything to anyone: 'They are two English from Bordeaux – say nothing or we'll all be shot.'

By now, their stomachs full of their first decent meal for eight days, Hasler and Sparks were reeling with exhaustion. Clodomir Pasqueraud would not hear of them sleeping anywhere but the bed of his two elder sons, Yves and Marc, on the first floor. They stripped down to their underclothes, leaving their outer garments to be hung out in front of the fire by Madame Pasqueraud. Then – for the first time since their launch from *Tuna* all those distant days and nights ago, and heedless of the hygienic uncertainty of mattress and bedclothes – they fell into the luxury of a real bed.

*

For Johannes Bachmann, in his headquarters in Nantes, 15 December was a less congenial day. Following an angry letter from Field Marshal Keitel at Supreme Headquarters in Berlin demanding greater vigilance, Bachmann issued a signal to his naval units. Headed 'Sabotage in Bordeaux on 12 December 1942', it gave a full resumé of what had happened and listed a series of actions he now required them to take. These mostly repeated the instructions already issued by Kühnemann, but added for good measure:

> Prisoners are to be segregated immediately. Keep a sharp watch over them. Escape is out of the question ... Should an explosive device be activated against the hull of a ship, the remainder of the hull and those of neighbouring ships should be searched immediately ... The foregoing instructions are to be carried out to the letter.[17]

The clang of stable doors being energetically shut once again reverberated across southwest France.

28

Unnecessary Dangers

16 December 1942

The Chiefs of Staff Committee met this morning in the conference room set aside for their use in the Cabinet war complex beneath the Treasury building in Whitehall. Item 3 of the minutes from that meeting reads:

> Lord Louis Mountbatten reported the apparently successful results which had been achieved by part of the 'Frankton' force.
>
> The Prime Minister said that he wished to record his appreciation of what seemed to have been an extremely gallant and enterprising operation.[1]

Such direct comments from Churchill to the Chiefs of Staff Committee on individual operations were if not unprecedented, then at least extremely rare.

By the time the Chiefs gathered in their underground bunker that morning, Hasler and Sparks would have been well on the next stage of their journey. The Pasqueraud household had risen, as usual, before dawn. Last night's storm had passed and day broke to reveal a thin haze covering a clear sky with light winds from the southeast and temperatures around six degrees. After a night of seductive comfort and the luxury of full stomachs, it must have been a temptation to the two Marines to linger with their generous hosts – and indeed, the Pasquerauds tried to persuade them to do so. But Hasler insisted on leaving early, conscious of the need to press on and the danger he brought his hosts if he and

Sparks had been spotted last night by someone in the village sympathetic to the Germans.

Mme Pasqueraud, who had blown the fading embers of last night's fire back to life, presented her guests with luxurious bowls of hot water to wash in, followed by breakfast of bread, jam and hot 'ersatz' coffee. The little woodman insisted that Hasler and Sparks should not march the next part of their journey alone, but should be accompanied, at least as far as the Pont de Vinade over the Charente river, by his two eldest sons, Marc and Yves.[2]

Meanwhile, Mme Pasqueraud prepared a picnic of bread and the cold leftovers of last night's chicken. Hasler asked for some water and the Marines' bottles were duly filled.

They said their reluctant goodbyes, promising to ensure that the BBC sent the agreed code word – 'Le poulet est bon' – as soon as they got back, and to visit them again when the war was over. Then the two fugitives and the two Pasqueraud sons made their way back up the track through the wood and turned north again, passing once more through St Preuil and then up a steep escarpment before beginning the long descent into the Charente valley. They were now in the Cognac region proper.

Four miles or so from St Preuil, they came to St Même-les-Carrières, which to all outward appearances was just like every other little town they had walked through. But, as they passed the Café du Commerce[3] and entered the town square, a bugle sounded and a host of German soldiers poured out of a nearby building and started to line up for parade, deliberately bumping and jostling the four men as they ran past them.[4] Hasler's subsequent report to MI9 indicates that he was 'informed' (probably by the Pasqueraud boys) that this German detachment had moved into St Même only a few days previously and were part of the force deployed to the area to search for the two fugitives.[5] Had Hasler and Sparks been on their own, it seems very probable that they would have been stopped. But since the Germans were looking for two men and what they saw was four, they were left alone.

Leaving the square, Hasler and Sparks were inwardly congratulating themselves on having escaped disaster when another German came running up the road past them straightening his tunic and doing up his belt. 'Obviously late for parade. I bet he gets a hard time from the sergeant-major,' muttered Sparks under his breath.

Two miles past St Même, they crossed over the Pont de Vinade. The Charente at this point is a fine wide river, navigable by small boats. They must have feared that there would be a road block here, but mercifully it was clear. It was here that Yves and Marc Pasqueraud left their charges to continue alone and returned home.[6]

The two Marines continued their journey, travelling northwest now along the line of the Charente and passing the small château at Triac, where they swung north once more. They stopped outside the hamlet of Lantin (the N141, now a dual carriageway, runs just north of the village) to dip into the picnic Mme Pasqueraud had given them, while trying to conserve as much of it as they could for later. When Hasler took a swig of his water bottle he discovered that the Pasquerauds had, unbeknown to either of them, filled both his bottles and Sparks' with wine. They emptied one bottle into a nearby stream and refilled it with fresh water. But they kept wine in the other.[7]

On then through rolling vineyard country, past the imposing château at Fleurac, through Vaux Rouillac – the largest town they had been through so far – and along a ridge crowned by another windmill, from where there are fine views of the Charente snaking away to the west. The two fugitives would have been in no mood to enjoy such delights, however, for by now they were very foot-weary – and ravenously hungry again. To their joy, they found a pile of potatoes and turnips by the side of a ploughed field, devouring them raw accompanied by their Horlicks tablets, which were supposed to aid the digestion of raw food.[8] It was growing dark now and had started to rain yet again. Hasler discovered that damp had seeped into their second escape compass and he had to resort to their next spare. Now there was only one left.

They were lucky to find a small, deserted, rat-infested hut at the side of a light railway south of the hamlet of Le Temple. Here they ate a little of Mme Pasqueraud's food and had a dry if not especially comfortable night lying uncovered on the bare concrete floor, wet to the skin, while the rain beat down incessantly outside.

If only SOE and Combined Operations had been cooperating with each other, the two fugitives could have safely ended their journey there in Le Temple. For this was another of de Baissac's key areas of activity and the centre of a ten-square-mile parachute landing site which would become, in just a month, one of his biggest and most heavily used reception areas.[9]

29

Moments from Disaster

17 December 1942

It must have looked at first like a balk of timber; or a crumpled piece of common flotsam washed up on the long wave-swept beach at Blois en Ré,[1] not far from where a canoe had been found three days previously. Closer examination revealed it was a corpse of a young man dressed in camouflage uniform.

When the broken, blood-drained body was examined, a red identity tag was found hanging on a cord next to his skin. The stamped lettering on it was arranged in a circle at the centre of which was 'R.C.', denoting that the wearer's religion was Roman Catholic. Round the outside, the crude lettering read 'Ply-X108881 Mne Moffatt. D. D-o-B 20-11-20'.[2]

They buried David Moffatt, the brilliant mimic, in an unmarked grave in the ridge of dunes behind the beach – as they did all the many unclaimed bodies washed up on this stretch of beach during the war.[3] He lies there somewhere, still.

Fifty miles to the southeast, Hasler and Sparks ate the last of Mme Pasqueraud's picnic in the shelter of their rat-infested railway hut and, stretching cold, stiff legs, set off through the rain – more persistent and determined than yesterday – heading north once again along little country roads.

Past Montigne the countryside changes once more. They were out of the wine country now and into rolling agricultural land with big fields separated by hedges and interspersed with small coppices – not unlike Salisbury Plain or the long rolling crests of the south Dorset hills. This is a land of wide views fading into distant valleys and long, vanishing ridges retreating towards the horizon. Big skies too – or there would have been, had the heavens not been shrouded in cloud and pouring down on them all day as they tramped on, along deserted country roads and muddy farm tracks: two tiny, bedraggled figures hunched against the weather and dwarfed by the endless, desolate empty landscape all around them.

They passed through the almost deserted villages of Bonneville and Mons, with its pretty Romanesque church and tower topped by a dark-slated steeple. There they turned north towards Oradour to avoid the large town of Aigre. Past Oradour, they picked up a cart track which took them across marshy fields bordering a small swollen brook which they crossed by stepping stones to arrive at St Fraigne lying in a low hollow in the hills.

By now it was approaching 1600 and getting dark. They had to find shelter for the night – and something to eat as well. In front of them was the little agricultural hamlet of Beaunac, its northern edge butting onto the road ahead.

Here, they decided, they would try their luck. They did not notice the German watch-tower just 200 yards from the edge of the village.

'No, not here. Go somewhere else,' said the woman at the first door at which Hasler knocked.

'*Nous sommes deux soldats Anglais,*' he said again, hopefully, at the second door.

'*Impossible!*' said the woman who had come to Hasler's knock, slamming the door in their face.

They tried a third house. The response was the same. 'Friendly little place,' offered Sparks.

'They're all frightened. Perhaps the Gestapo have been round here,' Hasler suggested.[4]

The fourth door they tried was that of a modest-sized farm gathered around a courtyard edged with large barns, one of which invitingly spilled hay from the arched doorway of a first-floor loft.

The woman who answered was too frightened to say anything and called her husband. André Latouche had been watching the men for some time.[5] He ushered them in, installed them in front of a blazing fire, gave them some bread and pâté and then took them up a ladder into the hay barn. Here, after motioning them to make themselves at home, he went back to his house, returning after a few moments with a lantern and another half loaf of bread.

'Do not move from here. It is dangerous in the village,' he said – and left them. Dog tired but with full stomachs, the two men fell almost immediately into a deep, exhausted sleep.

But it did not last long. An hour or so later, they were suddenly and rudely awoken by a young man called Lucien Gody.

'You must go at once! There are people in the village who do not want you here and they have sent for the police. Hurry!'

Hasler and Sparks bundled themselves down the ladder and out into the unwelcome night. It was still raining. They splashed their way up a track pointed out to them by Gody and stumbled through the darkness until they were clear of the village.[6] Here Hasler consulted his compass. It was sodden and unworkable. He pulled out his fourth and last compass and they sloshed their way through the night towards the little village of Souvigné along a flooded cart track – at least this would prevent them from being followed by dogs, Hasler confided to Sparks.

Suddenly, not far from Souvigné, they saw the unmistakable bulk of a haystack loom up out of the night. They scooped out a hole in its base and crawled in, pulling a wedge of hay behind them to close the entrance. At least it was dry and warm. And safe – they hoped.

Not long after Hasler and Sparks had made their escape from Beaunac, gendarmes flooded in and searched the village. After settling his visitors in his hay barn, André Latouche had decided that he could not take the risk and had to seek advice. He went to see Mayor Bineau at neighbouring Ébréon (the centre of the commune in which Beaunac lies) to ask what he should do. Bineau decided that the commune *garde champêtre* (a kind of community policeman), Monsieur Picot, should be informed. He in turn reported the incident to the gendarmerie at Aigre, the main town in the area. They passed the message on to gendarmerie headquarters in Angoulême, who ordered an immediate but (thanks to Lucien Gody) fruitless house-to-house search of Beaunac.

Hasler and Sparks had avoided catastrophe by the narrowest of margins. Once again, their luck had held. But there would be consequences.

Combined Operations' War Diary notes that, on this day, 17 December, Mountbatten received a copy of the 'German memorandum on English Sabotage Activities' in Bordeaux. This was almost certainly the full Bletchley Park decrypt of Commander Kühnemann's detailed report with diagrams sent to Berlin on 13 December (see Chapter 23).[7] Now London could stop guessing about Hasler's success; they knew for certain and in detail how much damage he and his little team had achieved with their two canoes and sixteen limpets.

30

Arrival and Arrest

18 December 1942

Early on the morning of 18 December, Captain Poirier, commander of the Cognac section of the 18th Legion, Gendarmerie Nationale, sent an urgent signal to all units reporting that late the previous afternoon, 'two suspect foreign individuals came to the hamlet of Beaunac ... and asked for food and shelter, saying that they had come from the coast'. A unit of gendarmes had been sent immediately to the village, but 'the two individuals had already left in the direction of Souvigné'. Poirier ended his message by ordering 'Active search required' and giving the fugitives' descriptions:

> **The First man:** Height about 1 metre 75; blond hair, bald, small moustache; clothes very worn indeed and of blue colour; shoes black; socks grey; no hat. Speaks French.
> **Second man**: Height about 1 metre 70. Clean-shaven; clothes dark grey; blond hair; cloth forage cap. Speaks no French.[1]

On the same day, the Regional Intendant of Police for the Gironde region wrote a letter to his colleague in Bordeaux reporting the information he had gleaned from German sources about Hasler's raid. Its final paragraph said:

> I am under instruction to keep these facts strictly confidential because of their delicate nature. But actually the information is

more or less all fully known to the local population who believe the sabotage to have been carried out by a British team who either came up the Gironde as far as Bordeaux, or were parachuted into the area.[2]

Despite the Germans' best efforts, the success of Hasler's raid was becoming common knowledge in Bordeaux and right across the Charente region.

When Hasler and Sparks crawled out of their haystack near Souvigné shortly after dawn, they were observed by a woman from the village who reported to the gendarmes what she had seen.[3]

Before starting on what he hoped would be the final leg of their journey to Ruffec, Hasler consulted his compass – his last. Only to find that it too was now contaminated by moisture, the little needle stuck and motionless. He blew on it, dried it as best he could, shook it hard. Finally the needle began to quiver and weakly swung to point north. It would be enough – just enough – to see them through the last miles.

They were on the edge of exhaustion now and weak with hunger, spurred on only by the proximity of Ruffec, eight miles away – and the promise of the assistance of friends who, as they thought, were looking out for them.

It rained a little at around 0800,[4] but the weather otherwise remained kind as they trudged by little field tracks through Raix, where they met the main road which runs through Villemorte to the town. Now they could see Ruffec, dissected by the main Paris–Bordeaux railway line, backed by woods and clustered around its ancient château perched on a high point above a tributary of the Charente.

Hasler and Sparks walked into Ruffec at around 1115, along the main road from Villefagnan which enters the town from the east.

It seems little short of a miracle that they had made these last ten miles travelling, mostly not on small tracks, but along substantial and well-used roads. The gendarmes knew what they looked like, where they had been the previous night – even which haystack they had slept in – and the direction they were heading. It is scarcely possible to believe that, given all these factors, the local gendarmerie could not catch them. Unless, of course, they did not want to.

It seems probable that – at least on this final march to Ruffec – it was not merely luck that saved Hasler and Sparks; it was also that the gendarmerie were content not to find them. This possibility is greatly strengthened by the fact that the Ruffec gendarmerie was at this time commanded by Lieutenant Henri Péyraud, a key Resistance figure who worked for both Lise de Baissac and Mary Lindell.[5]

Having finally reached their goal, Hasler and Sparks suddenly found themselves bewildered and uncertain. As they walked into town they looked expectantly into every face – and saw no reciprocal spark of recognition or interest. They stood hopefully on street corners, but no one seemed to notice them. They even passed close to a policeman on point duty – but he paid no attention to them either, although they looked – and smelt – like a pair of the most malodorous vagabonds. They spent an hour and a half wandering about, feeling increasingly exposed and depressed. All this effort – and for nothing?

In fact, contrary to what Hasler and Sparks believed, they had indeed been noticed. A local baker and Resistance activist, René Flaud, was returning in his baker's van from a passage across the Demarcation Line with escaping fugitives, when he saw the two men at the entrance to Ruffec, remarking to himself that, even by the standards of wartime vagrants, they looked unusually disreputable. They were spotted, too, by another member of Ruffec's Resistance organisation, Mlle Henriette Regéon, who was also driving back into town in a lorry. MI9's calculation that the two would be noticed on entering Ruffec had proved correct. It was their inability to warn the *Marie-Claire* line to look out for the fugitives that was the problem – thanks to Mary Lindell's refusal to take a radio and MI9's failure to provide any other form of effective communication with her.[6]

In fact, Mary Lindell was not even in Ruffec that day. She was in hospital recovering from a near fatal accident, a hundred miles away.

At about the same time as *Tuna* sailed from the Clyde, she had left Lyon at the start of a tour of her escape routes, completely oblivious of the twelve men who would soon be depending on her for their lives. Three days later, on 3 December, as *Tuna* made her way down the Bay of Biscay, Mary Lindell was investigating a new crossing point of the Demarcation Line close to Blois in the Loire valley.[7] Suddenly and without warning, a car driven by two pro-German French collaborators smashed into her bicycle, catapulting her high into the air to come crashing down on the car's radiator cap. She was carried to a nearby farmhouse, where the farmer pronounced her dead and began to dig a grave for her in the garden.[8]

She miraculously survived and was quickly transferred to hospital in the little town of Loches, where she was put in the care of a Resistance surgeon called Martinez.[9]

She spent the next few days fighting for her life, finally pulling through on 10 December (the day of Hasler's uncomfortable sojourn on the Île Cazeau) when her son Maurice was permitted by the doctor to pay her a visit – only to be told by his mother to return immediately to Ruffec and tell Gaston Denivelle to carry on 'the business' without her until she recovered.[10] According to Dr Martinez, this was unlikely to be soon. She would have to stay in hospital for at least five weeks to give time for her bones to heal. For now at least, Ruffec, the *Marie-Claire* line and those who depended on her to escape France, would just have to do without her.

Eventually Hasler and Sparks decided that, with money remaining from their escape francs, they would at least try to get something to eat. Needing to choose a cheap, working-class establishment where their clothes and rank odour would not be out of place and where there would, preferably, be few fellow customers, they looked at several restaurants, standing at the window and inspecting what was inside while pretending to study the menu. They saw the Hôtel de France (home of the Rouillons, Mary Lindell's headquarters and Lise de Baissac's main base in Ruffec) but its size, and the sight of the German swastika flying over its front door, not unnaturally put them off. About a hundred yards further on they found a little corner café/hotel called the Toque Blanche ('The Chef's White Hat'),[11] with a dozen or so working men lunching at tables inside. This seemed the kind of place they were looking for. With some trepidation, they pushed open the door and walked in, taking a seat in the corner as far away from their fellow diners as possible.

Their luck had held again. The proprietor of at least one of the restaurants they had looked at was known to have betrayed evaders to the Germans for money.[12] But not René Mandinaud, the owner of the Toque Blanche, or his two sisters Yvonne and Alix, who ran it. No more than a hundred yards from the German headquarters, the Toque Blanche was convenient for German officers – who were, at the time Hasler and Sparks walked in, billeted in the first-floor front rooms above. But the fact that the Germans were there did not mean they were welcome.

René Mandinaud was alone in the dining room when the two men entered.[13] He noticed that they looked soaked, bedraggled and close to exhaustion. A little later his sister Yvonne came in and went over to the two, thinking to herself that they were German deserters trying to avoid being sent to Russia. When Hasler spoke, his accent no doubt reinforced her judgement. He had already decided what to order – for without ration coupons (which had to be exchanged for almost all items on restaurant menus) he had little choice. The only thing they could have was soup. Lucas Phillips records the conversation that ensued:

'Du potage, s'il vous plâit. Et du vin.'

'Pour les deux, Monsieur?'

'Oui, Madame.'

'Bien, Messieurs.'[14]

'Two potato soups for the Germans,' Yvonne Mandinaud shouted to her brother at the stove, as she went back into the kitchen.[15] She returned a few moments later with two steaming earthenware bowls brimming with a nourishing brown liquid in which floated vegetables and broken bread.

'Cor, this is good. I could eat a bucketful of this scran,' whispered Sparks, gulping it down as fast as he could.

'Don't eat too fast,' Hasler whispered back. 'We've got to wait till the other customers have left.'

Their fellow customers began thinning out around 1400. But there were still too many in the restaurant. The two men's bowls were now empty. Yvonne Mandinaud came over again.

'Encore du potage, s'il vous plaît, Madame – pour les deux.'

'Et du vin?'

'Oui, Madame.'

They ate as slowly as they could. But by now the heat and the nourishment – and above all the wine – was beginning to tell on Sparks' ability to stay awake.

And still the three or four others in the restaurant kept talking. They seemed to be in the middle of an animated and extended conversation, but it was either in *patois* or spoken in a local accent so thick that Hasler could not understand a word of it.

Eventually Hasler decided he had to act. He took out the stub pencil from his escape kit and one of the few dry slivers of paper he had left and wrote, in the best French he could muster: 'We are escaping English soldiers. Do you know anyone who could help us?'

He then called for the bill and, when it was brought over by the *patronne*, handed her a five-hundred-franc note, into which he had carefully folded his message. He watched her closely as she took the note back to the till for change. She unfolded it, read the message and, without the slightest alteration of expression, wrote something below it, bringing it back to him folded in the notes of his change.

'Stay at your table until I have closed the restaurant.'[16]

There followed several very tense moments for the two fugitives. Yvonne Mandinaud shooed the remaining customers out, locked the door and disappeared for what seemed like an age; the two men were left to speculate that when she came back, it would be with a troop of Germans. When she returned to the dining room, however, it was to motion them into the kitchen. Here they were closely questioned by René Mandinaud as he cleared away the dishes.

'Who were you told to contact in Ruffec?'

'We were given no name. We were just told that friends of England would be on the lookout for us and would help us.'

'Why did you come here – to the Toque Blanche?'

'Because we were very hungry and this looked a good place.'

The brother and sister chatted among themselves at a speed Hasler could not follow. Then Yvonne said:

'You can stay here while we find someone to help you. Come with me.'

She took them up the back stairs to a room on the second floor separated from the others. She did not mention as she climbed the stairs that the Toque Blanche had two staircases – this one, and one at the front which was used by the German officers at the other end of the building.

The room into which she led them was a simple one, clearly made up for guests, with fresh linen on a double bed and recently swept floors.

'Here you are, Messieurs. My brother will not be able to go out until the evening. In the meantime you can get some sleep.'

'But we are very dirty, Madame, and I am afraid we will soil your sheets.'

She left for a few moments, returning with a hip-bath, a towel and some soap, followed by a large bucket of steaming water.

'Leave your clothes by the door – I will wash them.'

The two men stripped naked, enjoyed their first real wash since leaving *Tuna* nearly two weeks previously and, still naked, jumped between the sheets.

For a few moments Hasler was worried that their hosts had been so unsuspicious. Perhaps they had gone for the Germans? Perhaps this welcome was a ruse, perhaps it was a trap? Too bad, he concluded as sleep tugged him down – they couldn't very well fight their way out naked.

Suddenly he was awake again as he heard a noise outside the door – but it was only their clothes being taken away for washing. Then ... oblivion.

They were unaware that, during the afternoon while they were sleeping, the gendarmes called. A woman from Souvigné had seen two suspicious vagabonds emerging from a haystack that morning; had they been seen at the Toque Blanche? No, no one of that sort had been seen here, was the firm reply.

Against the odds, Hasler and Sparks had reached their first goal. In the middle of winter, with little sleep, less food and no comforts, they had travelled more than seventy miles through a countryside crawling with a vengeful enemy. They had navigated surreptitiously with the aid of four damp, tiny button compasses which would have not been out of place in a Christmas cracker and a map too large in scale to give them any real knowledge of the countryside around them or the hazards which lay ahead. One of them spoke no French at all, the other spoke it poorly and with a heavy German accent. The fact that despite all these impediments, they had made it to Ruffec in just six days is extraordinary testament to their endurance, determination, intelligence – and above all, luck.

Sadly, Hasler's luck was not shared by Jack MacKinnon and James Conway.

They had stayed *chez Jaubert* for the last three days, long enough for Louise Jaubert to wash their clothes, if not for Jack MacKinnon's abscessed knee to heal. During their stay they told the Jauberts that they had decided to catch a train from La Réole to Toulouse and then head for Bilbao in Spain.[17]

To reach La Réole, however, they needed to cross the Demarcation Line. After asking local Resistance members, smugglers and black-marketeers to help them, Louis Jaubert eventually found a reliable guide who promised to take the two fugitives across the Line and to the outskirts of La Réole. The two Marines left *chez Jaubert* late on the evening of 17 December having given their home addresses to their hosts, promising to write when they reached England and to visit the Jauberts again when the war was over. They stayed in Sauveterre-de-Guyenne that night, no doubt with another generous, brave French family, and crossed the Demarcation Line early on the morning of 18 December.[18]

At 0800 that morning, as they entered the town of La Réole on the road from Sauveterre, they passed an imposing town house, unaware that it served as the town's temporary wartime gendarmerie. Looking out of a window in her flat on the first floor, the wife of Captain Louis Olivier, the gendarmerie commander, saw two suspicious-looking men.[19] She called downstairs to her husband who was in his office with the station clerk, English-speaking gendarme Pierre Hennequin.

'The captain rushed out of the office and shortly afterwards called me to the window, where I saw two poorly dressed men, one with a limp, walking past six or eight metres in front of the house towards the town,' Hennequin reported later. 'The captain ordered me to stop them and bring them into the station. He often did this kind of thing – stopping passers-by who looked like strangers as they passed the gendarmerie and bringing them in for questioning. I went out and asked them to follow me into the station. It was immediately apparent that they were not French, as neither understood a word I said. One of them said the single word "Toulouse" several times in a very heavy accent. He was obviously English. I urgently whispered to them to be careful what they said as the captain was a German sympathiser and led them back to the house where Captain Olivier was waiting for us on the steps.'[20]

There is a full report in the La Réole gendarmerie records of the Marines' interrogation, which was conducted in English by Hennequin. MacKinnon is described as sporting a small black moustache and wearing a grey overcoat, black trousers, a blue sweater, a beret and shoes with (unusually) yellow socks. His rucksack contained a pocket-knife, a small metal saw 12 cm long, a compass, a watch, his escape box, some water sterilising tablets, a sweater, a spare pair of shoes, a pair of stockings, a Michelin map and 600 francs. Conway was dressed in a blue knitted jacket, grey trousers and shirt, a khaki overcoat, a black beret and sandals. His equipment was listed as an electric torch, a small metal saw, a pocket-knife, a rectangular box with his escape kit, some meat, a piece of bread, a pot of jam and 1700 francs.[21]

It is clear that the two men had worked out their 'cover stories' before their arrest, for when Hennequin started his questioning in English, the statements they gave were strikingly similar. MacKinnon's read:

I was a member of the British Force, which landed in Dieppe in September 1942 ... I was a volunteer for the Dieppe raid and was given a party of 30 men, all volunteers for this raid. We embarked on a boat that had no name. We landed at Dieppe, were in some street fighting, but were cut off from the harbour by the Germans. The ships then left and we were able to embark [sic]. Realising this we set off for the countryside and since that time, with one of my men, we have been living from farm to farm in the country with the intention of getting to Spain. It is not possible for me to give you the names of the people who sheltered us.[22]

Conway's said:

I was under the orders of Lt MacKinnon at the time of the Dieppe expedition in September 1942. After landing we were in some fighting. Our task was to destroy some factories. We were not able entirely to fulfill our task and, on being cut off from the rear by the Germans we were unable to embark again. We then left the town where we had dumped our explosives. We left behind our military clothing and the inhabitants of the area gave us some civilian clothes. We then lived in the country, but I cannot name the people who gave us shelter. It was our intention to go to Spain.

Hennequin attempted to mistranslate the two Marines' statements in order to put a more favourable gloss on them, but Olivier quickly spotted what he was trying to do, and took over their questioning.[23] Hennequin was sent to Artagnan in the Pyrenees, 180 miles away, the following day as a punishment.

The interrogation went on all day. Hennequin furtively continued to assist the two fugitives by advising them not to vary their initial story (even though he didn't believe it) because the Dieppe raid had been conducted by regular uniformed units and this would entitle them to be treated as prisoners of war. He seems to have won their confidence: as he notes in his post-war report, at one stage MacKinnon confided that they had not in fact come from Dieppe, but had landed from a submarine and been part of a team who had attacked German ships in Bordeaux harbour. Although the Germans had tried to keep this secret, everyone in La Réole had heard about it and in fact, he said, the BBC had already reported on it.

That evening MacKinnon was taken to La Réole hospital for treatment on his knee, while Conway was transferred to a cell in the town's prison two days later on December 21.

In Berlin and London, this too was a day of reports, letters and instructions. Field Marshal Wilhelm Keitel wrote another letter of excoriating criticism from Supreme Command of the Armed Forces (OKW) in Berlin to the German authorities in Bordeaux, lambasting them for their failure to prevent Hasler getting through, despite being given four days' notice of the raiders' intentions.[24]

In 10 Downing Street, Winston Churchill's Prime Ministerial box contained the usual ULTRA reports of German naval decrypts. These included the following item, dated 18 December: 'The steamships in Bordeaux which were attacked by a British sabotage party on the 12th are now known to have been heavily damaged.' Alongside this entry, 'C', the head of SIS, had written in his signature green ink: 'I am informing CCO' (i.e. Louis Mountbatten, Chief of Combined Operations).

Meanwhile, across the city, SOE were raising an Operational Instruction for the Despatch of Personnel and Stores by Air. This requested the RAF to parachute four containers and one package to de Baissac's drop site at the Moulin de Saquet, less than two miles from the Jauberts' house, which MacKinnon and Conway had left only the previous night.

31

Of Hospitals and Hospitality

19 December 1942

La Réole Hospital

La Réole Hospital records indicate that Jack MacKinnon was admitted for 'anthrax'[1] of the left knee and was attended by Dr Pierre Chavoix.[2] According to Captain Nightingale's post-war investigation, a permanent guard of one gendarme was mounted on his room.[3] But local sources insist that MacKinnon was left unguarded – though there was an injured gendarme called Clodomir Verchère in a nearby bed.[4]

Meanwhile, M. Blondy, the *juge d'instruction* at La Réole civil court, briefed 41-year-old lawyer Maître Marcel Galibert to conduct the defence of both MacKinnon and Conway and issued him with a permit to communicate with the two prisoners.

It is curious that although Olivier, a well-known German sympathiser, had been closely involved in the arrest and interrogation of the two men, there is no evidence that the Germans knew of their presence at this stage. Indeed, rather the contrary. In a post-war deposition, Marcel Galibert described how he began assembling his case for the defence of the two Marines by first visiting James Conway in prison:

He was dressed in rather worn working clothes ... I went to see him on several occasions and took him some books and cigarettes. Two days after our first meeting he asked me to write to his family, whose address he gave me, which I did at once ... On leaving the prison I went to the hospital. There I found another Englishman lying in bed with about ten young people from the college around him. He was in a ward with other sick people … visitors … brought him books, cigarettes and fruit … I told them that the Juge d'Instruction had put them under close arrest to prevent them from being handed over to the Germans and that in due course they would probably be freed. I said I would then endeavour to accompany them to the Spanish frontier.[5]

Given the circumstances of the two men's custody and the relaxed conditions of MacKinnon's stay in hospital, there is no reason to doubt that there was, at least at this point, a conspiracy to hide their presence from the German authorities. Gendarme Hennequin later gave evidence that, on the previous day, Captain Olivier had rung his superior at Montauban for advice about what to do with the prisoners, and had been firmly instructed to 'fix the matter for the Englishmen' – in other words, make sure they had the best chance of avoiding capture. The La Réole Procurator 'on being informed was also party to hushing up the affair'.[6]

La Réole, like Ruffec, was no ordinary French town at this stage of the war. Nor was its gendarmerie an ordinary gendarmerie.

From the start of the Occupation, La Réole's position on the 'Free French' side, close to the Demarcation Line, had made it a key staging post for SOE operatives, other British agents and escaping soldiers and pilots on their way in and out of France over the Pyrenees. Since 1941, Gaston Hèches had, it will be remembered, used La Réole as his main crossing-point over the Demarcation Line. When his escape line became subsumed into the SOE-run *Édouard* line, La Réole maintained a key position, with a number of agents in and around the town providing shelter, false documents and safe passage for those crossing into and out of the Occupied Zone. Robert Leroy had come through here on his many journeys to and from Tarbes, including the one in May 1942 when he took back to London the first written report on the blockade runners and detailed plans of the Bordeaux docks. He had last passed through just a month earlier, accompanying Mary Herbert on her way to Bordeaux.

La Réole was, therefore, like Ruffec, an important centre of resistance, with many active agents and sympathisers in the town and its surrounding villages including some of Claude de Baissac's early *Scientist* agents. In the late autumn of 1942, a new SOE network was established in the region. Known as *Wheelwright*,[7] this was led by one of F Section's most effective leaders, George Starr.[8] At the time MacKinnon and Conway were arrested, *Wheelwright* had at least fifteen agents in La Réole with more becoming active all the time. By the end of 1943 there were so many La Réole citizens in *Wheelwright* that a separate sub-network, *Philibert*, was set up in the town.

But La Réole's activities against the Germans were not confined to SOE. A separate Resistance group helped Jews escape from an internment camp in the Occupied Zone, smuggling them over the Demarcation Line, accommodating them, providing them with false papers and finally helping them to reach freedom.

Central to all these activities was a La Réole gendarme called Albert Rigoulet. The leader of a small group of La Réole Resistance agents who helped fugitive Jews and called themselves 'Les Rigoulets', he had been an early member of both Gaston Hèches' *Édouard* line and Claude de Baissac's *Scientist réseau* and in mid-1942 had masterminded an escape of Resistance agents from a German prison. In due course he would become the leader of the *Philibert* sub-network in the town.[9] Known as *Le Frisé* because of his mop of curly hair, Albert Rigoulet was a man of exceptional courage and enterprise. And he was at his most active at the time MacKinnon and Conway were arrested and questioned.

MacKinnon and Conway had unwittingly stumbled into one of the strongest Resistance centres in all southwest France.

About the time Maître Galibert was paying his first visit to Jack MacKinnon in La Réole Hospital, Yvonne Mandinaud was throwing open the shutters in Hasler and Sparks' bedroom in the Toque Blanche in Ruffec.

'You have slept well, Messieurs?'

She was assured that they most certainly had.

'Would you like something to eat?'

Sparks, whose ear had by now become attuned to the French verb *manger*, interjected before Hasler could answer:

'Cor, yes please. I could eat everything you have in the house.'

'What did he say?'

Hasler explained and a little later Yvonne brought them two trays laden with soup, meat, vegetables and some red wine. They ate and drank, still naked and sitting up in bed. Seeing their plight, she brought them replacement underwear.

As they sat in bed finishing their meal, dressed in their newly acquired underclothes, there was the sound of several male voices and the tramp of feet on the stairs, followed by a knock on the door. They tensed and looked at one another.

'Germans!' whispered Sparks.

'Go and see,' ordered Hasler.

'Why me?' said Sparks.

'Because I'm a major,' Hasler replied, unanswerably.

As Sparks struggled into his trousers there was another, more insistent knock. When he opened the door he found, to his relief, a small and respectful delegation made up of René Mandinaud and two other men, who quickly drew up chairs around the bed.

The previous night, after his restaurant closed, Mandinaud had gone to see his friend Jean Gaston Mariaud, the local tax collector (who was discreetly known in the town to have the right Resistance 'contacts'), to seek his advice on the unannounced arrival of the two strangers. After hearing Mandinaud's tale, Mariaud concluded that the first thing was to establish the two fugitives' *bona fides*. Were they really who they said they were, or was this a German trap? They normally had good warning of *colis* (parcels) who would require transportation over the Line, but these two had come out of nowhere. Mariaud had good reason to be cautious: he had himself been searched by the Germans in July 1941 on suspicion of assisting people to cross the Line illegally, and had spent a month in Angoulême prison before being released for lack of evidence.[10]

The two men quickly concluded that they would need the help of a retired Ruffec schoolteacher named Pailler, who had returned from teaching in England just before the war started.[11]

Either that night or the following morning, Mandinaud and Mariaud went to see François and Germaine Rouillon at the Hôtel de France. They were told that, although the Rouillons knew of *Marie-Claire*, they knew nothing of escaping British soldiers and advised that Mandinaud and Mariaud should make contact with Mary Lindell's old Red Cross nursing friend, Marthe Rullier, and the chief of the Ruffec Resistance,

Commandant Gua. Both confirmed that they had no knowledge of any English soldiers in the area, or any warning that such men were on their way. Rullier insisted (truthfully enough, since Mary Lindell was still recuperating in Loches Hospital) that she too had no idea where *Marie-Claire* was – but added that if the strangers did prove to be genuine, she might be able to help.

And so it was that, with M. Pailler acting as translator, the two Marines, still propped up in bed, were politely but firmly interrogated by the three Frenchmen sitting in a circle around them.

The interrogators carefully inspected the remains of Hasler's escape box, paying particular attention to the matches, the soap and the English lavatory paper. They asked the two strangers questions about England and what they had been doing. Finally they pronounced themselves satisfied. The clincher, apparently, was not anything the two men said or even the convincing nature of their lavatory paper, but Sparks' Cockney accent, which according to Pailler could never have been imitated by a German.

They were told to be ready to move after lunch.

At 1230, dressed in the old clothes the Mandinaud sisters had washed for them, supplemented by some newer ones which the two women had acquired, the Marines said their goodbyes to the sisters, who firmly refused Hasler's offer of payment. Jean Mariaud then led the way cautiously down the back stairs of the café, through the dining room and out into the street. Here they found a gas-powered baker's van with blackened windows driven by René Flaud.

They were unaware at the time that someone – probably Marthe Rullier – had, in the absence of Mary Lindell, arranged for the two fugitives to be inserted into the *Marie-Claire* escape line, which would now care for them all the way to Spain. Hasler and Sparks' position had changed again. They had now been relegated to the status of mere *colis*; packages to be moved at the whim of others without initiative, control, responsibility or volition. Hasler, writing to a French friend after the war, said of this moment: 'For us it was alarming to have to throw ourselves on the mercy of strangers ... for the first time we felt we had lost the initiative and were depending too much on good luck.'[12]

René Flaud picks up the story:

I received instructions to transport two 'packages' from the *Toque Blanche* café in the centre of Ruffec … my two 'packages' waited for me at the appointed hour and after I had picked them up I was to take them to the Demarcation line in the east … near a little village called Benest.

The two fugitives were very nervous and I had to re-assure them and ask them to keep as quiet as they could in the back as spot checks were frequent in this part of the country. Afterwards the journey passed without any hitches and I put my passengers down, as agreed, between the areas controlled by the *maquisards*.[13]

Flaud does not mention that, as he passed the tax office, he stopped the van and let in a fourth passenger. This was Fernand Dumas, one of Mary Lindell's *passeurs*, who would act as Flaud's navigator on the journey ahead. They left Ruffec and, following little country roads and village cobbled streets, completed the eighteen miles through Champagne Mouton to Benest without incident.

After about half an hour, Hasler and Sparks felt the van judder to a halt. The back doors were thrown open and the two fugitives were beckoned out, finding themselves at a small road junction on the edge of a wood. Flaud drove off without ceremony and returned to Ruffec. He entered the town past the tax collector's office, where he gave two beeps on his horn to indicate to Jean Mariaud that the two *colis* had been delivered. Then he called in at the Toque Blanche for a drink. To the Mandinaud sisters' anxious enquiries he responded simply: 'It was a piece of cake.'[14]

Back at Benest, Dumas used a branch to sweep away any tyre tracks and then led the two Marines to a secure hiding place a short distance into the wood. 'We are just southeast of Benest, close to the Demarcation Line,' explained their guide, who impressed Hasler by his professionalism and toughness. 'This line is still patrolled by the Germans and police dogs, even though the Germans have now occupied the whole of France. At twilight a guide will come here from the other side and will lead you across the line to your next house.'

The three men lay hidden in the wood until nightfall. Suddenly, and without any visible or audible signal that Hasler could detect, their guide stood up and made his way back to the edge of the road where he could be heard talking in a low voice to another man. It was almost dark when he returned accompanied by a younger man who looked like a farm worker and was to be their *passeur* for the next stage of the journey.[15]

Brief introductions completed, Dumas vanished into the night. With a curt 'Come with me,' their new guide led them off down a footpath through darkened wood and across silent fields. They crept along hedgerows, stopping every few minutes to listen to the sounds of the night as they made their way, pad-footed, over a mile or so of broken countryside.

Finally, at a little after 1930, the two Marines saw the shape of a single-story farmhouse loom out of the darkness. Leaving them behind a low wall, their guide went forward and knocked softly on the front door, which was quickly opened to let out a thin shaft of light from an oil lamp. After brief, murmured words between the two silhouettes in the doorway, Hasler and Sparks were motioned inside. There they were introduced to Armand and Amélie Dubreuille.

'We are friends of Marie-Claire,' said Hasler by way of introduction.

Hasler and Sparks were by no means home and dry. But they were now among dependable, loyal and efficient friends. The rest of their odyssey would not be without its dangers, but the most difficult and risky part was over.

For others who had risked their lives to help them, however, the dangers were about to begin.

32

Marvaud Saint Coutant and Mary Lindell

Christmas and New Year 1943

Marvaud Farm is set in close, hillocked countryside dotted with woods and coppices and watered by small streams. The farm building consists of a long, low, single-storey house accessed by a winding track, and set about with tumbledown sheds gathered around a rough farmyard littered with discarded farm implements and old machinery.

Though the grazing land here is good, the absence of nearby markets would have made farming a largely subsistence affair at the time of our story. The two young farmers who wrestled their livelihood from the land at that time were 26-year-old Armand Dubreuille and his 23-year-old wife Amélie, who lived there with their one-year-old son Michel and an elderly aunt.

Hasler noted when they arrived that the neat room into which they were ushered – containing a large double bed, a table, two chairs and a small stand with a bowl and china jug – looked as though it had been permanently laid out for guests. Armand Dubreuille was to say after the war that Hasler and Sparks were the first Englishmen they had accommodated[1] – a curious claim, since by December 1942 the *Marie-Claire* line had already passed a considerable number of escaping English soldiers and airmen 'down the line' to Spain. It may be however that the Dubreuilles, who could speak only French, had so far sheltered only French fugitives.

Armand Dubreuille's instructions to the new arrivals were firm and simple: 'I told them not to leave their room during daylight hours and to keep the two doors locked. They could get fresh air in the courtyard at night. If they needed the toilet during the day, they were to use the small privy by the stable, but they had to check first that no stranger was around. My wife and I were obliged to carry on with our normal life, so they would not see us at all during the day. My wife brought them dinner in their room that evening and I said we would talk more the next day.'[2]

The two men had to get used to one additional routine – a signal which indicated whether or not the coast was clear, for German patrols and passing hunters often wandered over the fields and through the woods nearby.[3] One of the doors from the room in which Hasler and Sparks were accommodated led out into the farmyard. Just beyond the door was a boiler with a metal cover, in which Amélie Dubreuille did her washing. If the cover was positioned one way, Armand instructed, it was safe to emerge; if the other, they must stay hidden.

On the morning following their arrival, after a hearty farmhouse breakfast of fresh bread, jam and heavily milked coffee made from roasted ground barley, Armand Dubreuille told Hasler that he had informed *Marie-Claire* by telegram that she had two *colis* to collect – so it should not be long before she came.

Beaunac, 22 December 1942

Early this morning, German troops descended in force on the little hamlet of Beaunac. It appears that the report written by the *préfecture* in Angoulême had ground its way through French bureaucracy until it finally came to the attention of the occupying powers, who reacted immediately.

The Germans, however, seemed not to know who they were looking for. They took away three villagers, Messieurs Bineau, Picot and Latouche, two of whom had, as far as we know, nothing whatever to do with Hasler and Sparks' appearance in the village. It may be that they wanted to interrogate these three in private to find out more details; or as often happened elsewhere, they were hostages against a demand from others to tell the full story.

On Boxing Day, the Germans returned to arrest another Beaunac resident (also not, as far as we know, directly involved), René Rousseau. Five days later, on New Year's Eve, Bineau, Picot and Latouche were freed, followed by two others on New Year's Day. All reported that, despite being interrogated separately, no violence had been used. But 43-year-old Lucien Gody (who had warned Hasler and Sparks), 28-year-old Maurice Rousseau and 16-year-old René Rousseau (the two Rousseaus were not related) were deported and never seen again. Apart from Blondie Hasler's men, the three from Beaunac are, as far as we know, the only others to lose their lives as a direct result of Operation Frankton.[4]

Marvaud Farm, Christmas 1942

When Armand Dubreuille originally agreed with *Marie-Claire* that he would act as the first key staging post for escapees on the Free French side of the border, it had been on the strict understanding that he would be warned of the arrival of *colis* two or three days in advance and that they would 'stay only a short time at Marvaud – two or three days at most – before being picked up for their further journey'.[5] Any longer would be most hazardous – there was, after all, a German post only 700 yards away.[6]

Now, at the Dubreuille farm, as day succeeded day with no sign of *Marie-Claire*, Armand became increasingly worried – and concerned for his family. He sent another telegram to Mary Lindell's flat in Lyon just before Christmas. But still nothing; silence.

Christmas came and went – celebrated with a greeting of '*Joyeux Noël*' from each of the Dubreuille family and a plate of pancakes delivered to the two guests by Amélie. Sparks later confessed that this was his lowest moment.

The Englishmen busied themselves reading newspapers and the few books the Dubreuilles left for them. All of these, of course, were in French, which Sparks could not read. There was nothing to talk about as the few subjects in which they shared an interest had long been exhausted. Hasler showed Sparks how to carve in wood, borrowing two knives from their host for the purpose. Sparks carved a somewhat misshapen elephant which he gave to the baby, Michel, for Christmas; Hasler himself made a remarkably competent carving of a little gnome with long ears, stub wings, a pointed hat and curl-toed shoes playing a flute.

They were increasingly bored. And Armand and Amélie were increasingly frightened by the risk of discovery. Yet still nothing happened. No telegram; no news; no figure on the winding track coming to collect the strangers whose prolonged stay could cost this little family their home, their future, their lives.

Loches Hospital, Christmas

Maurice, Mary Lindell's son, visited his mother in her sickbed in Loches Hospital on Christmas Eve 1942 bearing all the makings of a Christmas meal of turkey and seasonal trimmings. He explained that all was quiet, but that he was having more difficulty than he expected finding new guides over the Pyrenees to replace their previous guide who had been caught and shot.

On his return to Lyon he found what Armand Dubreuille had hoped he would have received several days previously: a telegram informing him that two English *colis* were awaiting collection.

He immediately retraced his steps to Loches to ask his mother for instructions. She ordered him to reply to Dubreuille's telegram immediately, saying that he would pick the two men up on 6 January. In the meantime he was return to Lyon and organise the reception for the new arrivals. She would discharge herself from hospital and follow him in a day or so.

La Réole, 29 December 1942

Early this morning two German NCOs called at La Réole gendarmerie. They told the gendarme on the desk, Maurice Drouillard, that they were from the *Sicherheitsdienst* in Bordeaux and demanded to question 'the two Englishmen'. Drouillard played for time; he knew nothing of this – he would have to refer the matter to his superior, Adjutant Estère. Estère told the Germans that, since the two Englishmen were under investigation by the local *juge d'instruction* for 'travelling illegally in France',[7] he had no authority to release them; the Germans should make their request through the normal legal channels. Estère then accompanied the two SD officials to the office of the local public prosecutor, where their request was refused. According to a deposition made by Drouillard after the war:[8]

> ... they left in a temper declaring that they would return that same evening.
>
> True to their word at approximately 2100 that evening a large detachment of Germans, armed with automatic weapons and numbering around fifty, suddenly appeared and encircled both the hospital and the prison. They took possession of the two Englishmen, Conway and MacKinnon (this latter was still under treatment in the hospital) in the presence of the Prosecutor.
>
> These two soldiers had been arrested on 18 December and placed in the hospital and the prison with the specific intention of avoiding us having to hand them over to the Germans.
>
> PS: I should add that about a quarter of an hour before the German soldiers arrived, that is at about 2045, we received a telephone call from the Vichy Minister of the Interior who ordered us to hand the two Englishmen over to the German authorities.

A record of the transfer of Conway, contained in the Departmental Archives of the Gironde, indicates that at 2330 he was returned his clothes and required to sign and fingerprint a document by which the French authorities 'placed them at liberty'.

They were then immediately rearrested by the Germans.[9]

Sadly, Maître Maurice Galibert, the man charged with the defence of MacKinnon and Conway, was not in La Réole to represent them. He was at the Red Cross office of the Social Services in Aid of Emigrants at 96 Rue Garibaldi, Lyon, where he was, at the request of his two British charges, in the process of sending reassuring messages home to their families. The substance of each brief message, written on the prescribed Red Cross form, was the same. That addressed to the MacKinnon family at 22 Clarendon Street, Glasgow read simply:

> Dear Mrs. MacKinnon,
>
> I expect that you and the family are rather well. Seen last week John, who was healthy and well.

It is a cruel irony that these messages were dated the very day the two Marines were taken away for imprisonment and interrogation by Friedrich Wilhelm Dohse and his SD team in Place Tourny, Bordeaux.

We are now presented with two questions.

First, given the overwhelming evidence that the authorities in La Réole had conspired to keep from the Germans the fact that MacKinnon and Conway were being sheltered in the town, how did they discover the two Englishmen were there? Were MacKinnon and Conway betrayed?

Second, since we also know that there was an active SOE circuit in the area, skilled and experienced in rescuing people and spiriting them away to freedom, how was it that the Germans got to the two Marines before the Resistance?

Here, once more, we can only speculate. We know that the head of the La Réole gendarmerie, Captain Olivier, was an active German sympathiser: indeed, he faced charges on this account after the war. So a betrayal would have been perfectly possible. But, if Olivier had betrayed the two men, he would presumably have done so immediately after their interrogation on 18 December. Why then did it take the Germans eleven days to move on the hospital?

It seems far more likely that MacKinnon and Conway fell into German hands not through betrayal, but because of poor security. Galibert's evidence indicates that MacKinnon was visited by students from the college who seem to have treated him as something of a hero; they brought him books and cigarettes. The whole town knew about the presence of the two men and there was, apparently, much chatter about them in homes, at La Réole secondary school and in the town's cafés. It is likely that the Germans, too, eventually picked up the local gossip. This conjecture is strengthened by the fact that, when they first arrived at La Réole gendarmerie on 29 December, the Germans did not appear to know who they were looking for – only that there were 'two Englishmen' in the town.

So why were the two Marines not rescued? If the whole town knew, then the *Wheelwright* circuit must have known, too – not least through Gendarme Albert Rigoulet, who lived at the time, with his wife Hélène and their three children, Michelene, Juliette and Jean-Pierre, at Rue de l'Abbatoir, no more than 200 yards from the hospital. Albert Rigoulet was, moreover, not the only French gendarme in La Réole who was helping the British. A newly uncovered file on Pierre Hennequin shows that he too had been unofficially helping 'the English' since early 1942 and after the war received the Franco-British Medal of Honour for this work.[10] It is thus almost inconceivable that the local SOE networks were ignorant of what everyone else in the area knew so well.

There is also evidence that Baker Street itself was aware of the situation, if not before the arrest, then very shortly afterwards. In his post-war testimony, Hennequin reported that a BBC broadcast in late December 1942 or early January 1943 specifically referred to the Marines' arrest on 29 December, pointing the finger at Captain Olivier for their betrayal. This transmission is confirmed in a post-war deposition made by another La Réole gendarme, Alfred Henry.[11] Unhappily BBC Archives at Caversham Park contain no records of broadcasts before December 1943, so these claims cannot be verified. But given the independent evidence of two gendarmes, it appears very likely that this broadcast did take place. If London knew and given that there were ten days in which to do it, why then did no one rescue the two Marines?

Even today, there is much rumour in the town to the effect that a rescue was imminent when the Germans arrived.[12] If that is so (and again no proof of it has yet come to light), then why did it take so long? Indeed, given that it was known in the early morning of 29 December that the Germans were aware of the two Marines' presence, why were they not spirited away before 2100 that night when German troops took matters into their own hands?

There appear to be two possible answers. Perhaps the La Réole Resistance believed that, despite the early morning SS visit to La Réole gendarmerie the two men were safe where they were and they could afford to wait until MacKinnon's knee had properly healed before launching him on the arduous journey over the Pyrenees into Spain. Or perhaps George Starr was awaiting instructions from London. At this time *Wheelwright* was not in wireless communication with Baker Street and had to rely on couriers to carry messages to other W/T operators, such as Roger Landes in Bordeaux. This would certainly account for the delay in getting signals backwards and forwards to *Wheelwright*.

Unfortunately, very little of SOE's signal traffic survives, and none of the surviving messages are from either *Wheelwright* or *Scientist*. So this too has to remain pure conjecture. Two points are clear, however.

First, if, as seems very likely, SOE headquarters did know of the presence of the two Marines in La Réole, either before or shortly after their arrest by the Germans, they said not a word about it to their colleagues in Combined Operations. And second, if Hasler and Sparks enjoyed almost charmed good luck throughout their escape, poor MacKinnon and Conway had no luck at all.

No. 10 Downing Street, London, end of December 1942

The regular 'SOE activities – Summary for the Prime Minister' report for the quarter ending December 1942 included a section marked 'France and the Low Countries', in which it was claimed that Blondie Hasler's attack was actually SOE's work: 'sabotage effected by SOE agents over the last three months has been considerable and includes: 1. An attack on five merchant ships in Bacalan and Bassens ...'[13]

A charitable reading of this claim might be that, having heard of the Bordeaux raid, knowing of the instructions for immediate attack on the blockade runners sent by SOE in mid-November and being aware that *Scientist* had received the explosive to do the job, Baker Street had genuinely concluded that the perpetrator was de Baissac and, in ignorance of the facts, ascribed it to him. But SOE could not have been in ignorance of the facts at this stage. Baker Street was not, at this point in the war, on the very restricted distribution list of ULTRA material.[14] So the only way they could have known about the attack in Bordeaux by early January, when their report was submitted to Downing Street, was from Claude de Baissac by way of Roger Landes' radio in Cenon. In which case, unless de Baissac himself claimed it was *Scientist*'s work (and we know from a later report that he did not), they would have known that SOE were not responsible for the attack and that they were therefore claiming a success – and the ensuing kudos from the Prime Minister – which was not theirs to claim.

We now know, though SOE did not at the time, that the Prime Minister was unlikely to have been impressed by SOE's claim. He had read the ULTRA reports, knew the raid was the work of Combined Operations and had already congratulated them for it. What Blondie Hasler, holed up in Marvaud Farm with four of his team dead and four more in German hands, might have made of the claim must be left to the imagination.

The interrogation of Bert Laver and Bill Mills would probably have started in the third week of December and carried on through Christmas, with Jack MacKinnon and James Conway joining them in the underground cells at Place Tourny over New Year. The questioning was conducted by a team made up of Naval Intelligence interrogators *Fregattenkapitän* Dr Krantz and *Hauptmann* Heinz Corssen, who were specially sent down to Bordeaux from Wilhelmshaven, and the Bordeaux SD under the command of Friedrich Wilhelm Dohse. Corssen had in fact been summoned to Bordeaux earlier to interrogate Sam Wallace and Bobby Ewart.[15] But only thirty-five miles from his base he had been hauled off the train and ordered to return home; Wallace and Ewart had already been executed.[16]

It seems likely that the Germans procured most of the information they managed to obtain from Laver and Mills, for on 3 January, only a week after the arrest of MacKinnon and Conway, the initial questioning was effectively completed. On that day a detailed summary of all the information obtained was sent in two long teleprinter messages to German Naval Intelligence at Wilhelmshaven and to Bachmann's headquarters in Nantes.

It is clear from these messages that the German team had obtained almost every detail about preparations for the raid, including the recruitment, names, living conditions and training of the two teams at the RMBPD in Eastney.

[The marines] received training while on a special course at Portsmouth. This course was run for 'Combined Operations'. The course included 30 men and was divided up into two sections. Each section received different training and was kept apart while on duty ...

They were billeted in barracks to begin with and later on in private houses in a small village on the coast near Portsmouth. Board and Lodging were paid by the Royal Navy. Captain Stewart and a Sub Lt. were the instructors, as well as a Sgt and several corporals ... The training consisted mainly of sport, duties aboard ship, navigation and firing with various weapons, other than German or French, as well as the use and attaching of limpet mines ...

About two weeks ago they were ordered aboard submarine P49 at Portsmouth [sic]. The reason for this draft and the task was not disclosed to them. According to their training they did not belong to the Commandos, but in spite of it expected to be shot on being arrested in Germany. Their superiors did not mention this at all, but rumours to this effect were circulating amongst those taking part in the course.

The 3 January telex also contained full details of the raid itself:

Canoe 'Crayfish' (crew Corporal Laver and Marine Mills) reached the target according to plan ... and carried out the mining of two ships. Five mines were stuck to the ship lying upstream and three mines to the ship lying downstream, all on the seaward side ...

The mines were attached between 2000 and 2300 (British time). The fuse set to detonate in 8 hours, with an alternative of 2½ hours either way. The 'Crayfish' then proceeded [to] ... the island of Cazeau, where she joined up again with (Major H.) Both boats ... landed separately a little to the north of Blaye; crew destroyed the boat and were arrested on 14th Dec. 1942 in Montlieu La Garde this side of demarcation line by French police and then handed over to the SD in Bordeaux. They were not assisted by French civilian population, and, according to the police, were still wearing the special rush-green uniform ...

Maj. Hasler and Marine Sparks of the 'Catfish' are still free ...

Of the ten saboteurs who took part in the mining operation, seven are indentified either as dead or prisoners. Exact and reliable personal descriptions of the two members of the crew of the 'Catfish' not yet captured and of Corporal Sheard of 'Conger' were to-day given to SD, Bordeaux, as a result of exhaustive enquiries made; also information concerning the intended crossing of the line of demarcation and the meeting points to be used ...

We do not know if torture was employed to obtain this information – but given the Gestapo practice of the time, it seems probable that it would have been. However, the presentation of Dohse's summaries suggests that torture, if used, would have been employed, not as the primary means of extracting information, but as a secondary means to complement the interrogators' main strategy. This would probably have followed the well-established practice of questioning each man separately and then dropping the information he gave (beyond name, rank and number) into the interrogation of the next man in order to persuade him that the Germans already had the whole story. By this means each successive scrap of information was used to add to the jigsaw until the whole picture was assembled.

Before passing 'armchair judgement' on these revelations, it is worth reflecting upon the historical context and the chilling reality faced by Hasler's young, inexperienced and – when it came to interrogation – unprepared raiders: capture, imprisonment, torture and the very real prospect of imminent execution.

To make an objective assessment of the information Dohse and his team were finally able to prise out of Hasler's men, it is important to remember two factors. First, all intelligence has a limited life. It is only of utility if it is timely enough to be used operationally by the enemy. So much of the intelligence in these summaries which related to the specifics of Frankton was, essentially, 'dead' information which was of no immediate tactical use to the Germans.

The details Dohse obtained about training methods and the future use of new weapons such as the human torpedo, would have been of more valuable long-term importance to the Germans, for, taken with the operational information on Frankton, it gave them a good idea of what to look out for and how to defend against it.

During defence exercises the units were instructed by Major Hasler that the use of special torpedoes should be expected, which would be steered by two men riding on them. Only the upper bodies of the men would be seen above the water. We refer to a report which comes from the interrogation of a sabotage unit captured in Norway.

The other vital piece of immediate intelligence Dohse would have sought, especially from MacKinnon and Conway, would have been information about the help they had obtained from the French population. There is an intriguing passage, very characteristic of Dohse, in Conway's interrogation report (which included a statement that MacKinnon remained completely silent): 'On grounds of gratitude the Marine [Conway] would not state the name of the village [which had assisted them]. It was decided not to force him to disclose the name, so as to prevent his becoming stubborn.' This seems to confirm that torture was not Dohse's weapon of first choice – but he would have had no compunction about using it, if and when it became necessary.

No doubt Conway was pressed further on this issue; no doubt Dohse's team would in the end have tried to 'force him'. But the only recorded German action taken against the local population as a result of Frankton was the deportation of Hasler and Sparks' helpers in Beaunac – and this was the result, not of information provided by the Marines but of reports from the local gendarmerie. As far as we know, no other lives were lost, no reprisals instituted and no heavyweight investigations of any sort carried out on the French men and women who had helped Dohse's prisoners. Which can only mean one thing. That on this, the most crucial matter of all, despite whatever means Dohse and his team employed, all of Hasler's Marines resisted.

33

The Long Road Home

Marvaud Farm, 6 January 1943

Armand Dubreuille was delighted and relieved to get Maurice Lindell's telegram before New Year saying that – at last – the *colis* would be collected on 6 January. But the final days dragged interminably. The fugitives wanted to continue their journey, while the Dubreuilles were feeling the strain of the prolonged suspense and the constant risk of discovery.

At one time Armand asked Hasler what they had done. He received the correct but curt reply: 'We did some good work, I think.'

Each evening the two Marines listened to the BBC with the Dubreuilles. The night before they were due to leave, Armand asked the two to send back a BBC message when they reached home and safety. Hasler replied: '*Le poulet est bon* can be for you, too.' But Armand demanded something special, so they fixed on '*Les poulets sont arrivés.*'

Maurice Lindell arrived at midday on 6 January. Armand brought him in to be introduced – a slim, good-looking young man, smartly dressed, with an air of gaiety about him and a manner of speaking English which, though according to Lucas Phillips almost accentless, was definitely not that of a native.

'I am sorry you have been waiting here for so long, but my mother got knocked down by a bus [sic]! She didn't get the message about you until after we had heard from Monsieur Armand that you had arrived. Now I am going to take you to Lyon where she is waiting for you.'

At first Hasler was somewhat taken aback. They needed to go west for the Spanish border. Lyon meant travelling east.

'Will you be able to get us through to Spain?'[1]

'Yes. But the route we were using is closed and we shall have to find another. You will be safe with us in Lyon.'

Maurice explained that they would ride by bicycle to Roumazières-Loubert station, eleven miles away, and then catch the night train to Lyon. 'I hope you can both ride. They're not very good bicycles. We have no tyres in France now – they are all on black market.'

The prospect of crowded trains and cities worried the two fugitives, who had spent their last weeks trying to avoid such situations. But Hasler confided to a complaining Sparks, 'Actually, the towns are probably safer than the isolated villages, where a strange face is spotted at once. Anyhow, these people are the experts and they risk more than we do. So we must just string along.'

After lunch Maurice explained another complication. They had no identity cards. Maurice had brought the right forms with him, but there was no camera at Marvaud. They would have to board the train without passing the ticket barrier, where there was always a policeman – or a German – inspecting papers.

'If anyone comes up and talks to you, pretend not to understand and say "Breton" in as guttural a voice as you can. There are still many Bretons in France who can't speak or understand French.'

When the two Marines said their goodbyes to their hosts, they again offered to pay for their keep, but as before the offer was firmly refused. They cycled off down the cart track and onto increasingly well-used roads, with Maurice, who only now announced that he could not ride a bicycle himself, sitting on one of their crossbars and chattering away to them in English. He seemed unconcerned, and acted as though this was the most normal thing in the world.

It was dark by the time they arrived at Roumazières, a railway junction town with a modest station but extensive marshalling yards. They were lucky to find a break in the fence close to the station. Maurice told them to wait there and look as casual as they could, while he bought the tickets. He would board the train and wave for them to join him. They should then walk up the railway track, avoiding the station. The two fugitives felt highly conspicuous, but in due course they saw Maurice's signal and made their way to the train without mishap, duly taking their places in a third class compartment full of sleeping people. Maurice talked loudly in English throughout the ensuing journey, which was long, tedious and full of stops and noisy shunting. As dawn broke they found themselves steaming slowly through the outskirts of Lyon.

At the station exit was a *contrôle* manned by gendarmes. Hasler and Maurice passed through without incident. But Sparks, carrying a parcel containing their British-labelled service underwear – which Hasler had insisted they keep to prove they were not spies – was stopped by one of the policemen. Sparks could not understand a word he said. Growing suspicious, the gendarme pointed at the package. In a panic, Sparks thrust it into his hands and fled. To his surprise he was followed neither by shouts nor hue and cry.[2]

The three men, unkempt and unshaven, made their way into the city on foot, stopping at a corner shop for Maurice to buy a paper and phone his mother. Hearing that the coast was clear, he led them straight to her flat.

Even when hobbling, with her arm in a sling and one leg in plaster, the diminutive Mary Lindell could still be an intimidating figure. Especially when, as always on such occasions, she was dressed in her Red Cross uniform, festooned with her full complement of medals. She took one look at Hasler's almost equally imposing and still oversized moustache and, pointing imperiously, commanded: 'Off!'

Hasler made little attempt to resist the removal of his moustache. But Sparks interjected 'Have a care, Ma'am: you're dealing with the pride of Pompey there!'[3]

Notwithstanding this mild protest, Mary Lindell took out a small pair of nail scissors, presented them to Hasler and packed him off to the bathroom to remove the offending item, which she pronounced was a mortal danger to them all because it 'stank of England'.[4] This from a woman whose public demeanour – along with her French accent – was without exception stridently, even scornfully English.

When Hasler emerged from the bathroom she inspected the tattered remains of his moustache, pronounced his handiwork insufficient and ordered him back to take off more. Finally satisfied, she gave them breakfast. According to Lucas Phillips, as they were tucking in, Mary explained:

'I am so sorry you were stuck at the farm for so long. My route across the Pyrenees has folded up[5] and I've got to try and open a new one. Meanwhile we are going to accommodate you in a large house in the northern suburbs – don't know the people myself but they are friends of my son and he says they're alright. We've only got one rule for Englishmen in our care – NO GIRLS. From past experience we know that once they meet a pretty girl, everything goes to hell. So we shall take care to keep them away from you. Now, I am going to take you along to a photographer so we can fix you up with proper identity cards.'

After lunch, still resplendent in her Red Cross uniform and medals, Mary shepherded them onto a crowded tram whose passengers she immediately started bossing about. Just before they reached their destination, the two Marines became separated from her.

'Here we are. We get off here!' she shouted to them loudly and in English, across the heads of the intervening passengers. Hasler and Sparks followed her out sheepishly, trying their best to pretend that they were nothing to do with this mad Englishwoman.

When they arrived home that afternoon with their new identities and false names,[6] Mary told them that she would very soon be making a trip to Switzerland and could if they wished carry a short message to the British Consulate in Geneva for transmission to London.

'May I code the message?' Hasler asked. 'It will be top secret material.'

'Yes. Anything you like, as long as it's short.'

Hasler wrote out a swift message, which he then encoded using the No. 3 Code he had been taught before leaving. This process involved two stages: the message was first put into cypher and then re-transcribed into what appeared at first sight to be a perfectly ordinary message of the sort a POW would send home. The first stage proved simple, but both Hasler and Sparks had forgotten how to do the second stage encoding. In the end Hasler had to trust that someone back in London would be able to decode his message despite the errors. He sent it back with his redoubtable host to be handed over to the British Consul and MI9 agent, Victor Farrell (code name *Bateman*), in Geneva.[7]

After dark that evening, Maurice took the two Marines to a large house on the banks of the Saône river in the northern suburbs of the city. They stayed here for twelve days before being moved on again.[8]

Commentators have suggested that Mary Lindell travelled to Geneva in order to receive treatment for her injuries. This may have been the secondary purpose of her visit, but we now know that she had an intelligence contact in Switzerland. Paul de Saugie was a Swiss intelligence officer who, probably operating with the informal agreement of his masters, provided intelligence to London and secret assistance to escaping Allied soldiers. It seems probable that de Saugie was a contact Lindell had been given by MI9 before she left London. De Saugie helped her cross the Swiss/French border by what seems to have been a well-frequented route using a magnificent Swiss-style villa adjacent to the small village of Ville-la-Grand, between Geneva and the French town of Annemasse.[9] The wall enclosing the villa's ornamental rose garden ran (it still does) along the edge of a sunken minor road (now the D15) which marks the Swiss/French border. Here Mary would wait until after dark, when she took up a position behind the garden wall with de Saugie and waited for the regular German foot patrol to pass along the frontier road below. She would then climb onto the wall, jump five feet down onto the road and cross to a farm track on the other side, following it for half a mile or so along a small stream until she reached the station at Ville-la-Grand.[10]

On her return from Switzerland Mary told Hasler and Sparks that she had been unable to re-establish her route across the Pyrenees and they would have to be handed over to another MI9 escape organisation, the *Pat* line. Introducing them shortly afterwards to a 'Mr Carter', she explained that he was the local representative of their new guardians who would take care of them from now on. It seems possible that Lindell was instructed by MI9 to make this handover while in Switzerland, for Lucas Phillips hints that there was at this time some disapproval in London of her cavalier ways.

Hasler and Sparks were now in the hands of arguably the most successful MI9 escape line in southern France. The *Pat* line was run by a former medical officer in the Belgian cavalry, Albert-Marie Edmond Guérisse, who has a claim to be among the bravest and most capable of all British agents in the Second World War.[11]

'Carter' separated the two Marines, sending Hasler to stay first with Mme Bonnamour, the French daughter of the manager of Barclays Bank near SOE headquarters in Baker Street, and moving him to a second flat a week later. Finally Hasler and Sparks were reunited in a large villa in the north of the city notable for its magnificent marble staircase, the piano in the loft (which Hasler played) and the pretty young Frenchwoman who cared for them.

In early February they were taken on another long overnight train journey to Marseille, accompanied by one of the *Pat* line's couriers,[12] a Parisian who spoke a little English and impressed Hasler by his calm demeanour and quick-wittedness, if not necessarily by his professionalism. He sat the two Marines in a third class carriage next to two German soldiers and insisted on addressing them in audible but very faulty English. They nevertheless made their destination without mishap. In Marseille they were housed with two RAF escapees in a well-furnished flat overlooking the Observatory Gardens, the family home of Mme Marie Martin, her husband and two daughters aged seven and eleven. Mme Martin, described as 'middle class, small, slim, dark, volatile and generous',[13] looked after a number of fugitives, performing prodigious (and dangerous) feats in the local markets to obtain enough food for her 'guests'. Her husband, a docker and dyed-in-the-wool Communist, insisted that, since Britain was now in alliance with Russia, she too must have embraced Communism and that therefore his two guests must be, like him, fellow travellers in the great cause – a view from which Hasler did not have the heart to disabuse him.

Over the next three weeks, the population of Allied escapees in the flat – mostly RAF men – fluctuated wildly, at one time reaching twelve. The two Marines fretted to move on but were told by Guérisse that they would have to be patient: there had been more trouble on the route over the Pyrenees and it was taking time to repair.

Hasler's message finally arrived at MI9's offices in St James's Square in the early hours of 23 February 1943. It was taken immediately to officer Ronnie Sillars. 'It was an evening I will always remember,' Sillars later wrote to Hasler.[14] Apparently, though MI9 had been 'tensely awaiting news', Hasler's coded report arrived much earlier than they had anticipated. At first none of the night staff could make head or tail of it, thanks to Hasler's mis-coding of the message. But one of MI9's best decoders, Wren 2nd Officer Mary Hamilton, though off duty at the time, happened to be in her office. Sillars finally asked her if she could do anything with it:

Marie Hamilton had both imagination and amazing skill as far as codes were concerned and it wasn't long before there was a volcanic eruption of cigarette smoke and ash as she leapt to her feet coughing: 'It's coming out! It's coming out!' She quickly had the code decoded. She was just 'fey' that night. Shortly afterwards the decoded version was on its way to Combined Ops by special Despatch Rider.

The decoded message read:

Tuna launched five cockles, seven Dec. Cachalot torn in hatch. Pad hatches. In bad tide race SW Pte de Grave, Coalfish lost formation. Fate unknown. Conger capsized, crew may have swum ashore. Cuttlefish lost formation nr le Verdon fate unknown, Catfish, Crayfish lay up in bushes Pte aux Oiseaux. Found by French but not betrayed. Ninth in hedges five miles north of Blaye. Tenth in field south end Cazeau. Eleventh in reeds thirty yards south of pontoons opp Bassens South. Attack eleventh. Catfish Bordeaux West three on cargo ship two on engines of Sperrbrecher two on stern of cargo ship three on smaller liner. Back together same night. Separate and scuttle cockles one mile north of Blaye. Sparks with me. Fate of Crayfish unknown.

There are two points of note about this message, which Hasler must have constructed with much thought. First, though he had been fully briefed by Bert Laver and Bill Mills about their part in the operation, no mention is made of this at all; second, in a message which was necessarily brief, Hasler nevertheless thought it important to devote space to mentioning the damage done to *Cachalot* by *Tuna's* forward torpedo hatch at the time of unloading.

Combined Operations' Chief Planning Committee happened to be in session when Hasler's report reached Richmond Terrace. As the minutes record, the committee 'Took note with satisfaction' but agreed that no publicity should be given to Hasler's success until further 'potential targets for similar operations' were examined.[15]

Late in February, when the crush in the flat had eased somewhat, Hasler and Sparks were joined by two downed RAF pilots, Flight Sergeant J.G. Dawson and Flying Officer Prince Paul Marie Ghislain Werner de Merode, a Belgian aristocrat who had joined the RAF after escaping from Belgium to Britain through Spain in 1941. On the last day of February 1943, the day after Hasler's 29th birthday, they were told to be ready to move at first light on the following day and were issued with a small canvas haversack and two pairs of *espadrilles*.

Early on the morning of 1 March, in the company of a French *passeur* from the *Pat* line, Hasler, Sparks, de Merode and Dawson boarded the train to Perpignan. They arrived in the ancient town in early afternoon after a journey through countryside bursting into spring, with the Mediterranean sparkling sapphire-blue in the distance. Here, after an hour's wait in a municipal garden, they were bundled into a rickety van with a fifth traveller, a young, cadaverous Frenchman with a rucksack and a bundle of books tied up with string. De Merode spoke to him at length and pronounced afterwards that he was a French intellectual fleeing the Germans.

The van headed off from Perpignan travelling parallel with the coast along minor roads, arriving, after a journey of forty-five minutes or so, at a point a little beyond the small town of Ceret, which lies eight miles inland from where the Pyrenees end their long descent into the Mediterranean, marking the southern extremity of the Franco-Spanish border. Here they left the van and were joined by two guides, swarthy Catalonian hillmen dressed in *espadrilles* and rough mountain clothes, complete with berets, crude rucksacks and, slung over their shoulders, sheepskin *botas* (gourds) filled with the local rough red wine. They parted company with their courier and set off behind the two guides, who moved off wordlessly to begin the long climb to the Spanish frontier.

Every previous description of the fugitives' journey over the Pyrenees closely follows that given in both Lucas Phillips' book and Bill Sparks' autobiography. These describe 'towering mountains, snow-covered, awesome and magnificent',[16] which they ascended in a dizzying climb up to barren snow-covered mountain passes where the air was so thin that they suffered 'high altitude distress' and had to fight for oxygen.[17]

In fact, their journey was very different. De Merode's account to MI9[18] (which Hasler himself, in his own MI9 report, referred to as an accurate description of this part of their journey) describes them crossing the border by Las Illas, a low saddle connecting Ceret in France with the Spanish village of Massanet de Cabrenys. At a height of 1850 feet, this col (the same one which Lise and Claude de Baissac had crossed on their way out of Spain nineteen months previously) is far too low to cause altitude sickness or oxygen deprivation, or even for snow in early spring unless the weather is exceptionally cold.

According to the German weather charts for 1 March 1943 the temperature in Perpignan at midday was sixteen degrees centigrade and the weather cloudy and calm, with the sky clearing into a fine evening by sunset.[19] It is very unlikely that there would have been snow on the col by March this year.

Las Illas (known in French as Les Illes) is also the name of a small village of maybe fifteen houses[20] surrounded by fine, stone-built alpine farms and pastures, nestling in a hollow just below the col on the French side. Accessed from the valley below by what is now a metalled road (but would in 1943 have been a motorable earth road), which peters out into a rutted track just short of the col, the village is gathered round a stout mountain hotel called the Hostal dels Traboucayres. Behind this is a smaller stone house which was, according to the villagers,[21] the patrol house for some fifteen German Alpine troops stationed here guarding the crossing with the assistance of a small detachment of French *milice* police and some customs men.[22]

The *passeur's* overnight refuge lay about three miles from the German house at Les Illes and two hundred feet or so below the crest which marks the Franco-Spanish border. The climb to this point is perhaps a little over a thousand feet and could have been accomplished in a couple of hours. No doubt the little party of escapers would not have been able to travel on the road but would have had to follow instead small sheep and animal tracks up the lower slopes, which are here thickly wooded with dark evergreen trees about the same colour and height as olive groves. Higher up the ridge these give way to deciduous woods, peppered with wild cherry (which would just have been coming into flower in late March) and flowering bushes. This would not have been a true climb, or even a mountain walk. But it would not have been easy either, for the slope is steep and the paths narrow, wet and slippery at this time of year. According to both Lucas Phillips and Bill Sparks, Hasler and Sparks, who had been living the lives of holed-up animals for nearly ten weeks, found the going hard and had great difficulty keeping up with the others.

They reached their night's refuge, a rough stone hut with a red-tiled roof, a little before dark. Here they lit a fire and ate some of their food before bedding down for the night. Looking back into France for the last time, they would have seen Perpignan lying far below them and beyond it, the long curving sweep of the coast, bounded on the right by the great expanse of the Mediterranean, now darkening in the evening light.

The following day they were on their way again at dawn. It must have been on this second day – another day of trial and exhaustion for Hasler and Sparks, to the annoyance of their companions[23] – that they crossed the sharp rock-strewn ridge-line which marks the frontier, probably about two miles or so north of the main crossing and the German patrol base in the village of Las Illas. Here, according to Lucas Phillips, the guides lost their way and the lead was taken over by the cadaverous French intellectual who, at one stage when they were enveloped in fog, had to climb on the shoulders of the others to establish their position by inspecting a road sign.

Hasler does not comment on his first view of freedom from the Spanish border – perhaps because, according to Lucas Phillips, the sky was overcast at the time. What he and his little party would have seen, however, was a landscape quite different from that they had left behind. The Pyrenean ridge at this point forms a sharp escarpment ascending abruptly out of the fertile plains of southern France. But the Spanish side is quite different, consisting of a succession of long, featureless, gradually descending wooded ridges, each a slightly darker shade of blue as they roll away into the distance. It would have been difficult to get lost on the climb up to the border where the features are sharply etched and

Figure 12

arranged in linear fashion, following the ridge. But once beyond the frontier they were in featureless, undulating countryside in which losing one's way, especially without a compass (Lucas Phillips confirms that none of them had one), would have been all too easy.

Massenet de Cabrenys, the first Spanish settlement they passed through, is a small, ancient mountain village roughly two miles from the frontier, its stone and cobbled streets so narrow that in some, two sheep can pass only with difficulty.

The party marched for a further two days, finally, according to de Merode's report, arriving at a small village five and a half miles north of the substantial Spanish market town and administrative centre of Bañolas.

Here they were put up in a hotel run by a Spanish member of the *Pat* line – only one, the Hotel Comte Tallafero in the little village of Besalú, conforms to de Merode's description and could have been used as a hotel in 1943. They stayed here or hereabouts for three or four days, until arrangements could be made to collect them in the back of a rattle-trap lorry carrying a number of porcelain WCs generously packed around with straw. This doubled as both a source of comfort and a means of concealment at the occasional road blocks through which they had to pass on their sixty-mile journey to the British Consulate in Barcelona.[24]

When they arrived in Barcelona, suddenly and without warning or goodbyes, their mysterious French companion disappeared. It was only later that they discovered why.

On the day Hasler's party crossed the Spanish frontier, Albert-Marie Guérisse met one of his recently recruited agents, Roger le Neveu (also known by his nickname, Roger le Légionnaire)[25] in the bar of the Café Super in Toulouse. Le Neveu, who had approached the *Pat* line in Marseille in January 1943 offering his services, had first been given a few small jobs to do and then, having passed the test, was given the responsibility of escorting a party of escaped airmen south from Paris. All arrived safely, as did a second party. But seven airmen in a third party had been arrested changing trains in Tours in February – only le Neveu escaped the arrests. Someone had obviously betrayed the line.

Guérisse's first question to le Neveu when they had settled into a discreet alcove was whether he knew who had betrayed the line in Paris. As le Neveu gave his one-word answer, 'Yes,' Guérisse felt a Gestapo Luger thrust roughly into his ribs. He was arrested and eventually taken first to Natzweiler-Struthof concentration camp in Alsace and then to Dachau, where he was condemned to death.

Hasler's luck had held again. His was the last *Pat* line escape party to get out of France. Had he and Sparks been any later they would probably have been 'rolled up' with the rest of the line after le Neveu's betrayal. Their cadaverous intellectual Frenchman had been, they were later told, a Gestapo agent and their two Catalan guides would almost certainly have returned home to be shot and their families deported.

It took a little time for the two Marines to convince a sceptical young Consulate reception officer that they were British. But this done, they were given a change of clothes and some spending money. Allied servicemen of military age found in Spain at this time of the war were detained by the Spanish authorities and incarcerated in appalling conditions in internment camps. For this reason, Sparks was not allowed to leave the Consulate. Hasler, however, though still less than thirty, with his bald pate and no doubt by now fast-recovering moustache, looked too old for military service, an impression no doubt supplemented by the rigours he had been through. He was allowed to rent a cheap room in the Hotel Victoria in the Plaça Cataluña, from where he wandered the streets and savoured the first real freedom he had experienced for four months.

News of the arrival of Hasler and Sparks in Spain seems to have reached London slowly, since a minute of the meeting of the Chief Planning Committee of 11 March (ten days after Hasler had crossed into Spain) notes, under the heading 'FRANKTON', that, following Hasler's coded message, 'no further news has been received concerning the personnel but this need cause no despondency'.[26] The day after, Hasler, signing himself with the name only his family knew him by, wrote chattily to his mother from the Hotel Victoria:

I am taking this first opportunity of writing to let you know that I am still flourishing and happy. I am sorry not to have been able to let you know before, but you know how things are these days! I hope you haven't been too worried about me – I'm afraid it isn't by any means the first time that you have spent waiting for me! I am very fit and happy.

I am supposed to be on my way home, but anything may happen, and I expect this letter will get home before I do. Don't worry about me in any case.

I have had a most interesting time since I last saw you. I have only just arrived here so the novelty has not yet worn off. I was here for a day in 1936, during the Civil War, but things are naturally much better nowadays.

There is quite a lot of food and drink to be had, but most of the things one can buy are rather expensive and appallingly bad quality. However there are compensations not to be found in England – no blackout, lots of bananas and oranges and even quite a few eggs.

> There is so little I can write about that I have now exhausted it.
> Hoping to be with you again soon –
>   Love George[27]

A few days after the arrival of the two Marines, the Barcelona Vice-Consul received a telegram; Hasler was to return to the UK with the 'utmost priority'. In fact it was over a week before a car took him, on 22 March, to Madrid, leaving poor Sparks behind to continue his subterranean existence in the bowels of the Barcelona Consulate. Hasler spent several days in Madrid as the guest of the naval attaché, visiting the Prado Museum and enjoying what Lucas Phillips describes as a 'gay round of parties' before another Embassy car took him and a newly acquired cardboard suitcase containing his few possessions to Gibraltar (by way of a night stop in Seville where he saw flamenco dancing and bridled at being in a bar full of German officers). He finally crossed over to British territory on the afternoon of 1 April, the day he had proposed as a dinner date with Dick Raikes on the bridge of HM/s *Tuna* on that black, star-spangled night half a lifetime ago.

Hasler was put on a plane back to the United Kingdom the following day, landing at Portreath air station in Cornwall on 2 April. From there he made his way to London to provide an initial debrief to Combined Operations. His completed operational report was submitted to Richmond Terrace on 8 April,[28] and a copy – unusually – sent to Gubbins at Baker Street. The following day, Hasler was back in Eastney, pouring his customary beer over his morning cornflakes and asking if anyone was interested in having a sail.[29]

On 12 April he returned to Combined Operations headquarters where he gave a fuller verbal report to the Planning Committee. Afterwards, only eleven days later than promised, he met Dick Raikes and his wife for lunch at Kettners Restaurant in Soho (in preference to dinner at the Savoy, because, according to Raikes, 'the food was better'). After the war, Raikes commented that Hasler appeared to have aged ten years in the four months since he had waved him goodbye from *Tuna*'s bridge.[30]

Bill Sparks' return to his homeland was neither so swift nor so enjoyable. He spent an extra week in the Consulate in Barcelona, where he whiled away the time learning bridge from two fellow RAF fugitives, before travelling to Madrid and thence by train to Gibraltar, arriving on 2 April.[31] Here, once again, the British were doubtful of his identity, keeping him locked up in a small cabin on the upper deck of the troopship on which he was sent home. Arriving back in Liverpool, Sparks was placed in the custody of the military police and ordered to report immediately to the Euston Hotel for further interrogation as soon as he reached London. He managed to give his escort the slip, however, and went home to see his parents in Finsbury Park before reporting to the Euston Hotel two days later. After finally convincing the authorities of his identity, he was taken to Combined Operations headquarters where he met Hasler, complaining in typical fashion that he had travelled through the whole of German-occupied southern France without being arrested, only to find himself locked up the moment he set foot back in Blighty. He was debriefed by MI9 on 20 April 1943.

It is curious that Hasler, normally so assiduous when it came to the care of his men, seems to have made no move to ease Sparks' journey back to the UK. It was as though, having spent four months with every fibre of his being concentrated on their welfare, only to have them taken from him two by two until just Sparks remained, he had now, with typical single-mindedness, decided to put the past behind him and concentrate on what was next.

According to Lucas Phillips, when the German spies in Bordeaux reported Hasler and Sparks' escape, Field Marshal Keitel sent a furious diplomatic cable to Franco complaining bitterly about the lack of seriousness shown by the Spanish authorities in policing their frontier – conveniently ignoring the fact that, in order to reach the Spanish border, the two Marines had first travelled with impunity across 700 miles of German-controlled France.

PART V

Aftermath

34

Bordeaux after Frankton:
The Triumph and Demise of *Scientist*

For Claude de Baissac and *Scientist*, Hasler's raid was irksome, but transitory; measured against his other activities it was a relatively minor event. True, the heavy German presence in Bordeaux harbour after Frankton forced them to abandon their primary objectives, the Bordeaux blockade runners. But there were plenty of other targets to be getting on with.

Beginning in December 1942, just a few days after Frankton, de Baissac launched a major campaign of sabotage throughout the Bordeaux area. Charles Hayes, working with Jean Duboué and a team of some forty Resistance fighters, carried out attacks on the rail network at Dax and La Réole, high-level pylons at Facture and junction boxes at Bayonne, rupturing the electricity supply to the entire regional rail system. De Baissac's men, no doubt with technical advice from the *cheminots* (railway workers), took advantage of the power failure to short-circuit the electricity systems, so that when the Germans reconnected them there were more violent explosions and more damage. The stoppages and reductions of traffic lasted several days.[1]

These were followed by attacks on the power station at Pessac on the eastern outskirts of Bordeaux, on an electricity substation at Quatre Pavillons (just 200 yards from the house in Cenon in which Roger Landes kept his wireless) and on some small steamships in Pauillac harbour, which were severely damaged. Although Hayes' demolition teams could not gain access to the city's dock area, they did manage to doctor a consignment of battery acid destined for the accumulators on the U-boats in the Bordeaux pens.[2]

In response the Germans took hostages on the day of each attack, executing them the following morning at Souges. After one attack in which forty Germans were killed, seventy-two hostages were taken at random and shot at dawn the next day.

The escalating scale of de Baissac's operations soon required more arms and explosives, which London was now able to supply in abundance. There were nine successful air drops to *Scientist* in the first five months of 1943, many in the Omet area, where Hasler and Sparks had spent an uncomfortable night in a rat-infested railway hut. By the end of August a further 121 drops had been made, giving *Charles le Démolisseur* some nine tons of explosive and causing a severe strain on the storage capacity of the underground cellars at Jean Duboué's Ancienne Villa Roucoule. De Baissac was now able to provide weapons for every member of his fast-growing organisation.

And that was the problem. *Scientist* was growing too fast; becoming far too widely known for its own security.

SOE's original strategy was to create small self-contained cells. But London were now beginning to prepare for the invasion of Europe, hoping that armed risings behind the German lines would make a major contribution to the Allied victory. This meant big organisations able to do real damage to German units. So when de Baissac signalled in mid-December 1942 (before Frankton) that he wanted to return to London to discuss the possibility of combining with the *Organisation Civile et Militaire* (OCM) which numbered thousands of ex-soldiers among its members, Baker Street saw, not danger, but a mouth-watering opportunity. De Baissac was picked up by Lysander on the night of 17–18 March 1943 and went immediately to Baker Street to be debriefed. His account of what happened in Bordeaux on the night of 11–12 December, described as 'A copy of a report of an interview between an officer in NID (Naval Intelligence) and a well-informed French Officer who was in Bordeaux up to the middle of March 1943',[3] arrived at Combined Operations headquarters on 2 April, the very day that Hasler arrived to give his version of the same events.

For the first time – albeit through the bypass of Naval Intelligence – SOE information gained from *Scientist* in Bordeaux had reached

Richmond Terrace. Both sides, it seems, had finally understood that there had been a tragic duplication of effort, although no records can be found in the surviving files of either organisation formally acknowledging this.

De Baissac returned to France by parachute on 14 April 1943 and made his way back to Bordeaux. Later that month, with his sister Lise, Roger Landes and Charles Hayes, de Baissac attended a large meeting in Cours Verdun at the house of the son of a French admiral, André Grandclément (*Bernard*).[4] Here Grandclément, who headed the Bordeaux 'chapter' of OCM, *France Vivra* ('France will live'), formally agreed to join de Baissac and bring with him the whole of his organisation. In return, Grandclément would be made deputy commander of the combined organisations.

But de Baissac and his *Scientist* colleagues were not the only players in the Bordeaux game in 1943. Friedrich Wilhelm Dohse was also active, and made a breakthrough in July 1943 with the rolling-up of SOE's *Prosper* network in Paris. One of those arrested, Christian Fossard, was found to have Grandclément's name in his address book. As a result, first Grandclément's wife and then, on 19 September, Grandclément himself were arrested, the latter in the Café de Madrid in Paris. Dohse immediately asked for Grandclément's transfer to Bordeaux where, in a brilliant counter-espionage play, he persuaded Grandclément that France's real enemy was not the Germans but the Communists. A deal was done in which Grandclément's own men were spared (to 'fight the Communists later, when the Germans had left') in return for the betrayal of the entire *Scientist* network. Grandclément's betrayal resulted in the recovery of vast amounts of weapons and explosives – a third of all weapons dropped – and the start of an energetic programme of arrests. It has been estimated that around 250 of *Scientist*'s minor agents were subsequently captured and shot or deported. The rest, including most of the major participants, fled or went to ground. It was the end of *Scientist* in Bordeaux.

Claude and Lise de Baissac escaped the purge. They had been flown back to Britain in August to keep them clear of the early ripples from the break-up of the *Prosper* network, with which they both had close connections.

Roger Landes managed to escape over the Pyrenees with the help of Gaston Hèches and the *Édouard* line, but was inserted back into Bordeaux in May 1944, charged with taking command of the broken remains of *Scientist* (now re-christened *Actor*) and rebuilding an organisation able to contribute to the liberation of France and the Bordeaux area when the day came. On 20 January 1944, SOE in London ordered that Grandclément should be executed for his treachery. Roger Landes arranged for London's orders to be carried out in July of that year when Grandclément, his wife and deputy were assassinated in his home in Bordeaux.[5] Despite strenuous efforts to catch him, Landes always managed to keep one step ahead of Dohse, who said after the war that he would have paid almost any sum for his capture. Despite Landes' contribution to the liberation of the Bordeaux area, he was expelled as *persona non grata* by de Gaulle (with whom he clashed) on the general's arrival in the city. He died in Britain, aged ninety-one, in July 2008.

By August or September 1943 it was plain to all that Mary Herbert, *Scientist*'s 'fragile' courier, was carrying de Baissac's baby. Warned in mid-September by Charles Hayes that 'there was trouble brewing'[6] as a result of the Grandclément affair, she fled north to Poitiers where she took refuge in Lise de Baissac's empty flat for the last months of her pregnancy, returning south in December to have her baby in a private nursing home in Talence, a southern suburb of Bordeaux. She named her child Claudine after her own *nom de guerre*.

In early 1944, Mary (still using her cover name, Marie-Louise Vernier) returned north to Poitiers with her baby, taking up residence again in Lise de Baissac's flat. On 18 February she was sitting up in bed giving the baby a bottle when the Gestapo burst in looking for 'Madame Brisse' (Lise's code name). Not finding her there, they took Mary away for questioning instead, leaving the infant in the care of her maid. Mary Herbert must have had remarkable presence of mind, however, for she eventually persuaded her interrogators that she had no connection with *Scientist* and was instead, as she claimed, a married woman from Alexandria whose husband had abandoned her with his child. Released by the Germans at Easter, she was able after some searching to find her child, who had been handed over to a local orphanage. The two took refuge in a small country house near Poitiers for the rest of the war and were finally reunited with Claude de Baissac in September 1944.

Two months after their reunion, de Baissac and Mary were married. The couple never lived together again, however, and in due course divorced so that de Baissac could remarry. According to one source, Mary committed suicide by hanging herself from a crab-apple tree in her garden on 23 January 1983.[7] Claudine is now married and lives in Los Angeles.

On the evening of 13 October 1943, Charles Hayes and Jean Duboué returned to the Ancienne Villa Roucoule, unaware that, thanks to Grandclément's treachery, the net was closing in on them. During the night, Hayes heard noises in the garden and, looking out of the window, saw that the house was surrounded by German troops. Realising that they were about to be attacked, Hayes, Duboué, his wife Marie-Louise (known as Louise) and his daughter Suzanne collected arms and ammunition from hiding places in the cellars and sheds around the house and stacked them at the windows, ready for battle. That night Hayes promised Suzanne, with whom he had fallen in love some months previously, that he would return after the war and marry her.

The siege of the Ancienne Villa Roucoule, which is still known as the 'battle of Lestiac', began at about 0100, with Hayes and Duboué dashing from window to window and letting loose volleys of Sten gun fire at the surrounding Germans in an attempt to give the impression that the house was defended by a large and well-armed group. The Germans tried several direct assaults on the house but were beaten back every time. At around 0300 Hayes and Duboué tried to smuggle the two women out through the back garden to the nearby river Garonne, but just as they were about to leave, Hayes took a bullet in the upper thigh. Having tried in vain to staunch the flow of blood, the two women insisted on staying to care for him. Hayes, unable to stand, sat on a chair at one of the windows and continued firing.

Just before dawn, a second bullet broke his right arm. Suzanne bound this up with her scarf as Hayes continued firing, using his left hand. Around 0500, Marie-Louise Duboué was also wounded, but in her case more seriously with a bullet in the stomach. Dohse called a ceasefire so that she could be safely evacuated. She was carried out unconscious by her husband and handed over to the Germans, who on Dohse's instructions sent her in an ambulance to St André's Hospital in Bordeaux. As soon as Duboué returned to the house, the fight continued.

By dawn, Dohse, who had called up reinforcements from local Wehrmacht units, had the house surrounded. He knew that sooner or later his opponents would have to give up and was content to wait them out. The battle went on for a further two or three hours, finally ending in mid-morning when, their ammunition exhausted, the fighters surrendered on a promise from Dohse that they would be treated as prisoners of war.

When the Germans searched the cellars and outbuildings of Duboué's house they found eighteen hand grenades and several boxes of detonators, ten 9mm machine guns, ten Colt pistols, numerous packs of explosive, 240,000 francs (the equivalent of £50,000 in today's money), a gold watch, several gold bars, a huge stack of ammunition and a suitcase containing a radio set[8] – all of which, according to the report made to the Commissioner of Police at Bordeaux, was of British origin and had been received by parachute. But they failed to discover further caches of arms and materiel in two of Duboué's hidden underground cellars. These were subsequently recovered and used by Roger Landes after his return to Bordeaux in 1944.[9]

On the following day, the Café des Chartrons was raided and its proprietor, Marcel Bertrand, deported. He was never seen again. The café itself was razed to the ground.

Having been sent to hospital to recover from her wounds, Mme Duboué escaped and returned to Lestiac. Afraid to go home for fear of being betrayed by her neighbours, she hid in the vines and was looked after by the local *curé* until the end of the war. When Claude de Baissac returned to Bordeaux with the Judex Mission[10] immediately after the city's liberation, he sought out Marie-Louise Duboué, found her 'in great need'[11] and arranged for her to be given an ex gratia payment of 25,000 francs (£5,250 today).

In May 1943, just before the Grandclément betrayal, London ordered the withdrawal of Robert Leroy, who had become, they decided, too unreliable and too much of a risk, largely due to his old problem – alcohol. On arrival back in England, he was declared '*brulé*': literally 'burnt'. This term can mean 'too widely known to the Germans', but in

Leroy's case it probably just meant burnt out. He was found a place in his old profession, the French merchant navy. After the war Leroy married and settled in Melom par Porspoder, two miles north of Finisterre and six from his native Brest.[12] In the post-war years he paid at least two visits to the Bordeaux area, and returned with his wife to see Gaston Hèches in Tarbes.[13]

Dohse's promise to treat Jean Duboué and Charles Hayes as 'soldiers' rather than terrorists was immediately broken by the Germans. Although Dohse travelled to Paris to intercede with his superiors on the grounds that he would have a much better chance of cleaning up the Resistance in his area if he could establish a reputation for keeping his word, Duboué was tried and deported to Wolfleben concentration camp. Here he was shot and wounded while making an escape bid and transferred to Mittelbau-Dora, the infamous underground slave-labour camp near Nordhausen in the Hartz mountains where the Germans constructed their secret V1 and V2 rockets. Here a runaway light railway wagon full of stones ran over him, necessitating the amputation of one leg in concentration camp conditions and without anaesthetic. Remarkably, he survived and reached Bordeaux on 2 May 1945, despite being in such poor health that he was immediately placed in the city's St André Hospital to recover.

After the war the French government gave pensions or emoluments to all who could prove they had fought for the liberty of France by serving in the Resistance – including those in SOE's RF Section. But Duboué, as a member of *Scientist*, had been in the British-controlled F Section and therefore was not accepted by the French as their responsibility. His SOE file contains a long and protracted correspondence, involving Claude de Baissac, between SOE and the Treasury in which Baker Street argued for the payment of a pension equivalent to the rank of a lieutenant in the British Army.[14] Despite a clear promise given to Duboué – and recorded in his file on 7 May 1943 – that he would be eligible for a post-war pension and 'disability or pension rights in relation to casualties incurred in our service', the Treasury after the war would grant him only a single ex gratia payment of 75,000 francs (£16,500 today), from which the 25,000 francs already given to his wife was deducted. The Treasury moreover insisted that, despite the promise made to him, Duboué should be refused a disability allowance on the grounds that this was 'a liability of the French

Government and not of SOE or any other British Government Department'.

Whitehall did however agree that he should be awarded the King's Medal for Freedom, which no doubt cost considerably less than the pension to which he was entitled.

Duboué was also awarded a further clasp to his existing Légion d'Honneur, the Croix de Guerre and the Médaille de la Résistance from the French government and, from the Belgian government, the Order of Leopold II. Extraordinarily, given the depredations he suffered at Buchenwald and Dora, he lived until the age of ninety, dying at Lestiac-sur-Garonne on 14 October 1986, just two months after his beloved wife Marie-Louise.

Suzanne Duboué was sent to the women's camp at Ravensbrück. She also survived and made her way back to Bordeaux – on foot – after the war. She subsequently married a M. Leglise, spent much of her life in the Congo and had a son whom she named Yves, after the *nom de guerre* of her lover, Charles Hayes. Suzanne, now approaching ninety, lived until recently in Nice where her son Yves and his wife and children also live.[15] In the summer of 2010, she went missing from her retirement home and was lost for several days, despite an extensive police search. Having eventually been found by the family dog hiding in a cave, she said she had seen the police searching for her but had hidden from them because she thought they were the Gestapo. Suzanne went missing again during the summer of 2011 and has not been seen since. Her family believe her body lies still undiscovered, somewhere in the ravines and rough country in the area.

Until now no clear evidence of the ultimate fate of Charles Hayes has come to light. He was seen for the last time by Jean Duboué in the exercise yard at the Fort du Hâ prison in Bordeaux, when he asked Duboué to pass a message to Suzanne that he would return after the war to find her.[16] Suzanne saw him for the last time, from a distance, when the two were brought for sentencing (she to deportation, he to execution by firing squad) before the Bordeaux German military tribunal.[17] His SOE file says variously that he may have died of his wounds or been executed at Gross Rosen concentration camp, but there is no evidence to support either of these speculations. However, in the course of research for this book, a document has come to light containing evidence from Otto Bernau,[18] a German cook who was in prison in Bordeaux awaiting execution for firing three shots, while drunk, at a portrait of Hitler.[19] Bernau describes sharing a cell with a British captain who precisely fits Hayes' description (wounded in the arm and leg while being arrested, 1m 65cm in height, of medium build, forty years old, bald, with a small moustache, and married before the war to a French wife who was killed on her way back to Britain). He continues:

> On 6th February 1944, the Captain was taken out of the cell for questioning. When he returned he had been beaten and ill-treated so much that he was unable to stand, eat or even sleep. On 16th February 1944 at 4 o'clock in the morning he was removed from the cell and did not return. This was the usual time that prisoners who were to be shot were taken from their cells.

Hayes was awarded a posthumous Military Cross after the war.

Yvonne Rudellat was captured near Blois by the Germans on 21 June 1943. She perished from typhus in Dachau concentration camp on 23 April 1945, just five days before the camp was liberated. Her identity at the time of her death was shown as Jacqueline Gautier, the cover name she had been given by SOE when she was first sent into France.

After his parachuting accident, Harry Peulevé was looked after by a Resistance family until his injury had improved enough for him to cross the Pyrenees in February 1943, just a few weeks before Hasler made his crossing and by the same route he was to follow (no mean feat, since Peulevé was still on crutches). He was parachuted back to France in September 1943, narrowly surviving after capture and a spell in Buchenwald, and ended the war with a DSO and MC for his actions.

Albert Rigoulet, the courageous La Réole gendarme, finally ran out of luck on 7 May 1944 when he was arrested in the town. He was deported to Dachau, but managed to survive against the odds. He returned to France on 1 June 1945, but his health had been so badly damaged by his experiences that he died six weeks later on 20 July.

Pierre Hennequin, the English-speaking gendarme at La Réole who questioned MacKinnon and Conway, deserted and joined the Resistance in the Savoie in August 1944, after his eldest brother was executed and two others sent to Auschwitz.[20] His boss, Captain Louis Olivier, was tried by a tribunal after the war for collaboration and suffered the minor punishment of the loss of his pension – a judgement which was overturned by a second investigation in 1948, when the pension was restored.[21]

Joseph Gagnerot, the betrayer of Laver and Mills at Montlieu-la-Garde, was arrested by the gendarme to whom he had betrayed them – Georges Rieupéyrout – on the day France was liberated. He was taken swiftly to the headquarters of the Gironde *maquis* in Reignac where he was summarily shot, though probably not for the betrayal of Laver and Mills, as he had also been involved in a number of other such incidents in the area.

Fire chief Raymond Brard, saboteur of German efforts to refloat the stricken Bordeaux blockade runners, survived the war and was awarded the Croix de Guerre. After the war he was made a Chevalier de la Légion d'Honneur for his resistance work. His sixteen-year-old accomplice Albert Juenbekdjian also survived and lives today in Cannes.

Despite remaining active on both the escape and sabotage fronts in Tarbes right to the end, Gaston Hèches, his wife Mimi and their restaurant survived the German occupation. Gaston's nephew, Dr Pierre Hèches, lives in nearby Argèles-Gazost, while his daughter, Denise, still lives in Tarbes.[22]

And Claude de Baissac? He and his sister Lise remained in Britain while *Scientist* was being dismembered. On 11 November 1943, the *London Gazette* announced that de Baissac had been awarded the DSO for his work against the Bordeaux blockade runners. An extract from the citation reads:

Intelligence from his organisation regarding blockade runners operating from Bordeaux has been graded very highly by the Ministry of Economic Warfare. The Admiralty have also expressed their appreciation of this information which they too rate highly.[23]

Claude and Lise were parachuted back into northern France in February 1944.[24] Here they raised *maquis* units which did outstanding work disrupting German communications, ambushing German troops and attacking German positions in the Departments of Orne, Calvados, Mayenne and Île et Vilaine during the battle of Normandy. For this work, Claude was awarded a bar to his DSO, making him one of the most decorated SOE agents in France.

Claude de Baissac retired to France after the war, remarried, and settled in Aix en Provence. His personal file in the Château de Vincennes includes an intriguing surveillance report written by the French security services about a visit de Baissac made to Casablanca in the mid-1950s as a 'representative' of one of the big Paris perfume houses, in which it is speculated that he was actually an agent working for the British SIS. De Baissac died in his sleep, aged sixty-seven, on 22 December 1974.

Lise de Baissac received the MBE[25] after the war and became a friend of Queen Mary the Queen Mother. During her SOE training, Lise had been allowed to make only five parachute jumps instead of the six required of her male colleagues – six being the minimum number needed to qualify for 'wings' during the war years. In 2003 – the year before her death at the age of ninety-one – the annual memorial service for SOE's F Section heroes at the memorial in Valençay, south of Orléans, saw Lise finally presented with the parachute 'wings' denied her in wartime.

35

Tea with Mountbatten and other Afterlives

Although there was no public acknowledgement in Britain of events in the Gironde, news slowly began to leak out to the participants' families and to those connected with the Royal Marines Boom Patrol Detachment in Eastney.

The first intimation of the fate of Hasler's men had come on 9 December 1942, when a London evening newspaper picked up on the German announcement that 'a small British sabotage squad was engaged at the mouth of the Gironde River and finished off in combat'. Reprinted the following day in a Portsmouth newspaper, the report was seen by Sergeant King, who showed it to Jock Stewart, temporary commander of the RMBPD in Hasler's absence.

The item was also spotted by sixteen-year-old Heather Powell at the White Heather in Worthing Road. Although neither Heather nor anyone else in the household had any reason to connect this brief report with No. 1 Section, some kind of premonition convinced her that it was connected with her beloved Bobby. Never a strong girl, Heather fell ill and was taken to hospital.

After their return to Eastney Barracks, Mrs Powell, presumably seeking to protect her daughter, asked that Norman Colley, Eric Fisher and Bill Ellery should not be sent back to Worthing Road. The three were in any case largely isolated and were not allowed to talk to other RMBPD personnel about the operation.

On 30 January 1943, the standard and impersonal 'Missing in Action' telegrams were sent out to the next-of-kin of all the Frankton raiders except 'Jan' Sheard's wife, Renee,[1] to whom the news had been broken personally by the chaplain of Plymouth Division Royal Marines on a visit to her home in Sussex Road, Devonport the previous day.

Then, for the families, there was silence: nothing to comfort, nothing to inform, nothing to relieve gnawing anxiety. Until on 29 March, when Sparks' and Hasler's families heard from the Admiralty that the two men had 'arrived in a neutral country'[2] but were instructed firmly not to make any attempt to contact their loved ones.

Sparks joined Colley, Fisher and Ellery in April 1943 and paid an early visit to Worthing Road, where Mrs Powell's first question was about those who had not returned. Sparks replied noncommittally that they would 'be along later'. Hearing that Heather was in hospital, he went to see her, but found himself again unable to satisfy her craving for news and commented afterwards that she was 'weak and unwilling to fight her illness'. Despite this, Heather was allowed home. But back in the guest house, the sight of the empty wardrobes where No. 1 Section had kept their clothes and equipment caused another bout of deep depression. She was diagnosed as having advanced tuberculosis; when her father was allowed leave to come home and see her, she told him that she had dreamt that they were all dead.

Heather died of her illness – compounded, they said, of a broken heart – the day before her seventeenth birthday.[3] Bill Mills' fiancée, Kitty Faulkner, who was also in fragile health and whom he was due to marry in December after returning from Frankton, also suffered a complete breakdown and died in the winter of 1943.[4]

On 6 April, four days after Hasler arrived back in England, a telegram for Mrs Moffatt, signed by the Officer Commanding Plymouth Division, Royal Marines, was delivered to 62 Wheatley Road, Lee Mount, Halifax. After the usual expressions of regret and condolences, it stated bleakly: 'From information received from a German Casualty List, the body of your son, David Moffatt, Mne Ply X 108881, was washed ashore on 17 December 1942 at Le Bloisenre [sic] and your son was buried on the Ridge of Dunes.'[5]

On 12 May, Mrs Moffatt received a second letter, this time from Mountbatten himself, whose curt phraseology says much about the 'stiff-upper-lip' attitudes of the age:

> I have only just heard of the news of the death and burial of your son.
>
> At the time he was lost at sea, David Moffatt was taking part in a hazardous Combined Operation, for which he volunteered.
>
> I cannot give you details of this operation, but it will comfort you to know that it was successful. Your son's life was not given in vain. I sympathise deeply and share with you in his loss.

For others there was what at first sight appeared to be good news. Marcel Galibert's letter, posted at the Red Cross office in Lyon more than three months previously, finally arrived at James Conway's Stockport home in early April, causing Mrs Conway – with what mixture of joy and relief we can only imagine – to write to Jock Stewart at RMBPD:

> I am happy to inform you I have had word from France that my son, Marine Conway 105763 is a prisoner, dated 29th December 1942. This was how the form was worded. 'have seen James last week, he is healthy and conveys New Year's greetings to you, don't worry'. I have sent the 25 word note to him [Galibert] as allowed, but up to now have received no further news.
>
> … Thank you for your sympathy during my time of anxiety, but I feel greatly relieved to hear he is alive.

Jack MacKinnon's mother, who seems to have received her letter from Marcel Galibert a little earlier,[6] followed swiftly by a comforting letter from Hasler dated 21 April,[7] no doubt reacted in the same way. But the two women's hopes were cruelly ill-founded. According to German reports, Jack MacKinnon, James Conway, Albert Laver and Bill Mills were actually executed by firing squad on 23 March 1943.

However, having spent the war years believing their sons to be alive, it was only three years later in 1946 that the MacKinnon and Conway families learnt the terrible truth. Mrs Conway told the papers:

Jim went with 11 other Marines in two-men canoes. His job was to fix limpet mines to German ships lying at Bordeaux. Something went wrong, and after the job was done, Jim and his companion Lieutenant John MacKinnon of Glasgow took to land and were captured. After that all I know is that they were taken to Paris for questioning. Then they were murdered without cause. Jim was only a baby. They can't hang the German leaders soon enough for me.

Marcel Galibert's letters were not the only correspondence from France received by the two families. After the war, Louis Jaubert wrote a series of letters to both the MacKinnons and the Conways, describing what happened when the two Marines stayed with him and his wife at Cessac and seeking news of them since.

As yet there is no firm evidence of what did happen to Jack MacKinnon, James Conway, Bert Laver and Bill Mills after 4 January 1943, the date on the German telex signal reporting the result of their interrogations.

Some have argued that, in conformity with the infamous Hitler Commando Order, they had been, like Wallace and Ewart, executed in the Bordeaux area immediately their interrogation was finished. But we now know from a signal sent by the German 85th Army Corps (stationed next to Bordeaux),[8] that all German units were firmly instructed in early January 1943 that, following the execution of Wallace and Ewart, 'Commando' prisoners were not to be executed until their intelligence potential had been fully exploited. Which is no doubt why this possibility was not even seriously considered by Captain Nightingale of the War Crimes Investigation Unit in his post-war examination of the events surrounding Frankton.

The German records (*Totenliste*) indicate that the four were buried in Bagneux cemetery in Paris[9] – but these should not, by themselves, be relied on. The German authorities were not averse to misrecording the fate of those executed under the Commando Order; indeed they had initially claimed that the four Marines, together with Wallace and Ewart, had 'Drowned in Bordeaux harbour', when in fact they died before German firing squads.

There is however corroborating evidence that MacKinnon, Conway, Laver and Mills were taken to Paris, perhaps for further exploitation of their information or for use for propaganda purposes (we know that the SD hoped to do just this when they sought a further delay to Wallace and Ewart's execution for additional detailed interrogation, but were overruled by Admiral Bachmann). A German paper marked MOST SECRET DOCUMENT, written in January 1944 by Major Otto Reichel[10] of German Military High Command, considers what propaganda action could be taken to counter the news of the execution of three Gestapo officers found guilty of war crimes in a trial held at Kharkov in the Soviet Union the previous month.[11]

Reichel looks at the cases of a number of Commandos and Special Forces troops captured by the Germans, to see if any of these could be exploited for counter-propaganda purposes. Among those listed are MacKinnon, Laver, Conway and Mills, against whose names it is noted: 'Noteworthy punishable offences committed on their flight have not been discovered up till now. All those captured were shot in accordance with orders on 23/3/43.'[12]

Nightingale took evidence from Reichel and concluded that his paper was substantial and should be taken seriously. Following up the lead, he found that it took him to four unmarked graves in Bagneux civil cemetery in 'the one hundred and eleventh division, first line, number fifty one'. He was informed by the French authorities that the bodies in these graves had been interred on 30 March 1943, a week after the supposed execution date, and that 'at first the Germans carrying out the burial would not disclose the identity of the four bodies, but later stated that they were "four high ranking German Officers"'.

Nightingale treated these German claims with scepticism. While it is true that the 111th division of Bagneux cemetery was at the time used for the burial of German military personnel, these were in the main soldiers of low rank. Nightingale considered it most unlikely that high-ranking German officers would have been buried there – and in an unmarked grave – rather than properly in the German military cemetery in Paris. In a telegram from the headquarters of the British Army in Paris dated 12 November 1945, he requested the assistance of a Home Office pathologist for an exhumation. Unfortunately, this revealed that the bodies had been cremated and that identification was thus impossible – a point which adds weight to the suspicion that these were the four

Marines, as it was common practice to cremate those executed under the Hitler Commando Order.[13]

The French municipal authorities have recently confirmed that according to their records, four urns – marked simply 1, 2, 3 and 4 – were buried by the Germans on 30 April 1943. These were however removed, along with other German military remains, on 21 and 22 April 1949 by the *Volksbund Deutsche Kriegsgräberfürsorge* (VDK), the German war graves authority, and relocated to the central German military graveyard at Champigny-St André, fifty miles west of Paris.[14] This cemetery holds the graves of over 2200 German soldiers. A search conducted in January 2012 revealed that one so-called 'comrade' grave at St André contains the remains of four unknown German soldiers, but according to the records (which could of course have been falsified), these were fallen from Normandy. The issue is complicated because, until 1949 when the records were handed over to the VDK, all German graves were the responsibility of the French authorities.[15]

A search of French cemetery records and those of the prison at Fresnes in Paris, where the Germans held all military and Resistance prisoners, has also regrettably proved fruitless. Nightingale listed a number of other cemeteries as possible sites for the graves, including Ivry, another Paris cemetery often used by the Germans to bury executed prisoners. However, a search of the records at Ivry, together with those of twenty other Parisian cemeteries carried out in late 2011, has thrown up no trace of the four Marines, or of any burials at this time which might be related to them.[16] We can only conclude that, as with other illegal executions carried out under the Commando Order, the German authorities of the time took considerable pains to hide the bodies of those they murdered.

And so we are forced back again into the realm of speculation. Taking into account his doubts that the Bagneux graves were those of high-ranking Germans and the proximity of the date of the bodies' interment to that of the presumed executions, Nightingale appears to have concluded that the cremation jars found in the Bagneux graves had by far the best claim to be the last resting place of the four Marines.[17] Unless new evidence comes to light,[18] it seems wise to conclude that he was right.

If so, then one more terrible irony is added to a story that has altogether too many: the remains of Jack MacKinnon, Bert Laver, Bill Mills and James Conway lie today somewhere in the German military cemetery at Champigny-St André, among the bodies of their enemy and under the flag and symbols of the nation against whom they were fighting when they lost their lives.

There has also been much speculation as to the exact site of the execution of Sam Wallace and Bobby Ewart. The site at which their death before Theodore Prahm's firing squad is recorded and commemorated annually is the wall of a concrete bunker at what was known at the time as the Château Dehez (now the Château Magnol) in Blanquefort. Today Blanquefort is a suburb of Bordeaux, but in 1945 it would have been a small town a short distance north of the city. The claim that this was the site of the execution is reinforced by the fact that Kriegsmarine units (and Italian navy divers) were stationed in the château during the war, and by some prominent bullet holes in the concrete wall of a nearby bunker.

But this site appears not to fit the facts given in Prahm's evidence (see Chapter 20). First, the bullet holes are far too large to have been made by small arms – they are much more likely to have been caused by something of larger calibre, perhaps a light anti-aircraft gun. Next, the bullet strike marks are too low to be appropriate for an execution, unless either the victims were seated, which we know they were not, or the ground has since been raised, for which there is no firm record. Most tellingly of all, the topography of the Blanquefort area does not conform in any way to that described by Prahm; it is neither sandy, nor wooded, nor isolated.

A second possibility has recently come to light. Just to the northwest of Blanquefort Château lies the village of Birehen, on the outskirts of which the Kriegsmarine had a base called Soustra. Some distance beyond the camp's southern boundary, close to a place called Les Pins (The Pines), there was, during the period of the German occupation, a large sandpit, Le Sablière d'Andrian.[19] Some believe that this sandpit may have been the execution site. But apart from the sandpit, the proximity to a known Kriegsmarine base and the local name referring to pine trees, little else seems to support this claim. Although there is evidence that

Kriegsmarine executions did sometimes take place on Kriegsmarine sites, there is no evidence that Soustra was used as a regular place of execution – or indeed that any executions took place there.

It is important, in assessing these rival claims, to remember that the Germans were meticulous about how and where they conducted executions. They were careful to keep these events away from prying French eyes, routinely conducting them in the large ex-French tank base at the Camp de Souges, set in a sandy area among extensive pine woods some four miles from the city. Here, starting with the Jewish protester Leizer Karp on 27 August 1940, the Germans executed more than 300 French Resistance fighters, hostages, gypsies, Jews and Communists. The site, now a memorial to those who died there, is still preserved exactly as it was during the war. True, it is to the northwest, rather than the northeast of Bordeaux, as claimed by Prahm – but as Prahm himself admits in a deposition made six years after the event, it was difficult to orientate himself during the journey because it was dark and he was in unfamiliar territory. In every other respect, however, the site conforms closely to Prahm's description, with a sandy bank to stop bullets behind the execution posts and buildings nearby in the trees, in just the position he describes, where the coffins of the two men were placed after the executions. Indeed, the presence of these buildings indicates strongly that this was not a site selected at random for the occasion, but rather part of a formal installation. The fact that the coffins of Wallace and Ewart were taken there straight after their execution also suggests a well-established routine and a proper burial process, rather than disposal in a hole in the woods.

Only one argument is advanced against the Camp de Souges. Prahm's report indicates that when the execution party arrived at the site, the posts to which the two Marines were tied had to be erected, whereas the execution posts at Souges today are permanent ones. But Souges today is a memorial and museum. The posts are permanent to show what it would have looked like. Given that the Germans did not like to advertise the details of their executions, it seems unlikely that they would have kept the site permanently set up; much more likely, posts would have been erected as the need arose and dismantled afterwards. This possibility is strengthened by Prahm's statement that 'The SD men dug in two posts, which were lying there', i.e. that the execution posts were already on site and had only to be erected – a description which reinforces other indications in Prahm's report that Wallace and Ewart were shot at a site frequently used for executions. The Camp de Souges thus remains incomparably the best candidate for the site of the execution of Wallace and Ewart.

The location of the graves of the two Marines, however, remains a mystery. The Germans, assisted by the local French authorities, were meticulous about recording both the deaths of those executed at Souges and the locations of their graves. But repeated searches of the local records have revealed nothing.

It may be that, in this instance, the Germans, conscious that the two men had been executed contrary to the rules and practices of war, again took steps to hide their place of burial. A post-war Red Cross report found that Wallace and Ewart were buried in the 'Prisoner of War cemetery' in Bordeaux.[20] Nightingale investigated this claim and found that there was no POW cemetery in Bordeaux, concluding that Wallace and Ewart's most likely last resting place was in the German military cemetery (*Soldatenfriedhof Nord*). If this is so, then their bodies too could have been among those of German soldiers exhumed and relocated, when the German war graves authority – this time in the early 1960s – removed all the German dead in their various military cemeteries in the area to a single regional military cemetery at Berneuil, some fifty miles north of Bordeaux.

According to the German records, the bodies of fourteen named German soldiers were moved from Bordeaux to Berneuil in 1962. The following year a further three bodies came to light in the Bordeaux cemetery; being unnamed, they were simply recorded as those of 'unknown German soldiers',[21] but were also transferred that year to Berneuil and reburied. The description provided by the VDK of the remains of these unknown soldiers and the equipment found with them seems strongly to indicate that they were Germans.[22] However, the German cemetery at Berneuil contains more than 8300 graves, of which (including bodies taken from other graveyards in the region) nearly 300 are those of 'unknown German soldiers'. Moreover no record was made of exactly where any other unknown soldiers transferred from Bordeaux in 1963 were finally interred.[23] So the possible site of the last remains of Wallace and Ewart cannot be identified, except to say that these too may well lie, like those of their comrades who were shot in Paris, under the flag and among the fallen of their enemy.

This leaves only one of the ten who left HM/s *Tuna* on the night of 7 December 1942 unaccounted for – George Jellicoe Sheard, who with David Moffatt was last seen when the two men, frozen and suffering from hypothermia, said goodbye to their comrades just inside the mouth of the Gironde and about two hundred yards from La Chambrette beach. Sheard, it will be recalled, was reported by the others to be in a worse state than Moffatt, whose body was washed up ten days later on the Île de Ré.

In the absence of any other information, all previous accounts have concluded that Sheard, like Moffatt, must have succumbed to the cold and that his body was lost to the Atlantic.[24] But now we have to consider the evidence of Jeanette Lhermet and her cousin Mano Etinette, who claim to have seen the body of a young man in sodden camouflage uniform which had been brought in by a German patrol from La Chambrette beach on the morning after their capsize. This evidence, which is widely believed in Le Verdon, seems to suggest that George Sheard made it to the beach and succumbed to the cold there.

But there are problems with this version of events. First, there are no German reports of the discovery of another body at Le Verdon. Given the severe reprimands handed down by the German authorities for the late reporting of the capture of Wallace and Ewart that morning, it is difficult to accept that the local German commanders in Le Verdon would have risked not reporting at all the existence of a third raider. We have, moreover, clear evidence from the interrogation reports that the Germans were never able to establish the whereabouts of George Sheard and believed that he had escaped to Spain with Hasler and Sparks. A large number of people of all ranks in the German camp must have seen the body, and it would have taken a conspiracy of silence of major proportions to have kept this evidence from superior German authority.

Second, if this *was* George Sheard's body, which would of course have carried his identity discs, then where was he buried? There is (or was) a small German military cemetery in the pine woods about sixty yards from the canteen at which Jeanette Lhermet worked. It has always been assumed in Le Verdon that the body Jeanette saw was buried there. This graveyard, like those in Bordeaux and elsewhere, was emptied in the 1960s and the bodies moved to the German regional military cemetery in Berneuil. The German war graves authority's records[25] show that, among the 214 bodies of German soldiers and POWs transferred from the German military cemeteries at Soulac and Le Verdon, there were five bodies with 'no clear identity', which the Germans believed to be either 'white' Russian (mostly Cossack) or Dutch.[26] It may be that one of these was that of 'Jan' Sheard, but there is as yet no firm evidence of this.

In short, Lhermet's evidence, while compelling, is not conclusive. What happened to Corporal George Sheard remains a mystery. His final resting place must, like those of his comrades, remain uncertain.

None of this information, or even the fact that Wallace and Ewart had been executed, came to light until after the war. Indeed, the presumption of death in the case of all of those declared missing was not made and announced to the families until July 1945, two months after the European war was over. With the exception of Mrs Moffatt, who knew the fate of her son, all the families spent the rest of the war hoping that their loved ones were still only 'missing' and might yet be found.

On Sunday 25 April, Blondie Hasler was invited to tea at the Mountbatten family home at Broadlands near Romsey. Here, in the presence of the assembled Mountbatten clan, he related for the first time the full story of Operation Frankton.

At about this time Mountbatten must have been considering what awards should be given to those who had taken part. His recommendation for Hasler concludes: 'Major Hasler's cool, determined and fearless leadership was in accordance with the highest traditions of the Royal Marine Corps – and he is strongly recommended for the highest recommendation permissible for a feat of this nature.' Hasler was simultaneously recommended for promotion to brevet major,

The phraseology used here is interesting. At first sight, 'the highest recommendation possible' means a Victoria Cross. But Mountbatten knew that one of the conditions for the award of a VC is that the relevant act of valour must have been observed and vouched for by a senior officer.[27] Hasler of course, *was* the senior officer and could not, by the nature of the operation, have been observed by anyone else. Which meant that, whatever his valour, Hasler could not receive the

VC – a fact tacitly acknowledged by that final phrase, 'for a feat of this nature'.

On 29 June 1943 the *London Gazette* announced:

For courage and enterprise:
　To be a Companion of the Distinguished Service Order (DSO):
　Captain (Acting major) Herbert George Hasler, OBE Royal Marines.
　The Distinguished Service Medal (DSM):
　Marine William Edward Sparks, Ply.X.3664.

The DSO is indeed the highest award that can be given 'for a feat of this nature'. The fact that, just four months after Hasler's award, Claude de Baissac received exactly the same medal for his work against exactly the same targets is only one more to add to the long list of curiosities in this extraordinary tale.

Mountbatten's recommendations also included, at Hasler's suggestion, Corporal Albert Laver and Marine William Mills. It was agreed that, if either returned to Britain, they should like Sparks be given the DSM. But, since the DSM cannot be awarded posthumously, it was agreed that, if the two Marines had been killed, they should only be mentioned in dispatches. Hasler also recommended Lieutenant-Commander L'Estrange and Dick Raikes for awards, but neither name appeared in the published honours list for Operation Frankton.

In October 1943, Churchill appointed Mountbatten Supreme Allied Commander South East Asia Command. Almost as soon as he arrived in Delhi, Mountbatten started bringing his Special Forces units[28] under a single command and appointed Hasler, now a 29-year-old lieutenant-colonel, Officer Commanding Special Operations Group (SOG)[29] at the Combined Operations naval base HMS *Braganza* in Bombay. Hasler later moved his base to Hammenheil in northern Ceylon. The unit made a contribution to Allied victory in the Far East which, in the opinion of many, has yet to be properly recognised.

Having rejoined the RMBPD on Eastney front, Bill Sparks, Eric Fisher and Norman Colley were sent to the Aegean where they saw service with the 'Earthworm Detachment' and were involved in canoe and small boat raids on German installations along the Aegean and Adriatic coasts. After the war, Fisher moved back to West Bromwich, where he worked as a printer. He married but had no children, and died in the 1990s.

Bill Sparks became a London bus driver immediately after the war. He took up a post in the 1950s as a police lieutenant during the Malayan emergency, returning to finish his working life as a London Transport bus inspector. In the late 1960s he launched a campaign for Hasler's DSO to be upgraded to a VC and for his dead comrades to be awarded the DSM, turning to his MP, Sir Bernard Braine, for help. Braine persuaded Sparks to campaign instead for a memorial at Poole, the home of the modern SBS. This was unveiled in 1983. In June 1988 Sparks, now remarried after the death of his first wife, found himself in financial straits and decided to sell his DSM. The medal fetched £31,000 at an auction which attracted a good deal of national publicity thanks to Sparks' claim that he had been forced to sell as a result of welfare cuts instituted by the then Conservative government.[30]

Bill Sparks DSM died aged eighty on 30 November 2002, sixty years to the day after he paddled into legend at the start of Operation Frankton.

Norman Colley also survived the war and afterwards worked for an engineering firm in Yorkshire, before first taking over his brother's bakery and confectionery firm and then becoming sub-postmaster in South Elmsall near Pontefract. He lives there still, a sprightly and alert 92-year-old with razor-sharp memories of Frankton and the comrades he served with.

According to Norman Colley's recollection, Bill Ellery, the 'crafty Cockney', went 'absent without leave' from the RMBPD shortly after *Tuna*'s return to Devonport. There is no indication of this on Ellery's service record. But it may very well be that his 'absence' was simply 'overlooked' because he had recently returned from Operation Frankton (as was Sparks' brief 'absence' after arriving at Euston when he took two days off to see his parents). This was just the kind of thing that Hasler – despite his outward appearance as a disciplinarian – would have expected the RMBPD to do for one of his men who had just returned from operations. But if Ellery did, in naval parlance, go 'over the wall' early in 1943, then he did it again a year later. His service record shows that he deserted on 2 December 1943. This time he spent twenty-seven days 'on the run', for which he received a punishment of 182 days' detention.

The reason for his behaviour, which seems so out of character with others in the RMBPD, is something of a mystery.

After the war Ellery returned to Pimlico where he and his wife brought up six children. He worked for some time for the Gas Board and later delivered *Hansard* for the House of Commons.[31] He died in 1999 at the age of eighty-four.

There is good reason to believe that one of the canoes sent on Frankton, *Cachalot*, still survives. It is displayed in the Combined Services Military Services Museum in Maldon, Essex. A small cut on the starboard side just forward of the Number One's seat – in precisely the position described by the only living witness from that night, Norman Colley – is, according to fabric and X-ray tests carried out by scientists and experts from the University of Bradford in January 2012, consistent with the damage *Cachalot* is said to have suffered on the night *Tuna* disembarked Hasler and his men and which caused Hasler to leave Ellery and Fisher behind (see Appendix B for full details).

The afterlives of the other main players in our story also deserve mention. Mary Lindell continued to smuggle Allied fugitives across the Demarcation Line and pass them on to other escape lines for the final leg of their journey home. She also paid several more visits to the British Consulate in Geneva, on one occasion carrying vital information about a convoy of blockade runners leaving Bordeaux, enabling the Allies to intercept and sink them at sea.

She finally paid the price for her obstinate refusal to take precautions and was arrested in a spot check at Pau station in southwest France on 24 November 1943.[32] While being taken north, Mary tried to escape by jumping from the train at Châtellerault, south of Tours, but was shot three times in the head by her guard. She should have died from her wounds but, once again, survived and was sent to recover in Dijon prison. Here a fellow inmate, the recently arrested young SOE agent Yvonne Baseden,[33] was alerted to her presence by the hearty rendition of English songs emanating from a neighbouring cell. The two women eventually shared a cell before being transferred to Ravensbrück concentration camp. Here Mary took over the running of the prison hospitals, browbeating medicines and supplies out of her German captors, who swiftly christened her '*Die arrogante Engländerin*' ('the arrogant Englishwoman'). In the last months of the war Mary spirited her young SOE colleague away on one of the relief buses whose passage had been negotiated by Count Bernadotte, head of the Swedish Red Cross. In due course, Mary followed. Returning briefly to London via Sweden, she eventually went back to France, taking up residence again in her flat in Rue Erlanger after the liberation of Paris. In 1969 she finally received an OBE for her wartime work, an award that seems as tardy as it does meagre when set against her achievements. She died in 1986.

Her 'right hand man', Gaston Denivelle, also survived the war after being arrested several times and escaping. He eventually joined up with the *maquis*, with whom he fought with great distinction, and was awarded, after the war, the King's Medal for Courage in the Cause of Freedom by the British government, the American Medal of Freedom with Palm by the USA and the Croix de Guerre by the French.

Germaine Rouillon, who with her husband François ran the Hôtel de France in Ruffec, was arrested and deported on 23 May 1944. She was never seen again. After the war she was posthumously made a Chevalier of the Légion d'Honneur.

Albert Guérisse, the founder and leader of the *Pat* line, was sent to Dachau, where after terrible torture he was condemned to death. But by now the advancing Allies were at the gates of the camp. When Dachau was liberated Guérisse refused to leave the camp before the Allies agreed to take care of the other inmates. After the war he became one of the most decorated people of the Second World War, receiving among other awards the George Cross and a knighthood from Britain and a peerage in the rank of count from the King of Belgium. Mme Martin, together with her husband and two young daughters, who had cared for Hasler and Sparks in Marseille, were arrested after the collapse of the *Pat* line, deported and never seen again. Le Neveu, the *Pat* line traitor, was later horribly executed by the Resistance.

So far as is known, all the other *Marie-Claire* agents involved in the escape of Hasler and Sparks survived the war. Hasler went back to Bordeaux several times and always took care to see those who had helped him. He kept his word to revisit La Présidente Farm in 1961, to find that Alibert Decombes had died in 1949. But he was able to thank his son Robert and returned to see him several times in later years. In 1961, at Mary Lindell's suggestion, Clodomir Pasqueraud, the 'Fiery

Woodman', and others who had helped Hasler and Sparks were invited to London by the Commandant General Royal Marines and formally thanked for their actions, each being presented with a small gilt 'Globe and Laurel' badge, the symbol of the Royal Marines. In a letter to Pasqueraud of 9 February 1961 Hasler wrote thanking his host 'from the bottom of my heart, for risking so much and helping us so generously, on that far off rainy night'.

Two of the remarkable French women who risked all to help Hasler's Marines are still alive today. Jeanne Baudray, who helped Hasler and his men at Pointe aux Oiseaux, subsequently became Mayor of St Julien-en-Médoc and still lives there today. Amélie Dubreuille, who with her husband Armand looked after Hasler and Sparks at Marvaud Farm, is a frequent attender at Frankton memorial events.

On 21 April 2012, Anne-Marie Bernadet (later Farré), who met Jack MacKinnon while herding her cows, died peacefully at the home she shared with her son, his wife and her charming grandchildren in St Médard d'Eyrans.

As a result of the war crimes investigation into the executions of 'Sailor' Wallace, Bobby Ewart, Jack MacKinnon, James Conway, Bert Laver and Bill Mills, it was decided that Admiral Johannes Bachmann should be tried for war crimes. But it was discovered that he had, apparently, been killed in the last days of the war. One of the most senior men in the department[34] which dealt, among other matters, with the execution of Hitler's Commando Order in German Supreme Headquarters, Colonel Werner von Tippleskirch, was tried at Nuremberg in his stead in 1948. At the same time the Nuremberg court also tried Lieutenant-General Walter Warlimont for a number of war crimes, which included playing a role in the execution of the six Marines.[35] Bill Sparks was called to give evidence and did so. Blondie Hasler however declined a similar invitation – perhaps another example of his lifetime's aversion to revisiting the past. He was subsequently criticised by Sparks, who felt that he was letting down the memory of his men. Tippleskirch was eventually acquitted of direct involvement in the executions, but Warlimont was sentenced to life imprisonment.

Theodore Prahm survived the war and gave evidence to Captain Nightingale's subsequent war crimes investigation. No further action was taken against him.

Ernst Kühnemann was still in charge of the Port of Bordeaux when the town was liberated by the French. As such he was responsible for putting into effect a massive plan of destruction so that the port would not fall into Allied hands. With huge quantities of explosive pre-positioned along the quays and waterfronts of the *Port de la Lune*, local wine merchant Louis Eschenauer was tasked by the French to open negotiations with Kühnemann (whose family were themselves wine producers in Germany) to prevent the city's destruction.[36] In the event, before these could be concluded, a junior German naval officer called Heinz Stahlschmidt blew up the warehouse in which were stored the 4000 detonators to be used in the destruction, so saving the city.[37]

Lieutenant Künesch, the Place Tourny SS officer who was probably responsible for any torture used on Hasler's Marines, committed suicide in 1945 to avoid capture by the Allies.[38]

Friedrich Wilhelm Dohse, Bordeaux's unusual Gestapo chief, left the city on 28 August 1944 on posting to Denmark, where he was captured at the end of the war. Having been returned to Bordeaux on 24 June 1947 and imprisoned in the Fort du Hâ,[39] where he had incarcerated so many prisoners, he was finally tried before a French tribunal in Bordeaux in April and May 1953, an event much publicised throughout France. Dohse finally received the relatively mild sentence of eight years in prison, but was immediately released as he had already served this time since his capture. He later became something of a minor celebrity in Bordeaux. The light sentence was almost certainly due to the remarkable evidence given in Dohse's favour by his old adversary Jean Duboué:[40]

You treated us as soldiers, I must say … I'm only sorry you weren't on our side. You are a skilful man who destroyed the Resistance in our region. As far as you are concerned, in the battle which opposed us, I must in truth state that I found in you a dangerous adversary, but an honest enemy with a strong sense of honour and of patriotism.

Nevertheless, in my opinion I must recall with what a spirit of hatred and without respect for human dignity, the methods employed by your other compatriots against men guilty of nothing more than sacrificing themselves to defend their country, are unworthy of a great nation and of a civilised people.

36

Placid Waters

Blondie Hasler was never destined to be a quiet, career-minded post-war soldier; he was too restless and eccentric for that. He left the Royal Marines in 1948 and dedicated the rest of his life to his many other pursuits and enthusiasms, the chief of which was, as ever, sailing – especially across the Atlantic and preferably single-handed.

His deeply practical bent and, in the words of Lucas Phillips, 'ardour for contriving and devising things', produced a string of inventions which included a £500 ocean racer, a cabin heater, stiff sails, a 'self-tailing' rope winch, a one-man flying machine which he called an ornithopter, the Hasler Floating Breakwater and even an improved coathanger. None of them, however, excited commercial interest, apart from the Hasler pendulum servo gear. This was immediately adopted on a wide scale and is still the essential component of all self-steering rigs used by yachtsmen on single-handed voyages. But since Hasler had not taken the precaution of patenting the device, he received none of the benefit. Like so many inventors, Hasler was good at ideas, but very bad at marketing them.

He also pursued environmental living (long before its time), hill farming, drawing, and writing, especially for *The Observer*. He searched (with typical thoroughness) for the elusive Loch Ness monster, wrote plays and musicals, played his jazz clarinet, painted, composed poetry and conducted hydrographic surveys: his book on harbours and anchorages on the north coast of Brittany is still regarded as a model of its kind.[1]

It was typical of Hasler's other-worldliness in practical matters that among these preoccupations was not included making enough money to live on. With a meagre Royal Marines pension of £450 per year he soon found himself in straitened circumstances.[2] In 1956, David Astor, a close friend from Combined Operations days, wrote to Mountbatten expressing his concern about Hasler's condition:

> I know how much you admire Lt Col 'Blondie' Hasler. [He] is a bachelor who lives extremely modestly, sometimes in lodgings and sometimes aboard a small yacht. I believe that one reason he hesitates to get married is that he cannot afford to maintain a wife in reasonable circumstances ... He has a great capacity for inspiring men, particularly younger ones, and one feels that there ought to be a use for him somewhere ... All I wish to do is to draw your attention to his personal situation in the hope that you may know of some special way in which such a superb man can be made better use of.[3]

Mountbatten wrote back in rather bewildered tones, saying that while he had done what he could to involve the Royal Marines, '[Hasler's] views on employment are unusual. He wants to get as much capital as possible with the ... eventual aim of farming and ... writing a play!'

In fact, Hasler's financial situation deteriorated steadily during the mid-1950s, even forcing him to lay up his beloved yacht and live in lodgings while working for the government on a six-month assignment. By now his main hope of improving his finances was a play called *The Tulip Major*, which ran briefly and to reasonable reviews in Dundee but otherwise failed to take off. He received £50 from Lucas Phillips for advice on the writing of *The Cockleshell Heroes* and was also paid for his work as technical advisor on the Columbia Pictures film of the same name (he hated the picture so much for its inaccuracy that he escaped the country to avoid it, leaving his mother to represent him at the royal gala premiere while he spent the evening alone in a bar in Boulogne). Hasler wrote two more plays, but these too failed to generate interest.[4]

Hasler finally found a job as consultant to a firm called Dracone Ltd, set up to manufacture and market the invention of a much-admired friend, Sir William Hawthorn. The Dracone was a giant floating rubber sausage towed behind tugs and designed to transport large amounts of bulk liquid, such as petroleum and crude oil. Hasler's employer paid him the princely sum of ten guineas a day. Now he could get married!

Hasler's search for a wife was conducted with the same focus, determination and thoroughness as his paddle up the Gironde and his search for the Loch Ness monster. He describes the chase in his diary, writing in 1958:

17 May. Being now for the first time able to keep a wife am about to make a real effort to find one – HJ? Plan would be for wife to help set up family business (Hasler Boats Ltd – to make folding boats of all sizes) in lieu of any other insurance policy.

21 June. Have thought seriously of marrying P but am also about to start on H.J.

August. No longer thinking of marrying P or HJ or Z. Present possibilities DBS, DGB

An entry from later in the year notes: 'All prospective wives rejected me, [now] waiting for HJ without confidence.' But by January 1959, after a friend has donated him enough furniture to rent a flat, he is more optimistic:

Dracones looking brisk so I will stay with them. No longer looking at Diana B or HJ. Priority for week-ends. 1. Wife Hunt (nothing in sight but about to renew acquaintance with Georgie.) 2. Convert pram dinghy for sailing. 3. Have a boat in commission – inclination to enter the trans-Atlantic race.

And by June or July:

Sudden avalanche of girl friends – Poll (in Med cruising), Cynthia (Sailed last Sunday), Belinda (just approaching), Sue (not answering). Possible matrimonial order B, C, S, P but don't know what I've got to offer first three. Must guard against tendency to 'cheese off' in middle of wooing. Remember, marriage is urgent.

But early the following year, 1960, he is becoming more choosy:

> February. Girlfriend order C, S, P but not sure I can face marriage
> with any of these. It must be somebody who will help me in my
> work and with boat as well as run home.[5]

Eventually Hasler's single-minded campaign to find a wife paid off. In
July 1961 the younger sister of a past girlfriend, twenty-year-old Bridget
Fisher, agreed to help him search for the Loch Ness monster. After a
courtship spent bucketing around in sailing boats and chasing mythical
monsters in all Scottish weathers, Bridget finally accepted Hasler's third
proposal on St George's Day 1965 and they were married on 30 October.
Hasler was fifty-one, his bride twenty-five. It proved a most inspired and
loving partnership and opened the way to a final stretch of calm, sunlit
waters in Hasler's life.

The couple settled in a small hill farm in Argyll in 1975. Hasler's latter
years were spent with his wife and two children happily 'pottering
about' (as Blondie would have put it) in boats, growing various crops,
raising a few cattle and learning how to plough a straight furrow in his
ancient Ferguson tractor. He died of a heart attack on 5 May 1987 and is
survived by his wife, daughter Dinah, son Tom and five delightful
grandchildren.

Bridget Hasler still lives a simple life at their Argyll home, where I
visited her in October 2010 for help and advice in writing this book.
Blondie's drawings and pictures hang on the wall, along with the little
flute-playing pixie he carved while staying with the Dubreuilles at
Marvaud Farm. There is a piano and sheets of music among a jumble of
books, papers and artefacts from his wide-ranging and remarkable life.
The front windows look over fields and woods leading down to the arm
of a narrow sea loch of pristine clarity; about as wide as the channel
which separates the Île Cazeau from the vineyards of Margaux. Its
surface is dotted with small boats lying at safe anchorage on the placid
sunlit water. It is difficult to imagine a more appropriate final 'lying-up
position' for Blondie Hasler's restless, questing, inquisitive, awkward,
challenging spirit.

37

In Memoriam

At a moving ceremony in the spring of 2011, a magnificent memorial representing, in abstract form, men emerging from the sea, was unveiled at the mouth of the Gironde, just 200 yards from where George Sheard and David Moffatt said their last goodbyes to their colleagues. It is dedicated to the Frankton raiders and the brave French people who assisted them. Those present at the unveiling included relatives of the Frankton Marines, Blondie Hasler's widow, two children and five grandchildren, and three of the women[1] who gave the Marines succour and assistance on their escape.

The memory of the Frankton raiders has been painstakingly preserved in France by Frankton Souvenir, founded by ex-French paratrooper François Boisnier MBE,[2] who was responsible for uncovering many of the details which have made this book possible. Frankton Souvenir, under their new president, Erick Poineau of Le Verdon, organise an annual Frankton memorial service. They have also, with the help of funds from the SBS Association, the Royal Marines Corps Fund and the RM Historical Society, arranged for the erection of memorials at all the key places on the operation and subsequent escape, including the Quai des Chartrons and the Toque Blanche.

The war memorial at the little town of Montlieu-la-Garde, which records the French fallen of two world wars, also contains a small marble plaque remembering the lost lives of Marines Albert Laver[*] and Bill Mills.

---

[*] At the time of going to press Wirrall Council are considering naming a street in the town after Bert Laver.

A walking itinerary called the Frankton Trail (again established thanks to Frankton Souvenir) now follows the escape route taken by Hasler and Sparks. The seventy-mile route starts near the point where *Catfish* made her last land-fall beneath the Château de Segonzac[3] and ends at the Toque Blanche, running from the great vineyards of the Blaye district, through the open heathland and conifer woods of the Landes du Terrier Pêle and on through the vineyards of Cognac to the rolling agricultural country around Ruffec. Along the trail each place where Hasler and Sparks were given shelter is marked with a memorial to the brave French families who helped them. It is not an arduous route for anyone used to walking. There are plenty of fine vineyards and small châteaux along the way to lift the spirit and speed the journey and a scattering of small bed and breakfast establishments and village restaurants for weary travellers, tired feet and empty stomachs.

In Britain, there is a stone memorial to the raiders at the Amphibious Training Centre Royal Marines, Poole, the home of the modern-day SBS. David Moffatt is commemorated on a plaque in St Bernard's Church, Halifax. His name orginally appeared as a 'Mercantile Marine', rather than a Royal Marine, on the Roll of Honour of the City of Halifax's fallen in the Second World War. The mistake was eventually noted and, in a ceremony at Halifax Town Hall in December 2007 the Roll was amended and rededicated in the presence of his family.[4] Jack MacKinnon is remembered, also inaccurately, (his name is spelt incorrectly) on a memorial at Firth of Lorn, Oban.

At North Corner Quay in Devonport, close to the spot where the Sheard family house, 3 East Cornwall Street, used to stand, there is a memorial to members of the Sheard family who served with such distinction and courage in the Second World War. The inscription reads:

IN CELEBRATION AND IN HONOUR OF NORTH CORNER HEROES DURING WORLD WAR II 1939–1945 Sheard G – Operation Frankton. Sheard M – British Empire Medal. Sheard W H – Distinguished Service Medal. Siddall H – P.O.W. Stalag VIIA & VIIIB. Yabsley T – George Medal

A blue plaque marks Bill Sparks' post-war council house in Poundfield Road, Loughton, Essex.

Memorials to Claude de Baissac's *Scientist* team are far more rare and less well cared for. An unkempt memorial by the side of the road in Lestiac-sur-Garonne commemorates the 'battle of Lestiac' and marks the site of the Ancienne Villa Roucoule, which has since been demolished to make way for a road-widening scheme. A square has been named after Gaston Hèches in Tarbes and a plaque erected marking his restaurant. In La Réole, a square has been renamed Place Albert Rigoulet after the town's remarkable and courageous gendarme. At Valençay Charles Hayes' name is inscribed on the memorial to those who lost their lives in SOE's F Section. And that is all.

Jean Duboué's Café de Commerce was the single building on the Bordeaux quays to be hit by a bomb during the American air raid on the city in May 1943.[5] The structure was completely destroyed, and has been replaced by Molly Malone's Irish pub. The site of the Café des Chartrons has also been reconstructed – as an archway. On neither building, nor anywhere else along the quays, is there a memorial, plaque or sign dedicated to the memories of Jean Duboué and his colleagues, who risked so much to assure the discomfiture of their enemies, the victory of the Allies and the liberty of their country.

38

Epilogue

Combined Operations' decision that there should be no publicity for Operation Frankton 'as we might want to repeat the operation'[1] was followed, in August 1943, by serious consideration of that very possibility. The feasibility study (which eventually advised against the mission) contains a telling passage giving Hasler's opinion:

> The previous operation was carried out in a condition of almost flat calm which is most exceptional and the odds are against it ever occurring again. In spite of the calm weather two of the five canoes capsized at the mouth of the river and Major Hasler is of the opinion that, under any other sea conditions, it is unlikely that any of the canoes would get through the race [sic].[2]

On 25 September 1943, a similar action took place on the other side of the world which probably matched Frankton for courage and daring. In Operation Jaywick, a mixed British and Australian party under the command of Major Lyons of the Gordon Highlanders launched their canoes from an ex-Japanese fishing boat, the *Krait*, to attack and sink six merchant ships in Singapore harbour. All those involved returned home safely. However, in a later attempt to repeat the operation all the raiders were discovered before launching their attack, captured and subsequently executed.

Later, in June 1944, another canoe-based raid, involving Eric Fisher, was launched on German shipping in Portolago, Leros, sinking several small merchant and naval vessels. The two operations confirmed what

Frankton had illustrated, that canoe-based special operations could play an important strategic role.

After the war the Royal Marines were given the task of developing that role, taking over from the Army Special Boat Sections. In late 1954 a new headquarters was established for the SBS at Poole in Dorset, where they are still based today and from where they have sent operational units into every theatre of action in which Britain has been engaged since the Second World War.

Although the existence of Operation Frankton was never publicly acknowledged during the war, the story became widely publicised afterwards and played a role in boosting post-war national morale. During the 1950s, when Britain was struggling to make the long, slow, grim ascent out of wartime penury, a number of books were published with the purpose of cheering the nation by reminding us of our 'finest hours'. There were no less than twenty-two of these, many of them made into films.[3] Though (like Lucas Phillips' *Cockleshell Heroes*) thrillingly and often very competently written, their authors did not have access to many of the sources available to us today, and painted a largely black and white picture of flawless heroes, peerless heroism and an irredeemably black-hearted enemy. Their public appeal lay in their role as morale boosters in dark times, rather than as balanced historical works.

But today, seventy years on – and with the advantage of access to sources closed in the immediate post-war years – it is possible to make a more rounded assessment of the achievements and implications of Operation Frankton.

Measured only against its strategic purpose – to sink Bordeaux blockade runners – Frankton cannot be considered a success. The ships were empty and the tide at its lowest when Hasler's limpets detonated. They mostly sank a few feet onto the mud; the *Tannenfels* and *Dresden* were refloated on the next tide. The *Portland* was repaired, loaded with machine tools and spare parts and ready to sail for Japan in February 1943, just a few weeks after Hasler's attack.

There are those who claim that de Baissac's *Scientist réseau* were still 'months away' from being ready to launch their attack when Hasler and his men placed their mines. They insist that it is 'simply not true', as SOE's historian Professor M.R.D. Foot has said, based on a now lost post-war document he had seen, that the *Scientist* team had 'reconnoitring parties actually on the quayside making their last recce before they attacked the following night' when Hasler's limpets went off.[4]

The claim that *Scientist* were not yet ready rests on two assertions. The first is that the 60 lb of explosive de Baissac had received by parachute at the end of November 1942 was insufficient to conduct his attack. But, as we have already seen, this is to misunderstand the difference between Hasler's attack and that planned by de Baissac. Hasler had to try and sink the ships from the *outside* while they were stationary, and so needed large charges to blow holes in their steel sides big enough to sink them alongside the quay. As SOE had made clear to de Baissac, however, they envisaged him using small charges which would be strategically placed on the *insides* of the ships with the aim of disabling their control mechanisms and puncturing small holes when the ships were under way.

The second is the admission in de Baissac's London debriefing report of 23 March 1943 that 'owing to the almost complete lack of supplies he has been forced to confine himself almost entirely to the organisation, as opposed to the active side, of his mission'. But any reading of this report makes it clear that, in making these comments, he was referring not to his December activities (attacking the blockade runners), but to his new mission of raising an army of 3–4000 men.

Even in the absence of available documentary evidence, there is much solid fact to support the proposition that *Scientist* was both ready and able to conduct its attack by the time Hasler and his men arrived in Bordeaux. First there is Buckmaster's mid-November 1942 call to *Scientist* for 'sabotage immediately … against all shipping which used the port of Bordeaux'[5] – a call he would hardly have made unless he believed *Scientist* was ready. Second, there is de Baissac's own statement that, at the time of Hasler's attack, 'In spite of the comparative lack of material, *Scientist* was well on the way to organising an attack on his shipping targets by the introduction of … explosives through the dockers and the paint sealers working on the vessels.'[6] Next there is SOE's claim in late December 1942 that the success of Frankton was their own – indicating perhaps that they believed this action was imminent, rather than months away. And finally there is an operational review recorded in Buckmaster's diary in February 1943, in which he stated that, far from being short of supplies, Bordeaux had 'good W/T, stores OK'.[7]

In the end, however, the strategic target set by Selborne of closing down blockade runner traffic out of Bordeaux was achieved not by Combined Operations but by his own organisation, SOE. In September 1943 the Admiralty wrote to Baker Street congratulating *Scientist* on providing intelligence from Bordeaux on the blockade runners which had enabled the Allied navies, who now had sufficient resources, to deal with them at sea: 'Ground intelligence from Bordeaux ... has virtually put an end to blockade running between Europe and Far East this year. The stoppage of this traffic is of the highest importance as the supplies ordered are vital to the Japanese.'[8]

But the fact that the exploits of Hasler and his team had little or no impact on the Bordeaux blockade runners did not mean that they had no impact on the Germans at large – or on the French, particularly in the southwest of the country.

The German reaction to discovering that they were vulnerable to attack in what they regarded as one of their safest harbours was not confined to the panicky actions of Kühnemann and Bachmann in the days after Hasler's limpets exploded. Operational studies based on Dohse's interrogation reports were widely distributed, especially to Kriegsmarine commanders, and new security measures, involving the deployment of extra manpower, were taken to defend the Germans' other harbours on the Atlantic seaboard.

Among those present in Bordeaux on 12 December to witness the effects of Hasler's limpets was *Korvetten-Kapitän* Peter Popp. He was later sent to act as an instructor in one of the Kriegsmarine's training establishments and made wide use of Operation Frankton in his lectures. His views on the importance of the operation were outlined in a post-war deposition made to Nightingale's war crimes investigation:

In his opinion, this particular operation in the Gironde was the outstanding Commando raid of the war. He cited it as an example of outstanding merit in all his lectures whilst employed as an instructor in mines and explosives ... He often quoted to his class that it would be just as feasible for these Commando boys to start from a point between Heligoland and Cuxhaven and come up the Elbe as far as Hamburg.[9]

The effect of Frankton on the spirit of French resistance is rather more difficult to quantify. Suffice to say, however, that Frankton came at a moment when German belief in their own invincibility was at its highest and French confidence in their ability to resist was still relatively low. Following Frankton, there was a sharp increase in *Scientist*'s sabotage operations against the Germans in the Bordeaux area – but this was, as we know, provisioned for, planned and ordered by Baker Street before Frankton took place. Nevertheless, the fact that German ships had been successfully attacked in the middle of Bordeaux must have had a beneficial effect on de Baissac's ability to recruit agents to his cause and facilitate operations in the area – indeed the report on de Baissac's debriefing admits as much: 'This attack indirectly did Scientist some good as he [de Baissac] was popularly reputed to be the author.'

There was a marked increase in Resistance activity across France in 1943 and it would be reasonable to suggest that, at least in the southwest, the attack on Bordeaux (widely known and talked about across the region) and the fact that two of the perpetrators had been able to evade capture right under the Germans' noses, acted as encouragement to this.

So, were the results achieved worth the price paid? Was Frankton really worth the loss of eight brave young men? Here it is necessary to avoid judging the decisions made by a nation struggling for survival in 1942 against the rather more genteel standards of today.

Speaking of Frankton, Professor Foot commented that we should remember 'An old-fashioned phrase from the eighteenth century; look at the butcher's bill. It cost ten [sic] very good Commandos. Himmler was killing Jews at the rate of about ten thousand a day. Was this a lot?'[10] To our eyes that may be a brutal way of looking at it. But it is probably an accurate assessment of the calculation Hasler's superiors made when they launched Frankton. Mountbatten, as we know, 'did not expect them to come back',[11] but he sent them nevertheless.

But would Mountbatten still have sent them if he had known about *Scientist*? Did he in fact know about *Scientist*?

A careful study of the available evidence reveals nothing to suggest that Combined Operations knew of the simultaneous SOE operation in progress on the Bordeaux quayside. On the other hand, although there is no proof that SOE knew of Frankton, it seems extremely likely that they were aware, at least in general terms, of what Combined Operations were planning in the Gironde.

There are two reasons for this assumption. First, confirming that Baker Street had no trouble finding out what was happening at Richmond Terrace, is SOE liaison officer Major Wyatt's observation to Baker Street of 14 August 1942: 'No difficulties are being experienced in keeping in touch with plans and operations at COHQ (Combined Operations Headquarters).'[12] Second is the fact that, on 1 September, just three weeks after Major Wyatt's memo, SOE's Brigadier Colin Gubbins was himself at Richmond Terrace, encouraging Combined Operations to mount a raid on the Bordeaux blockade runners (see Chapter 8). Given Gubbins' seniority and the acknowledged national importance of the task, it seems most improbable that, having encouraged Combined Operations to address the 'Bordeaux problem', SOE would have dropped the matter there, rather than following it up.

But what if Mountbatten *had* known of SOE's plans; that the Frankton plan was not, to quote his own phrase, 'the only one which offers a good chance of success'?[13] Would he then have approved Hasler's plan?

It must be a near-certainty that the answer here is no. The raid, as envisaged by Hasler, would most probably have been cancelled.

And what about the Chiefs of Staff? If *they* had known about SOE's assets and capabilities on the quayside in Bordeaux – if they too had understood that this was not the only plan which offered 'a good chance of success' – would they have approved the operation in the form proposed by Mountbatten? Here too the answer is, almost certainly not.

This, as we have seen, is not because of the risk to Hasler's men. It was rather because Frankton also put at severe risk something which was, at this stage of the war, much more important – a capital ship: a submarine. At the height of the Battle of the Atlantic, the request to deploy a submarine would never have been approved if a better solution had been on offer.

Professor Foot believed that, if Mountbatten had known what SOE were doing, his first action may not, however, have been to stand Hasler down immediately: 'He would probably have gone to see Hambro, who was SOE's Executive Head, or Gubbins and said: "Now look here, why don't you let me do this instead?" He was anxious always to do anything that would bring credit to Mountbatten and would have tried to talk SOE out of doing it and letting him do it instead.'[14]

Following this hypothesis, Mountbatten might have argued that, if *Scientist* were to do the job, the inevitable consequence would be heavy German reprisals against the Bordeaux population: after all, fifty Bordeaux hostages had been shot in reprisal for the assassination by BCRA agents of a single German officer, Hans Reimer, in the autumn of 1941. But if, on the other hand, Combined Operations were to carry out the operation, then only those who took part would be at risk and the local population would be spared (which is in fact what happened). This would have been a powerful argument. For, despite their barbarity, reprisals *did* often work. Attacks by Resistance units resulting in the execution of hostages often alienated local communities who felt that, after the fighters had gone, they were left to pay the 'butcher's bill'.

But what if instead of competing over who should do the operation, Combined Operations and SOE had decided to cooperate? The short answer is that Frankton would have had a much better chance of real success and placed far fewer lives at risk.

Intriguingly, this was precisely the possibility canvassed in the undated and unauthored Admiralty docket put before the Chiefs of Staff when they considered the Bordeaux problem on 7 August 1942: 'The whole expedition, together with a stock of limpets, could be moved from the submarine to a hideout within striking distance of Bordeaux and kept there long enough to enable the canoes to deliver a series of attacks with limpets timed to explode after the last attack had been delivered and the expedition had withdrawn.'

Apart from its obvious good sense, this proposal opens up an interesting possibility. Was this suggestion, like Churchill's original demand to emulate the Italians' daring, also modelled on how the Italians did these things? In September 1941, the Italian Navy mounted a brilliant attack by underwater swimmers launched from a submarine, on British shipping in Gibraltar and afterwards smuggled the raiders out of Spain using their network of secret agents.[15] After a second attack on British ships in Gibraltar using surface swimmers operating from a secret agent 'safe house' in Algeciras in July 1942 (just weeks before the Chiefs of Staff met on 7 August), the raiders were again smuggled out of Spain by the Italian secret agent network.[16] It seems that Rome did not experience the same difficulty as London when it came to persuading its secret organisations and its Special Forces to work together.

This is exactly how the modern-day SBS would, conditions permitting, conduct a deep-penetration canoe operation against enemy ships in a protected harbour at the end of an estuary. They would try to avoid paddling their canoes through the 'front door' of a strongly defended harbour, as Hasler was forced to do, and would instead look at the possibilities of mounting the operation through the 'back door', landing to one side of the harbour entrance where the defences would be lighter. They would then carry their canoes over a suitably narrow area of hinterland and launch them *within* the estuary and from *behind* the main line of harbour defences.

As it happens, Bordeaux is uniquely well placed for just such an attack. Two long arms of water go deep into the hinterland both north and south of the entrance of the Gironde. The northern arm begins at La Tremblade and runs almost thirty miles inland as far as Saujon, seven miles east of, and directly behind, Royan; the southern consists of a large bay almost fifteen miles deep called the Bassin d'Arcachon, which reaches inland to a point twenty-five miles due west of Bordeaux. Neither inlet would have been as heavily defended as the Pointe de Grave – and the northern inlet would probably not have been defended at all. Both offer significantly less hazardous seaward drop-off points for a submarine than the strongly defended (not to say RAF mined) entrance of the Gironde, as well as shorter and less hazardous paddles for canoes; neither are subject to tidal disturbances of the magnitude that occur around the mouth of the estuary.

Given de Baissac's resources and extensive network, it would surely have been relatively easy for him to pick up Hasler's team at a prearranged rendezvous point on one inlet or the other and transport them overland to the target area (we know de Baissac had access to heavy trucks, for there is a photograph of *Charles le Démolisseur* and Jean Duboué standing alongside one not long after Frankton). An ideal place to have relaunched Hasler's canoes would have been from the banks of the Garonne upstream from Bordeaux, perhaps somewhere a few miles below Jean Duboué's house at Lestiac-sur-Garonne, where the river is still tidal. This would have enabled Hasler to avoid the hazards of the entrance to the Gironde, the risk of discovery on the way down, the exhaustion and the losses among his team. He could have caught the start of the ebb tide to sweep him down to Bordeaux harbour, coming from behind the German harbour defences rather than from in front of them. Having planted their limpets, his team could then have continued – with the ebb still behind them – to a point a few miles downstream from the city for a second rendezvous and pickup by *Scientist,* say an hour after planting their limpets. This would have left them ample time to destroy their canoes and be spirited away to a safe house long before the limpets went off. It would then only have been a matter of waiting for the hue and cry to die down before they could have been smuggled securely through Gaston Hèches and the *Édouard* line, over the Pyrenees – and home.

This would, moreover, have given Hasler much more scope to choose his time of attack so that the ships were full, rather than empty. And, not being so constrained by the times of the tides, it would have enabled him to set his limpets to explode when the water was high, rather than at flat low water. Along with the lost lives, one of the tragedies of Frankton was the lost opportunity to strike a more effective blow against the enemy.

By the time Frankton was over, those in Whitehall were at last beginning to recognise the need for better cooperation. On 4 January 1943, the Chiefs of Staff Committee discussed the 'conflicting interests' of SOE, Combined Operations and SIS. One of its conclusions was that 'the planning of all clandestine sea-borne operations, whether originated by Combined Operations, SOE or SIS, would be coordinated by the Admiralty ...'[17]

Although no record survives of any formal post-operational study of the lessons learnt from Frankton (there are, by contrast, many on other Combined Operations raids of the time), things did finally begin to change when it came to cooperation during the early and middle months of 1943. Professor Foot comments from his time in Richmond Terrace:

After it became clear in London that there had been a major mix-up between two services, a controlling officer was [required by the Chiefs of Staff] to be appointed. One was never given his name. One was given the telephone number of the Admiralty switchboard and anybody planning a raid would be given that number and would ring up and say 'Good morning. My name is so and so and I work for such and such a service. I am talking about Operation Shovel, latitude so and so, longitude so and so, dates so and so'. He would say 'Very good' and put the receiver down. Five minutes later one's telephone would ring and a voice would say 'Shovel, no' and the receiver would go down again.[18]

No doubt there was closer liaison between Richmond Terrace and Baker Street, at least in part, as a result of Frankton. But other, larger forces may have been more influential in pushing for this. For one thing, Combined Operations itself was getting out of the 'small raid' business altogether. Britain, with the US behind her, was now strong enough to begin planning to return to the offensive on mainland Europe. Already minds were turning away from 'butcher and bolt' operations towards preparations for full-scale invasion. The first large-scale combined amphibious landing, Operation Torch – the landings in North Africa – took place a month before Frankton was launched. When Hasler returned to Combined Headquarters in April 1943, the word on everyone's lips would have been 'Husky', the code name for a second such operation, the Allied invasion of Sicily, which took place in July 1943.

The truth is that, although inter-service cooperation became a key principle of Allied operations after Frankton, it was only in a minor way because of Frankton. In the era of small-scale raids, when Frankton was conceived and planned, the atmosphere in Whitehall had been one of suspicion, rivalry and competition. Now, with the future of Europe at stake and large-scale operations involving many tens of thousands of troops the order of the day, only the closest cooperation would do. As the tempo of events increased, a full-scale liaison and coordination structure was created in August 1943. In time, this would be able to coordinate all Whitehall's clandestine structures into a single, seamless whole in support of Combined Operations' most triumphant enterprise, Operation Overlord: the invasion of Europe and the largest amphibious operation of all time.

One of the final ironies is that among the most successful SOE agents parachuted in to France to support Combined Operations' assault on the D-Day beaches by creating havoc behind German lines in Normandy was Claude Marie Boucherville de Baissac.

One other important legacy can be attributed to Frankton. Although the Special Boat Section was in existence before Hasler led his men into the Gironde, it was Frankton which proved that this kind of operation could have genuine strategic value. In this sense, the attack is regarded by those in the modern Special Boat Service as the founding event of their unit.

And with good reason. Even today, when the employment of Special Force units for strategic purposes is widely accepted, Operation Frankton stands out. There have been many deeper penetrations into enemy territory using external means of insertion such as aircraft, parachutes, jeeps and helicopters. But when it comes to penetrations conducted without any external assistance, few compare with Hasler's seventy-mile paddle into the Gironde. Moreover, when it comes to escape and evasion, Hasler's and Sparks' long journey home has rarely if ever been equalled.

Conducted as they are at the extreme limits of what is feasible, all Special Forces operations depend in some measure on luck – and Frankton is remarkable for that, too. Although in the early days fate struck blow after blow against Hasler and his men, from the moment Hasler entered the harbour of Bordeaux, luck became his constant companion. And one of his greatest strokes of luck was to have an enemy who was unimaginative, panicky, badly coordinated and made crucial mistakes. Without these he would probably not have got through; and almost certainly he would never have got away.

Finally, it is important to judge the achievements of Hasler and his men on Operation Frankton by the context of the time. Nowadays, Special Forces operatives are carefully selected. Only the best will do. Blondie Hasler's men were perfectly ordinary, 'just a good cross section of average young fellows': a milkman whose best friend was his horse; a man who went on to be a London bus driver; a Glasgow coal merchant's clerk. Hasler's achievement in investing these ordinary men with the skills, courage and self-confidence to undertake such an extraordinary mission marks him out as a leader of men similar in both approach and achievement to Sir Ernest Shackleton.

Nowadays, Special Forces receive extensive training in combat survival, how to handle interrogation, advanced escape and evasion techniques, language skills and first aid procedures. Hasler's men had almost none of this; they had no proper extraction plan, no outside support. To have done what they did on such skimpy preparation and without any external support is remarkable. True, they struggled to resist the sophisticated interrogation of Friedrich Wilhelm Dohse. But how could one expect more from ordinary young men who had received no special preparation whatsoever for such a situation?

I am especially struck by the achievements of MacKinnon, Conway, Laver and Mills during their attempts to escape and evade their pursuers. These were young men who had never been out of Britain – perhaps never been very far from their own home community before they joined up. They suddenly found themselves in the middle of a foreign land, of whose culture, habits and geography they knew nothing and of whose language they could speak not a word. I am amazed that they lasted so long and got so far. In the end, they were captured not because of their own actions, but because their luck ran out – and that can happen to anyone.

In assessing the achievements of Hasler's Marines, we should remember one final fact – their equipment. They had no special equipment beyond the 'Cockle suits' Hasler had designed for them and the 'escape boxes' they largely made up for themselves. Otherwise they used the ordinary equipment provided to regular forces. Woollen gloves, not waterproof ones, in that bitter cold. No sleeping bags. No waterproof covers. No special rations. No lightweight wireless sets. No GPS, of course. By the standards of the equipment and support provided to Special Forces today, Hasler's raiders carried out Operation Frankton alone and naked against both the elements and a vastly superior enemy. Their hardiness and endurance was truly extraordinary.

No amount of Whitehall infighting, no petty inter-departmental jealousies, no squabbling rivalry, no intrigue, no deception, no stupidity, can detract from the extraordinary bravery, endurance and determination of the young men who followed an outstanding leader, Blondie Hasler, into the mouth of danger on that bitterly cold night of 7 December 1942. Or from the acts of generosity and courage of the ordinary French men and women who, in helping them, struck a blow not just for the liberty of their country, but for the cause of humanity itself.

In an age of easy living when we are rarely faced with the need to choose between ourselves and something greater, they should be an inspiration to us all.

APPENDIX A

'OPERATION FRANKTON'

Summary of Verbal Orders
Issued by Military Force Commander

Reference: Special Sectional Charts, Sheets 1-21, issued on a scale of 1 set per boat.

Information

1. (a) Attacking force will consist of 2 Officers and 10 O.R's of R.M.B.P.D. in 6 Cockles Mk.II. operating from one 'T' class Submarine.

    (b) Detailed intelligence of enemy dispositions, targets and approach route as extracted from intelligence summaries, charts, maps and air photographs supplied by C.O.H.Q. and given verbally to the attacking force, with frequent revision by question and answer.

Intention

2. To sink the 12 largest merchant ships (excluding tankers) lying in the BASSENS-BORDEAUX area.

Method

3. General Attacking force with all equipment will leave CLYDE area in H.M.S. TUNA a.m. 30th November 1942, carrying out day and night disembarking exercises en-route in INCHMARNOCK area. Submarine will arrive off the entrance of the GIRONDE approximately 5th December, and will hoist out entire force on first suitable night after 5/6th December, starting point being approximately 9.5 miles 259 degrees from Pte. de la NEGRE[1]. Force will enter the Estuary and proceed towards BORDEAUX by stages, lying up by day and travelling by night on the flood tide. On the first convenient night the attack will be delivered with limpets at H.W. slack, after which force will withdraw

---

1   Sic. It is presumed that this should be Pte. de la Negade.

down the Estuary on the ebb as far as possible. At L.W slack crews will land on the East bank, scuttle boats and equipment and escape overland via Spain to the U.K.

Preparatory Period.
4. See Appendix 'C'

Stores and Equipment
5. Appendix 'C' gives a complete list of stores and equipment in various categories.

Stowage in Submarine and Disembarkation Drill.
Are given in Appendix 'C'.

Before giving the order to commence hoisting out, the Captain will give last-minute estimate of the magnetic bearing and distance of the headland 2.5 miles N.N.E. of Pte. de la NEGADE. This will be set on compass grids.

Approach Course
8. Will be as stated in para.6 until I mile offshore, after which, boats will follow the coast to Point 'X', which is a point, I mile due North (Magnetic) of Pte. de GRAVE. At this point the C.O. will decide which side of the Estuary is to be taken for the first lying up place by each division, guided by the following limits:–

To Reach Point 'X'	Latest time of Passing	Remarks
ST. SEURIN DUET	2 hrs before H.W. BREST	Nearest site on E. Bank
CHENAL DE TALAIS	I hr before H.W BREST	

9. At some stage during the first night's passage the Force Commander will give final instructions to 'B' Division (3 boats) which will then proceed independently under its own C.O. for the remainder of the operation.

Formation.
10. Whilst both Divisions are together, formation will be. 'A' Division in arrowhead followed by 'B' Division in arrowhead. When the leading boat stops, 'B' Division will close and each boat will come alongside the boat ahead.

Passage-making will only take place in darkness. No attempt will be made to move in daylight in foggy weather. Boats should keep out of the buoyed channel, but must not move close along the shore.

Lying Up.

12. Sectional Charts have the coastal areas marked in colours as follows:

> Red...   within half mile of a known enemy position.
> Yellow... "   "   "   "   "   "   habitation.
> Green... More than half a mile from a known habitation.

It must however be remembered that the information may not be up to date, and that unplotted German batteries and defensive positions may be well camouflaged and invisible at close range in daylight. This, together with the fact that coast-watchers may use powerful glasses, makes it essential for all ranks to keep right under cover in daylight, even in apparently deserted areas. Ranks may stretch their legs after dark as opportunity offers.

13. Each group of boats lying up will maintain a concealed sentry at all times.

The Advanced Base

14. The advanced base from which the attack is to be launched, must be selected in accordance with the limits imposed in Appendix 'D'.

15. During the day at the advance base, the following will be carried out:

(a) Complete the fuzing of all limpets, cable and wire cutters, in accordance with the drill laid down in Appendix 'E'.
(b) Restow cargo bags as shown in Appendix 'F'.
(c) Fold breakwaters and stow compass below.

The Attack

16. Boats will move off from their advanced base in accordance with the timetable in Appendix 'D', checking their timing as frequently as possible en route. The final approach will be made as close as possible to the river bank.

17. Allocation of boats to targets is as follows:

'A' Division
Catfish (Major Hasler, Mne Sparks), Crayfish (Cpl Laver, Mne Mills), Conger (Cpl Sheard, Mne Moffat)

'B' Division
Cuttlefish (Lt McKinnon, Mne Conway), Coalfish (Sgt. Wallace, Mne Ewart), Cachalot(Mne. Ellery, Mne. Fisher).

Target Area

BORDEAUX, West Bank   Catfish, Crayfish.

BORDEAUX, East Bank   Conger, Cuttlefish.

BASSENS, North and South Quays   Coalfish, Cachalot.

18. The Objectives of each boat are as follows:–

(a) Primary. Two limpets on each of the four largest merchant ships (excluding tankers) in their target area. The two limpets are to be placed 5ft. below the waterline in the following positions:–

'A' Division Boats. On the upstream end of each ship one limpet just past amidships and the other midway between there and the upstream end of the ship.

'B' Division Boats. On the downstream end of each ship one just short of amidships and the other midway between there and the downstream end.

In addition, Catfish and Cuttlefish carry one cutter and one wire cutter each, to be placed during the withdrawal on any vessel lying in the stream. This vessel will have been noted on the way upstream and if of sufficient size these two boats will reserve a pair of limpets each for her.

(b) Secondary Objectives.(only to be attacked if it is impossible to get at the full quota of primary objectives).

In order of choice:–

(i) Large tanker in the target area (two limpets from each boat all between midships and stern.)

(ii) Any smaller vessels (except submarines) in the target area (one limpet from each boat. 'A' boats on upstream end and 'B' boats on downstream end).

(iii) Any vessels not in the target area which may be encountered during the withdrawal, down to and including dumb lighters.

The Withdrawal

19. Boats will proceed downstream on the ebb with caution, avoiding the ship channel and the middle ground banks and keeping well out from the shore. At L.W. slack they will select a suitable landing place, land their two bags of escape equipment, then destroy reserve buoyancy in the boat and scuttle it with all remaining equipment. Then proceed independently in pairs in accordance with the escape instructions (verbal).

20. On reaching a British Consul in Spain, he is to be informed that the part consists of Combined Operations personnel escaped from a raid, but no further details.

Action to be taken in Various Emergencies.

21. If the submarine should be surprised on the surface with any boats out on the casing, the fore-hatch will immediately be closed. Crews on deck will inflate life jackets, load their boats get in and fasten the cover. If the submarine should dive, they will endeavour to float clear and proceed independently with the operation. Or, if ordered by the Captain from the bridge, crews will withdraw via the conning tower hatch, having first destroyed the reserve buoyancy of the boat.

22. Once clear of the ship, any boat losing the remainder of its formation will take the prescribed action to rejoin. If this fails, it will continue the operation independently.

23. If approached by any other vessel, evasive action may be taken until the vessel gets nearly close enough to see the canoes. At this stage boats will stop and remain stationary in the lowest position.

25. If hailed or fired at from the shore, boats will stop in the lowest position and allow the tide to carry them clear. They will never attempt to paddle away or shoot back.

26. If approached by a person of apparent French nationality whilst lying up, crews will remain concealed until sighted, then get hold of him (or her), explain they are English and instruct them not to tell anybody they have seen you. Children should be told to tell the above to their parents and nobody else. Do not detain such people long or harm them unless they are behaving suspiciously.

27. If approached by one or more soldiers of apparent German nationality, remain concealed until sighted. Then kill them as silently as possible, and conceal the bodies preferably below H.W. Get away as soon as it is dark, regardless of the state of tide.

28. If a boat gives the S.O.S. signal for any reason, only the remaining boats of its division will go to its assistance. If the distance is reasonable and the area a safe one, an attempt may be made to get the damaged boat and crew ashore. Otherwise, the boat will be scuttled and the crew left to swim for it with their No. 5 bag.

Any crew unable to reach their objective will:

(a) Make every effort to scuttle or conceal their boat and equipment.
(b) Go to the nearest safe lying-up place and remain there until 4 days after leaving the submarine.
(c) Escape by the route laid down.

29. If the alarm is raised during the attack, boats will not withdraw, but will use their own initiative to press home the attack at the earliest opportunity.

Security
30. (a) All charts covering area North of BLAYE will be destroyed or concealed as soon as the area has been passed. This will be done whilst lying up in daylight.

Air photographs will be destroyed or concealed at the advanced base.

All remaining charts and papers will be scuttled with the boat, except for the escape gear.

Annexe I

NOTES ON PREPARATORY PERIOD

R.M.B.P.D. was formed on 6th July 1942. Period 6th July-28th October was spent based in Southsea, training in canoeing, handling of various types of assault boat under oars and paddles, swimming, weapon training, shallow water diving, and motor boat driving.

Outline proposals for 'FRANKTON' were submitted 22nd September 1942. Passed by the Examination Committee 15th October 1942. Revised Outline Plan completed 18th October 1942, having been provisionally accepted by F.O.S.

No. 1 Section R.M.B.P.D. was selected to train for this operation under O.C. R.M.B.P.D. as Force Commander. The following programme was carried out:

(a) 31st October–7th November

In H.M.S. FORTH with 6 Cockles Mk.II, developing the technique of hoisting a boat out fully loaded (480 lbs. load including the crew) by means of a tackle and an extension girder 4 ft. long on the muzzle of the gun of a 'T' class submarine. Training included dummy limpet attacks on 'JAN VAN CELDER' and 24 hrs. training in P. 339 in Inchmarnock area.

(b) 10th–14th November

Carrying out exercise 'BLANKET' (attack on DEPTFORD from MARGATE, via River SWALE). Very useful exercise.

(c) 19th–29th November

In H.M.S. FORTH, preparing and packing stores, testing hoisting gear under full load, swinging compasses, field training ashore, fuzing limpets etc. Period included one day's day and night training in limpet attacks on 'JAN VAN GELDER' in Loch Long.

(d) 50th November–5th December

On passage in H.M. S. TUNA briefing crews, study of air photographs and reconnaissance reports.

Annexe II

EQUIPMENT LIST

Boats Gear	H	S	L	M	W	E	Remarks
Cockles Mk. II	I	I	I	I	I	I	
Double paddles Mk. II, prs.	3	3	3	3	3	3	
Handgrips Mk.II, prs.	I	I	I	I	I	I	
Bailers	I	I	I	I	I	I	
Sponges	I	I	I	I	I	I	
Buoyancy bags	2	2	2	2	2	2	
Cargo bags, sets	I	I	I	I	I	I	Set of 5
Magnetic holders	I	I	I	I	I	I	
Codline fms	20	20	20	20	20	20	
Sounding reels, 16 fms	I	I	I	I	I	I	
Repair bags	I	I	I	I	I	I	Each containing Bostick cement, patching canvas, needle, waxed thread, oil bottle, waste, tyre, patch, rubber solution, spare split pins and copper tacks.
Sectional charts sets	I	I	I	I	I	Iø	
Log pads	I	I	I	I	I	Iø	Containing tide tables and spare paper.
P.S compasses	I	I	I	I	I	Iø	
Corrector for	I	I	I	I	I	Iø	
Monoculars	I			I	I		

Item							Notes
Pencils	2	2	2	2	2	2	Half size, sharpened.
Dim reading torches	I	I	I	I	I	I	
Spare reading torches	I			I			
Spare bulb for	I	I	I	I	I	Ix	
Protectors, G.S	I	I	I	I	I	Iø	
Camouflage nets	I	I	I	I	I	I	Special light type.
Watches, pocket GS	I	I	I	I	I	Iø	Waterproofed.
Spare torch batteries	2	I	I	I	I	I	
Wire cutters		I				I	
Screwdrivers		I				I	
Marline spikes		I				I	
W.T. matches, tins	2	2	2	2	2	2	
Camouflage cream, tins	I	I	I	I	I	I	
Escape kits							
Pieces of chalk	2	2	2	2	2	2	
Whiting line, 4 fm.lengths	2	2	2	2	2	2	
Weapons & Explosives							
Silent Sten 9 mm.			I		I		
Magazines for			4		4		Each filled 32 Rds.
69 grenades	2	2	2	2	2	2	Fuzed
Limpets, rigid, 6 magnet	8	8	8	8	8	8	Fuzed A.C. and sympathic
Ampoule boxes	2	2	2	2	2	2	Each contained 4 red, 4 orange ampules. 4 soluble plugs. 2 tins luting.
Limpet spanners	I	I	I	I	I	I	
Placing rods	2	2	2	2	2	2	

Food & Medical

Compact rations, days	10	10	10	10	10	10	Each day contains 3 boxes, 1 tin meat and 1 tin cheese.
Water cans, ½ gallon	5	5	5	5	5	5	Filled
Benzedrine, boxes	1	1	1	1	1	1	Each day contains 20 tablets
Water sterilising sets	1	1	1	1	1	1	
1st field dressings	2	2	2	2	2	2	
Iodine bottles	1	1	1	1	1	1	
Toilet paper, packets	2	2	2	2	2	2	
Morphia syringes	2	2	2	2	2	2	
Hexamine cookers	5	5	5	5	5	5	Varnished
Dixie, (5 pint)	1	1	1	1	1	1	With lids
Foot powder (tins)	1	1	1	1	1	1	
W.T. ditty boxes	1	1	1	1	1	1	
Cough lozenges, tins	1	1	1	1	1	1	
Laxative pills, tins	1	1	1	1	1	1	
Cups	1	1	1	1	1	1	

Carried in Parent Ship

Camouflage cream, tins	2
Mk.II slings and spreaders,	1 set
Slip book	1
Girder for 4" gun	1
Purchase tackle	1
Wire preventer pendant	1
Preventatives	12

Seasick tablets, tubes	12
Boats' envelopes	6
Air pumps	1
Spare P.S. compass	1
Box of instructional models	1
Mineral jelly, lbs	2
Pads for boats	6
Needles and twine	
Photographs	
Orders	
Intelligence reports	

Carried on the Men

Canoes[2]	1	2	1	2	1	2	1	2	1	2	1	2	
Cockle suit, complete	—	—	—	—	—	—	—	—	—	—	—	—	With knife sheath sewn on.
W.T. trousers, prs	—	—	—	—	—	—	—	—	—	—	—	—	
Socks, prs	—	—	—	—	—	—	—	—	—	—	—	—	
Denim trousers, prs	—	—	—	—	—	—	—	—	—	—	—	—	
Braces, prs	—	—	—	—	—	—	—	—	—	—	—	—	
Belts, light	—	—	—	—	—	—	—	—	—	—	—	—	
Pants, long thick, prs	—	—	—	—	—	—	—	—	—	—	—	—	
Vests, woolen, long sleeves	—	—	—	—	—	—	—	—	—	—	—	—	
Seaboot stockings, prs.	—	—	—	—	—	—	—	—	—	—	—	—	
Blue balaclavas	—	—	—	—	—	—	—	—	—	—	—	—	
V-neck sweaters	—	—	—	—	—	—	—	—	—	—	—	—	
Blue scarves	—	—	—	—	—	—	—	—	—	—	—	—	
Handkerchiefs	—	—	—	—	—	—	—	—	—	—	—	—	
Reliant lifejacket	—	—	—	—	—	—	—	—	—	—	—	—	
Gloves, 3 compartment, silk	—	—	—	—	—	—	—	—	—	—	—	—	
Gloves, 3 compartment, wool	—	—	—	—	—	—	—	—	—	—	—	—	

2 These are listed by the initials of the Canoe No. 1s. So H = Hasler, S = Sheard, L = Laver, M = MacKinnon, W = Wallace, E = Ellery.

Item	1	2	3	4	5	6	7	8	9	10	11	Notes
Red and green identity discs.	2	2	2	2	2	2	2	2	2	2	2	
P.T. shoes, brown, prs.	1	1	1	1	1	1	1	1	1	1	1	
Twine, 12"-long pieces.	6	6	6	6	6	6	6	6	6	6	6	
Web belts & holsters	1	1	1	1	1	1	1	1	1	1	1	
.45 Colt	1	1	1	1	1	1	1	1	1	1	1	Includes one in gun
Magazines for	3	3	3	3	3	3	3	3	3	3	3	Each loaded 7 rds.
Knives, fighting	1	1	1	1	1	1	1	1	1	1	1	
Bird calls		2		2			2		2			On lanyards.
Clasp knives	1	1	1	1	1	1	1	1	1	1	1	
Sheet of paper	1	1	1	1	1	1	1	1	1	1	1	Lining Ditty Box.

In the Bags

Item	1	2	3	4	5	6	7	8	9	10	11	12	If required
Short pants, prs	2	—	2	—	2	—	—	—	—	—	1	2	
Toothbrush & paste	—	—	—	—	—	—	—	—	—	—	—	—	
Towel	—	—	—	—	—	—	—	—	—	—	—	—	
Handkerchiefs	—	—	—	—	—	—	—	—	—	—	—	—	
Sea water soap pieces	—	—	—	—	—	—	—	—	—	—	—	—	
Razor and blades	—	—	—	—	—	—	—	—	—	—	—	—	
Shaving brush	—	—	—	—	—	—	—	—	—	—	—	—	
Felt-soled boots, prs	—	—	—	—	—	—	—	—	—	—	—	—	
Spare laces for, prs	—	—	—	—	—	—	—	—	—	—	—	—	
Socks, prs.	—	—	—	—	—	—	—	—	—	—	—	—	
Roll-neck sweater	—	—	—	—	—	—	—	—	—	—	—	—	
Spare woollen gloves, prs	—	—	—	—	—	—	—	—	—	—	—	—	
Cigarettes	20	20	20	20	20	20	20	20	20	20	20	20	
Extra matches, bos	—	—	—	—	—	—	—	—	—	—	—	—	

ESCAPE GEAR

Binoculars	I	Additional reading torch	I
Dim reading torch	I	Matches (From W.T.T.)	I
Matches (from W.T.T.)	I	Escape kits (complete)	I
Escape kits (complete)	I	Spare compact rations	
Watch	I	First field dressing	I
Spare compact rations		Iodine bottles	I
Benzedrine boxes	I	Morphia syringe	I
First field dressing	I	Tin, water	I
Morphia syringe	I	Pills, water	I
Foot powder (tin)	I	Pencils	I
Tin water	I	Camouflage cream	I
Pills boxes	I	String, of, pieces, fms	4
Needle and thread	I	Toilet paper, pkts	I
Oil bottle	I		
Pencils	I		
String, of, pieces	4		
Water sterilising set	I		
Toilet paper, pkts	I		

APPENDIX B

Cachalot

In the course of my research for this book, I visited the Combined Military Services Museum (CMSM) at Maldon in Essex to view a number of items related to the Frankton raid, including a canoe which was said to be the only surviving production Cockle Mark II of the sort used by Hasler's Marines. There has for some time been suspicion that this canoe is in fact *Cachalot*. This is based on the following facts:[3]

1. The canoe in the CMSM was discovered in the early 1980s on the site of the Saro works on the Isle of Wight by Mr Gerry Lockyear, from whom it was obtained by Richard Wooldridge for renovation and display at the CMSM.
2. At the time the canoe was found, it was in a very damaged state with large holes in the front and back decking.
3. In the course of renovation, some very faint lettering was found on the starboard bows. Only one letter was positively identifiable – an 'O' which appeared to have been painted in the style used for Second World War stencilling. It was also noticed that a small tear had been repaired on the starboard side just forward of the Number One's seat.
4. It is established service practice that damaged equipment is returned to the original manufacturer for repair.
5. The Saro works on the Isle of Wight, where the Frankton canoes were manufactured, produced only twenty-six production models of the Cockle Mark II, before the contract for these canoes was moved to the Parkstone Joinery in Poole some time in 1943. So it would appear likely that the 'CMSM canoe' was manufactured by Saro.

---

3 I am indebted to Quentin Rees for the technical details of the Mark II contained in his books *Cockleshell Canoes* and *Cockleshell Heroes: The Last Witness*. Also his email to Richard Wooldridge of 21 August 2011, which summarises his findings.

6. The pilot models of the Cockle Mark II (all built by Saro) had a beam
    of 30.5 in. The final production models had a beam of 28.5 in. The
    'CMSM canoe' has a beam of 28.5 in. Furthermore the 'CMSM canoe'
    has a curved bow and stern, whereas the stern and bow of all later
    versions of the Mark IIs were straight.

7. From these facts it can reasonably be presumed that the 'CMSM
    canoe' is one of the twenty-six original Saro production models, six
    of which were taken by Hasler on Frankton.

The damage to *Cachalot* which caused the craft and crew to be sent
below was, according to Hasler's report, made by the 'hatch claws' on
Tuna's forward torpedo-loading hatch. Hasler even referred to this, and
to the need to pad the hatches, in his very short first coded message back
to London, carried by Mary Lindell to the British Consulate in Geneva.

On 10 January 2012 a team led by Sonia O'Connor from Bradford
University visited Maldon at my invitation to conduct tests with X-rays
and other imaging on the Cockle Mark II displayed at the museum.
These revealed two facts; that there were, indeed, faint letters visible
below the paintwork – an 'O' and possibly a 'C'. And that the damage on
the starboard side forward of the Number One's seat consisted of two
sets of marks: some gouges in the paintwork, and a tear. Though the size
of the tear seems smaller than one might have expected, the presence of
gouge marks in the paintwork seems to confirm that these could have
been made by a blunt instrument, such as *Tuna*'s hatch claws.

Both of these facts add weight to the proposition that the canoe at the
Combined Services Military Museum in Maldon, is indeed *Cachalot*.

Notes

Unless otherwise specified, all official documents cited are held in the National Archives, Kew.

1 London 1942

1   'If a submarine sinks two 6,000 ton ships and one 3,000 tanker, here is a typical account of what is lost: 42 tanks, 8 six-inch howitzers, 88 twenty-five pound guns, 40 two-pound guns, 24 armoured cars, 50 Bren carriers, 5,112 tons of ammunition, 600 rifles, 428 tons of tank supplies, 2,000 tons of stores and 1,000 tanks of gasoline.' Official report.

2   Minutes of the ninth (1942) meeting between MEW and naval staff, held at the Admiralty on Tuesday 16 June 1942, ADM 199/549. Courtesy Mark Bentinck.

3   The German crews even had their own blockade runner's cap badge featuring a speeding merchant ship with a German eagle on its prow, smashing through an iron chain. For an example, see the archive of François Boisnier, Barbézieux-St-Hilaire, France.

4   Extract from Admiralty docket on attack on French Biscay ports (PD 0183, 5 October 1942), First Sea Lord Records, ADM 205/24. Courtesy Mark Bentinck.

5   One intelligence report from the SOE *Scientist* network listed a typical suite of arms on these blockade runners as 'one 120mm gun fore and aft, a gun turret amidships [with] at least one 75mm, two 20–40mm guns amidships and on either side naval guns of possibly 75mm, besides which there were several machine guns, bofors, pom poms and other light guns'. Claude de Baissac debriefing, 24 March 1943, HS 9/75.

6   At the time the beaches south of the mouth of the Gironde were also being considered as a possible future invasion site, and/or a potential target for a large-scale raid of the sort subsequently (and disastrously) carried out in Dieppe.

7   *After the Battle* 11 (November 2002), p. 4.

8   The Japanese word for 'evergreen' or 'fir tree'. Of the three previous attempts by submarines to break the blockade, all had been sunk. The *Momi* attempted the same journey in March 1944 carrying a cargo of molybdenum, tungsten and, again, gold. Arriving in the south Atlantic after D-Day, she was warned off continuing to Lorient by the Germans. So she rendezvoused with a German submarine off the Cape Verde Isles to receive fuel, an Enigma machine, the latest German radar detector and two German radio operators. A short while later, she was found and sunk by a US task force in the southern Atlantic.

9   Churchill, memo to General Ismay, 6 June 1940, CAB 120/414.

10 Hugh Dalton, *The Fateful Years* (London: Muller, 1957), p. 368.

11 From which SOE was specifically excluded, except when an invitation was extended requiring their presence.

12 J. Beevor, *SOE Recollections & Reflections 1940–1945* (London: Bodley Head,1981), pp. 75–6.

13 When SOE's prize *Prosper* network in Paris was rolled up by the Germans in mid-1943, 'Claude Dansey marched in, clapped his hands and declared "Great news, Reilly. Great news . . . One of the big SOE networks in France has just blown up."' Robert Marshall, *All The King's Men* (London: Fontana, 1988), p. 193. Reilly was personal assistant to Menzies.

14 Memo to DCD/A and DCD/O, 19 July 1942, HS 8/275.

15 There were in fact *six* SOE sections. In addition to F, RF and DF Sections, there was also EU/P Section (which dealt with Poles outside Poland), AMF (which ran agents into the south of France from Algeria) and the 'Jedburghs', combined SOE/SAS/OSS uniformed fighting units parachuted in behind German lines just after D-Day.

16 In all F Section inserted 172 British, 92 French, 46 American and 15 'others' into France as secret agents (325 in total). Of these 12 were killed, 45 executed, 30 became POWs and 38 were reported missing. Of the 1720 British agents landed, no fewer than 108 became casualties, of whom 88 never returned. SOE post-war evaluations, HS 8/42.

17 Despite this near prohibition, whose aim was to keep the two organisations as separate as possible, there was much more crossover than appeared on the surface. RF Section was largely staffed at headquarters level by British officers and recruited a number of British citizens as agents in the field – the most famous being Wing Commander Yeo-Thomas, alias 'Le Lapin Blanc' (the White Rabbit). After the war, however, the French government strongly discriminated against F Section agents. While showering RF Section survivors with recognition and medals, de Gaulle gave almost none to either the British F Section agents or those among the French population who helped them.

18 The genesis of BCRA was rather muddled. It started when de Gaulle appointed Dewavrin as the head of his secret intelligence organisation, known as *Service Renseignements* (SR) in July 1940, while appointing another colleague, Raymond Lagier, in charge of his clandestine operations agency, *Service Action* (SA). The two were combined under Passy to form the BCRAM (the M denoting *militaire*) in January 1942. There was a further simplification into the *Bureau de Renseignements et d'Action* (BCRA) in the summer of 1942.

2 Bordeaux 1940–1942

1 http://www.tundria.com/trams/FRA/Bordeaux -1930.shtml

2 For the third time in its history, the two previous occasions being the Franco-Prussian War of the nineteenth century and the First World War.

3 Mark Seaman, *Special Operations Executive: A New Instrument of War* (London: Routledge, 2006), p. 65.

4 Reimer, an Abwehr colonel, was killed with a knife and his body weighted and dumped in Bordeaux harbour by members of the BCRA-controlled CND *Réseau*. Reimer's briefcase contained the plans for the fortifications then under construction at the mouth of the Gironde. In one of the most notable intelligence coups of the early years of the war, these plans, together with those of the entire German 'Atlantic Wall', were subsequently smuggled back to London and later proved invaluable in the planning of D-Day.

5 Although FTP was Communist led, not all its members were Communists.

6 http//pedagogie.ac-toulouse.fr/lyc-sarsan-lourdes/CONCOURS%20RESISTANCE/groupe1.htm

7 During the course of the war, the organisations and *réseaux* which sprang out of Duboué's original *A.S. Réseau* involved no less than 916 agents, of whom 23 were shot or hanged, 14 were interned and never seen again and 256

were deported, only a hundred of whom returned after the war. Jean Duboué, *Historique du Réseau 'Denis – Aristide – Buckmaster'*, Les Archives Nationales, Valenciennes.

8 'La Gironde sur occupation. Groupes homologues. A.S. Gironde', www.ffi33.org/groupes/asgironde/asgirondeo.htm

9 These two agents were recruited in Bordeaux in the early months of 1941 by Gilbert Renault Rémy, the head of the BCRA-controlled CND (*Confrérie de Notre-Dames*) *Réseau*.

10 Henri de Grandmaison, *Rémy – le plus grand agent secret de la France libre* (Paris: Les Chemins de la mémoire, 2004), p. 20.

11 See Raymond Brard's personal files, 16P 87939 and 0039 3289-40, Château de Vincennes, Paris. Brard was also president of the Bordeaux Boxing, Weight Lifting and Girondin Wrestling Club, whose headquarters (together with the centre for Brard's secret activities) was in a gym in the Impasse Sainte Ursule about 400 yards back from the Quai des Chartrons. By the time of Frankton, Brard's organisation numbered around 110 agents, mostly drawn from members of the Port Fire Service and the gym at Impasse Ursule.

12 The spelling and even the ordering of the two words *Phidias* and *Phalanx* appear in the records in variable forms.

13 Letters from Albert Juenbekdjian, held in the Royal Marines Museum, Eastney; Juenbekdjian, interview with François Boisnier, 14 March 2000.

14 Juenbekdjian letter. The same point about non-cooperation between *Scientist* and Brard is also made in a letter dated 5 March 2000 from Raymond Lager (alias *Bienvenue*) to Raymond Muelle. Boisnier archives, Barbézieux. Noreen Riols reports that the lack of shared information between the two sections often meant duplicate parachute drops to the same location within days of each other.

15 Denise Hèches, interview with the author, Tarbes, 29 March 2011.

16 Denise Hèches interview, 29 March 2011. See also Gaston Hèches, *The Companions of Little Gaston: Adventures of the Resistance in Bigorre*, trans. C.D. Russell (privately printed, December 1949).

17 Denise Hèches interview, 29 March 2011.

18 So called after Colonel 'R's' code word, *Édouard*. The Colonel was known as *Edward the First* and may even have been Claude Dansey (second-in-command of SIS) himself. Dansey is known to have been personally involved in setting up the first escape networks just before the war started so that his agents had a 'railway home' during the conflict. He was assisted at the time by Donald Darling (code name *Sunday*).

19 Rigoulet was a member of a number of French and SOE *réseaux* over the war years from 1941 onwards. The source of his involvement with the *Édouard* line is contained in documentation held at the *mairie* in La Réole.

20 HS 8/155.

21 Ibid.

22 It has proved impossible to establish the identity of *Robert*.

23 Known as '*Radio Londres*', this was established in 1940 and broadcast throughout the war. It was operated by General de Gaulle's Free French Forces and used both for propaganda purposes and to pass coded messages to French and British agents operating in the country. It broadcast twice a day – from 1330–1430 and 1930–2115. There were usually 40–45 messages in the lunchtime broadcast and 60–70 in the evening one (HS8/446). Each broadcast opened famously with the phrase '*Ici Londres. Les Français Parlent aux Français. Attention! messages importants pour nos auditeurs!* (This is London. The French speaking to the French. Listen carefully! Important messages for listeners.) The lunchtime broadcast ended '*à 2115 vous attendez des autres messages pesonnels*' (at 2115 there will be further personal messages). The messages which followed each carried a

prearranged meaning and proved a highly effective way of communicating with the clandestine structures, not least because they significantly reduced the traffic over clandestine wireless networks. They did, however, cause some amusement among listeners – typical examples being 'Jean has a long moustache' and 'There is a fire at the insurance agency.'

24 'La Gironde sur occupation', www.ffi33.org/groupes/asgironde/asgirondeo.htm

25 SOE set up a special 'Shipping Section' very early in its existence. It seems very likely that they were the main taskers and coordinators of all SOE's port activities in Bordeaux until early 1944.

26 HS 8/831. Fidelity's first lieutenant at the time was a Belgian called Albert Guérisse, later to become head of MI9's 'Part-Line' and one of the most decorated agents of World War II.

27 HS 7/121, p. 6.

28 HS 8/155.

29 Duboué, Historique du Réseau 'Denis – Aristide – Buckmaster'.

30 This information comes chiefly from Leroy's debriefing, which took place on 6 September 1943 after his final return to the UK. HS 9/75.

3 Blondie Hasler and the Blockade Runners

1 'Blockade Runners', minute from Lord Selborne to the Prime Minister, 9 May 1942, HS 8/897.

2 In this case, his earlier written reports passed back through Hèches in Tarbes and Robert in Tours. Leroy's own written report (and plan of the Bordeaux quays) did not reach Baker Street until he returned three weeks later on 29 May 1942.

3 Lucas Phillips, Cockleshell Heroes (London: Heinemann, 1956; Pan Books, 1957), p. 11. This and all subsequent references are to the Pan edition.

4 Director of Plans, letter of 12 August 1942 to the First Sea Lord. First Sea

Lord Records, ADM 205/24. Courtesy Mark Bentinck.

5 Extract of the minutes of the 189th meeting of the Chiefs of Staff Committee held on 25 June 1942, ADM 199/549. Courtesy Mark Bentinck.

6 Lucas Phillips, Cockleshell Heroes, p. 12.

7 DEFE 2/217.

8 For much of the personal information in this chapter, I am indebted to Hasler's widow, Bridget.

9 Lucas Phillips, Cockleshell Heroes, p. 26.

10 Southby-Tailyour papers.

11 Details of Hasler's service record are from the Hasler papers.

12 Not, as is sometimes imagined, his moustache, which he did not grow until later.

13 Southby-Tailyour papers.

14 David Astor, letter to Ewen Southby-Tailyour, 3 May 1989.

15 D.J. Orr, letter to Ewen Southby-Tailyour, 10 May 1989.

16 Ewen Southby-Tailyour, Blondie (London: Leo Cooper, 1998), p. 17.

17 The friend was Colonel J.R. Phillips, who was at the time training the first Royal Marines Commando. He was subsequently awarded a posthumous VC in the Dieppe raid. Southby-Tailyour, Blondie, p. 37.

18 He sometimes wrote under the pseudonym 'Charles Tyndall', which he used especially for his less serious articles.

19 Letter to Tom Coombs, 12 January 1984. Hasler papers.

4 Buttercup and Her Daughters

1 Founded by Johannes Klepper in 1906, the firm is still in existence today and still supplies operational canoes to the modern SBS.

2 'War – Suggestions from the Fleet', AFO 3669. PD 08135/39, 30 November 1939.

3 Known until the early 2000s as the Special Boat Section.

4 G.B. Courtney, SBS in World War Two (London: Robert Hale, 1983), p. 119.

5 All submarines are known as 'boats'.
6 Obituary of Col. David Sutherland, *Daily Telegraph*, 8 January 2006.
7 Gerald Montanaro papers, Liddell Hart Centre for Military Archives, King's College, London.
8 Quentin Rees, *The Cockleshell Canoes: British Military Canoes of World War Two* (Stroud: Amberley, 2008), p. 86; Southby-Tailyour, *Blondie*, p. 51.
9 Goatley, a deeply serious man not much known for his humour, had already designed a 12ft 4in folding assault boat in 1937, 1000 of which had already been manufactured by Saro and were in regular service.
10 It was at this meeting that the term 'Cockle' was decided on – one about which Hasler, incidentally, was not enthusiastic.
11 Minutes of a meeting held at CO headquarters at 1400 on 9 March 1942 to discuss the detailed staff requirements for an improved design of two-man canoe. K/14/3/111410.
12 Rees, *Cockleshell Canoes*, p. 94.
13 The Mark II was somewhat slower than the Mark I. Hasler, training notes, p. 27.
14 'differences from Mark II . . . less stable. Crew must learn to balance together and not to wobble when paddling.' Hasler, training notes.
15 It is interesting to note that the first sailing boat which Hasler built – from instructions in *Boy's Own Paper* – at the age of fourteen or fifteen, was also flat bottomed. It was described by him as 'a sort of flat bottomed punt' which he admitted lacked seaworthiness, but in which he nevertheless sailed extensively in the Solent area. Southby-Tailyour, *Blondie*, p. 5.
16 Rees, *Cockleshell Canoes*, p. 82. Also DEFE 2/842. This decision of Courtney's was not lightly made. Hasler's diaries note many visits by Courtney to see Hasler at Eastney in June, July and August 1942, during which he watched and discussed the development of the early versions of the Mark II.
17 COHQ War Diary, 16 December 1942, DEFE 2/5.
18 Rees, *Cockleshell Canoes*, p. 93.
19 Norman Colley, email to the author, 21 August 2010.

5 An Idea Born in the Bath

1 Previously the Inter-Services Training and Development Centre.
2 This was a two-man craft, or swimmer delivery vehicle, capable of either surface or underwater operation. It carried at the front a large explosive charge about the same size as a torpedo warhead, which was detached and hung under the keel of the target vessel. These were known by the Italians as *Maiale* or pigs (referring probably to the difficulty of handling them under water). Later British versions were called 'Chariots'.
3 Winston S. Churchill, *The Second World War*, Vol. IV, *The Hinge of Fate* (London: Cassell, 1951), p. 750.
4 According to a letter from Mountbatten to Tim Wiltshire of 1985, Hasler was sent to CODC specifically because of his authorship of the earlier paper. See Southby-Tailyour, *Blondie*, pp. 48–9.
5 Letter to Lt Tim Wiltshire RM, 1985. Quoted in Southby-Tailyour, *Blondie*, p. 49.
6 Lucas Phillips, *Cockleshell Heroes*, pp. 28–9.
7 Today Lumps Fort houses a small municipal garden. The concrete constructions carrying the wartime boom are still visible at low tide.
8 Southby-Tailyour, *Blondie*, p. 62.
9 Hasler diary, 21 April 1942.
10 If Hasler really did think this, he was wilfully and conveniently ignoring both the established SBS units set up by Montanaro and Courtnay which were doing exactly this.
11 The idea of a wholly Royal Marine unit was actually Hussey's: 'He originated the idea of an all RM unit.' Hasler diary, 23 April 1942.
12 Hasler diary, 24 April 1942.
13 Lucas Phillips, *Cockleshell Heroes*, p. 38.
14 Memorandum BP 60, ADM 202/310.

15 Agenda for RM Boom Patrol Detachment Meeting, Appendix C, ADM 202/310.

6 RMBPD

1 Lucas Phillips, *Cockleshell Heroes*, p. 43.
2 Sound-only interview with William Pritchard-Gordon, recorded August 1984 on behalf of the Imperial War Museum. Interview No. 8266, Reel 4. I am indebted to Tom Keene for drawing my attention to this fascinating interview, which also features in his doctoral thesis, 'Beset by Secrecy and Beleaguered by Rivals: the Special Operations Executive in Western Europe 1940–1942 with Special Reference to Operation Frankton', University of Plymouth, 2011, p. 191.
3 From pre-war years until my time in the Royal Marines, all other ranks (i.e. not officers) carried either two or three letters before their service number indicating where they had joined the corps. The prefix for Chatham-enlisted men was CH12345678 (denoting their number), for Portsmouth-enlisted men it was PO12345678, and for those enlisted at Plymouth it was PLY12345678. All Hasler's men at the time the RMBPD was formed were PLY, Plymouth-enlisted men, who formed the Plymouth Division.
4 Bill Sparks, interview 8397/03/1, Imperial War Museum sound archives.
5 Norman Colley, interview with the author, Pontefract, 2 August 2010.
6 Southby-Tailyour, *Blondie*, p. 68.
7 Fred Phelps came from Winsham in Somerset. His sister, Olive Pyne, remembers Hasler and No. 1 Section calling unannounced at their mother's house at 6 West Street, Winsham, near Chard, on their way back from an exercise in the early autumn of 1942, when Mrs Phelps gave them all breakfast. The canoes parked outside were a talking point in the village for weeks.
8 This house remains today almost exactly as it must have been when No.

1 Section lived there, though there is, curiously, nothing to mark the fact.
9 The RMBPD seems to have had a second dog, as a letter of the time from MacKinnon refers to a St Bernard as well.
10 Sparks interview, Imperial War Museum.
11 Originals held with the Hasler papers, with copies in the Royal Marines Museum, Eastney.
12 Sparks interview, Imperial War Museum.
13 Colley interview with the author, 2 August 2010.
14 Author interview with Peter Ellery, Bill Ellery's son, Pimlico, 4 August 2011.
15 Colley, interview with the author, 2 August 2010.
16 Now renamed the Taswell Arms.

7 The Die is Cast

1 COS (42) 223(0), Friday 7 August 1942, DEFE 2/217.
2 DEFE 2/217.
3 'German–Japanese Blockade running', ADM 199/549. Courtesy Mark Bentinck.
4 Minutes of the 111th Examination Committee Meeting, 8 September 1942, DEFE 2/3.
5 Norman Colley, interview with Dr Tom Keene, 5 January 2011. Colley says he only got rid of these 'hooves' after the war.
6 Hasler diaries.
7 Lucas Phillips, *Cockleshell Heroes*, p. 72.
8 Ibid.
9 Lucas Phillips, *Cockleshell Heroes*, p. 74.

8 *Scientist*

1 HS 7/75.
2 Many of these were in requisitioned country houses – giving rise to the sardonic joke that SOE really stood for 'Stately 'Omes of England'.
3 History of the AL/Q Sub-Section, HS 7/14.
4 Colonel Rémy (code name for Gilbert Renault), *Les Soldats du silence: Mémoires*

d'un agent secret de la France Libre (Paris: Éditions France Empire, 1998) p. 57.

5 Both men were deported and, remarkably, survived, making their way back to France after the war. Later one of the pilot boats on the Gironde would be named the *Jean Fleuret*.

6 Resumé of SOE activities in various theatres of war, 26 June 1942, HS 8/274. This broad form of words remained in all SOE's activity reports to the Cabinet up to at least April 1943 – that is, until after the Bordeaux raid had been carried out.

7 His SOE file records that he was born in Tananarive in Madagascar, but this is described as a 'tale' by his daughter Claudine Pappe. Clothilde Blanc, email to the author, 19 February 2011.

8 A French exam, named after a seventeenth-century French mathematician, taken at the end of school – roughly the equivalent of the British A level.

9 This information comes from de Baissac's official resumé in his SOE file. But another document on his file which appears to have been written by him, says that he got fed up with formal education and left his studies at nineteen to work in a friend's bank, returning to Mauritius in 1926 and then leaving to join his father's mica business the following year. According to this account he returned to France in 1932 to become the publicity agent for a film company, leaving this in 1936 to become the *chef de commerce* in the Society for Industry and Mining of the North Alps Region until the outbreak of war. It is impossible to determine which account of de Baissac's early life is accurate, for they both contain aspects typical of de Baissac's 'rolling stone' character.

10 There is some confusion about his rank. His file in the French archives, at the Château de Vincennes in Paris, records that he was a second lieutenant. But according to his SOE resumé, he had an 'anonymous war' as a mere '*Soldat 2ème classe*'.

11 Clothilde Blanc, interview with the author, Paris, 31 January 2011.

12 Simone Pezzani, née Baissac, at 4 Pump Road, The Temple.

13 Claude de Baissac's personal file, HS 9/75.

14 David Nicolson, *Aristide: Warlord Of the Resistance* (Barnsley: Leo Cooper, 1994), p. 6.

15 The brother of the actor John Gielgud, Lewis Gielgud's real interests were far more artistic than military. He had written several novels and plays and had travelled widely as Under Secretary for the Red Cross before the war.

16 Buckmaster's history of SOE, HS 7/121.

17 Code name *Author*.

18 AIR 27/956.

19 SOE drops always took place in the few days before and after the full moon – known as 'the moon period'. This was so that pilots and reception committees could take advantage of the extra light provided by the moon. Night commando raids (such as Frankton) were (and still are) always conducted in the 'no moon period', in order to take advantage of the deeper darkness at these times. The moon phase here is taken from http://eclipse.gsfc.nasa.gov/phase/phases1901.html

20 Now Nîmes-Arles-Camargues international airport.

21 De Baissac's personal SOE file, HS 9/75, indicates that F Section subsequently recommended him for an MBE for 'saving' Peulevé on this occasion. The citation, which bears little resemblance to de Baissac's own report, reads: 'Lt de Baissac, in spite of his own injury, succeeded in getting his brother officer to safety without being detected, saved their kit and W/T set, made all the arrangements for medical care for Peulevé, finally installing him in a clinic, where he made a good recovery.' This description is so far at variance with the facts that it gives rise to the suspicion that SOE were medal chasing – not in order to get recognition for de Baissac, but to get recognition for themselves.

22 A rather exotic name for what was in reality a converted sardine trawler.

23 SOE code name *Soaptree*.

24 Before moving to Baker Street, SOE began its life in cramped offices in the St Ermine's Hotel, not far from the Ebury Court Hotel.

25 She was known in SOE communications as *Jacqueline*.

26 Duboué's Café des Marchands had been taken over by the Germans at this stage.

27 Also pronounced *Saquette* in the area. Its exact position is Lat 44° 42' 30" N, Long 00° 09' 16" W. Taken from Operation Report of 161 Squadron (Tempsford), AIR 20/8452. The building now on this site, a very pretty, low, single-storey farmhouse next to the ruins of the old mill, is run as a *chambre d'hôte* by a charming English couple called Val and Vito Traill. The site, which is well sheltered from prying eyes by woods, is now a vineyard. Visit to Targon area by the author, 3 April 2011.

28 Yves Leglise and Suzanne Leglise (née Duboué), interview with the author, Nice, 30 January 2011.

29 Raymond Henry Flower was an ex-RAF Leading Aircraftman. He escaped from France in June 1940 and was transferred from the RAF into SOE in April 1942. After training he was parachuted back into France on 27 June 1942 with instructions to form a network in the Tours area with the primary task of receiving parachute drops of people and stores. He was not a great success as an SOE agent in the field and was eventually withdrawn from France back to England on 15 May 1943 because he was completely 'blown' to the Germans. He finished the war as a member of SOE staff.

30 The full list of handwritten initials at the top of de Baissac's report is: D/R – David Keswick, Regional Controller NW Europe; D/F – Leslie Humphries, i/c DF or Escape Section; FL/1 – Flight Liaison Officers either André Simon or Major Vaillant de Guelis; FL4 – Lieutenant-General Barabier; FM –

Gerry Morel; FP – Colonel Robert Bourne-Paterson, F Section's Planning Officer and Buckmaster's second i/c; FV – Vera Atkins, F Section Intelligence Officer.

31 Minutes of 111th Examination Committee Meeting, 1100, 1 September 1942.

32 Robert Lyman, *Operation Suicide* (London: Quercus Press, 2012), p. 70.

33 SOE code name *Artist*.

34 138 Sqdn Ops Record Book, AIR 27/956.

35 History of Lise de Baissac's life provided by Clothilde Blanc.

36 Lise de Baissac personal file, HS 9/77/1

37 HS 9/880/8.

38 SOE code name *Stanislas*.

39 He was dropped with four containers, nine packages and another agent, Gilbert Norman (*Archambault*).

40 Boisrenard near the village of Mer.

41 Stella King, *Jacqueline: Pioneer Heroine of the Resistance* (London: Arms and Armour,1989), pp. 237–9.

42 De Baissac debrief, 26 March 1943, HS 6/566.

43 Landes' debriefing on return to the UK, HS 6/574.

44 Between 31 October 1942 and 18 January 1944, Landes transmitted 321 messages to SOE and received 221. HS 9/880/8. Unfortunately none of these messages survived the post-war fire which destroyed many SOE records.

45 Three fellow F Section passengers were landed with her: Marie Thérèse Chêne, Odette Sansom (*Lise*) and George Starr (*Hilaire*).

46 SOE code name *Jeweller*. Her *nom de guerre* was Claudine.

47 Squadron Leader Beryl E. Escott, *Heroines of SOE* (Stroud: History Press, 2010), p. 7.

48 Churchill, whose alias was *Raoul*, had arrived in Cannes to set up the *Spindle* circuit in August. Odette Sansom, one of Mary Herbert's fellow passengers on *Sea Dog*, was to be his courier and became his lover. They were both captured, in large measure because of their own insecurity, and saved their lives by pretending to be not only married but also related to the British Prime Minister. They did in fact marry

after the war. As a result Churchill was later to describe Mary Herbert as 'too fragile for our kind of work'.

49 Professor M.R.D. Foot, interview with the author, 12 October 2010.

50 These reports were distributed very widely within SOE, being seen by almost everyone who mattered from Gubbins downwards. Significantly, however, the distribution list included no one in Combined Operations. On 17 February 1942 Wyatt met Mountbatten, who asked how widely his reports were distributed in SOE and 'expressed his horror' at how many people in SOE knew so much of what was going on in Combined Operations. COO/SOE Liaison Officer's report No. 54, 17 February 1942. HS 8/819.

51 Wyatt, Liaison Officer's Report, 14 August 1942, HS 8/819. Also Keene, 'Beset by Secrecy and Beleaguered by Rivals', p. 334.

52 Wyatt's eventual replacement was Major H.M. Romilly, who took up his post of SOE Liaison Officer at Combined Operations in December 1942.

9 Approval and Preparation

1 The word 'Frankton' appears in Hasler's diary for the first time on 21 September.

2 These little 'toy' compasses, each about the circumference of a shirt button, were manufactured by Messrs Blunt, instrument makers, in The Old Kent Road, who made no less than 235,853 of them during the war. John Nichol and Tony Rennell, *Home Run* (London: Penguin Books, 2008), p. 85.

3 At this stage of the war, there were fewer than thirty submarines in operation in home waters.

4 In an interview after the war with Ewen Southby-Tailyour, Raikes described L'Estrange as 'a rather shadowy figure . . . very fluent in French and . . . an expert on that part of the French coast'.

5 Romilly, Wedlake and Mowl. DEFE 2/4.

6 This stipulated that planners should not go on operations where they might fall into enemy hands because they knew too much. Mountbatten also considered Hasler too valuable to the further development of small boat raids to be risked in this enterprise.

7 Operations Committee minutes, 28 October 1942, DEFE 2/5.

8 Minutes of 119th Examination Committee, Richmond Terrace, 20 October 1942, DEFE 2/5.

9 Minutes of Combined Operations Committee meeting, 28 October 1942, DEFE 2/4. There seems to be some confusion of dates here, since according to other documentation, the decision to let Hasler lead the operation had already been agreed by Mountbatten by this date. It may be that there is some lag between the actions taken and the date they are recorded in the minutes.

10 Hasler was normally a most rational and unemotional man – at least to strangers. It is thus indicative of his desperation to lead his men on Frankton that he considered the 'main difficulty' to be their standard of seamanship, rather than the huge concentration of German troops in the area, the fact that he was dealing with one of the world's most dangerous estuaries and the near impossibility of any of them getting away alive.

11 Major David Stirling, otherwise known as The Phantom Major, was famous for leading his own deep-penetration raids on German airfields in the North African desert.

12 Lucas Phillips, *Cockleshell Heroes*, p. 79.

13 Minutes of 120th Examination Committee, 27 October 1942, DEFE 2/4.

14 Lucas Phillips, *Cockleshell Heroes*, p. 80.

15 Letter from Louis Mountbatten, Chief of Combined Operations, to the Secretary of the Chiefs of Staff Committee, 30 October 1942, DEFE 2/218.

16 Minutes COS (42) 306th Meeting, 3 November 1942, Item 3, CAB 81/51.

10 Hasler's Men

1 The Cockle Mark II did not have a rudder, so the canoe had to be steered by use of its paddles. The modern Klepper canoes used by the SBS are fitted with rudders, controlled by foot pedals, which are operated by the person sitting at the rear. So in modern canoes, the Number Two is the canoe commander, has the compass and is responsible for navigation.

2 Unless otherwise indicated, the biographical and service information in the following personal sketches is taken from each man's personal service record file, held by Director Naval Personnel, Room 48, Disclosure Cell, West Battery, Whale Island, Portsmouth.

3 This happened on 31 July 1942. Norman Colley, email to the author, 30 March 2011.

4 Ply X 3644, Marine William Edward Sparks, born 5 September 1922 in Holborn, London.

5 He had originally intended to follow his father and brother into the Royal Navy, but was sidetracked into the Royal Marines by an alert recruiting sergeant.

6 Lucas Phillips, *Cockleshell Heroes*, p. 104.

7 Ex Po/x 105495 Marine John Withers MacKinnon, born 15 July 1921 in Oban, Argyll.

8 Letter to Mrs MacKinnon of 21 April 1943. MacKinnon family archive.

9 Lucas Phillips, *Cockleshell Heroes*, p. 105; Ken Brotherhood, email to the author, 13 March 2012.

10 Ply X 665 Sgt Samuel Wallace, born 24 September 1913 in Dublin.

11 Rees, *Cockleshell Canoes*, p. 172.

12 Colley, interview with the author, 2 August 2010.

13 Lucas Phillips, *Cockleshell Heroes*, p. 102.

14 Ply X 108880 Marine Robert Ewart, born 4 December 1921 in Springburn, Glasgow.

15 Colley, interview with the author, 2 August 2010.

16 Ibid.

17 Ibid.

18 Ply X 3091 Cpl Albert Frederick Laver, born 29 September 1920, Birkenhead, Cheshire.

19 Among other duties on board, the Royal Marine detachment on most major warships manned one, and sometimes two, of the ship's gun turrets – usually X and Y turrets at the stern of the ship. Right up to the time I joined the Royal Marines the nomenclature 'X' and 'Y' was carried forward into the designations of Royal Marines Commando troops. My first posting as a Royal Marines 2nd Lieutenant in 1960 was as the third officer in X Troop, 42 Commando Royal Marines in the Ear East.

20 According to Lucas Phillips, Laver was Jock Stewart's partner when the pair set the RMBPD record for a long-distance paddle – thirty-four miles in a single night.

21 Ply X 108159 Marine William Henry Mills.

22 Mr Edward Collett. Lucas Phillips, *Cockleshell Heroes*, p. 103.

23 *Kettering Guardian*, 11 January 1946.

24 Ply X 1369 Marine George Jellicoe Sheard.

25 A shortened version of 'Janner', the term used in the Royal Navy (and elsewhere) for a Devon man.

26 Quentin Rees, *Cockleshell Heroes*, p. 176.

27 Ply X 108881 Marine David Moffatt.

28 Lucas Phillips, *Cockleshell Heroes*, p. 103.

29 Ply X 108875 Marine William Alfred Ellery.

30 Colley, interview with Dr Tom Keene, 5 January 2011.

31 Sparks, *Last of the Cockleshell Heroes*, p. 34.

32 Rees, *Cockleshell Heroes*, p. 187.

33 Ply X 108151 Marine Eric Fisher.

34 Fisher was to prove that he was more than capable of this kind of work. Nevertheless, given Sparks' comments and hints from other accounts, it may be that at this stage he was not one of the strongest members of Hasler's team.

35 Ply X 108877 Marine Norman Colley.

36 Norman Colley, email to the author through Jean Rose, 30 March 2011.

37 Colley interview with the author, 2 August 2010.
38 Rees, *Cockleshell Heroes*, p. 191.

11 *Marie-Claire*

1 MI9's headquarters, known as the 'London Transit Camp', were first in the Metropole Hotel in Northumberland Avenue (close to Richmond Terrace) and then the Grand Central Hotel opposite Marylebone station (close to SOE headquarters at Baker Street). However the organisation also had a number of 'safe houses', of which the one in St James's Square was the best known. Nichol and Rennell, *Home Run*, p. 25. After the war, Neave wrote his own story in his two principal books, *They Have Their Exits* (London: Coronet Books, 1980), and *Saturday at MI9* (London: Coronet Books, 1971).
2 Neave, *Saturday at MI9*, pp. 197–8.
3 The information in this section, including the quoted dialogue, comes from Barry Wynne, *The Story of Mary Lindell: Wartime Secret Agent* (London: Robin Clark, 1980).
4 *Women of Courage: Mary Lindell*, Yorkshire TV, 1990.
5 Lindell's description. Denivelle lived in the Place d'Armes, close to the *mairie* in Ruffec.
6 Donald Caskie, who also had the nickname 'The Tartan Pimpernel', had been rector of the Scottish Kirk in pre-war Paris.
7 Péyraud was commander of the Ruffec *gendarmerie* from early 1942 to mid-1943.
8 Henri Gendreau and Michel Regéon, *Ruffec et les Ruffécois dans la guerre de 1938 à 1945* (Ruffec: Editions La Péruse, n.d.), p. 160.
9 Also known as the Grand Hôtel de France.
10 Wynne, *Story of Mary Lindell*.
11 *Women of Courage: Mary Lindell*.
12 M.R.D. Foot and J.M. Langley, *MI9: Escape and Evasion 1939–1945* (London: Bodley Head, 1979), p. 86.

13 Foot and Langley, *MI9*, pp. 141, 142.
14 In October 1942, Groome was parachuted in as radio operator for one of MI9's other networks, the *Pat* line. He was arrested when his radio was tracked down by a German radio direction finder and, with a revolver pointed at his head, was ordered to transmit to London. He managed to send his signal without including the prearranged safety code, so alerting London that he was in German hands. Later, while under interrogation, Groome jumped out of a window thirty feet above the street and managed to make good his escape, only to be betrayed by a passer-by while hiding from his pursuers in a doorway. He was subsequently sent to a concentration camp, but managed to survive the war. Foot and Langley, *MI9*, pp. 141–3.
15 Lyman, *Operation Suicide*, p. 148.
16 Ussel is some thirty miles west of Clermont-Ferrand. Thalamy field, otherwise known as the Aerodrome d'Ussel, is today largely derelict, though one runway remains in occasional use.

12 A Thickening of Plots

1 The RMBPD war diary describes the weather conditions for each day.
2 She flew the Dutch flag and had a Dutch crew.
3 'Scran' has several meanings in naval slang. The word can mean food. It can also be used for personal possessions left lying around a ship, which is then placed in the 'scran bag' to be redeemed on payment of a small fine. But the term 'scran bag' can also be used to describe an untidy or scruffy person or thing, which is undoubtedly the intended meaning here. In normal parlance it would translate as 'the old rubbish heap'. German interrogation report, January 1942, ADM 1/18344.
4 Colley interview with the author, 2 August 2010.
5 According to Denise Hèches, Juliette Latour was the wife of one of Mimi Hèches' cousins. Her address when she

was first recruited was in Rue de la Denise, but she later moved to the Rue Latour, some 300 yards further from the quayside.

6 File 16P 175257 and *Artist* liquidation files, Château de Vincennes, Paris.

7 SOE war diary, October–December 1942, HS 7/245.

8 The six were Gaston Denivelle, Ernst-Henri Gua, Germaine Rouillon, Pierre Cottu, Leopold Marais, Fernand Lavaud, Henri Péyraud. Gendreau and Regéon, *Ruffec et les Ruffécois dans la guerre*, p. 167.

9 The small rural market town of Ruffec seems to have had more than its fair share of action during the war. Apart from being the centre of two British spy rings and a key transit point for two escape lines smuggling Allied servicemen and agents out of France, it was also the home of two German regiments of young conscripts doing their military service. De Baissac debriefing, 21 and 23 August 1943, HS 6/566.

10 This appeared to be common practice. Victor Gerson, the head of SOE DF Section's *Vic* line, cooperated closely with the MI9 escape lines in his area. But both sides agreed that they should keep this fact hidden from their bosses in London. Conversation with Professor M.R.D. Foot, 7 February 2012.

11 A full report on this raid is given in ADM 179/228.

12 In fact, Hitler's order was applied retrospectively to commandos captured even before it came into effect. Seven commandos captured during Operation Musketoon, a joint Combined Operations/SOE raid on the power station feeding an aluminium plant at Glomfjord, Norway on the night of 17–18 September 1942, were taken from Colditz to Sachsenhausen concentration camp and executed on the afternoon of 22 October, four days after Hitler's order was issued. Their bodies were immediately cremated.

13 The general order to shoot commandos was actually broadcast in a Wehrmacht communiqué on 7 October, three days after Operation Basalt and eleven days before Hitler signed the formal written version. The communiqué said, 'In future all terror and sabotage troops of the British and their accomplices, who do not act like soldiers, but rather as bandits, will be treated as such and will be ruthlessly eliminated in battle, wherever they appear.'

14 Colley interview with the author, 2 August 2010.

15 King, *Jacqueline*, p. 235.

16 In fact provoking a German invasion of Vichy France (sometimes known in Whitehall as 'Petanie') had long been a British war objective. In an October 1941 letter to his Foreign Office opposite number, discussing SOE's sabotage operations in France (such as they were at the time), Gladwyn Jebb of SOE commented: 'If, on the other hand, they should result in such confusion as to provoke a German occupation of Petanie, nobody, I understand, would be better pleased than the Foreign Office.' Boisnier archives, Barbézieux.

17 Messages given to Roger Landes for de Baissac, HS 9/880/8.

18 Mary Herbert's debriefing, 30 January 1945, HS 6/566.

19 Lucas Phillips, *Cockleshell Heroes*, p. 91.

20 Lucas Phillips, *Cockleshell Heroes*, pp. 91–2.

21 COHQ War Diary, DEFE 2/4.

22 HS 7/121.

23 The parachute information in this chapter comes from Air Drops 1942, AIR 20/8256; 138 Sqdn Op. schedules, AIR 20/8306; 138 Sqdn Op Instructions 1941–1942, AIR 20/8334; Ops: 188 and 161 Sqdn, AIR 20/8343; 138 Sqdn Op. Reports Aug–Dec 1942, AIR 20/8452; 161 Sqdn Op. Reports April 1042–January 1943, AIR 20/8456; 138 Sqdn Op. Reports May 1943, AIR 20/8476.

24 SOE code name *Printer*. The other agent parachuted with him was France Antelme, code name *Bricklayer*, who was destined for another circuit.

25 Suzanne Duboué and Yves Leglise, interview with the author, Nice, 30 January 2011.

26 Suzanne Leglise, letter of 10 May 1993. Leglise papers, Nice.

27 HS 9/681/3.

28 Ibid.

29 Suzanne Duboué and Yves Leglise, interview with the author.

30 Lyman, *Operation Suicide*, p. 71.

31 Both Hasler and Colley are clear that, even at this late stage, MacKinnon did not know of the operation ahead – but he must at the very least have had his suspicions after this afternoon's training.

32 Sparks, *Last of the Cockleshell Heroes*, p. 40.

33 Rees, *Cockleshell Canoes*, p. 175.

34 Sparks, *Last of the Cockleshell Heroes*, p. 40.

35 This operation very nearly descended into farce even before it started. The plan was for the three agents to paddle ashore in a rubber dinghy, attached to the submarine by a long rope. Once safely on the beach they were to flash a blue lamp and the submarine crew would then haul the dinghy back, thus releasing both parties to go their separate ways. The three agents, who had perhaps enjoyed a little more than was wise of the submarine's hospitality (and especially His Majesty's rum ration), insisted on shaking the submarine crew by the hand and passionately declaring '*Vive la France!*' to each in turn. They then loaded themselves and their radio into the dinghy and began paddling with a will – on the precise reciprocal course to the one they had been given, straight out into the Atlantic. Disaster was only averted by the submarine crew hauling them back. Once back at *Talisman*, the secret agents insisted on another round of hand shaking and declarations of '*Vive la France!*' before being pointed in the right direction and paddling off to carry out their mission.

36 For which he was, after the war, invalided out of the Navy.

37 HM/s *Tuna*'s sailing orders, DEFE 2/216 and 217.

38 Ibid.

39 François Boisnier and Raymond Muelle, *Le Commando de l'Impossible* (Paris: Trésor du Patrimoine, 2003).

40 Dick Raikes, interview with Ewen Southby-Tailyour.

13 Fortress Gironde

1 These were units of the 4th Artillery Regiment under Major Karl Burdach. Alain Chazette, *La Forteresse de Royan-Pointe de Grave* (Editions Heimdal, n.d.), p. 33.

2 Sébastien de Vauban, Louis XIV's great military architect. He also constructed the forts at Blaye and Royan. This was the date when the German construction unit *Baukompagnie 4/211* arrived at Soulac charged with designing and overseeing the construction of the fortress in the Pointe de Grave area, using mainly forced labour supplied by the German Organisation Todt.

3 This wish was not to be granted.

4 Nightingale's analysis, WO 309/1604.

5 This is not a hotel, as its name suggests, but the home of the city council.

6 It was almost totally destroyed by Allied bombardment in 1945.

7 Dominique Lormier, *Bordeaux 1940–1944: La Base Sous-Marine, Questions de Mémoire* (Editions CMD), p. 15.

8 Jean Fernandez, interview with the author, August 2010.

9 Lormier, *Bordeaux 1940–1944*.

10 The Germans certainly believed it to be so.

11 The total distance paddled by Hasler and his team, including during his withdrawal after the attack, was 91 nautical miles.

14 Planning, Tides and Escape

1 Atmospheric pressure can also significantly affect tidal levels, with high pressure suppressing the levels of high tides and accentuating the depth of low tides. Tide tables assume a

standard atmospheric pressure of 1013 millibars (mb). The atmospheric pressure at the time when Hasler entered the Gironde was 1025 mb (diminishing during following days as the high pressure moved away). This would have had the effect of marginally lowering the level of high tides and accentuating the depth of low tides in this period.

2   Lucas Phillips, *Cockleshell Heroes*, Appendix A.

3   1025 millibars. Weather chart for 7 December 1942, Met Office Library and Archive.

4   A recommendation that was rejected because 'L'Estrange was only eligible for a periodic [that is in respect of meritorious service over a period] recommendation because his services were not operational' and that he should therefore be recommended for recognition in the New Year's Honours list of 1944. Minutes from the Naval Secretary and Deputy Naval Secretary, 6 and 12 May 1943, DEFE 2/217 418659.

5   The modern coefficient for the Pointe de Grave is: for High Water Pointe de Grave, add ten minutes to the time of High Water Brest. For Low Water Pointe de Grave, subtract ten minutes from the time of Low Water Brest. These differentials occur and can alter because of a combination of two factors. The first, which delays the onset of the ebb tide, is caused by the fact that the general tidal flow at this point of the Atlantic coast is from south to north, across the mouth of the Gironde. This produces a 'blocking' effect across the mouth of the estuary, holding back the ebb until it is strong enough to force its way through. The second variable element, which has the effect of delaying the start of the flood tide, is caused by the fact that the fresh water flow of contributory rivers into the Gironde, especially in winter and during spring tides when the river and estuary volumes are higher, adds to the strength of the ebb flow which has to

be overcome before the flood tide can dominate.

6   'Red within half a mile of an enemy position, Yellow within half a mile of a known (area of) habitation, Green more than half a mile from known habitation.' Hasler's summary of verbal orders, DEFE 2/218 418659.

7   Hasler's outline plan, 21 September 1942.

8   According to Lucas Phillips, Hasler's preference for the east bank of the Gironde was partly because this bank was rather more sparsely populated, but chiefly because, on the west bank, his Marines coming ashore in the early morning would be silhouetted against the rising sun in the east. Hasler was nothing if not a meticulous planner!

9   Indeed, this is one of the major surfing sites in France and the national surfing championships are frequently held here.

10 For example, the RMBPD diary entry for 19 September has both sections 'landing and leaving beach through breakers'. But given that there are no true surf beaches anywhere on the south coast of Britain, the waves they would have negotiated would not have been more than those which would characterise a blustery day on the beach.

11 Though, interestingly, among the Hasler papers at his home in Argyll is one detailed description of how to negotiate big surf.

12 Colley, email to the author, 21 August 2011.

13 Since Hasler's raiders used a magnetic compass, all his bearings were in relation to magnetic north, rather than true north. The variation between the two in this area in 1942 being 9° 24' west, with an annual decrease in the differential of 11' every year.

14 So much so that in the mid-2000s a whole new island of sand began to appear in the mouth of the Gironde, a short distance from the Cordouan stack. This will in due course, experts say, become established as a permanent

and habitable island as more and more sand and mud is washed up onto it.

15 ISTD prepared a special report for Frankton, ISTD C/95. This drew heavily on two previous ISTD topographical surveys on the Gironde, which were carried out prior to the Frankton raid, when Fleuret and Gaudin were still active. These earlier surveys contain much detailed and up-to-date topographical information preceded by the phrase 'it is reported that . . .' It seems very likely that these were the product of reports from Fleuret and Gaudin. ISTD C/95 also contains a number of photographs drawn from previous ISTD reports which show the Gironde islands and banks and were clearly taken from a ship on passage in the estuary. It seems very probable that these also were taken clandestinely either by Fleuret or Gaudin in the course of their duties as Gironde pilots.

16 Hasler's final report, DEFE 2/217. See also Appendix B.

17 This headland is actually named after St Aldhelm, not St Alban, though the latter name is more commonly used by locals and fishermen. I have paddled a fully loaded canoe through these overfalls and they are indeed very uncomfortable.

18 Hasler's own phrase for the overfalls at Portland Bill – having passed through them on 19 August 1935, saying that, on this occasion and despite their ferocious reputation, the overfalls 'would hardly have worried a duck punt'. Hasler papers.

19 DEFE 2/217.

20 Hasler diaries, 31 May 1942.

21 Operation Frankton – Appendix II Intelligence, DEFE 2/217 418659.

22 Interestingly, the Pilot for Langstone and Chichester harbour uses almost exactly the same language, warning of 'Breakers [which are] particularly hazardous when a strong ebb tide is flowing.'

23 ISTD C/95 includes a paragraph quoting from this section of the Pilot verbatim.

24 The Bay of Biscay Pilot of 2000 (p. 5) contains the following warning about the southern approach to the estuary mouth: 'Overfalls [in this area] are severe and dangerous. Do not attempt to enter the estuary . . . if there is any swell or on the ebb tide . . . only use the south entrance in . . . favourable tidal conditions.' This area, which is known to local fishermen as Le Chaudron du Diable (The Devil's Cauldron), was also the site of the capsize, in 1997, of a 55ft long, 24 tonne pilot vessel from Bordeaux. The pilot, Claude Businelli, survived and the boat was subsequently recovered. Boisnier, Le Commando de l'Impossible.

25 Penrose's notes here have faded to indistinction, so it is impossible to be certain of this notation, but the markings seem to indicate turbulent water and, since there are no other hydrological hazards here, it is probably safe to assume that this is what is indicated.

26 Carte de L'Embouchure de La Gironde d'après la reconnaissance hydrographique faite en 1874.

27 ISTD C/21.

28 Southby-Tailyour, Blondie, p. 104, fn 12.

29 In the Hasler papers there is a somewhat over-coloured article from around the mid-fifties, probably penned by a journalist, which contains Hasler's manuscript amendments in pencil. In this he makes it clear that these tide rips were 'something the Admiralty hydrographers missed'.

30 Colley interview with the author, 2 August 2010.

31 There is a fine example of this escape box, together with the maps the Marines carried, in the Combined Services Military Museum in Maldon, Essex.

32 This drug seemed to have been in very wide use by the services during the war, not just for operational but perhaps even for recreational use, including by Hasler himself. There are even mentions in his diaries of 'Benzedrine parties' in Eastney.

33 M.R.D. Foot in his book MI9: Escape and Evasion says, 'Particular care was taken

to provide them [Hasler's team] with advice, including cover stories' (p. 85). Norman Colley has no recollection of either advice or cover stories being provided to the raiders and these are not mentioned in any of the post-raid accounts.

34 Norman Colley confirms that they were all well aware of this rule.

35 Professor Michael Foot, interview with the author.

36 Southby-Tailyour, *Blondie*, p. 88.

37 Rommel's Army Group B for instance simply ignored the order and put captured 'commandos' in POW camps. The 85th Army Group (positioned next door to Bordeaux) did the same to parachuted *'Fallschimispringer'* (parachuted 'commandos') – as against *'Fallschimijaeger'* – parachuted regular troops. (Email with Peter Lieb 27 March 2012.)

38 Colley interview with the author, 2 August 2010.

15 The Start of the 'Little Adventure'

1 The date of sailing appears to have been changed. The minutes of Meeting 122 of the Examination Committee of Combined Operations of 10 November 1942 indicates that an earlier sailing was originally planned, but this was changed to 29 November and then, it appears, delayed a further day. DEFE 2/4.

2 Colley interview with the author, 2 August 2010, and subsequent emails.

3 *Tuna's* log, 30 November 1942.

4 This description is taken from an undated article, 'Operation Frankton', written after the war by *Tuna's* chief coxswain, Petty Officer William Stabb DSM, copies of which are in the Royal Navy Submarine Museum, Gosport, and in the papers of Mrs Kiltie, Sam Wallace's sister, Plymouth.

5 Stabb, 'Operation Frankton'.

6 Stabb, 'Operation Frankton'.

7 All records from eyewitnesses at the time confirm that *Tuna's* crew and Blondie's Marines did indeed 'dress ship' in this fashion on departure from the Clyde. See especially the interview with Norman Colley of 2 August 2010. Nevertheless, advertising that *Tuna* had a special party of Marines on board seems a most odd thing to have done, given the high security which surrounded Operation Frankton. Any sharp-eyed observer could easily have noted that this was not a normal submarine patrol, but one dedicated to an unusual and clandestine purpose.

8 Every ship, and especially metal ones, carries its own powerful magnetic field. This can cause serious inaccuracy with magnetic compasses. But much more importantly, it is this field which sets off magnetic mines. 'Degaussing' is the technical term for removing, as far as is possible, a ship's magnetic signature.

9 Hasler's diaries.

10 Colley interview with the author, 2 August 2010.

11 Lucas Phillips, *Cockleshell Heroes*, p. 106.

12 Sparks, *Last of the Cockleshell Heroes*, p. 45.

13 Lucas Phillips, *Cockleshell Heroes*, p. 108.

14 Colley interview with the author, 2 August 2010.

15 Sparks, *Last of the Cockleshell Heroes*, p. 47.

16 *Tuna's* log shows this exercise as taking place at 'Kilmarnock Water', but written underneath are the words 'Scalpsie Bay' (also known as Kilchattan Bay). In fact Kilmarnock island is on the other (western) side of the Isle of Bute. But this would have necessitated *Tuna* rounding the headland at the southern end of Bute and then sailing some way north, meaning that she would have had to retrace her steps when she continued her journey down the Clyde later that evening. Furthermore, whereas Scalpsie Bay offers a good lee to the southwesterly wind which, *Tuna's* log records, was blowing at the time, Kilmarnock island is fully exposed when the wind is in this quarter. I have therefore taken Scalpsie Bay as the accurate location for these canoe disembarkation exercises. Today,

Scalpsie Bay is popular for its sandy beach and nearby seal colony.

17 *Tuna's* pilot, Gordon Rowe, wrote a post-war account of *Tuna's* part in Frankton (A1945/195/1, now in the Royal Navy Submarine Museum, Gosport). In this he says that Raikes blew and vented his buoyancy tanks so as to raise and lower *Tuna* for each canoe launch. But this is not mentioned by any other eyewitness. Nor does it make sense. Once *Tuna* was trimmed down as far in the water as Raikes thought prudent in the prevailing sea state, she would have stayed at this trim rather than wasting time altering it for each canoe launch. Moreover, however gently buoyancy tanks are emptied and filled, the operation is always somewhat noisy and Raikes would have wanted to keep the noise down as low as possible at this point, for obvious reasons. So I have chosen to ignore Rowe's description at this point.

18 A well-known submarine practice. When carrying passengers, small submarines such as *Tuna* did not have enough space for every man to have a bunk. 'Hot bunking' means that a person coming off watch takes over one of the empty – and still warm – bunks of those going on watch.

19 Stabb, 'Operation Frankton'.

20 Colley interview with the author, 2 August 2010.

21 Colley TV interview with Dr Tom Keene, 5 January 2011.

22 The minutes of the Examination Committee meeting this day indicate that 'a brief [on Operation Frankton] would be required for the Prime Minister about 5 December'. DEFE 2/5.

23 *Tuna's* maximum surface speed was fourteen knots; her speed when dived and on electric propulsion was eight knots for an hour and a half or two knots for twenty hours.

24 Sparks, *Last of the Cockleshell Heroes*, p. 49.

25 Colley interview with the author, 2 August 2010.

26 Submarines are at their most vulnerable on the surface, so their lookouts tend to be sharper than on other ships. Their job is much assisted by the fact that submarines, being so low in the water, are very difficult to see, especially when bow on and with a black land mass behind them. Other vessels are easier to spot, because from a low angle more of them shows up against the horizon. Raikes prided himself on *Tuna's* lookouts, regarding them as the best in the Submarine Service. This made a major contribution to the fact that she survived the war, sinking five U-boats and an ocean-going tug, severely damaging another U-boat and successfully keeping track of numerous German capital ships so that they could be found and attacked by the RAF and Royal Navy surface ships.

27 Stabb, 'Operation Frankton'.

28 The full MI9 escape instructions have been lost. This extract comes from a passage quoted by Hasler in a letter to war crimes investigators dated 27 October 1945, DEFE 2/218.

29 Raikes' after-operation report speaks of 'tens of hundreds of [fishing] boats' which were 'most marked along the 100 fathom line. On one occasion there were ten of them within two miles of me. And of course being fishing boats they were facing north one minute, east the next.' Ewen Southby-Tailyour, taped interviews between 2 May 1995 and 8 November 1996.

30 Rowe, A1945/195/1.

31 Raikes' after-action report to Flag Officer Submarines, DEFE 2/218.

32 Lucas Phillips, *Cockleshell Heroes*, p. 112.

33 Colley interview with the author, 2 August 2010.

34 *Kettering Guardian*, 11 January 1946.

35 Email from Ken Brotherhood to the author, 13 March 2012.

36 Rees, *Cockleshell Heroes – the Final Witness*, p. 175.

37 Frankton papers, Royal Marines Museum, Eastney.

38 Conducted in November 1942, this was the first British airborne operation to use gliders. Its target was the Vemork Norsk Hydro chemical plant in Norway, which produced heavy water

for the Nazi atomic weapons programme. The raid was a complete failure and all its participants were either killed in glider crashes or captured and executed by the Germans. A second, successful raid carried out by SOE agents alone became the basis for the film *The Heroes of Telemark*.

39 HS 8/222.

40 The navigational term for establishing one's position by taking a bearing on two or more fixed points on the land. A fix can also be obtained by taking a bearing on a single point, if the distance from that point is known or can be calculated. An astral fix uses stars or the sun for the same purpose.

41 Lucas Phillips, *Cockleshell Heroes*, pp. 118–19.

42 Commander J.R.H. Bull DSC RN (retd), 'Submarine Special Operations – a personal story'. Hasler papers.

43 Document sent to the author by Ewen Southby-Tailyour containing the transcript of an undated interview with Raikes carried out in the course of writing his biography *Blondie*.

44 Ibid.

45 HM/s *Tuna* patrol report for period 30 November–13 December 1942. Submarine Museum, Gosport.

46 In his after-action report Raikes wrote, with typical bluntness, 'The plan quite evidently required extreme accuracy in navigation, even allowing for the rather touching faith of the authorities in the accuracy of the positions given by the RAF – a faith which I did not share.' The majority of submarine losses in both world wars were from mines, many of them due to navigation errors. In the Royal Navy's submarine service, navigation was often described as 'by Guess and by God'.

47 Rowe, A1945/195/1.

48 Hasler's verbal orders.

49 Ibid.

50 Ibid.

16 Black-Faced Villains

1 Bull, 'Submarine Special Operations', p. 4.

2 This lighthouse is 223ft (68m) high, making it the tenth tallest traditional lighthouse in the world. Sometimes known as the 'Patriarch of Lighthouses', Cordouan is also the oldest lighthouse in France. It was designed by leading Paris architect Louis de Foix, and is something of a Renaissance masterpiece, being an amalgam of a royal palace, a cathedral and a fort. It was started in 1584 and completed in 1611.

3 HM/s *Tuna*, patrol report for period 30 November–13 December 1942. Submarine Museum, Gosport.

4 Stabb, 'Operation Frankton'.

5 This was the aerial reconnaissance ordered by Combined Operations Planning Committee on 17 November (see Chapter 12) for the day after Hasler's planned disembarkation from *Tuna* and was conducted without the knowledge that this had been delayed twenty-four hours. Interpretation report 4309 of 8/12/42, AIR 34/330. Today a Special Forces commander could receive this last-minute information by encrypted signal in the hours, even minutes before his operation started; no such facility existed in Hasler's day.

6 Raikes report to Flag Officer Submarines, DEFE 2/218.

7 Stabb, 'Operation Frankton'.

8 Lucas Phillips, *Cockleshell Heroes*, p. 96.

9 In peacetime the Cordouan stack shows, like all other lighthouses, a flashing and occulting red and green light, divided into sectors. But, according to locals, the Germans changed this to a constant white light during the war years.

10 Stands for 'Hydro Effect' in naval parlance, but is almost always taken to mean the noise of a boat or its Asdic.

11 Submariners refer to this as the 'periscope standards'.

12 Rowe, A1945/195/1. There is a discrepancy between Rowe's account and that of Lucas Phillips and Raikes at this point. Rowe does not mention that Hasler was on the bridge. But the other two, whom I have followed in this narrative, are clear that he was. And it

seems only logical that he should have been there at this point, as he would have wanted to see the sea state before making the decision that the operation should commence.

13 This passage of dialogue is as recorded in Lucas Phillips, *Cockleshell Heroes*, pp. 116–19.

14 There is a discrepancy in Raikes' report on timing. He says that he started the operation by surfacing *Tuna* at 1957 hours, but that the boats were all out on the casing by 1845 (i.e. twelve minutes earlier than he surfaced). Moreover the first German radar report was at 1950 (seven minutes before *Tuna* surfaced). Both Raikes and Hasler agree that the canoes paddled off at 2022 hours (see Annexe I). We know from several sources that the time it took to launch all the canoes was forty-six minutes. So I have taken 2022 hours as the correct time for the canoes to depart and subtracted forty-six minutes to give *Tuna*'s surfacing time, which also seems to broadly fit with the first signalled report of *Tuna*'s image on the German radar.

15 This part of the exchange is taken from Ewen Southby-Tailyour's post-war interview with Raikes.

16 Raikes interview with Dr Tom Keene, Dorset, 1 April 2004.

17 'They were young, they were great . . . A fine bunch of young chaps. They were full of fun, but very serious with it all. Blondie, of course, was totally serious in the job . . . My crew were very impressed with them.' Raikes interview with Dr Tom Keene, 1 April 2004.

18 Email from Clive Evans, 30 September 2011.

19 In his post-war interview with Ewen Southby-Tailyour, Raikes claims it was he, not Hasler, who gave this order. See also Dr Tom Keene's interview with Raikes, 1 April 2004. But Norman Colley, who was on the casing that night and saw the damage, is certain that it was Hasler who personally inspected *Cachalot* and gave the order to strike her below.

20 Lucas Phillips, *Cockleshell Heroes*, p. 119. Lucas Phillips has Fisher shout this to Moffatt as they paddle off, but all other witnesses – and crucially Norman Colley – insist that Fisher, like Ellery, followed *Cachalot* below and was not on the casing when Hasler paddled off.

21 Lucas Phillips, *Cockleshell Heroes*, p. 123; Sparks, *Last of the Cockleshell Heroes*.

22 Lucas Phillips, *Cockleshell Heroes*, p. 123.

23 The night sky observations mentioned in this and succeeding chapters are taken from http://www.heavens-above.com, adjusted for the latitude and longitude of Hasler's positions during his entry into the Gironde and for the appropriate time during the night of 7/8 December 1942. I am most grateful to Dr Steve Bell, Head of HM Nautical Almanac Office, UK Hydrographic Office in Taunton, for all other information on the times, positions and aspects of sun and moon rise during the period 7–13 December 1942.

24 Hasler papers.

25 Hasler, final report.

26 Colley interview with the author, 2 August 2010.

27 Raikes' operational report. Some reports have *Tuna* diving at this juncture. But her log makes it clear that she withdrew on the surface, no doubt relying on the dark mass of the land behind to hide her from the prying eyes of the German patrol boat.

28 Copies of these signals are held in the Royal Marines Museum, Eastney. W310 is a strongpoint marked on German defensive maps of the time as S310. See the maps in Chapter 13 and Alain Chazette, *La Forteresse de Royan-Pointe de Grave* (Editions Heimdal, n.d.), pp. 38–42.

29 Johannes Bachmann's diary.

17 The Pointe de Grave

1 Sparks, *Last of the Cockleshell Heroes*, p. 52.

2 Lucas Phillips, *Cockleshell Heroes*, Appendix A.

3   I am grateful to Guy Hannaford, Archive Research Manager, UK Hydrographic Office, Taunton, Somerset and his team for the work they did with the French Hydrological Office in Brest to reconstruct the tidal conditions on this and the following nights of Operation Frankton, upon which all the tidal calculations in this and the following chapters are based.

4   See Annexe I.

5   There is a curious discrepancy between accounts here. Both Hasler and Sparks subsequently insisted that they lost Wallace and Ewart when they failed to reappear after passing through these overfalls (though Hasler seemed somehow to know that they had not capsized there, insisting correctly that they had paddled on to be wrecked further down the coast). Wallace himself, however, is reported in a later account as saying that he was suffering so badly from seasickness that he was 'detached [by Hasler] with the instruction to go into hiding on shore and to carry out the orders at a later date than that agreed upon'.

6   Much of the detail and all the dialogue for this part of their journey is taken from Lucas Phillips, *Cockleshell Heroes*, pp. 129–32.

7   There is a contradiction about the position of this third tidal rip. In Hasler's main report (see Appendix B) he says that, while picking up Sheard and Moffatt, 'the tide carried the Party round the Pointe de Grave, not more than a quarter of a mile offshore and through a third but less violent tide race' (i.e. when they were going through the third overfalls, they were on the Pointe de Grave's seaward side). But in his intelligence report, he quotes the position of the third tidal overfalls as being 750 yards northwest, that is on the estuary side of the Pointe de Grave. Locals tell me that the right position is the one given in Hasler's intelligence report – i.e. they encountered this tide rip *after* they had passed the Pointe de Grave and were on its estuary side. On a visit to the Pointe de Grave in August

2010, I watched a small motor boat about 20ft long get into difficulties in a tide rip in just this position.

8   Hasler's intelligence report.

9   Hasler could not have known at the time that these were units of the local Inshore Squadron, whose commander, Captain Max Gebauer, had been dining with Admiral Bachmann in Royan that evening and had been present when the message from the German radar station reporting unusual activity opposite Montalivet had been brought in. Gebauer's presence at this dinner was a prelude to his squadron's inspection by the Admiral later on this morning. Gebauer was in fact commander of the German Naval Anti-Aircraft School in Dax, but was currently deputising for the normal squadron commander, Captain Lipinski, who was on leave (see Gebauer's evidence to the Nightingale Inquiry of 25 June 1948, WO 309/1604).

10 'Pusser's' is a Royal Navy term for 'official issue'.

11 See his message to London of February 1943 (Chapter 33).

12 Bridget Hasler, Blondie's wife, concurs with this judgement. Interview with the author, 8 October 2010. In his interview with Ewen Southby-Tailyour, Raikes also comments that Hasler never showed his emotions.

13 317m, to be exact. The Môle is still in existence, though in a very decrepit state, having been severely damaged by the Germans at the end of the war in order to prevent it being used by the Allies.

14 According to Hasler's report the distance was 0.75 miles.

15 Hasler papers.

18 The Pointe aux Oiseaux

1   Small local fishing vessels in the Gironde. The term also applies to larger vessels, such as pilot boats. A *chaloupe* – pronounced 'kaloupe' – can be rowed, or powered by either a sail (in the case of older vessels) or a small diesel engine (in the case of more modern ones).

2 Jean Fernandez (Lhermet's son), interview with the author, Pointe de Grave, 16 August 2010.
3 Admiral Bachmann's War Diary, Boisnier archives, Barbézieux. English version from a French translation by Peter Siddall.
4 Evidence of Max Gebauer, 25 June 1948, WO 309/1604.
5 Ibid.
6 Fallingbostel in Lower Saxony, Germany, was the site during the Second World War of two prisoner-of-war camps, Stalag XIB and Stalag 357.
7 Evidence of Max Gebauer, WO 309/1604.
8 According to the evidence of Franz Drey in WO 309/1604, Helmut Harstick was a trained German lawyer and prosecutor. He was at the time deputy to Major Glatzel of Divisional Intelligence. He was assisted by a Lieutenant Weidemann, who acted as translator.
9 Evidence of Franz Drey, WO 309/1604.
10 Lucas Phillips, *Cockleshell Heroes*, p. 142.
11 Lucas Phillips, *Cockleshell Heroes*, p. 143.
12 This account, which comes largely from an interview with Jeanne Baudray by the author on 16 August 2010, differs markedly from that given in Hasler's report (see Appendix B). Hasler says that the canoes were already hidden when the fishermen arrived, but he felt it right to approach them in case they were discovered. He also reports that shortly after the boats emerged from the St Vivien channel, they were joined by the women from St Vivien who brought their men breakfast. But it seems curious that the women should carry breakfast the mile or so from the Port de St Vivien when their men had just sailed down from there. Finally, the practice of the fishing families of St Vivien is for wives to accompany their husbands on the family *chaloupe* and to help gather the oysters. Hasler does however mention being brought food that evening. On the presumption that the account given here is the more accurate one, it seems likely that

Hasler's initial plan was to paddle a short way up the Chenal de St Vivien. His canoes would thus have been better hidden from the main traffic on the estuary – but they would also have been much more vulnerable to discovery by German patrols along the banks of the Chenal.
13 Sparks in his book says there was only one ship, but Lucas Phillips stipulates 'six or seven'. There is also an account of this incident in an account called 'Blondie Hasler and the Cockleshell raid on Bordeaux' in the Hasler papers.
14 Sparks was right. According to a later analysis based on photographic evidence, one of these was the *Portland*, heading for a berth at Bassens South and a target for Laver and Mills in three nights' time. Intelligence report from the Director of Naval Intelligence (DNI), 3 May 1943, DEFE 2/217.
15 Sparks, *Last of the Cockleshell Heroes*, p. 62.
16 Lucas Phillips, *Cockleshell Heroes*, p. 146.
17 Lucas Phillips, *Cockleshell Heroes*, p. 145.
18 This appears, from other corroborating facts, to have been actually the point marked S301 on Fig. 3 Chapter 13.
19 A member of Admiral Marschall's staff, Naval High Command.
20 A naval POW transit camp.
21 Evidence from Feiffer, 21 March 1948, WO 309/1604.
22 Copies of German signals held at the Royal Marines Museum, Eastney. Translated by Christine Tochtermann.
23 Statement of Wolf Junge, 10 April 1948, WO 309/1604.

19 La Présidente Farm

1 La Présidente Farm no longer exists. It was demolished to make way for a nuclear power station in the 1960s.
2 In Hasler's report and that of Lucas Phillips, this conversation took place in the evening as the Marines were leaving when, according to Hasler, their silhouettes were spotted by the farmer etched out against the dusk light reflected off the river. But both Sparks in his autobiography and the interviews

carried out by François Boisnier after the war seem to confirm that this first encounter took place in the morning, not the evening.

3 Dialogue taken from Boisnier, *Commando de l'Impossible*. Boisnier interviewed Decombes's son after the war.

4 Lucas Phillips, *Cockleshell Heroes*, p. 145.

5 Aerial Interpretation Report 4319 of 12 Dec 1942, AIR 34/330.

6 In 1960, four young officers who joined the Royal Marines in the same year as me, Jake Hensman, Peter Cameron, Mike Hodder and Brian Mollan, carried out the first re-enactment of the Frankton raid and escape and wrote a very good report on what they discovered. They visited La Présidente Farm and, with the help of the farmer's son, identified the ditch in which the raiders hid. They searched for Hasler's tommy gun in the mud, but were unable to find it. Their report is held at the Royal Marines Museum, Eastney.

7 Corssen was a specialist Naval Intelligence interrogator based at Wilhelmshaven in Germany and was on his way down to Bordeaux to conduct the further interrogation of the two Marines. See the Nightingale War Crimes Investigation, WO 309/1604.

8 Southby-Tailyour, *Blondie*, p. 113.

9 Also known as Île Nouvelle. Hasler's reports refer to this as 'Desert island' but do not positively identify it. But this speculative identification, made by François Boisnier, seems to fit the facts better than any other island in this small archipelago.

10 See Hasler's intelligence report for two nights later.

11 This story, for which I am indebted once again to François Boisnier, came to light during the Frankton commemorations in 2001, when Jean Raymond approached Bill Sparks and said: 'I am happy to meet you after so many years, in memory of the fright you gave my father and me fifty years ago . . .' But, of course, this could not have been Sparks as he was with Hasler on Île Bouchard, and so could only have been MacKinnon and Conway.

According to Raymond the encounter took place on the night of 8–9 December. But this is very unlikely, as at 2000 that night the tide would have been at full ebb flow, making it impossible for MacKinnon and Conway to have made any headway against it. It is technically possible that they had lain up the previous day very close to Fort-Médoc and had just left their lying-up position hoping to make somewhere close by before lying up again to wait for the tide to turn (as Hasler was doing in the same area). But this would have meant them making far greater progress the previous night after losing Hasler at the Môle at Le Verdon than would have been possible. I therefore conclude that the timing given by Raymond for this encounter was right, then the night must have been 9–10 December, rather than the night before.

12 The *Sicherheitsdienst* or military security was founded by Himmler. The SD's Bordeaux headquarters at this time were in a rather beautiful eighteenth-century building which is now the Hôtel de La Marine (headquarters of the French Marine Service).

13 Bachmann diaries.

14 In the course of making the BBC 2 docudrama *The Most Courageous Raid of World War II*, I visited these cells, which remain broadly as they would have been in 1942. Many prisoners, chiefly from French Resistance organisations, were incarcerated here before being deported or shot. The walls still bear the marks they left, especially those ticking off the passing days.

15 This was the overarching structure combining all German police and security in the region.

16 Referred to as the 'Leiter IV' section.

SS-Rasse und Siedlungshauptamt (Race and Settlement Authority) file on Wilhelm Dohse, held at the Bundesarchiv in Berlin. Dr Sabine Dumschatt, email to the author, 7 November 2011. Dohse became something of a legend, even among the French, for his work in Bordeaux. As a result his rank was later exaggerated, not least by Roger Landes, who described him as a *Hauptstürmführer* (roughly captain). But his actual rank was *Hauptscharführer*, roughly equivalent to a WO II. Later in the war he was promoted to SS *Unterstürmführer* (which means he finally became an officer). It was most unusual for a WOII to have officers under his command. See Jacques Villette, 'Pour la Réhabilitation de Maurice Papon', http://www.maurice-papon.net/documents/dohse.htm

17 Villette, 'Pour la Réhabilitation de Maurice Papon'.
18 Ibid.
19 Ibid.
20 Evidence from a French witness, W309/1604.
21 Michel St Marc, interview with the author, Cauderan, Bordeaux, 4 April 2011. M. St Marc, a retired local schoolteacher, has made a special study of what happened to Lt MacKinnon and Marine Conway during and after Operation Frankton.

20 Approach and Execution

1 Hasler papers.
2 Because of the blocking effect of the prevailing south–north ocean current off the mouth of the Gironde, there is a longer period of slack water after the end of the flood tide than after the end of the ebb. This tends to increase the further one goes up the estuary.
3 There are many speculative variations of exactly what happened to Conway and MacKinnon at this point. I have used, as the basis for this account, Conway's own description (see *Sicherheitsdienst* report of 19 December 1942, ADM 1/18344), which has been adapted only (e.g. on the point relating to the Bec d'Ambès) where the geography does not make sense, or where it could reasonably be presumed that he was dissimulating to protect local people.
4 Evidence of Prahm, WO 309/1604.
5 Probably Hans Luther, rather than Friedrich Dohse.
6 Deposition taken on 29 April 1948 for the Nuremberg War Crimes Tribunal.

Boisnier archives, Barbézieux, and WO 309/1604. I have made very minor alterations to this text to make it easier to read, without in any way altering its meaning. When assessing Prahm's account of his allegedly minor and reluctant role in this and the correspondingly larger role played by the 'head of the SD', allowance should be made for the fact that this was a deposition to a War Crimes tribunal which could have resulted in a charge being made against Prahm himself.

21 Priming the Weapon

1 Bachmann later issued an official signal to this effect. See WO 302/1604.
2 From the Archives of the Third Reich, seized after the war, and taken to the USA. Boisnier archives, Barbézieux; National Archives and Record Administration (NARA), Washington.
3 There is some confusion about the name and function of this ship, which is also referred to as the *Python* – but since it was referred to by Raymond Brard of the Bordeaux Port Fire Service as the tanker *Cap Hadid*, it seems appropriate to stick with that name.
4 Believed to be the *Schwannheim*.
5 The quay at this point is divided in two, the southern portion being the Quai Carnot while the northern is the Quai des Chartrons. For ease I have referred to it all as the Quai des Chartrons throughout. Just to confuse matters further, the Quai Carnot is the name for the dockside edge of a street called the Quai Bacalan, named after what was at the time the working-class suburb of Bordeaux.
6 HS 8/222.
7 HS 7/121. See Chapter 13.
8 Duboué, *Historique du Réseau 'Denis – Aristide – Buckmaster'*.
9 Lucas Phillips puts the time of high water at midnight, but that does not concur with the tide tables of the time.
10 Known as the SMD Pattern Sympathetic fuse. These fuses, which were themselves of doubtful reliability, were only finally

produced for operations, 1 July 1942, which meant that Hasler's team would have been using one of the earliest versions. I am much indebted to Lt Col (retd) N.A. Bonney for his advice and help on the history, design and development of the limpet mine. His letter to the author of 18 December 2011.

22 Attack

1 Hasler in his final report said he could not identify which way the *Tannenfels* was pointing. However, Schnöppe's photographs make it clear that she was pointing downstream, so Hasler's first limpets must have been planted on her stern.
2 Lucas Phillips, *Cockleshell Heroes*, p. 161.
3 I suspect Hasler meant 'double paddles' here. He no longer needed single paddles for reasons of stealth and they would have been much slower, when what he needed now was speed.
4 Lucas Phillips, *Cockleshell Heroes*, p. 164.
5 Ibid.
6 The tide must have turned against them before they reached Bassens South as the aerial photographs taken next day show a large collection of ships, mostly merchant ships, alongside the southern quay on the Garonne's east bank. Interpretation Report 4344 of 21 December 1942, AIR 34/330.
7 Lucas Phillips, *Cockleshell Heroes*, p. 166.
8 Ibid.
9 Ibid.

23 Bangs and Blame-Dodging

1 The steel plates from which merchant ships were constructed at this time were less than an inch thick. National Maritime Museum, Greenwich.
2 Named after Charles E. Munroe, who discovered it in 1888 while working at the Naval Torpedo Station at Newport, Rhode Island in the United States.
3 The *Cockleshell Heroes* film shows the ships – models made of balsa wood –

being blown to smithereens. That too was pure Hollywood.
4 Jean Trocard, interview with the author, Bordeaux, 30 March 2011. M. Trocard was a conscripted labourer in Organisation Todt.
5 Bachmann diaries. Boisnier archives, Barbézieux; WO 309/1604.
6 The Italian navy had thirty submarines in Bordeaux, supported by 1800 crew members, 400 workers and technicians and 700 armed marines. Boisnier, *Le Commando de l'Impossible*.
7 Report of an interview of Naval Intelligence Department and a well-informed French officer who was in Bordeaux up to the middle of 1943 (almost certainly de Baissac), 3 April 1943, DEFE 2/219.
8 Evidence of *Korvetten-Kapitän* Peter Popp to the Nuremberg court, ADM 1/8344.
9 In the submission for a post-war medal for Brard in his file in Vincennes, he claims the sinking of the *Cap Hadid* as one of his major acts of sabotage during the war. Amongst Schnöppe's photographs is a picture of a totally flooded *Cap Hadid* resting on the bottom alongside the Quai des Chartrons.
10 Certificate of activity in the Resistance dated 15 January 1946, signed by Raymond Brard. Royal Marines Museum, Eastney.
11 A copy of this letter in German and French is held in the Royal Marines Museum, Eastney.
12 It cannot be said that the Germans lacked improvisational skills. This unusual use for bacon rashers is described in Schnöppe's notes.
13 I am most grateful to Richard Wooldridge of the Combined Services Military Museum for alerting me to this fascinating evidence, and to Jak Showell for his help in finding Schnöppe's photos and putting me in touch with the U-Boat Museum in Germany which holds Schnöppe's papers.
14 German document in the possession of the Combined Services Military Museum, Maldon, Essex, translated by Peter Siddall with minor textual amendments by the author. This comes

(as do the photographs) by courtesy of the Schnöppe Collection held at the U-boat museum in Cuxhaven, Germany.

15 SOE's historian Professor M.R.D. Foot in an interview with Dr Tom Keene, 26 January 2004. Quoted in a BBC TV documentary researched, written and produced by Dr Keene and transmitted in March 2004. In a telephone conversation with the author on 25 April 2011, Professor Foot confirmed that, in his researches for his book *SOE in France*, he had had sight of a document (now regrettably lost) which confirmed this.

16 Combined Operations report of February/March 1943, DEFE 2/14.

17 Interpretation Reports 4325 of 13 December 1942 and 4344 of 21 December 1942, which was a much fuller analysis of the same photo run and may have been called for after London heard of the operation's partial success.

18 German signals held at Royal Marines Museum, Eastney.

19 Boisnier, *Le Commando de l'Impossible*, p. 150.

20 An intriguing note in Kühnemann's journal dated a week later indicates that there may indeed have been a subsequent court-martial, but it resulted in everyone being exonerated: 'In the course of an inquiry led by the Court Martial into security, no shortcomings were found.' Boisnier archives, Barbézieux.

21 Information extracted from captured enemy documents, 12 July 1946, DEFE 2/218.

24 The Start of the Long Walk

1 Hasler's first brief report to MI9 – MI9/s PG (-) 1140, now in the Southby-Tailyour papers – makes specific mention of a railway line at this point. But it seems likely that he confused this with a line they would have crossed on the second night, as the escape map he used makes no mention of a railway line at this point. The road they crossed

is now the D255 from Blaye north to Royan.

2 Lucas Phillips, *Cockleshell Heroes*, p. 178.

3 In an interview conducted by François Boisnier after the war, M. André Montaut related how his father, Michel Sauvaître, a resident of Fours at the time, had told him of seeing two half-submerged canoes drifting down the Gironde opposite the Île Bot that morning. M. Sauvaître also told his son that the Germans had erected several lines of barbed wire in the field behind the spot where Hasler landed and it was probably these, rather than wires supporting vines, that he and Sparks had encountered. Vines were not grown in these fields below the Château de Segonzac until well after the war, he claimed.

4 Only one wood in this area conforms to Hasler's description and that is the one near the tiny hamlet of Espangle, GR 685050045 on Sheet 1535 O of the French 1:25,000 *Carte de Randonnée* 'Blaye – Bec d'Ambès'. In this case, the stream referred to by Hasler is the Ruisseau de Fours. Visit to the area by the author, 15 August 2010.

5 The information relating to the *Cabane Fume Bas* is based on interviews conducted with Mme Solange Gacis and Mme Lucienne Bernard by François Boisnier on 11 March 2004. Boisnier archives, Barbézieux.

6 Boisnier archives, Barbézieux. Long abandoned and in a state of dilapidation, the cabin was bought many years after the war by a local family. While carrying out its renovation the new owners found under the floor the remains of what appeared to be military equipment, almost certainly left behind by Laver and Mills after they had unloaded *Crayfish*.

7 Letter of 14 January 2003 to François Boisnier from Michelle Ringearde, the daughter of Maurice Marchais, who related hearing her parents talk of this event. Boisnier archives, Barbézieux. It seems likely that, in mentioning Angoulême here, the two Marines were indicating the general direction they were heading in without giving

away the name of their actual destination, Ruffec.

8 There is a copy of one of these maps in the Boisnier archives, Barbézieux. See too François Boisnier's notes analysing the maps, also in the Boisnier archives. In addition, three original maps survive – one held by a family in the area, one at Combined Military Services Museum, Maldon, Essex and one 5 by Peter Ellery, the son of Bill Ellery. Each has a crayon mark tracing the approximate course of the Demarcation Line between the *Zone Occupée* and the *Zone Non-Occupée*.

25 Begging Clothes and Braving Daylight

1 Paul Addison, *Churchill: The Unexpected Hero* (Oxford: Oxford University Press, 2005).
2 For the discovery of this important signal, I am indebted to Robert Lyman, who quotes it in *Operation Suicide*, p. 245.
3 The figures for the relative percentages of the civil population categorised as 'Resistant' in the rural and urban areas of Gironde region at this time were: Resistant in rural areas: 81.88%. Resistant in urban areas: 18.12%. Philippe Souleau, *La Ligne de Démarcation en Gironde* (Fanlac, 2003), p. 227.
4 Lucas Phillips describes Hasler and Sparks making this approach together. But Sparks' autobiography is clear that he was left behind in hiding and only called in when the coast was clear. This is the correct escape and evasion procedure and the one Hasler taught his Marines.
5 Lucas Phillips, *Cockleshell Heroes*, p. 185.
6 Lucas Phillips, *Cockleshell Heroes*, p. 187.
7 'Bekänntmachung/Avis'. Boisnier archives, Barbézieux.
8 Research by Michel St Marc of Cauderan and the German reports on the interrogation of the two Marines, WO 309/1604.

9 Designed by German architect Gustave Eiffel who is best known for his greatest the Eiffel Tower.
10 Bull, 'Submarine Special Operations'.
11 Colley interview with the author, 2 August 2010.

26 Hunger, Betrayal and Refuge

1 Raymond Furet, interview with François Boisnier, May 2000.
2 Chez Ouvrard, where there is a memorial to Laver and Mills, has now been fully renovated by an ex-French para and his young family who bought it in 2005. Visit by the author, August 2010.
3 Evidence given by Georges Rieupéyrout to Captain Nightingale of the War Crimes Investigation Unit, Montlieu, 5 November 1945, WO 309/2011. According to Rieupéyrout the events described here took place on 17 December, but this must be a mistake arising from the fact that the evidence was given three years later, since this date does not conform with other evidence – see especially the German interrogation reports.
4 An intriguing footnote to this incident is contained in Rieupéyrout's 1945 evidence. After the arrest of Laver and Mills, he ordered that a search should be carried out of the whole Chez David area. About a hundred yards away, the search party stumbled across a British officer, two men and a wireless set. They were not arrested because Rieupéyrout did not wish to hand them over to the Germans and the matter was kept secret. In his debriefing in London of 27 August, Claude de Baissac mentions that his radio operator, Roger Landes, confirmed that he was aware of an SIS team in the La Réole area who were operating on the same wavelengths as he was – indicating once again the crossover and lack of liaison between SIS and SOE in the area. File HS 6/566. There is an airfield suitable for light aircraft nearby which was used by the Germans – so this

mystery group may have been in the area on reconnaissance, preparatory to mounting an attack on the airfield.

5 Evidence of Georges Rieupéyrout, WO 309/1604.

6 In fact, the Combined Operations badge of anchor, wings and a tommy gun.

7 Jules Bergéon, interview with François Boisnier, May 2000. Bergéon, aged twenty-five in 1942, had been mobilised in 1940 and served in Syria. Taken prisoner by the British at Saint-Jean d'Acre, he was repatriated and later joined the Resistance movement.

8 The map has stayed in the Gaujean family ever since.

9 Episode on the Cockleshell Heroes raid in the *One Day* TV series made by Les Films de Jack Febus co-productions, broadcast on Fr3 Aquitaine. On a DVD distributed by Frankton Souvenir. Boisnier archives, Barbézieux.

10 ZN 2007/1/008691, Archives of the French Gendarmerie, Château de Vincennes, Paris. My translation.

11 Discussions between Jean Fernandez and the author, 10 August 2011.

12 This street is now known as the Rue de la Madame Seiglière.

13 Louis Jaubert, letter to Mrs MacKinnon, 14 September 1945.

14 The information on this encounter comes from evidence collected by Michel St Marc from Edouard Pariente after the war and from Captain Nightingale's war crimes investigation in 1945. WO 309/1604.

15 Louis Jaubert's evidence dated 2 Nov 1945 given to Captain Nightingale's War Crimes Investigation team, WO 309/1604.

16 File note of a telephone conversation of 14 December 1942. Royal Marines Museum, Eastney. Translated by Christine Tochtermann.

17 Naval Headlines 528 1100, 14 December 1942, HW 1/1220.

18 Edward Llewellyn, Prime Minister Cameron's Chief of Staff, No. 10 Downing Street, email to the author, 6 June 2011. In fact the Whitehall convention is that red ink is usually reserved for the use of the Foreign Secretary when signing off documents. But Churchill adopted this practice for himself during the war.

27 The Fiery Woodman and the Quarry Workers

1 Archives Départementales de la Gironde, 100W, SC 907. Quoted in *Cessac*, a local history of the town of Cessac in the A la Découverte de l'Entre-Deux-Mers series (L'ASPECT, 2011), p. 130. Translation has been amended slightly by the author for reasons of clarity and context.

2 Nightingale manuscript notes, WO 309/1604.

3 Drey deposition to Nightingale, WO 309/1604.

4 This has now been converted into a splendid tarmacked cycle track.

5 From a post-war interview with Edouard Pariente conducted by François Boisnier. Boisnier archives, Barbézieux.

6 Southby-Tailyour, *Blondie*, p. 138.

7 Sparks also refers, in a letter to Ewen Southby-Tailyour of 15 February 1998, to a diary he kept which 'is in the safekeeping of a very good and well known friend'.

8 As with the previous chapters on Hasler and Sparks' escape, much of the detail here is taken from Lucas Phillips' *Cockleshell Heroes*, in this case p. 195.

9 Lucas Phillips, *Cockleshell Heroes*, p. 191.

10 This 1930s-constructed garage with its stepped gable is still there, as are the now redundant pre-war fixing points for the telephone lines.

11 The modern D1 bypasses the village to the west but in those days the road would have run through it.

12 The information in this chapter – and especially the section that follows – has been put together from four separate sources: Lucas Phillips, Sparks' autobiography, evidence taken from Robert Patience by François Boisnier and a live interview with Patience on

the Cockleshell Heroes episode of the *One Day* TV series.

13 In Lucas Phillips' book he is described, rather unkindly, as a dimwit – but, even leaving aside the offensiveness of the term to modern ears, there is no support for this in other witness evidence, including that of François Boisnier who interviewed the main players after the war. It is on his evidence that much of this part of the story is based.

14 These have since been largely cleared and replaced with vines.

15 At the time of my visit here in August 2010, the house was in the process of being lovingly restored by a young vineyard worker and his family.

16 This element of the story is taken from Bill Sparks' account in *Last of the Cockleshell Heroes*. This appears to be, in most other details of the escape phase, rather unreliable both as to chronology and events. On this phase of Frankton especially, Lucas Phillips appears the more reliable source.

17 Bachmann diaries. Boisnier archives, Barbézieux; WO 309/1604.

28 Unnecessary Dangers

1 DEFE 2/5 and 2/218. There is a hopeful note at the bottom of the page from the COHQ War Diarist: 'Bring up [i.e. draw attention to this minute] when Frankton Force returns.'

2 The fact that Hasler and Sparks were accompanied by Yves and Marc Pasqueraud was well documented after the war (not least during Hasler's own post-war visits to the area). Curiously however, they are not mentioned in either Lucas Phillips' book, or in Sparks' own, or in Hasler's subsequent post-escape report to MI9.

3 Now renamed the Café du Centre (2 Route de St Preuil, 16720 St Même-les-Carrièrres), this is run today by Valerie and Nathalie Marguet. St Même seems to have quite strong English connections. During the war a crashed British airman was given refuge in an

attic in the village and remained there, pretending to be a deaf mute, from 1943 to the end of the war. The whole village knew of the subterfuge but no one said anything to the Germans. The late Ronnie Barker had a holiday home in the village, which still sports an English B&B catering for tourists.

4 Sparks, *Last of the Cockleshell Heroes*, p. 80.

5 MI9/SPG (-) 1140, WO 208/3314–7.

6 In 1944 the two young men were deported to Germany, apparently for some offence to do with the black market. They were never seen again.

7 Sparks, *Last of the Cockleshell Heroes*, p. 89.

8 Sparks, *Last of the Cockleshell Heroes*, p. 81.

9 De Baissac debrief, 26 March 1943, HS 6/566.

29 Moments from Disaster

1 Note of 3 May 1943, quoting 'German Sources', DEFE 2/217. The precise translation from German of the place at which Moffatt's body was found reads 'Le Bois Enre', which caused some bewilderment at the time since no such place could be identified on any map. In fact, this turns out to be a corruption of 'Le Blois en Ré', strongly suggesting that this information came from an ULTRA decrypt, since in code there is no space indicated between the words; the decrypter would thus have read the words as 'Enre' rather than 'En Ré'.

2 Only one identity tag belonging to the participants in the raid survives – that worn by Bill Sparks, which, together with his Combined Operations shoulder flash and escape maps, can be seen at the Combined Services Military Museum, Maldon, Essex.

3 The beach and the dunes are still much as they would have been in 1942. In 1965 a well-known and much-respected pilot on the Gironde, Emile Rivière, was drowned at the estuary's mouth, not far from where David Moffatt and George Sheard capsized. His body too was recovered close to this spot.

4 Wellington used to say that the key art of generalship was to 'see what was on the other side of the hill'. Hasler too seemed to have an uncanny ability to sense the unseen. As with Wallace and Ewart, when he rightly judged that they had not capsized in the first tidal overfalls but had been wrecked further down the coast, he may have been right on this occasion. In a conversation with the young Royal Marine officers who followed Hasler and Sparks' trail in 1961, Lucien Gody's wife related that, about a week before Hasler and Sparks arrived in Beaunac, two Germans dressed as fleeing British soldiers had come to the village begging for food, in an attempt to flush out local sympathisers to the British cause. Cameron, Hensman, Hodder, Mullen report, Royal Marines Museum, Eastney.

5 Boisnier, *Le Commando de l'Impossible*, p. 180.

6 In his autobiography, Bill Sparks says that as the two ran out of the village, they passed the gendarmes running in. But other sources indicate that the police did not reach Beaunac until some time after the two marines had fled.

7 The British had been reading the German Dockyard code, known as the *Werftschlüssel* (WS), since April 1940, though some changes to it caused Bletchley temporary difficulties in October 1941.

30 Arrival and Arrest

1 Folio 94, Gendarmerie national archives, Château de Vincennes, Paris.

2 Rb/sl of 18 December 1942. Supplied by Odile Jurbert, Archives nationales, CARAN, 11 rue des Quatre Fils, 75003 Paris.

3 Information from Mme Mandinaud. Cameron/Hensman/Hodder/Mullan report, August 1960. Royal Marines Museum, Eastney.

4 Meteorological office records for Angoulême.

5 The two Mandinaud sisters were at pains to make this point when first interviewed in Ruffec after the war by the young Royal Marines officers who met them in August 1960. Cameron/Hensman/Hodder/Mullan report, Royal Marines Museum, Eastney.

6 Gendreau and Regéon, *Ruffec et les Ruffécois dans la guerre*, p. 127.

7 Blois is just five miles southwest of *Monkeypuzzle*'s Boisrenard DZ, where Lise de Baissac had parachuted into France ten weeks previously.

8 Wynne, *Story of Mary Lindell*, pp. 125–6.

9 Wynne, *Story of Mary Lindell*, p. 127.

10 Wynne, *Story of Mary Lindell*, p. 126.

11 On pre-war postcards it is shown as the Café des Sports.

12 Sparks' report to MI9, MI9/B/PG (-) 1162, WO 208/5582.

13 Once again there are conflicting accounts of the chronology of the events in the Toque Blanche this afternoon. Some say it was Alix who served the Marines, some Yvonne, while René Mandinaud's own account (see Gendreau and Regéon, *Ruffec et les Ruffécois dans la guerre*) insists that he served them. I have chiefly followed René Mandinaud's account here, but amended it to include the account of Lucas Phillips where that seems appropriate and is confirmed by other sources (as in the case of the dialogue and the role of Yvonne, the waitress).

14 Lucas Phillips, *Cockleshell Heroes*, p. 204.

15 Cameron/Hensman/Hodder/Mullan report, Royal Marines Museum, Eastney.

16 While the basic outlines of what happened next are the same, the chronology between the three primary accounts – that in Lucas Phillips' book, approved by Hasler; that of François Boisnier, which came largely from post-war interviews, and that of Bill Sparks in his autobiography – differs considerably. I have chosen here to follow Lucas Phillips' chronology but to add local information (especially from Boisnier) where it appears both relevant and convincing.

17 Letter from Louis Jaubert to Jack MacKinnon's mother, 14 September 1945. Family archive.

18 Evidence from Louis Jaubert. *Épopée sur la Gironde*, a research publication by students of Lycée Jean Renou, La Réole, in the possession of the Mairie de La Réole.

19 Deposition made by Lt Jacques Aubertin in respect to Commander Louis Olivier who was at the time under arrest in Nancy, 3 November 1945, WO 309/1604. Also Michel St Marc, interview with the author, 4 April 2011. This information was given to M. St Marc by Mme Chavoix, widow of the local doctor who acted for the *gendarmerie*.

20 Pierre Hennequin file SHD, GR 16P 289649, Bureau Résistance et Seconde guerre mondiale, Château de Vincennes, Paris. Author's translation.

21 Archives Départementales de la Gironde, Series Y 2034W.

22 WO 309/1604.

23 Ibid.

24 Note by Buckmaster to his regional controller from France, dated 14 April 1944, in which he refers to the fact that Keitel's letter has come to light as part of a package of papers captured from the Germans. Buckmaster, after quoting from the letter, adds: 'This operation can be identified with the often-reported attack on the blockade runners, which was instigated originally by Scientist (de Baissac) but never claimed by him officially as it could not be proved that it was his group that carried it out. The two men arrested must have been local adherents, because we do not know anything of their activities.' The phrase 'local adherents' may well have been a reference to saboteurs outside SOE's control – possibly BCRAM networks in Bordeaux – such as Raymond Brard's *Phidias-Phalanx*. This letter is also referred to in a letter from Duncan Stuart dated 25 January 2002.

31 Of Hospitals and Hospitality

1 One possible reason for recording that MacKinnon was suffering from anthrax – a contagious and deadly, but rather unusual condition – was to discourage further investigation by higher authorities, especially the Germans.

2 In 1944, Dr Chavoix joined George Starr's SOE F Section *Wheelwright* circuit.

3 Deposition taken by Captain Nightingale, WO 309/1604.

4 Verchère was in fact admitted to hospital six weeks before MacKinnon and left five days before he was arrested. Despite this he was accused by the Resistance after the war of being there to keep an eye on MacKinnon. Taken from research in the hospital records. Michel St Marc, letters to the author of 1 September 2011 and 30 April 2012.

5 One of the difficulties in trying to reconstruct exactly what happened to MacKinnon and Conway in La Réole is that nearly all the evidence comes from Captain Nightingale's war crimes investigation. It seems likely that the facts will have been shaped to present the best picture possible in the context of the Allied victory and the possibility of a war crimes trial.

6 Deposition by Lt Aubertin in respect of Commandant Olivier, 3 November 1945, WO 309/1604.

7 This started as the *Hilaire* network, changing its name to *Wheelwright* sometime in mid-1942.

8 Code-named *Hilaire*, Starr had been one of Mary Herbert's fellow passengers on the felucca *Sea Wolf* when she landed near Cannes in November.

9 Rigoulet file, 16P 511589, Château de Vincennes, Paris.

10 Gendreau and Regéon, *Ruffec et les Ruffécois dans la guerre*, p. 148.

11 Again, there are conflicting accounts as to the exact chronology of events (and even of some of the substance) during Hasler and Sparks' stay in Ruffec. I have based this account on what appears to

me to be the most reliable outline – that given in Lucas Phillips (although he and at least one other account add a night at the Toque Blanche which simply wasn't there). I have supplemented Lucas Phillips' outline story with details given in later, mostly local accounts where these seem to be appropriate and are not directly contradictory.

12 Letter to Robert Chaussois, 3 January 1968. Quoted in Lyman, *Operation Suicide*, p. 230.

13 Letter to Ewen Southby-Tailyour, 8 August 1997.

14 René Flaud, interview with François Boisnier. Boisnier, *Le Commando de l'Impossible*.

15 Probably Maxime Delavergne, the owner of 'Farm A' at La Manguinerie (See Chapter 11), as he was the normal guide for crossing the line. Gendreau and Regéon, *Ruffec et les Ruffécois dans la guerre*, p. 153.

32 Marvaud Saint Coutant and Mary Lindell

1 There were however many escaping Allied servicemen and Jews who passed through Marvaud during the later years of the war.

2 Armand Dubreuille, interview with François Boisnier, November 2002.

3 Sparks, in *Women of Courage: Mary Lindell*.

4 There is a memorial to them and to Hasler and Sparks' visit in the village of Beaunac.

5 Dubreuille, interview with François Boisnier, November 2002.

6 *Cockleshell Heroes, One Day* TV series.

7 Evidence of Maurice Drouillard to Captain Nightingale, 2 November 1945, WO 309/1604; again, when reading this, account should be taken of who it was given to, and when. Also *Épopée dans la Gironde*, by students of Lycée Jean Renou, La Réole. Author's translation.

8 Evidence of Maurice Drouillard, WO 309/1604..

9 Archives Départmentales de la Gironde, Series Y 2034W. With thanks to Michel St Marc, who discovered this.

10 SHD, GR 16P 289649, Château de Vincennes, Paris.

11 In relation to the arrest of the two Marines, Henry commented, 'Radio London broadcast identified Captain Olivier' as being responsible. *Archives du Service Historique de la Défense*, File 33E, p. 73. Information courtesy of Michel St Marc.

12 St Marc, interview with the author, 4 April 2011.

13 HS 8/22.

14 According to Professor M.R.D. Foot, 'SOE was (like half the War Cabinet) outside the *Ultra* loop . . . [But] Gubbins had a private arrangement with Ismay [Deputy Secretary (military) to the War Cabinet], of which "C" did not need to know. Ismay kept on his desk a file into which he put any *Ultra* telegram that he thought might interest Gubbins who called on him once a week, read the file, but took no notes.' Prof. Foot, email to the author, 20 June 2011.

15 Nightingale investigation, WO 309/1604.

16 On their journey to Bordeaux, Krantz and Corssen stopped off in Paris to determine the exact circumstances of the execution of Wallace and Ewart. In their post-war depositions to the Nuremberg War Crimes investigation, they said that their principal purpose had been to question the legality of the killing of the two Marines. But there must be some suspicion that they were at least as concerned about the hasty execution of the two raiders before their full intelligence potential could be realised as they were about the legalities. It would not be surprising if, in the course of their enquiries they had not also suggested that this was one of the reasons for the German authorities' failure to stop Hasler getting through. After the interrogation of the four Marines was concluded on 5 January, Corssen and Krantz returned to their base. A few days later Corssen was sent back to

Bordeaux to see if more could be extracted from Hasler's men. Learning nothing to add to the report already sent, he finally returned to Wilhelmshaven on 15 January 1943.

33 The Long Road Home

1 Lucas Phillips, *Cockleshell Heroes*, p. 214.
2 Sparks, *Last of the Cockleshell Heroes*, p. 104.
3 *Women of Courage: Mary Lindell*.
4 Ibid.
5 One of her *passeurs* for the Pyrenees section, a Catalan called Rouag, had been arrested and shot.
6 Lucas Phillips says that they continued to wear their identity discs, but this cannot be accurate. After the war Sparks' identity disc was returned by Armand Dubreuille, through the British Embassy, to his family. (It is now at the Combined Services Military Museum in Maldon, Essex.)
7 Farrell was an SIS officer who also worked for MI9. His cover was to act as Consul General in Geneva. He was closely involved in assisting a number of French Resistance circuits that used Geneva; probably the most famous of these was the *Gilbert réseau* run by Colonel Groussard and a Swiss, Marcel Durupthy.
8 Hasler's Escape and Evasion report, MI9/S/PG (-) 1140, WO 208/5582.
9 Apart from being divided up into flats, this villa and its magnificent but slightly unkempt garden, remains today much as it must have been in 1943. Visit by the author, 14 August 2011.
10 *Women of Courage: Mary Lindell*.
11 Code name Lt Cdr Patrick Albert O'Leary RN. Three months previously Guérisse himself had paid a visit (courtesy of de Saugie?) to see Farrell at the British Consulate in Geneva after his radio operator Tom Groome (the one Mary Lindell had refused to take with her) had been arrested.
12 According to Lyman, *Operation Suicide*, p. 274, this was Fabian de Cortès.
13 Lucas Phillips, *Cockleshell Heroes*, p. 221.

14 Ibid.
15 Combined Operations Chief Planning Committee meeting, 23 February 1943, DEFE 2/8.
16 Sparks, *Last of the Cockleshell Heroes*, p. 127.
17 Perhaps when writing this Lucas Phillips had in mind the other main escape route across the Pyrenees, run by the *Comet* line, the 7000ft high Col de Pecouch in the Massif de Couserans. This lies further north, midway up the Pyrenean chain, and requires a four-day trek and a total altitude gain and loss of 20,000ft. It is a much more taxing route on which more than 100 escapers died from exposure, cold and German ambushes. A commemorative trek is conducted annually along this route, known today as *Le Chemin de la Liberté*. The BBC journalist Edward Stourton has done a programme on this route and is writing a book on it.
18 MI9 S/PG (-) 1131, WO 208/5582.
19 Met Office Library and Archive, email to the author, 29 June 2010.
20 These have now been augmented by many holiday houses scattered in small colonies in the woods.
21 Visit to the area by the author, 3 April 2011. The house is currently let as a *Gîte de France*.
22 On the front wall of the hotel there is today a stone plaque commemorating the 450,000 Spaniards who fled across the col to freedom during the Spanish Civil War, including Presidents Mañuel Azana, Lluis Companys and José Aguirre who passed through in 1939. Today the Spanish side of the col is accessed by a metalled road that reaches all the way to the summit. Here another memorial commemorates the terrible times of misery when nearly half a million Spanish men, women and children used this crossing to escape into exile. When the Germans occupied France, the flow of refugees switched direction; thousands of Frenchmen, mostly heading for England, crossed to spain by this route (the road up to the col is now renamed *La Route des Evadées de la France*). The French fugitives of the Second World War have their

memorial here, too – it is positioned near one of the houses tucked into a wooded valley some distance below the ridge-line which marks the Spanish/French border.

23 In his autobiography, Sparks describes how de Merode threatened to put him on a charge on his return to UK for his failure to keep up. Sparks, *Last of the Cockleshell Heroes*, pp. 130–1.

24 The British Consul at the time was Sir Henry Farquhar, who reported to the Spanish Ambassador, Sir Samuel Hoare. Hoare, himself an ex-career SIS officer, intensely disliked SOE and MI9, regarding them as 'more trouble than they were worth'. MI9 had two other agents in the Iberian peninsula: Martin Creswell in Madrid (code name 'Monday') and Donald Darling ('Sunday'), who was responsible for, among other things, initial debriefing in Gibraltar.

25 http://.rafinfo.org.uk/rafescape/guerisse.htm

26 Minutes of the Chief Planning Committee, 11 March 1943, DEFE 2/8.

27 Southby-Tailyour, *Blondie*, p. 119.

28 Combined Operations War Diary, 8 April 1943, DEFE 2/10.

29 Southby-Tailyour, *Blondie*, p. 121.

30 Comment made to Royal Marines historian Mark Bentinck and François Boisnier. Bentinck, email to author, 4 July 2011.

31 Letter from Casualty Department War Office, 2 June 1943. Royal Marines Museum, Eastney.

34 Bordeaux after Frankton

1 De Baissac debriefing, 21–23 August 1943, HS 9/75.

2 Though it was claimed by some that two U-boats were sunk in consequence. See Foot, *SOE in France*, p. 248.

3 Combined Operations War Diary, 2 April 1943, DEFE 2/10.

4 Code name *Bernard*.

5 HS 7/252 signal to Plygone of 20 January 1944.

6 Mary Herbert debriefing, 30 January 1945, HS 6/567.

7 http://en.wikipedia.org/wiki/Mary-Katherine-Herbert. While there is sufficient rumour and anecdote in SOE circles about Mary Herbert's suicide to require serious consideration of the claim, I have been unable to find any further source to corroborate this.

8 Report of 20 October to the Principal Commissioner of Police in Bordeaux. Leglise papers, Nice.

9 Description of the battle in the Leglise papers, Nice.

10 An inquiry led by Maurice Buckmaster which started work in 1944. Its purpose was to find and root out French collaborators and those connected with the German occupation, especially in the police and Gendarmerie.

11 Duboué personal file, HS 9/452/4.

12 Leroy personal file, Château de Vincennes, Paris.

13 Denise and Pierre Hèches, interview with the author, 29 March 2011.

14 Duboué file, HS 9/452/4.

15 When I visited her with my daughter in February 2011, Suzanne, who had lost some of the stability of her mind, took one look at me and said: '*Vous n'êtes pas Anglais. Vous avez le visage d'un Allemand*' ('You're not English – you have the face of a German!') and refused to speak to me on the grounds that I was a Gestapo interrogator. She was however happy to speak at length to my daughter, especially when we were joined by one of her Resistance colleagues, who was with her father in Dora.

16 Suzanne Leglise, letter of 1993. Leglise papers, Nice.

17 There is a moving letter in Charles Hayes' SOE personal file, HS 9/681/3, from Suzanne Duboué to Maurice Buckmaster, dated 9 July 1945, seeking information on her lover.

18 I discovered this document when looking through the papers (WO 309/1604) relating to the Frankton war crimes investigation. Included was a paper containing this testimony from Bernau. It seems that it was included because it was thought the officer might have been MacKinnon.

19 Bernau's sentence was subsequently commuted to twelve years' penal servitude which he served in Ostfriesland concentration camp, surviving a mass slaughter when 4500 fellow inmates were killed wholesale with the use of anti-aircraft cannon. He survived the war.

20 Hennequin file SHD, GR 16P 289649, *Bureau Résistance et seconde guerre mondiale*, Ministry of Defence, Paris.

21 Olivier's file, National Gendarmerie archives, Château de Vincennes, Paris.

22 Denise and Pierre Hèches, interview with the author, 29 March 2011.

23 WO 373/93.

24 Lise was offered the chance to return to the Bordelais, but volunteered instead to accompany her brother.

25 Disparity between the awards given to men and women of the SOE was – and remains – a scandal, which has recently been the subject of a debate in the House of Lords led by Baroness Crawley of Edgbaston.

35 Tea with Mountbatten and other Afterlives

1 Renee Sheard was killed in an air raid on Plymouth when a bomb hit her house, 21a Sussex Road, Ford, on 13 June 1943. There is some speculation that she was pregnant at the time, but there is no firm evidence supporting this. A letter dated 12 July 1943 in the documents held at Royal Marines Museum, Eastney advises that, following Renee's death, George Sheard's next-of-kin details should be changed to those of his mother at East Cornwall Street.

2 It seems very likely that there would have been some earlier informal contact with Mrs Hasler and perhaps also with the Sparks family in February when Hasler's coded message sent by way of Mary Lindell and the Geneva Consulate arrived – but there is no record of this.

3 Lucas Phillips, *Cockleshell Heroes*, p. 234.

4 *Kettering Guardian*, 11 January 1946.

5 Combined Operations War Diary, 16 April, DEFE 2/8.

6 Her letter was postmarked as having passed through the GPO sorting office in London on 5 March 1943.

7 MacKinnon family archive.

8 Peter Lieb, Konventioneller Krieg oder NS-weltanschauings krieg? Kriegführung und Partisanbekämpfung in Frankreich 1943/44, Munich, Oldenburg 2007, pp. 114–45.

9 ADM 1/18344. The German attempt to cover up the facts was clumsy. They claimed in Death List 269 that although MacKinnon, Laver, Conway and Mills were 'drowned in Bordeaux harbour', they were buried in Bagneux, Paris.

10 Otto Reichel was a judge before the war and president of Plauen county court in Vøgtland.

11 Hans Reitz, Wilhelm Langfeld, Reinhard Retzlaff. They were hanged on 19 December 1943.

12 Reichel report, 12 January 1944, DEFE 2/218 418659.

13 As for example the first to be executed under Hitler's order, the seven commandos captured during Operation Musketoon on 17–18 September 1942 (see Chapter 12, fn 12).

14 Letters from Edouard Vergriete, Conservateur of Bagneux archives, to the author, 28 September 2011, and from Pascal-Hervé Daniel, Chef du Service des Cimetières, Paris, 10 January 2012.

15 Email from Arne Schrader of *Volksbund Deutsche Kriegsgräberfürsorge*, 7 February 2012.

16 Bureau des Cimetières, Paris, letter to the author, 28 September 2011.

17 Telegram in WO 309/1604.

18 It would be intriguing, in this year of the seventieth anniversary of the Frankton raid, to find out what a modern DNA investigation might reveal.

Catherine Bret-Lépine and Henri Bret, *Années sombres à Blanquefort et dans ses environs, 1939–1945* (Blanquefort: Publications du GAHBLE, Groupe d'archéologie et d'histoire de Blanquefort, 2009), pp. 131–3. Courtesy of Michel St Marc, Cauderan, Bordeaux.

19 No trace of this report has been found in the archives of either the International Committee of the Red Cross in Geneva or in those of the French Red Cross. Correspondence with the author, December 2011.

20 Arne Schräder of the *Volksbund Deutsche Kriegsgräberfürsorge*, email to the author of 17 November 2011

21 'Cadaver 1. Boots, parts of field-grey uniform height: 168 cm, 30–40 years old. Cadaver 2. parts of field-grey uniform, navy badges, rest of officers signs, height 171 cm, 20-25 years old. Cadaver 3. Boots, parts of field-grey uniform, steel helmet, German belt "*Gott mit uns*" ("God with us"), height 168 cm, age 20.' Schräder, email to the author, 7 February 2012.

22 Conversation with Julien Hauser Berneuil, representative of *Volksbund Deutsche Kriegsgräberfürsorge*, 2 January 2012.

23 Among the papers examined during the Nightingale investigation is a translation of a German document (probably a Bletchley intercept) recording that, on 18 December, the date when Moffatt's body was found on the Île de Ré, the *second* body of an Englishman was found at the same spot, but only 'one of these was presumed to be a saboteur'. This lead was followed up but produced no further information, leading to the presumption that the second body was not that of one of the raiders. ADM 18344 – 418659.

24 Colonel Michael J. Haller, Military Attaché in the German Embassy, London, email to the author, 15 July 2011.

25 Letter from Arne Schräder to Col. Michael Haller, attached to email from Haller to the author of 30 September 2011.

26 This is one of the reasons why the vast preponderance of VCs go to junior officers and other ranks. It seems however that, later in the war, this rule may have been relaxed somewhat as VCs were given to the commanders of X-craft midget submarines for their attacks on the *Tirpitz*, which could also, by their nature, not have been observed by a senior officer. Operation Source, September 1943.

27 Among whom he was known as 'The Batty Lord Mount'.

28 Originally called the Special Boat Service Units – the name was changed to avoid confusion with Army units of the same name.

29 Sparks' DSM was bought by Conservative peer Lord Michael Ashcroft, who outbid by £1000 a joint offer of £30,000 put together by Bill Sparks' son, Terry – himself by then a Royal Marines officer – and the Royal Marines Museum, Eastney.

30 Peter Ellery, interview with the author, 4 September 2011.

31 See liquidation files for the *Marie-Odile réseau*, Château de Vincennes, Paris.

32 Yvonne Burney (née Baseden), interview with the author, 18 January 2011.

33 Qu (Quartermaster's) Department.

34 Warlimont was Deputy Chief of the Operations Staff in Keitel's headquarters and as such the officer responsible for ensuring that Hitler's Commando Order was carried out.

35 Michel St Marc, letter to the author, 1 September 2011.

36 Stahlschmidt immediately deserted to the French Resistance (possibly through Raymond Brard's *Phidias-Phalanx réseau*). He later changed his name to Henri Salmide, married a Frenchwoman, became a naturalised French citizen in 1947 and worked the rest of his life in the Bordeaux Port Fire Brigade. It is sometimes forgotten in Bordeaux that the survival of the city was also due to a deal made between the Germans and the Resistance which gave them 'free passage' out of the city.

37 Jacques Villette, 'Pour la Réhabilitation de Maurice Papon'. http://www.maurice-papon.net/documents/dohse.htm. Also Dominique Lormier, *Bordeaux brûle-t-il? ou, La Libération de la Gironde, 1940–1945*.

38 Villette, 'Pour la Réhabilitation de Maurice Papon'.

39 This statement is an amalgam of the verbal evidence given by Jean Duboué and a personal letter written by him to Dohse for use in his trial. The original documents are in Duboué's papers held by the Leglise family in Nice.

36 Placid Waters

1 Those who wish to know more of this extraordinary man's life can do no better than read Ewen Southby-Tailyour's excellent biography, *Blondie* (Barnsley: Pen and Sword, 1998).
2 His co-creator of Cockle Mark II received an annual pension of £150.
3 Southby-Tailyour, *Blondie*, p. 196.
4 They were titled *The Veteran Yachtsman* and *The Long Voyage*.
5 Southby-Tailyour, *Blondie*, pp. 204ff.

37 In Memoriam

1 Jeanne Baudray, Amélie Dubreuille and the late Anne-Marie Bernadet (married name Farré).
2 Awarded by Her Majesty on 24 October 2011 for his services to the preservation of the Frankton memory.
3 The trail actually starts closer to the point where Blondie and Sparks disembarked, but the Château is the first place on which a plaque is fixed marking the beginning of the route.
4 Letter from the Mayor of Calderdale, Councillor John Hardy; 15 June 2012.
5 This fact gave rise to a good deal of leg pulling by Duboué's friends, who used to tease him: 'See, that's what your English friends do for you in return for all the help you give them.'

38 Epilogue

1 Combined Operations War Diary, 3 May 1943, DEFE 2/1.
2 DEFE 2/217 418659.
3 *Cockleshell Heroes, The Dam Busters, Reach for the Sky, 633 Squadron, The Great Escape, The Wooden Horse, The White Rabbit, The One That Got Away, The Colditz Story, Ill Met by Moonlight, Carve Her Name With Pride, The Red Beret, Appointment with Venus, The Guns of Navarone, Above us the Waves, The Cruel Sea, The Enemy Below, The Battle of the River Plate, The Court Martial of Billy Mitchell, Stalag 17, 5 Fingers, the Shetland Bus.*
4 Professor Michael Foot, interview by Tom Keene, 26 January 2004. In a telephone conversation with the author on 25 April 2011, Professor Foot confirmed that, in his researches for his book *SOE in France*, he had had sight of a document which confirmed this.
5 HS 7/121.
6 De Baissac's debriefing of 23 March 1943, HS 9/75, and Appendix D.
7 Buckmaster, F Section History, p. 9, HS 7/121.
8 Foot, *SOE in France*, p. 277.
9 ADM 1/18344.
10 Foot, interview with Dr Tom Keene, 2004.
11 Lucas Phillips, *Cockleshell Heroes*, p. 72.
12 Wyatt, Liaison Officer's Report, 14 August 1942, HS 8/819; Keene, 'Beset by Secrecy and Beleaguered by Rivals', p. 334.
13 DEFE 2/216; Lucas Phillips, *Cockleshell Heroes*, p. 3.
14 Foot, interview with Dr Tom Keene, 2004.
15 The Italian submarine was called *Scire*.
16 In December 1942 – the month of Frankton – the Italians mounted a third attack using the merchantman *Olterra*, anchored at Algeciras on the Spanish side of Gibraltar bay as a claudestine base for their attackers. On this occasion the British were alerted and the raid failed. But the Italian base was not compromised and the *Olterra* was used for two further – successful – raids on Gibraltar harbour. In each case the raiders were then smuggled out of Spain by Italian secret agents.
17 Chiefs of Staff Committee of 4 January, DEFE 2/6.
18 Foot, interview with Dr Tom Keene, 2004.

Bibliography

1940 – Objets, documents et souvenirs du patrimoine militaire. Montreuil: Gourcouf Gradenigo, 2010.

A la Découverte de l'Entre-Deux-Mers – CESSAC. L'Association pour la Sauvegarde du Patrimoine et de l'Environment du Canton de Targon, 2011.

Addison, Paul. *Churchill, The Unexpected Hero.* Oxford: Oxford University Press, 2005.

Boisnier, François and Muelle, Raymond. *Le Commando de l'Impossible.* Paris: Trésor du Patrimoine, 2003.

Bret-Lépine, Catherine. *Années sombres à Blanquefort et dans ses environs, 1939–1945.* Blanquefort: Publications du GAHBLE, Groupe d'archéologie et d'histoire de Blanquefort, 2009.

Chazette, Alain. *La Forteresse de Royan-Pointe de Grave.* Editions Heimdal, n.d.

Clark, Freddie. *Agents By Moonlight.* Stroud: Tempus Publishing, 1999.

Cobb, Matthew. *The Resistance.* London: Simon & Schuster, 2009.

Costello, John and Hughes, Terry. *The Battle of the Atlantic.* London: Collins, 1977.

Downton, Roger and Sandra. *In War Heroes Wake.* Poole: Travellers Joy Publishing, 2005.

Épopée dans la Gironde. Research publication by students of Lycée Jean Renou, La Réole.

Escott, Squadron Leader Beryl E. *The Heroines of the SOE F Section: Britain's Secret Women in France.* London: The History Press, 2010.

Foot, M.R.D. *SOE in France.* London: Whitehall History Publishing in association with Frank Cass, 2004.

Foot, M.R.D. and Langley, J.M. *MI9 Escape & Evasion 1939–1945.* London: Bodley Head, 1979.

Gendreau, Henri and Regéon, Michel. *Ruffec et les Ruffécois dans la guerre de 1938 à 1945.* Ruffec: Editions La Péruse, n.d.

Hèches, Gaston. *The Companions of Little Gaston: Adventures of the Resistance in Bigorre,* trans. C.D. Russell. Privately printed, December 1949.

Henry, Jean-Marcel. *Marais Sanglants: Le Médoc en Guerre 1944–45.* Éditions Le Pas Perdus, 1985.

Jérosme, Pierre. *De l'Engagement de la nation française dans la triste aventure du gouvernement de Vichy*. Paris: L'Harmattan, 1994.

Keene, Dr Tom. 'Beset by Secrecy and Beleaguered by Rivals: the Special Operations Executive in Western Europe 1940–1942 with Special Reference to Operation Frankton'. Doctoral thesis, University of Plymouth, 2011.

King, Stella. *Jacqueline: Pioneer Heroine of the Resistance*. London: Arms & Armour Press, 1989.

La Seconde Guerre Mondiale en Gironde par les textes. Archives départementales de la Gironde, 2006.

Lormier, Dominique. *Bordeaux brûle-t-il? ou La Libération de la Gironde 1940–1945*. Bordeaux: Dossiers d'Aquitaine, 1998.

Lucas Phillips, C.E. *Cockleshell Heroes*. London: Pan Books, 1956.

Lyman, Robert. *Operation Suicide*. London: Quercus Press, 2012.

Marshall, Robert. *All The King's Men*. London: Fontana, 1989.

Neave, Airey. *Saturday at MI9*. London: Coronet Books, 1971.

Neave, Airey. *The Little Cyclone*. London: Coronet Books, 1973.

Neave, Airey. *They Have Their Exits*. London: Coronet Books, 1980.

Nichol, John and Rennell, Tony. *Home Run*. London: Penguin Books, 2008.

Perrin, Nigel. *Spirit of Resistance: The Life Of SOE Agent Harry Peulevé DSO MC*. Barnsley: Pen & Sword, 2008.

Rees, Quentin. *Cockleshell Heroes: The Final Witness*. Stroud: Amberley Publishing, 2010.

Rees, Quentin. *The Cockleshell Canoes: British Military Canoes of World War Two*. Stroud: Amberley Publishing, 2008.

Rémy, Colonel. *Les Soldats du silence: Mémoires d'un agent secret de la France Libre*. Paris: Éditions France Empire, 1998.

Robertson, K.G., ed. *War, Resistance and Intelligence: Essays in honour of M.R.D. Foot*. Trowbridge, Wilts: Leo Cooper, 1999.

Seaman, Mark, ed. *Special Operations Executive: A New Instrument of War*. London: Routledge, 2006.

Souleau, Philippe. *La Ligne de Démarcation en Gironde*. Périgueux: Fanlac, 2003.

Southby-Tailyour, Ewen. *Blondie*. Barnsley: Leo Cooper, 1998.

Sparks, William with Munn, Michael. *The Last of the Cockleshell Heroes*. Barnsley: Leo Cooper, 1992.

St Marc, Michel. *Le Canton de Targon sous l'Occupation 1939–1945*. Villenave d'Ornon: AAPA, 2007.

St Marc, Michel. *Periplus in Gironde of Two Heroes of the Operation 'Frankton'*. Villenave d'Ornon: AAPA, 2011.

Villette, Jacques. 'Pour la Réhabilitation de Maurice Papon'. http://www.maurice-papon.net/documents/dohse.htm

Voisin, André-Roger. *L'Odyssée du Commando Frankton*. Paris: L'Apart, 2011.

Wynne, Barry. *No Drums, No Trumpets: The Story of Mary Lindell*. London: Arthur Barker, 1961; reprinted Robin Clark, 1988.

Ziegler, Philip, ed. *Personal Diary of Admiral Lord Louis Mountbatten*. London: Collins, 1988.

Index

Page numbers in *italic* refer to illustrations